Fictions of Presence

Studies in the Eighteenth Century
ISSN: 2398–9904

This major series from Boydell & Brewer, published in association with the British Society for Eighteenth-Century Studies, aims to bring into fruitful dialogue the different disciplines involved in all aspects of the study of the long eighteenth century (c. 1660–1820). It publishes innovative volumes, singly or co-authored, on any topic in history, science, music, literature and the visual arts in any area of the world in the long eighteenth century and particularly encourages proposals that explore links among the disciplines, and which aim to develop new cross-disciplinary fields of enquiry.

Series editors: Ros Ballaster, University of Oxford, UK; Matthew Grenby, Newcastle University, UK; Robert D. Hume, Penn State University, USA; Mark Knights, University of Warwick, UK; Renaud Morieux, University of Cambridge, UK

Previously published

Material Enlightenment: Women Writers and the Science of Mind, 1770–1830, Joanna Wharton, 2018

Celebrity Culture and the Myth of Oceania in Britain, 1770–1823, Ruth Scobie, 2019

British Sociability in the Long Eighteenth Century: Challenging the Anglo-French Connection, edited by Valérie Capdeville and Alain Kerhervé, 2019

Things that Didn't Happen: Writing, Politics and the Counterhistorical, 1678–1743, John McTague, 2019

Converting Britannia: Evangelicals and British Public Life, 1770–1840, Gareth Atkins, 2019

British Catholic Merchants in the Commercial Age, 1670–1714, Giada Pizzoni, 2020

Lessons of Travel in Eighteenth-Century France: From Grand Tour to School Trips, Gábor Gelléri, 2020

Political Journalism in London, 1695–1720: Defoe, Swift, Steele and their Contemporaries, Ashley Marshall, 2020

Fictions of Presence

Theatre and Novel in Eighteenth-Century Britain

Ros Ballaster

THE BOYDELL PRESS

Published in association with

First published 2020
Paperback edition 2024
The Boydell Press, Woodbridge

ISBN 978 1 78327 558 8 (Hardback)
ISBN 978 1 83765 127 6 (Paperback)

The Boydell Press is an imprint of Boydell & Brewer Ltd
PO Box 9, Woodbridge, Suffolk IP12 3DF, UK
and of Boydell & Brewer Inc.
668 Mt Hope Avenue, Rochester, NY 14620–2731, USA
website: www.boydellandbrewer.com

A CIP catalogue record for this book is available
from the British Library

To Phil, Frances and Stuart, who are always with me

Contents

Part 3. Consumers: What is Seen

Acknowledgements

I am a late and reluctant convert to theatre history. Students, scholars and colleagues have helped me to get there. Student actors sometimes appeared flighty, but I've come to admire the fierce energy they bring to finishing their work and taking their audience with them. I wrote this book over the five-year period that I served as the senior member of the Oxford University Dramatic Society. The creative presence of the actors, directors and producers with whom I worked is felt everywhere in these pages. So too the doctoral students I have supervised over the same period, who have written so well about theatre, the eighteenth century, women writers and performers: Azlina Aziz, Sarah Barnette, Kitty Gurnos-Davies, Kimberly Marsh, Rathika Muthukumaran, Camille Pidoux, Honor Rieley. Special thanks to Dr Anna Senkiw, first my doctoral student and later my research assistant, who checked citations and prepared my online bibliography, as well as holding long and fascinating conversations with me about eighteenth-century celebrity culture. Research is always the better for doing it with others and I thank here the other research assistants who have given support along the way: Ellen Brewster, Grace Egan, Kathleen Lawton-Trask, Anne-Claire Michoux, Ben Wilkinson-Turnbull. They have sustained me through their willing embrace of my enthusiasm for the present, the now, in all its rich and redolent fictitiousness.

There are colleagues at Oxford to whom I owe particular intellectual debts. The teaching and research of Dr Ruth Scobie always inspire me and prompt me to think further and responsibly. I have called often on the depth, scope and generosity of Dr David Taylor's knowledge of the eighteenth-century stage. Professors Christine Gerrard, Nicole Pohl and Abigail Williams have been the best of companions here at Oxford in communicating the excitement and energy of eighteenth-century culture, and the research in which we engage. Professor Karin Kukkonen has been a brilliant interlocutor, first at Oxford and after from Oslo. She has kept me on my toes with her understanding of how the novel found its feet through theatre in the period, as well as with her command of cognitive theory.

I have benefited from the expertise of many scholars of the theatre and the novel and acknowledge them here, while reserving the claim for any errors to myself: Misty Anderson, Marcie Frank, Lisa Freeman, Judith Hawley, Robert D. Hume, Georgina Lock, Elaine McGirr, Ian Newman, Felicity Nussbaum, David O'Shaughnessy, Gillian Russell, Rebecca Tierney-Hynes, David Worrall.

I've had kind welcome from those who work in the theatre now. James Dacre and John Manning invited me in to the Royal & Derngate Theatre, Northampton, where I held a Knowledge Exchange Fellowship 2014–15. That experience altered my point of view, to think about process rather than product. And, I hope, made this book much better for it.

Mari Shullaw has been a wonderful editor at Boydell & Brewer, reading every draft with wise understanding. The Huntington Library, California, hosted me for two weeks exploring the Larpent manuscripts. The Bodleian Libraries, especially the English Faculty Library, and Christ Church Library (which hosts an extraordinary archive of theatre history: the Brady Collection), are superb places in which to research, with well-informed, patient curators. Vanderbilt English Faculty hosted me as Drake Lecturer in 2018 and gave me a chance to rehearse my ideas with a knowledgeable and appreciative audience; special thanks to Professor Bridget Orr whose thinking on eighteenth-century theatre sparked my own in new directions.

I thank the editors who have commissioned essays which have informed the argument in this monograph. Sections in Chapter 14 'The Mimic' have been reworked from my article, 'Rivals for the Repertory: Theatre and Novel in Georgian London', *Restoration and Eighteenth-Century Theatre Research*, 27, no. 1 (Summer 2012), 5–24. Arguments about Sarah Fielding and Jane Collier's *The Cry* in Chapter 15 'The Critic' were worked through in different form in two earlier of my published essays: 'Satire and Embodiment: Allegorical Romance on Stage and Page in Mid-Eighteenth-Century Britain', in a special issue of *Eighteenth Century Fiction*, ed. Daniel O'Quinn and Gillian Russell, *Georgian Theatre in an Information Age: Media, Performance, Sociability*, 27.3–4 (Spring-Summer 2015), 631–660; and '"Thoroughly to unfold the labyrinths of the human mind": Distributed Cognition and Women (Novelist)'s Representation of Theatre in Eighteenth-Century England', in *Distributed Cognition in Enlightenment and Romantic Culture*, ed. Miranda Anderson, George Rousseau and Michael Wheeler (Edinburgh UP, 2019), 170–86.

My family have been there for me at every stage. My parents, Roger and Rosemary Ballaster, and my siblings, Cathy and Rufus, are always kin and kind. My partner, Phil Harriss, has not only joined me with good heart in feverish expeditions to productions of eighteenth-century plays. He has edited my writing with loving precision. He and our children, Frances and Stuart, improve me in every way.

Introduction: Being There

Maria Villiers, aspiring playwright and country girl, has spent a whole month in London without yet attending a play. She finally seats herself at a performance of Robert Jephson's *Braganza* at Drury Lane, securing a stage box that will show her to advantage.[1] 'Maria,' we are told, 'was absorbed in expectation; she forgot herself; she thought of nothing but the entertainment she was going to receive.'[2] Her special anticipation is reserved for the 'admirable actress' who is to play the principal character, the Duchess of Braganza, Louisa. In the final act of the tragedy, Louisa heroically resists the violent threats of Portuguese rebels:

> The last scene arrived; the distress rose; the great actress, whom Maria had so eagerly expected, pierced the veil which the languid power of declamation had thrown round her; she burst forth in a blaze which aroused every dormant spark of sensibility, even in the most inattentive of her auditors.
>
> Filled with the noblest enthusiasm, the divine fire of genius, she appeared almost more than mortal.
>
> It was Louisa herself, the indignant queen, the tender wife, the steady heroine, the generous victim to the happiness of her people.
>
> Her voice, her look, her attitude – the whole *tableau* was striking beyond description.
>
> But you must have heard her, grasping the tyrant's arm, pronounce, 'Feel! do I shrink, or tremble?'

[1] *Braganza* premiered at Drury Lane on 17 February 1775 and ran for nineteen performances in its first season. Mary Ann Yates (1728–87), close personal friend of the author Frances Brooke, played the part of the Duchess. Mary Ann Yates and Frances Brooke co-managed the King's Theatre with their husbands as joint leaseholders from May 1773 to 1778. On the history of this period of the theatre, see Ian Woodfield, *Opera and Drama in Eighteenth-Century London: The King's Theatre, Garrick, and the Business of Performance* (Cambridge: Cambridge University Press, 2001).

[2] Frances Brooke, *The Excursion*, Book 4, ed. Paula R. Backscheider and Hope D. Cotton, Eighteenth-Century Novels by Women (Lexington, KY: University Press of Kentucky, 1997), p. 56.

to form any adequate idea of the excellence of her performance.

> Every heart was chilled with terror, respiration was suspended through the whole house; the dagger seemed pointed at each particular bosom, and the shout of exultation on her breaking from the traitor (whose part was admirably sustained) also spoke the danger real.[3]

Frances Brooke – playwright, theatre-manager and novelist – here describes that moment when a theatrical performance comes to life, its audience not simply spectating but inhabiting the same affective space as the actor. The collective shout of the audience speaks the danger 'real'. Brooke's narrator describes a scene she admits she cannot match (the reader needs to have been there, she tells us, to realise the power of the moment). The shared experience of being there is not something that can be reproduced in print. It is necessary to hear the line pronounced to have that experience. Nonetheless, Maria is our surrogate for that experience and the print fiction, the novel of *The Excursion*, gives us access to a viewer's affective response and, in so doing, claims a different kind of presence peculiar to *its* capacities of mediation. Brooke's novel situates us with Maria, her heroine. Indeed, it provides us with an opportunity to inhabit the theatre with Maria, to observe not only an embodied performance on stage but the experience of other audience members, of being with them, at the scene of performance.

Maria is, however, no ordinary member of an audience nor an ordinary heroine in a novel; she is also an author and aspiring playwright. This may be her first visit to the London stage but she is already a playwright. Maria, a theatregoing novice, it is confirmed, 'was satisfied; her warmest ideas of theatrical perfection were realised; she was on fire to give her tragedy to the public.'[4] Just before her trip to the theatre, Maria reviews the contents of the portmanteau she has brought with her to London: an epic poem, a novel and a play. She wildly overestimates their value at one hundred pounds for the poem, two hundred for the novel and five hundred for the play and its 'copy', i.e. publication.[5] Maria's play is refused by the manager

---

[3]   Brooke, *The Excursion*, pp. 56–7. The play concerns the coup after the death of Philip II of Portugal against his successor, Philip III, led by Antão Vaz de Almada, Miguel de Almeida and João Pinto Ribeiro. The rebels were defeated and John, 8th Duke of Braganza, was established on the Portuguese throne on 1 December 1640. There were obvious parallels with England's Civil War, regicide and restoration of monarchy over the same period.

[4]   Brooke, *The Excursion*, p. 57.

[5]   Ibid., p. 55. Judith Milhous and Robert Hume identify a slow increase in the price paid for 'copy' (copyright) to playwrights from the late seventeenth century to the end of the eighteenth century. They combine the sums of mainpiece benefits (the

of the patent theatre to which she sends it.[6] We hear nothing about the fortunes of Maria's novel or epic poem, but the author Frances Brooke did enjoy considerable success as a novelist and a translator of French fiction in the 1750s and 1760s before finding the appreciation as a writer for the stage that she so clearly craved throughout her career with tragedies and operas at Covent Garden in the 1770s and 1780s.

Brooke's career is one in which the theatre and the novel are repeatedly interrelated. However, I have opened with this passage from a novel describing the immersive experience of a scene from the theatre, to place centre-stage the contemporary preoccupation with art's capacity to invoke 'presence'. Competing claims to presence, this book argues, fuel the rivalry between the stage play and the novel of the period. And that rivalry is a productive one that also nourishes in each mode the development of new techniques – and self-consciousness about those techniques – designed to stimulate the mimetic sense-experience of their consumers.

This book is about the different ways, shaped through competition, in which the novel and theatre in Georgian London strove to give their consumers a sense of 'being there'. I argue that the production of 'fictions of presence' is found in the projection of 'persons' – authors, characters, consumers. It is, I believe, in the tracing of the life of such persons across medias and genres that we can come to recognise the centrality of 'presence-effects' to the formation of a new aesthetics in the period: an aesthetics based on the turn from meaning (allegory, partisan analogy, rhetoric) to sensation and sense-experience. This process is not one of leaving theatre behind for the new form of the novel as the dominant vehicle for the transmission of story. Far from it. In the elusive play of the presence of the 'rival' art form, we can see each form of media (theatre and novel) advancing toward a transformed aesthetic.

First, though, to elaborate further the slippery quality of 'presence'. Presence is in many ways the antithesis of its near synonym, representation. Representation re-presents. Presence is present. Representation communicates meaning. Presence does not communicate. Hans Ulrich Gumbrecht distinguishes between presence-effects and meaning-effects and sees aesthetic experience as an oscillation – indeed the result of a tension – between

---

profits of each third day) with average publication fees paid to playwrights. By the 1770s, when Brooke's novel is published, the average theatre benefit is £195 and the average publication fee £130 (*The Publication of Plays in London 1660–1800, The Panizzi Lectures* [London: the British Library, 2015, p. 202]).

[6]   Frances Brooke sent to manager of Drury Lane, David Garrick, a tragedy called *Virginia* which he refused. Garrick produced instead Samuel Crisp's *Virginia* in 1754 and Brooke published her unperformed play in 1756.

the two. 'What is "present" to us (from the Latin form *prae-esse*) is in front of us in reach of and tangible for our bodies.'[7] For Gumbrecht, presence is produced ('brought forth' or 'pulled forth'); it is envisaged as a kind of birthing. He quotes Jean-Luc Nancy: 'Coming (being in the birth, being a birth), existence misses a sense as meaningful "sense". But this missing itself makes sense, and makes sense, our sense, the sense of exposed beings.'[8] Rather than making sense (meaning), presence occupies the senses. Where meaning unfolds through time, presence produces 'a spatial relationship to the world and its objects.'[9]

Presence is nonetheless something that 'happens', takes place in time. Gumbrecht understands Martin Heidegger's concept of 'Being' as that which takes the place of 'Truth' (the Platonic absolute). It is not something that is known but something that happens: 'Being is that which is both unconcealed and hidden in the happening of truth' and in art it is not found in 'meaning' but in 'things'.[10] To be experienced, Being must – paradoxically – cease to be, or cease to be being, since by definition it exists prior to culture and prior to a culture's meaning-systems:

> in order to be experienced, Being would have to become part of a cul-
> ture. As soon, however, as Being crosses this threshold, it is, of course,
> no longer Being. This is why the unconcealment of Being, in the hap-
> pening of truth, has to realise itself as an ongoing double movement of
> coming forth (toward the threshold) and of withdrawing (away from
> the threshold), of unconcealment and of hiding.[11]

Think of the relation of forestage and stage in the eighteenth-century playhouse. Some of the boxes are located at the sides of the forestage by the doors through which the actors exit and enter. Sliding flats and backdrops give the illusion of three dimensions on the stage behind. The body of the actor moves from stage to forestage as part of the business of constructing the fiction of a being both 'in' the fictional narrative and at its threshold with the audience. This is how audiences experience the actor's 'presence' on stage in time and space and it is a form of knowing 'Being'; it is what we can know *of* Being through an aesthetic relation to it.

---

[7]   Hans Ulrich Gumbrecht, *The Production of Presence: What Meaning Cannot Convey* (Stanford, CA: Stanford University Press, 2004), p. 17.

[8]   Jean-Luc Nancy, *The Birth to Presence*, trans. Brian Holmes and others (Stanford, CA: Stanford University Press, 1994), p. ix.

[9]   Gumbrecht, *Production of Presence*, p. xiii.

[10]   Ibid., pp. 68, 69.

[11]   Ibid., p. 70.

We recognise that Being as a fictional production, while still experiencing it as corporeal presence.

And Being moves in space on at least three dimensions. In this book I map those three dimensions onto the cultural geography of the novel–theatre nexus according to three different categories of fictional 'person': the author, the character and the consumer (the spectator at the theatre or reader of a print text). My interest is in fictional 'person' – however and however variously embodied – as the space and place of 'Being'. I propose that the mid-eighteenth century is a particularly fertile time – precisely in the self-consciousness about the encounter between two media, two sites of 'making' Being (theatre and novel) – for the turn from Being as something to be 'known' through 'meaning' to Being as something to be 'experienced' through the 'senses'.

Aesthetic 'presence-effects' impress on us the qualities of Being; as Heidegger makes clear in *Being and Time*, 'being' is not coterminous with 'beings' (persons) 'we can conclude that "being" ["*Sein*"] is not something like a being [*Seiendes*]'.[12] However, 'to work out the question of being means to make a being – one who questions – transparent in its being'. Being [*Dasein*] can be and is made transparent in other forms than 'beings' or 'persons';[13] Heidegger tells us it is found 'in thatness and whatness, reality, the objective presence of things [*Vorhandenheit*], subsistence, validity, existence [*Dasein*], and the "there is" ["*es gibt*"]'.[14] However, the rendering of fictional persons – especially in corporeal or textual forms – is the testing ground for the capacity of art to make being transparent *in* its being. It is just such a working out of the question of being that we can observe in the presentation of persons and the competition to claim more or less transparent 'presence' between theatre and novel as mediators of story in the period.

Presence is not presented through a single dimension. According to Gumbrecht, it is presented through at least three. The first dimension Gumbrecht labels as vertical and in this book I map it onto 'character', the imagined person or body who occupies the space of the stage or the consciousness of the reader. This is simple 'being there', or the 'emergence into being there and with occupying a space'.[15] Heidegger uses the term *phusis*

12 Martin Heidegger, *Being and Time*, trans. Joan Stambaugh, rev. Dennis J. Schmidt (Albany, NY: State University of New York Press, 2010), pp. 3, 6.
13 Throughout this book, I capitalise 'Being' when I refer to Heidegger's 'Dasein' and leave 'being' in lower case when I refer to the lesser order sense of persons, or identity, or living agents, or a sense of self.
14 Ibid., pp. 5–6.
15 Gumbrecht, *Production of Presence*, p. 69.

(nature) which he defines as 'emerging sway, the standing there-on-itself, constancy'. The corporeality of the actor, in contrast with the presentation of person in print, plays an important role in the making of what we commonly call 'stage presence'.[16]

A second dimension follows from the first. In this occupying of space, Being offers itself to 'somebody's view (as an appearance or as an "ob-ject" as something that moves "toward" or "against" an observer)'.[17] This dimension, of the horizontal (the idea, look, what is seen), I map onto fictional persons presented in the novel and theatre who read or watch narratives on the page and stage; the presence of these meta-fictional 'types' of consumer (mimic and critic) is represented as effecting performance within the work (play or novel) and beyond it: in the social world of reviewing, attending, describing contemporary works of fiction. Indeed, their presence takes the shape of a kind of performance itself.

Both the vertical and horizontal dimensions of presence are contained within a third 'dimension' Gumbrecht derives from Heidegger's account of *Being and Time*, that of 'unconcealment'. Unconcealment is the first movement which is completed by a second movement ('happening') of 'withdrawal' to complete the experience of Being-in-the-world. This dimension I relate to the fictional person of the 'author', a being made in and of the artwork rather than existing prior to it. In our example of Frances Brooke's account of the performance of Robert Jephson's 1773 play, *Braganza*, we see this effect of unconcealment and withdrawal. The tragic performance of the actor, its *phusis*, holds sway over the audience and commands their response, a response that mirrors affect and closes the space between both parties. But equally, the narrator's invocation of a complete world in a prose fiction promises a different kind of sway: an immersive capacity to dip into characters' consciousness, that of the narrator, of locale, scene, space – an entire field of knowing: not confined to nor indeed accessed through 'meaning' but rather through a set of sense-experiences produced through presence-effects. The presence of 'Being' requires this second moment of withdrawal after initial unconcealment to complete itself. Put another way, the author is a 'presence-effect' whose effectiveness rests on necessary withdrawal from 'full' visibility or total presence (such as is offered in the moment of heightened sense afforded by the actor or character).

Thinking in this way about fiction on stage or page requires us to suspend our diachronic habits of interpretation. We need to move away from a sequence of cause and effect which begins the artwork in the mind of an

---

[16]   See Jane Goodall, *Stage Presence* (London and New York: Routledge, 2008).
[17]   Gumbrecht, *Production of Presence*, p. 69.

author and sees it realised (in print or performed form) for a consumer. Our focus is rather on the artwork which exists in and for itself in the moment of being. Insofar as a temporal dimension exists, it is in that sense of being in the present tense; in other words, to 'be there' is to be *present at that moment* of becoming: to be in the 'present' of the art work. And yet these moments of becoming and being are also moments of loss (of a past, of that present).

Our understanding of what constitutes 'performance' has been enlarged alongside the development of new forms of media such as photography, film and sound-recording. It has also been enriched by a deeper interrogation into the variety and forms of performance in periods before such technologies and by thinking of how it contrasts and relates to other forms ephemeral and punctual. Stuart Sherman reminds us of the punctual synergy of consulting the periodical and playbill in the morning and attending play time in the evening: 'Convergent shapers of public thought and feeling, the press is "present" at the playhouse as the playhouse is present in the press.'[18]

Joseph Roach observes that performance memorialises lost pasts and produces versions of those pasts, particularly in the revival of 'living memory' against a 'historical archive of scripted records'.[19] Performance makes something absent present in the moment of performance. The term *performance*, he notes, following Victor Turner's etymology, derives from the Old French 'to furnish forth', 'to complete', 'to carry out thoroughly'.[20] Performance, Roach concludes, 'stands in for an elusive entity that it is not but that it must vainly aspire both to embody and replace.'[21] Performance theorists understand theatre as a 'memory machine' and acting as a form of 'ghosting', bringing present or bringing forth a past performance alongside re-animating a part (usually that of a person).[22] Narratives, characters, performances are recycled and apparently reanimated in the repertory. It might seem then that, contrary to our commonplace expectations, theatrical performance – in its very liveness and its acts of surrogation – offers a

---

[18] Stuart Sherman, 'Garrick among Media: The "Now Performer" Navigates the News', *PMLA*, 126, no. 4, Special Topic: Celebrity, Fame, Notoriety (October 2011), 967.

[19] Joseph Roach, *Cities of the Dead: Circum-Atlantic Performance* (New York: Columbia University Press, 1996), p. 11.

[20] Victor Turner, *From Ritual to Theatre: The Human Seriousness of Play* (New York: PAJ, 1982), p. 13.

[21] Roach, *Cities of the Dead*, p. 3.

[22] See in particular Marvin Carlson, *The Haunted Stage: The Theatre as Memory Machine* (Ann Arbor, MI: University of Michigan Press, 2003).

compelling reminder of absence and loss to its spectator, precisely through the presence of its etymological kin, the spectre.

As Emily Hodgson Anderson describes it, the actor David Garrick turned this experience into an artform and his own particular claim to novelty. In Garrick's ephemeral performances that replaced and displaced those of actors who had previously taken those parts, 'loss itself becomes an inheritance to be experienced and passed on', an experience for his audience to recall and recycle. Garrick as actor is 'revered for an artistry that cannot remain'. Embodiment becomes a reminder and an act of commemoration of loss, the performance always anticipating its conclusion and future acts of surrogation when other actors render the part.[23]

The novel by contrast – in its claim to be 'novel' rather than an act of surrogacy and in its invocation of the non-representable through the medium of print – offers a promise of plenitude and presence, a life in the mind of its reader to which that reader can punctually return and which the reader can reinhabit. As we shall see, it was precisely in drawing the worlds of theatre and novel into comparison that ideas of aesthetic 'presence' took shape in the Enlightenment, detaching theatre from its older associations with ritual and bringing it into dialogue with modern fields of performance which novels played an important role in shaping. Indeed, the 'novel' ghosts the 'theatre', recycling plots and characters in acts of surrogation that turn the theatre into a form of what Elizabeth Freeman terms 'temporal drag', the 'collective political fantasy' which exteriorises 'disavowed political histories' as a 'mode of bodily adornment', making a 'forward movement a drag back'.[24] Periodical news, reviewing culture, printed play texts, also play their parts in generating Enlightenment fictions of 'presence'. However, novel and theatre are relatively autonomous fields, each assemblage drawing on a shared set of elements and engaged in a common traffic in a cast of persons intradiegetic and extradiegetic whose co-presence generates fictional narrative. It is those persons of author, character and consumer – and the fiction of their lives extending beyond and between the artistic fields of theatre and novel – that provide the focus of the discussion in this book.

Presence is an elusive effect. Both theatre and novel are preoccupied with the fear that what is designed as presence may be experienced as absence when the consumer meets the product and engages with it as artwork. It is no surprise, given what we have seen concerning the anxiety of

---

[23] Emily Hodgson Anderson, *Shakespeare and the Legacy of Loss* (Ann Arbor, MI: University of Michigan Press, 2018), pp. 3, 9.

[24] Elizabeth Freeman, *Time Binds. Queer Temporalities, Queer Histories* (Durham, NC and London: Duke University Press, 2010), p. 65.

surrogation and the embeddedness of loss in every performance, that the production of presence – or rather the failure to produce presence – on the eighteenth-century stage is a consistent source of comedy and satire. The bodily presence of the actor can inhibit the force of the presence-effect of role. Consider Charlotte Charke's comical account published in 1755 of a strolling player friend's struggle to deliver the part of the Queen in Dryden's *Spanish Fryar*. The good-natured actress has lent the actor who plays Torrismond her stockings because his were full of holes and his costume requires more display of leg than her own. Having 'no business' with the Queen in her part of Lorenzo, Charke observes her from the wings:

> I found she spoke sensibly, but to my great Surprise observed her to stoop extremely forward, on which I concluded she was seized with a sudden Fit of the Cholic, but she satisfied me of the contrary; and on her next Appearance I remarked that she sunk down very much on that Side I stood between the Scenes, on which I then conjectured her to be troubled with a Sciatick Pain in her Side, and made a second Enquiry, but was answered in the Negative on that Score: Upon which I desired to know the Reason of her bending forward, and sideling so?
>
> She told me 'twas a Trick she had got. *'Tis a very new one, then*, said I, *for I never saw you do so before*; but I began to suspect something was the Matter, and resolved to find it out. Presently the Royal Dame was obliged to descend from the Stage into the Dressing-Room, and made a Discovery, by the tossing up of her Hoop, of a pair of naked Legs.[25]

Here, a superfluity of the bodily concerns of the actor inhibits the performance of anything other than 'sense', the communication of bare meaning. The actor's presence undercuts the potential for that other form of histrionic presence that unites audience and actor. While corporeality holds out the promise of presence, it can also impede the aesthetic experience of presence. Paradoxically, the presence of the actor and the presence of the 'real' paraphernalia of the stage, such as props, flats, lights – indeed, the presence of other bodies in the audience – risk undermining the spectator's immersion in the fictional 'real'.

Novels (such as Brooke's *The Excursion*) frequently go to the theatre to invoke the experience of an encounter with the art of stage presence. They usually do so to test and demonstrate the sensibility of their protagonists,

---

[25] Charlotte Charke, *A Narrative of the Life of Mrs. Charlotte* Charke [1755], ed. Robert Rehder (London and New York: Routledge, 2016), p. 97.

as well as invite their readers to think carefully about the ethical impli-
cations of mechanical responses to the stimulation of passions produced
by stage performance. Gillian Russell notes the ubiquity of the allusion to
theatregoing, to specific plays and performances in Georgian novels. She
concludes that 'an art form and cultural institution that was regarded with
suspicion on account of its shameless reliance on presence was often used
to enhance the reality effect of these narratives.'[26] Maria, we should remem-
ber, attends a 'real' performance (Frances Brooke's friend the actress Mary
Ann Yates did play the part of Louisa in the stage play in February 1775).
Stages and plays become props within the novel that enhance the claim to
be representing the now, the 'novel', the curious, the present: they afford the
reader the opportunity to 'be there'.

These descriptions of moments of experiencing theatrical presence in
the novel are moments of 'first time' encounter: with the longed-for performance of a leading actor, with a play that is the rage of the town or a
favourite from print. And they are often punctuated by a pause in which a
disappointment is experienced. Presence is not just spatial but temporal.
Temporal drag is present in that moment when the performance fails to
live up to its reputation: when the spectator feels they are viewing something of the past, worn out. This may be an effect sought by a new form of
media claiming its own novelty by comparison with the familiar and the
hackneyed: but it is usually followed by a moment of electrifying reversal
when the intradiegetic spectator is, like Maria Villers, suddenly aware of
the force of the performance in real time.

While theatrical performance is invoked for these reality effects, it is,
then, often called upon as a negative example of a vulgar species of presence that the novel's aesthetic diplomatically evades. The absence of 'body'
in printed prose fiction comes to be articulated as a means of conjuring
'real presence' – spirit, consciousness, a precious interiority – to which an
art form reliant on embodied performance can only gesture. Novels claim a
special magic to cross the barrier of skin and flesh on behalf of an audience
hungry to inhabit other beings from the inside. And they do so discreetly,
in the development of a realist style that increasingly tunes out the voice of
a narrator. In other words, the novel manufactures being without making
visible its workings – the pulleys, the thunder run, the tired costumes, the
creak of the sliding flat, so familiar to a knowing theatre audience.

---

[26]   Gillian Russell, 'The Novel and the Stage', in Karen O'Brien and Peter Garside, eds,
*The Oxford History of the Novel in English. Volume 2: English and British Fiction
1750–1820* (Oxford: Oxford University Press, 2015), p. 515.

Conversely, attention to the importance of theatrical effects as a means to produce affect – such as situation, point, gesture, music – in the shaping of new practices of narration in the novel might lead us to enlarge the scope of those novelistic practices we habitually understand to communicate 'presence'. Free indirect discourse or internal monologue, for instance, certainly plays an important part in building up the claim to a present 'interiority' for a reader of the novel. However, novels can also include direct authorial address to reader and/or protagonist, variation in the style and tempo of dialogue and narration, sudden reversals of plot, forms of novelistic narration that overtly imitate dramatic technique (the hybrid form of the 'dramatic novel'). All these have been overlooked, perhaps precisely because they appear to belong to the province of theatre.[27]

Jenny Davidson points to the ways in which close attention to gesture and to vocal tone learned through attending theatre translated into what we see as the new naturalism of the novel, while printed versions of plays added stage 'directions' in language learned from the novel.[28] Recent accounts of the imbrication of theatre and novel call attention to the ways in which theatricality interrupts novelistic interiority, both to call attention to the manufactured nature of the fiction of mind in prose fiction and to acknowledge the limitations of interiority as a mode of (collective political) being. Anne Widmayer parallels narratorial irony with those acts of parabasis (chorus commentary, actor's asides) in the theatre: moments when the fiction of 'being' elsewhere is interrupted and the present-ness of theatrical action or narratorial telling is foregrounded.[29]

'Presence' is often claimed to be the special prerogative of theatre as an art form. Theatre only exists when a spectator is present at an action (on a stage). Cormac Power in *Presence in Play* (2008) helpfully distinguishes

---

[27] David Kurnick diagnoses a form of stage envy among novelists from George Eliot to James Joyce, who resist the interiority and individualism of novelistic narration by contrast with the social and collective identity afforded by theatre, in his *Empty Houses: Theatrical Failure and the Novel* (Princeton, NJ: Princeton University Press, 2012); see also Marcie Frank's account of Elizabeth Inchbald's translation of dramatic situation into affective effects of narration other than free indirect discourse in her article, 'Melodrama and the Politics of Literary Form in Elizabeth Inchbald's Works', in *Georgian Theatre in an Information Age: Media, Performance, Sociability*, ed. Daniel O'Quinn and Gillian Russell, special issue of *Eighteenth-Century Fiction*, 27, nos. 3–4 (2015), 707–30.

[28] Jenny Davidson, 'Restoration Theatre and the Novel', in *The Oxford History of the Novel in English. Volume 1: Prose Fiction in English from the Origins of Print to 1750*, ed. Thomas Keymer (Oxford: Oxford University Press, 2017), pp. 435–49.

[29] Anne F. Widmayer, *Theatre and the Novel from Behn to Fielding*, Oxford University Studies in the Enlightenment (Oxford: Voltaire Foundation, 2015), p. 3.

between different forms of presence in theatre (although all these forms may exist in any one performance event): making-present (the fictional representation unfolding in time before an audience), having-present (the auratic presence of the actor or the artwork that is in some sense 'before' the audience) and being-present (the literal contingent co-presence of the actor, the play and the audience). We can see that Brooke is mindful of all three in her novelistic rendering of the ecstatic 'being there' of Maria Villiers. Power, however, argues not that 'presence' is the special property of theatre but rather that 'theatre... has the potential to interrogate our experience of the present'.[30]

That interrogation is prompted by the tension between what Gumbrecht terms 'presence-effects' and 'meaning-effects' which constitutes the always-hybrid aesthetics of both theatre and novel. To complicate our analysis further, the experience of being present at the action of the play or the novel was evidently not as differentiated in the eighteenth century as we might have assumed: novels served as dramatic 'scripts' to be read out loud by household members to each other; and play scripts were purchased (by those who were regular theatregoers and those who were not) to be read quietly and alone. We need not assume that the reading of a play script in published form among friends and family was always an attempt to recreate the experience of attending a performance of that play, nor that novels were always read by a single and silent reader first before they were shared between a group of readers. Both had and have a 'presence' at the moment of performance – and in subsequent performances, whether under new circumstances or not.

It might seem that the novel and theatre do not exist as separate categories of fiction in this period. As Joseph Roach shrewdly observes 'the separation of drama from fiction is an arbitrary function of twentieth- and twenty-first century academic specialisation.... Georgian playwrights and novelists were not simply connected, they were frequently the same person'.[31] Certainly by the mid-eighteenth century both plays and novels were recognised as 'fictional' in the sense that they trafficked in narrative, often invented but not always – historical plays and novels were acknowledged to be fabricated simulations based on the 'real'.

'Novel' was a term used for plays. George Colman's satirical afterpiece about a young woman obsessed with modern novels, *Polly Honeycombe* of

---

[30]   Cormac Power, *Presence in Play: A Critique of Theories of Presence in the Theatre* (Amsterdam and New York: Rodopi, 2008), p. 7.

[31]   Joseph Roach, 'Afterword: What Now?', in *Georgian Theatre in an Information Age: Media, Performance, Sociability*, ed. Daniel O'Quinn and Gillian Russell, special issue of *Eighteenth-Century Fiction*, 27, nos. 3–4 (2015), 733.

1760, is subtitled *A Dramatic Novel*. Conversely, novels could be presented and laid out as though they were plays. A novel entitled *The Disguise, A Dramatic Novel* of 1771 asserted in its preface that 'Epistolizing, journalizing, and narrating, have been so hackney'd, that Novels grow unprofitable to the writer, and insipid to the reader', to defend a decision to present an entire and complexly plotted three-volume novel as dialogue in a play.[32] Oliver Goldsmith's *She Stoops to Conquer* (first performed 15 March 1773 at Covent Garden Theatre) was submitted to the licenser under the title 'The Novel: or, Mistakes of a Night'.[33] To recognise that the same term is used for printed prose fiction and plays in performance to refer to works that concerned contemporary events or plots does not assume that consumers could not differentiate between the effects and experiences of the media through which they experienced them. The apparatus whereby fictional images of the real are delivered to mind was part of the mental conception of that mediation: book and stage communicate very different image-schema.

Tobin Nellhaus sketches the emergence in the eighteenth century of a new 'image schema' for cognition modelled on the written line rather than the action and points structure of the traditional theatre. Print is increasingly the medium of understanding of 'practical life' (the almanac, the conduct book, the legal contract). The theatre, Nellhaus argues, responds with a sentimental drama that offers an account of character developed on a sequential line of response, which is in turn replicated in the mind of the spectator.[34] In *Novel Minds: Philosophers and Romance Readers, 1680–1740* Rebecca Tierney-Hynes argues for a similar paradigm shift or new image schema founded in the vision of text in the mind, in place of the sight of the body in performance. In other words, the increasing significance of prose renderings of character produces a necessary shift in the cognitive ecology of the (previously) dominant mode in performing personhood: the theatre.[35]

---

[32] 'Preface', in *The disguise, a dramatic novel*, 2 vols (London: J. Dodsley, 1771), vol. 1, p. vi.

[33] Oliver Goldsmith, *The Novel; or, Mistakes of a Night*, LA349, The Huntington Library, San Marino, California.

[34] Tobin Nellhaus, 'Performance Strategies, Image Schemas, and Communication Frameworks', in *Performance and Cognition: Theatre Studies and the Cognitive Turn*, ed. Bruce McConachie and F. Elizabeth Hart (London: Taylor and Francis, 2006), pp. 77–94.

[35] Rebecca Tierney-Hynes, *Novel Minds: Philosophers and Romance Readers, 1680–1740*, Palgrave Studies in the Enlightenment, Romanticism, and the Cultures of Print (Basingstoke: Palgrave, 2012).

Vital to that ecology was, of course, an audience. 'Being there' entails not only feeling one's own presence at the scene of a performance but also that of being with other minds. To feel 'present' and to feel the 'presence' of others are profoundly interconnected. The moments of presence produced through works of art referred to here are not necessarily moments when the consumer of that work feels him or herself to be most alert and conscious of being, but rather when others seem to most fully occupy that consciousness: when presences are felt. It is perhaps unsurprising that supernaturalism is so often the occasion for the sense of 'others' being present or presented to us.

One of the recurrent scenes of such presence in the history of eighteenth-century theatre is the opening of William Shakespeare's *Hamlet* in which characters speak of the tricks of memory that manifest in the 'mind's eye'. Bernardo has reported to Horatio sightings on the watch of an armoured figure who looks like the dead king, Old Hamlet. The Ghost stalks on stage and interrupts Barnardo's account. Horatio concludes, 'A mote it is to trouble the mindes eye';[36] in other words the 'portentous figure' is an illusion, a speck ('moth' or 'mote') or spectre conjured by a troubled memory in a time of war. Hamlet returns to Denmark from Wittenberg and expresses his regret that his mother has so swiftly remarried after his father's death and to that father's brother. Hamlet comments, 'My father, me thinkes I see my father'. Horatio asks, 'Where, my lord?' to which Hamlet responds, 'In my mind's eye', providing Horatio with his opening to report the visitation of the ghost the night before.[37]

The scene that stuck in the theatre audience's 'mind's eye' was that of the ghost of Old Hamlet appearing to his son. This was associated in particular and for some time with the expressive and affective skills of Shakespeare's recognised champion, David Garrick. The myth that Shakespeare himself had taken the part of Old Hamlet only served further to promote Garrick's claims to reanimate the spirit of England's greatest playwright on his Drury Lane stage. As Emily Hodgson Anderson reminds us, theatre is often a place to memorialise the dead. 'But theatre is also, necessarily, the space of life, where tributes to the past are paid by the living, breathing bodies on the stage.'[38]

---

[36]   William Shakespeare, *Hamlet*, Act 1, scene 1, line 111, *Modern Critical Edition*, ed. G. Taylor, J. Jowett, T. Bourus and G. Egan (The New Oxford Shakespeare) (Oxford: Oxford University Press, 2016). Oxford Scholarly Editions Online doi:10.1093/actrade/9780199591152.book.1, p. 2001.

[37]   Ibid., Act 1, scene 2, line 182, line 183, line 184, line 185, p. 2007.

[38]   Emily Hodgson Anderson, 'Theatrical *Tristram*: Sterne and *Hamlet* Reconsidered', in *Georgian Theatre in an Information Age: Media, Performance, Sociability*, ed.

Hamlet may also have had particular resonance for eighteenth-century audiences because it is a play in which the hero struggles to read other minds while other characters struggle to read his. Recent attempts to introduce cognitive theory to literary analysis have tended to emphasise the experience of reading as a training in 'mind-reading'. This is not only a means of making connection with other minds through empathy but also a necessary survival strategy. Blakey Vermeule describes 'Machiavellian intelligence', the social behaviour whereby we learn to anticipate in order to function in a social group. We scan other people, she notes, because we have to compete with them. Fiction trains us in the processes of simulation and inference necessary for social agency in an 'offline' context.[39] Karin Kukkonen brings the insights of '4E cognition' – cognition that is embodied, extended, enacted and embedded in environments and bodily experiences 'beyond' the brain and mind – to the history of the rise of the novel: as a new way to configure the embodied dimensions of written language. She notes the importance of theatre to the novel as a model of a lifeworld technology, a form of mediation that trains its readers in an expert *techne* or embodied practice.[40]

The eighteenth century sees the flourishing of theory of mind (John Locke, George Berkeley, David Hume, Edmund Burke, David Hartley) alongside a discourse of aesthetics; historians of literature have recognised in this burgeoning theory a new self-consciousness about the effect and affect of the sensory stimuli of art.[41] The growing sense of aesthetic experience as a solitary reflex of mind may be related to the repeated efforts to contain the opportunities for communal response in public assembly in the space of the theatre. At significant moments the theatre's presence – especially in the shape of urban buildings where increasingly large numbers congregate to watch performances with topical resonance – was purposely suppressed or put into abeyance because of the public risk of riot: from suppression in the mid-seventeenth century in the Protestant republic, to the emptying of houses in favour of the scenes of public trial around the

---

Daniel O'Quinn and Gillian Russell, *Eighteenth-Century Fiction* Special Issue, 27, nos. 3–4 (2015), 674.

[39] See Blakey Vermeule, chapter 2 'The Cognitive Dimension', in *Why Do We Care About Literary Characters?* (Baltimore, MD: Johns Hopkins University Press, 2010), pp. 21–48.

[40] Karin Kukkonen, 'Introduction' and chapter 4, 'Fielding: A Lifeworld of Books', in *4E Cognition and Eighteenth-Century Fiction. How the Novel Found Its Feet* (Oxford: Oxford University Press, 2019), pp. 1–7, pp. 107–50.

[41] See Jonathan Kramnick, *Actions and Objects from Hobbes to Richardson* (Stanford, CA: Stanford University Press, 2010).

Popish Plot and Exclusion Crisis of the late 1670s, to the passing of the Licensing Act in 1737 and the Old Price Riots of 1809 at Covent Garden Theatre. Professional writers for the theatre turn to print narrative at these moments to maintain an income and sustain their skills. As David Kurnick observes, it is inaccurate to see the history of the novel as marked by a decisive turn from the invention of fictions on stage to the page. Rather, from Aphra Behn to Samuel Beckett, 'the novelistic turn to and away from the living theater was not a punctual event but has been an ongoing aspect of novelistic development'.[42]

This book pays attention to a particular stage in the novel's development, from the passing of the Licensing Act in 1737 to the rise of melodrama in the last decade of the eighteenth century. In part, it does so because this is a period of theatrical and novelistic history often overlooked and rarely addressed in terms of how the two genres mutually informed each other's development. Where conclusions are drawn, they are to the novel's advantage: that the Licensing Act sends the drama into decline and catalyses the novel in its place.[43] I argue, rather, that this is precisely the period in which the two modes enter into a dynamic, competitive dialogue with each other. Novels begin to be brought on to stage as props; their plots and characters are referred to as 'offstage' rivals to those of the stage. Likewise, characters in novels attend the theatre, discuss its affects and effects. Novelistic dialogue is rendered as though it were stage dialogue. In this mid-century period, the collocation 'dramatic novel' is brought into being to refer both to a short stage play and to a print fiction written as though it were a long play text.

In order to bring to life this energetic exchange over the nature of aesthetic presence between the theatre and the novel in the mid-eighteenth century, I do not offer a chronological account. Rather, I look in turn at the different but shared elements that go to constitute the generic fields of both theatre and novel, the coexistence of which are necessary for the transmission of presence effects from producer to consumer: authorship, character, forms and audience.

Various terms have been fielded in recent years in literary history to capture the multifarious and multivariant elements that go to make up aesthetic events. These new coinages seek to avoid the familiarity and second-handedness that now attach to the notion of 'representation': from

---

[42]   Kurnick, *Empty Houses*, p .2.
[43]   See Jones DeRitter, *The Embodiment of Characters: The Representation of Physical Experience on Stage and in Print 1728–1749*, New Cultural Studies (Philadelphia, PA: University of Pennsylvania Press, 1994).

the application of theory of 'assemblage' to the eighteenth-century stage to the notion of 'mediation'. David Worrall draws on the actor-network theories of Manuel DeLanda and Bruno Latour, derived from the account of social assemblage given by Gilles Deleuze and Félix Guattari in *A Thousand Plateaus*.[44] He employs these to argue for theatre as a form of 'social assemblage' in Georgian London, constituted from a dynamic and unstable set of component parts: ideological, material, symbolic.[45] Clifford Siskin and William Warner in *This is Enlightenment* suggest a new vocabulary to capture the 'new' attention to the means of transmission in the production of knowledge, meaning and aesthetic effect. 'Mediation' is defined by John Guillory in his introductory essay to their collection, 'Enlightening Mediation', as 'a process whereby two different realms, persons, objects, or terms are brought into relation'.[46] These important resituations of our critical vocabulary invite the eighteenth-century literary historian to attend to the systemic complexity of artistic practice, to recognise that meaning and effect are not the simple product of a single creative imagination, but rather of collective, sometimes conflicting, intentions and agents human and non-human.

Closest to my critical position, and also engaged in shaping the growing field of theatre-novel studies, is Marcie Frank's *The Novel Stage: Narrative Form from the Restoration to Jane Austen*. Frank argues that the history of media shift must be told in terms of genre and she charts the ways in which the narrative form of the novel was mediated by the drama through the eighteenth century. Her focus is on those genres that travel between novel and drama: the tragicomedy, the melodrama, the comedy of manners. By the end of the eighteenth century, she concludes the relation to have shifted from one of conjunction, novel-and-drama, to one of disjunction, novel-or-drama.[47] My interest in 'person' is rather different and I hope complementary, arguing for the emergence of an aesthetic of 'being' that is shaped in the, to some extent, purely contingent encounters of theatre and

[44] Gilles Deleuze and Félix Guattari, *A Thousand Plateaus: Capitalism and Schizophrenia*, trans. Brian Massumi (Minneapolis, MN: University of Minnesota Press, 1987).

[45] David Worrall, *Celebrity, Performance, Reception: British Georgian Theatre as Social Assemblage* (Cambridge: Cambridge University Press, 2013). See also Manuel DeLanda, *A New Philosophy of Society: Assemblage Theory and Social Complexity* (London and New York: Continuum, 2006); Bruno Latour, *Reassembling the Social: An Introduction to Actor-Network Theory* (Oxford: Oxford University Press, 2007).

[46] John Guillory, 'Enlightening Mediation', in *This Is Enlightenment*, ed. Clifford Siskin and William B. Warner (Chicago, IL: University of Chicago Press, 2010), p. 52.

[47] Marcie Frank, *The Novel Stage: Narrative Form from the Restoration to Jane Austen* (New Brunswick, NJ: Rutgers University Press, 2019).

novel in the eighteenth century. Frank, like Emily Hodgson Anderson and Francesca Saggini, sees novel-writing as a mode in which women writers in particular could experiment with theatricality and express their often frustrated ambitions as playwrights in the more competitive market of theatre: Frances Burney, Maria Edgeworth and Jane Austen shape their novelistic style by referencing – whether in repudiation or imitation – the mimetic and embodied characteristics of stage performance.[48] In the analysis that follows, issues of presentness, presentation and representation acquire sharp relief when they centre on women stage performers.

'Person' and 'persons' take their place within systems grammatical and social. And systems are not static, unchanging entities. Systems of genre, as Clifford Siskin identifies in *System*, thrive on adaptation and absorption of elements they conceive as 'extraneous' to their own workings: knowledge is made this way.[49] My interest lies in how sense-experience (rather than the ontological or epistemic knowledge Siskin addresses) is rendered through system. And the shaping or making of a separate category of the 'aesthetic' in the mid-eighteenth century is reliant, I hope this book will demonstrate, on a 'new' attention to the 'presence-effects' rather than 'meaning-effects' of art in the context of productive rivalry between established and insurgent/new and old forms.[50]

I am, then, especially interested in those 'presence-effects' that are tied to persons. And this because the most significant distinction between theatre (as performance) and the novel (as book) lies in corporeality: that theatre (even in its printed form) is constituted on the fiction of being in the presence of 'other' bodies: the actors and the audience. The novel, by contrast, is constituted on the fiction of being in the presence of consciousnesses more fully present to us than embodied beings. I insist that these are 'fictions' – coherent systems of aesthetic effect that require on the part of all those who participate in them a sense of distance from the 'real'. For example, audience members at the theatre know that they do not respond appropriately by seeking to intervene in the action, which is not to say that this is not an action happening in real time in the same space as they occupy.

So, each section of this book is organised according to the different persons – embodied or not, whether 'author', 'character' or consumer 'type' –

[48] Ibid.; Anderson, *Eighteenth-Century Authorship*; Francesca Saggini, *Backstage in the Novel: Frances Burney and the Theater Arts* (Charlottesville, VA: University of Virginia Press, 2012).

[49] Clifford Siskin, *System. The Shaping of Modern Knowledge* (London and Cambridge, MA: MIT Press, 2017), pp. 29–36.

[50] See Caroline Levine, *Forms: Whole, Rhythm, Hierarchy, Network* (Princeton, NJ: Princeton University Press, 2015).

who are the testing ground of the success of the 'presence-effect' of the artwork. There are of course other vehicles of 'presence-effects' in both the novel and the theatre: contenders would include sets, scenes and props in the theatre; plots of relative plausibility and implausibility (and cases are made for superior credibility on both sides); peritexts such as prefaces, epilogues and prologues that testify to immediacy, liveness and authenticity of sources. However, my claim – tested through the book – is that 'Being' is deeply associated with 'beings' and that the theatre/novel nexus of the mid-eighteenth century is a field in which there is vigorous contestation over the relative value of the aesthetics of producing a fiction of present 'Being' through corporeality and embodiment, print person and persona. The language of 'character' is thus central to the book as a whole. I am not interested in a taxonomy or historical account of the development of character types here, but rather in identifying the kind of work that character can do in conjuring a strong sense of presence. Hence, I investigate characters whose dynamic presence extends beyond the range of the genre that 'births' them.

My chapters are organised into three parts addressing different aspects shared by novel and theatre: authorship, characterisation and reception. In each section, a particular dimension of presence is explored. Part 1 considers four authors who wrote both for the stage and in the genre of the novel: Eliza Haywood, Henry Fielding, Charlotte Lennox and Oliver Goldsmith. We observe the different ways in which they conjure their own presence in their works both novelistic and theatrical. Authors walk on stage in plays, they invoke their 'other' lives biographical and as writers in and of an-other genre (as novelists in the theatre, as playwrights in the novel), they imagine what it is to be in the mind of a reader or audience-member. And yet they are also subject to displacements: repeatedly threatened by acts of ghosting, excommunication and vanishing by other presences (rivals for power in the playhouse, characters who refuse to submit to authorial management, inattentive or over-attentive audiences). Presence is forged in the dynamic of 'unconcealment and withdrawal', to produce what Gumbrecht translates as 'composure', the art of 'letting things be' in Heidegger's characterisation of *Dasein*'s contribution to the unconcealment of 'being'.[51] Composure in the face of such threats is the author's property across the theatre and novel: he or she is 'made', brought into being through this dynamic.

Part 2 turns to the issue of character. Here, I seek to move away from a simple dichotomy between stage character and novelistic character, to demonstrate rather how the interaction between the two modes worked

[51]   Gumbrecht, *Production of Presence*, p. 71.

to generate a sense of 'being there' or 'being with' characters who had lives beyond, between, across and indeed outside their fictional performance. Put simply, certain 'characters' of mid-eighteenth-century culture acquired a status and a mobility (across genres and time) that moved beyond 'type'. In this sense, character 'occupies space': it not only comes increasingly to stand at the centre of the artwork (epistolarity, melodrama, turns plot into vehicles for the delivery of 'attitudes' and states of consciousness to a spectator hungry for presence-effects), it also extends beyond a single work into a network or system of allusion and intertextual reference.

Our concern here lies not in measuring the different capacity of the mediums of theatre and novel to deliver character, but rather in the ways that character appears to escape the confines of media, to gain an independent being beyond the determinants of genre and mediation. We consider in turn: Lady Townly from Colley Cibber's completion of Vanbrugh's earlier play as *The Provok'd Husband* (1728), a part made famous first by Anne Oldfield and claimed as their star turn by many actresses through the eighteenth century; Samuel Richardson's serving-maid romance heroine, Pamela, the publishing sensation of 1740 whose presence and sway is felt in a series of subsequent dramatic and novelistic texts; Ranger, the rakish enabler of Benjamin Hoadly's *The Suspicious Husband* (1747), a part written for David Garrick and a play that was debated and defended by other playwright-actors such as Charles Macklin and Samuel Foote; and finally Tristram Shandy, the eccentric autobiographer of Laurence Sterne's cult fiction, who both appears (and disappears) in adaptations on stage and page.

The third section examines the ways in which the presence of the reader of the novel and the presence of the theatre audience are constructed and contrasted in the eighteenth century. This presence-effect of 'appearance' and 'idea', the 'what is seen', operates on a horizontal axis: the gaze or look of the audience member at the stage or the gaze of the reader at the page. What is there (*phusis*) offers itself to view. I look in this chapter at the conversion of the potentialities of viewing in theatre and novel into 'persons' designed to police the borders of ethical looking for an eighteenth-century audience learning to adapt to new image schema.

The (female) mimic and the (male) critic are fictional presences at performance on stage and page. Both are characterised as 'errant' forms of consumer, their behaviours a kind of present admonition to audiences and readers that helps to shape an absent 'ideal'. In each case I chart the sense of a rivalry between the modes of theatre and novel. The theatre casts the mimic as a female novel reader who walks on to the stage and applies a set of unreal norms to the 'real' world she inhabits. The novel casts the mimic as a female theatre-addict too vulnerable to affect and unable to achieve the critical distance required to assure moral behaviour in the 'real' world that prose fiction claims to represent. The theatre casts the critic as a man preoccupied with letter over spirit. And the novel casts the critic as a man preoccupied with his own performance. In this chapter the fluidity we have observed of single fictional persons more or less embodying or existing in relation to a 'real' person is less evident. Novel and theatre use fictional persons associated with rival media to bring into being the kind of reception they seek for themselves. Here, the *cause* of a failure to be present with a work is laid at the door of an alternative form of mediation as a means of advocating the superior affordance of its own form of mediation. The character of the consumer (the quality of their power of consumption) is complemented by the character of the art-object consumed (the quality of its power of converting presence-effect into ethical experience).

PART 1

Authors: Unconcealment and Withdrawal

Chapter 1
Introducing the Authors

What does it mean to be an author of novels or plays in the Georgian period? Authorship was certainly not associated with originality and ownership of one's own work. Authors tended to characterise themselves as subject to the desires of others – their audience, their booksellers, their kin – and driven to put their work into the public domain out of necessity rather than pride. Works were 'authored' by those desires and the hand that wrote was that of a scribe. This may of course have been the conventional modesty topos or a familiar kind of complaint that all labour produces. But here too we might say that what *is* – authorial Being – lies elsewhere than in the consciousness of the writer. Indeed, it was often perceived to lie in the imagination of the audience or reader.

Writing for the novel and writing for the theatre were often compared, and they were compared in conventional terms: the playwright is seen as one among many who bring a performance into being, whereas the novelist is envisaged as a solitary creator. In this, the playwright is not necessarily at a disadvantage or less likely to acquire recognition. There is some safety in numbers: a play's composition through plural makers may well hit popular taste(s) with more certainty and in that variety. Moreover, a play is tested in performance and the audience can express a desire to see the performance repeated or not. The novel – composed in isolation, put into print before it is exposed to its audience – speculates in lonely autonomy about its potential reception in the many minds of its readers.

Statistics appear to bear out this distinction. Even the most successful works of fiction had little market penetration by comparison with theatrical performances. Michael Suarez summarises prose fiction's place in the print market: *Robinson Crusoe* went through six editions of 1,000 copies each in its first four months, and *Pamela* sold some 20,000 copies in fourteen months. The average edition size for fiction 1770–99 was 500 copies and few novels went into second editions. Between 1703 and 1753 – the period in which the novel is emerging as a popular challenger to dramatic fiction – fiction publication (counting by titles) represents 'slightly less than 3.5 per cent of all surviving titles'.[1]

Few novelists could make a living from their labours and perhaps it should come as no surprise – if rather a depressing realisation – that this may have been one reason why women appear to have had more success in this genre of creative writing than others of the period. Literate women supported by their kin could afford to experiment in this market. Someone determined to make a living from their writing would be better to seek employment in the playhouse; Milhous and Hume estimate that one-third of the author's income from a single play came from publication and the remainder from benefits and payments from the theatre.[2] However – especially after the introduction of the Licensing Act in 1737 – there were very few opportunities for staging new plays and only two theatres licensed for the production of spoken drama in London. The rewards for play over novel-writing were higher, not only in terms of possible earnings, but also in terms of reaching what David Worrall terms 'density' in audience. Worrall calculates that by 1800 the annualised number of theatre seats available for sale in London was in excess of one million (for a population of some three million).[3] And, of course, the fictions told through theatre were accessible to those with low levels of literacy if they had the wherewithal – or were provided with it by their employers in the case of servants – to meet the relatively low cost of a ticket to the theatre; the cheapest seats were one shilling in the gallery.[4]

Nonetheless, numbers in an audience do not necessarily guarantee attention and the Georgian theatres were notoriously noisy, rowdy places at which people congregated to be seen, as much as to see a performance. Sales of individual printed texts or print-runs of titles are not necessarily a marker of how many people read a work (or returned to it many times to contemplate and reconsider it). Certainly, those who wrote about

[1]   Michael Suarez, 'Toward a Bibliometric Analysis of the Surviving Record, 1700–1801', in *History of the Book in Britain: Volume V 1695–1830*, ed. Michael F. Suarez and Michael L. Turner (Cambridge: Cambridge University Press, 2009), p. 48.

[2]   Judith Milhous and Robert Hume, *The Publication of Plays in London 1660–1800*, p. 202.

[3]   Worrall, *Celebrity*, p. 40.

[4]   See Robert D. Hume, 'The Economics of Culture in London, 1660–1740', *Huntington Library Quarterly*, 69 (2006): 487–533. Hume compares costs. Novels cost 1–2 shillings per volume and were usually published in three volumes. Earnings for most of the population averaged £50–£100 per annum and Hume estimates that annual maximum leisure money from such earnings approximates £16. Play texts cost sixpence to one shilling.

authorship for the theatre and the novel often distinguished the quality of attention an author might expect.

Samuel Foote characterises the playwright as a drudge torn between the conflicting demands to feed a hunger for novelty on the part of critics and to meet the huge variety of taste among the general audience. This variety is calibrated according to the class-expectations easily identified by ticket price – gallery, box and pit:

> Severe their Task, who in this critic Age,
> With fresh Materials furnish out the Stage!
> Not that our Father's [*sic*] drain'd the comic Store;
> Fresh Characters spring up as heretofore—
> Nature with Novelty does still abound;
> On every Side fresh Follies may be found.
> But then the Taste of every Guest to hit,
> To please at once, the Gall'ry, Box, and Pit,
> Require's [*sic*] at least — no common Share of Wit.[5]

In the concluding triplet Foote marks the author's separation from his audience formally by the introduction of a third line to the easy matching of a couplet (hit/pit now admits a third term, wit) and by exploiting the double meaning of 'common' – the author must not have things in common with the audience, nor be common like that audience, in order to have the wit to hit the diversity of taste beyond the pit.

By contrast the novelist does not enjoy this kind of co-presence with an audience, although ironically this levels the distinctions between the author and those who consume her or his works. In order to attract an audience's attention, the novelist needs to speak for the common interest rather than display an errant or uncommon wit. In an uncommonly witty and outspoken essay on the topic of the difference between the dramatic writer and the novelist, Elizabeth Inchbald identifies two types of novel reader:

> There are two classes of reader among this public, of whom it may not be wholly from the purpose to give a slight account. The first are all hostile to originality. They are so devoted to novel-reading, that they admire one novel because it puts them in mind of another, which they admired a few days before. By them it is required, that a novel should

---

[5]   Samuel Foote, 'Prologue', *The Author*, in vol. 1 of *The Dramatic Works of Samuel Foote, Esq; to Which Is Prefixed a Life of the Author*, 4 vols (London: J.F. and C. Rivington, R. Baldwin, T. Cadell, W. Lowndes and S. Bladon, 1788 [1789?]), p. B2.

be like a novel; that is, the majority of those compositions; for the minor part describe fictitious characters and events merely as they are in real life: -- ordinary representations, beneath the concern of a true voracious novel-reader.[6]

One class of reader looks for the novel to fulfil expectations and not to offer fresh or unusual representations: this convinces that the action is real. So much so, that Inchbald complains such readers tend to ignore the real sufferings and injustices happening on their doorstep while they weep over the unhappiness of a distressed heroine. Readers of the other class, possessed with good sense, read astutely enough to recognise their own faults or inconsistencies in the characters depicted in the novel and set about trying to correct them, hoping to make an even greater contribution to society.

Inchbald concludes that the novelist enjoys great freedom by comparison with the playwright:

> The Novelist is a free agent. He lives in a land of liberty, whilst the Dramatic Writer exists but under a despotic government.—Passing over the subjection in which an author of plays is held by the Lord Chamberlain's office, and the degree of dependence which he has on his actors – he is the very slave of the audience. He must have their tastes and prejudices in view, not to correct, but to humour them. Some auditors of a theatre, like some aforesaid novel-readers, love to see that which they have seen before; and originality, under the opprobrious name of innovation, might be fatal to a drama, where the will of such critics is the law, and execution instantly follows judgement.[7]

Inchbald's Jacobin radicalism leads her to argue that the novelist has more freedom to portray the 'real' world, a world in which the virtuous poor are not unremittingly grateful to a sympathetic gentry but may rather be resentful, inclined to see the wealthy as owing them a living. The novelist has the freedom to portray these relations – as indeed did Inchbald and her fellow radicals Thomas Holcroft and William Godwin in their experimental fictions – where the dramatist is confined by a conservative audience.[8]

---

[6]   Elizabeth Inchbald, 'To the Artist', in *The Artist: A Collection of Essays Relative to Painting, Poetry, Sculpture, Architecture, the Drama, Discoveries of Science, and Various Other Subjects*, 1, no. 14 (1807), 11–12.

[7]   Ibid., 16.

[8]   See Gary Kelly, *The English Jacobin Novel 1780–1805* (Oxford: Oxford University Press, 1976).

Inchbald's is a relatively high-minded account of the motives for writing in either genre or both. The evidence through the century points to the fact that those authors who had careers in the theatre only turned to the novel when the theatrical opportunities were slim or imperilled. And few only made a living from one or the other unless they had other financial stakes in the media itself. David Garrick, actor-manager of Drury Lane from 1747 to 1776, and George Colman the elder, manager of the Haymarket from 1777 to 1789, did not write novels. Few successful novelists of the period did not write for the theatre as well as print. Daniel Defoe and Samuel Richardson are exceptions to this rule, and it is striking that both had careers that were deeply embedded not only in writing for print but in the business of publication. Defoe was editor of *The Review* from 1704 to 1713, whereas Richardson ran a printing house near Salisbury Court close to Fleet Street from 1719 to his death, seeing into print some 10,000 items. The publishing house may have provided for these authors an alternative to the theatrical 'house' as the site for the production of their presence.

Most authors had what we might now call 'portfolio' careers. Sir Richard Steele was a hugely successful playwright, but also a retired soldier, a Member of Parliament, and the co-author of several successful periodical ventures. His co-editor-author of *The Tatler* and *The Spectator*, Joseph Addison, was also a Member of Parliament, playwright and much-admired poet. Such hybrid careers bred hybrid forms and modes in the works of fiction they produced, whether written first for stage or print or both.

In this section we focus on four authors who wrote both for the stage and in the genre of the novel: Eliza Haywood, Henry Fielding, Charlotte Lennox and Oliver Goldsmith. These authors have not been selected because they excelled in one or other genre, although all of them did in at least one. But rather because all four of these authors consistently investigate the sense of what it is to be 'there' at the action of fiction. And, more importantly, they all reflect on the place of the 'author' in that dynamic experience. In the work of all four we can see elements from one mode of fictional presence migrating to the other. The traffic between techniques learned in the theatre to the novel and back again is continuous and noisy. The process forms a history of presence, its repeated unconcealment and withdrawal, for each author.

The careers of these four writers span from the second decade of the eighteenth century to the end of the seventh: the high point of Georgian rule, from George I's established reign to the early years of George III before the latter's decline into mental illness. I consider the works and authors in chronological order, with the caveat that differences between them may have as much to do with the individual author and the peculiar kind of the presence he or she brings to acts of creation, as they do with the shifting contexts of the market for fiction over this fifty-year period.

This era was also one when the stage fell under attack from a ministry seeking to consolidate its authority by suppressing oppositional voices – most obviously in the passing of the stage Licensing Act in 1737, which brought an end to Henry Fielding's relatively successful career as a playwright and theatre manager. Clauses prohibited new theatres from performing or receiving payment for acting new plays, and one in particular provided that no new dramatic work could be performed unless:

> a true Copy thereof be sent to the Lord Chamberlain of the Kings Household for the time being fourteen days at least before the acting representing or performing thereof together with an account of the Playhouse or other place where the same shall be and the time when the same is intended to be first acted represented or performed signed by the Master or Manager ... of such Playhouse or Place or Company of actors therein.[9]

The effect of the Licensing Act for playwrights was not simply to suppress presence-effects, although it certainly contracted an already very competitive market. Few plays were refused licences after 1737;[10] the licensers did not usually turn down works so much as amend texts or make suggestions for alterations. Censorship rather takes place before the submission of scripts, with managers of the theatres commissioning far fewer new plays and relying on those already licensed or old plays from before the Act well established in the repertory.

However, the very fact that the 'play' to be licensed was understood to be present in the form of a written script transcribed by the prompter put increasing weight on the 'text' as the play and gave the author more visibility. Of course, performance might introduce all sorts of political reference and allusion not visible in the written form of the text: through impersonation of well-known characteristics of political and other celebrities, for instance. These elements, not identified in a written playscript, are usually

---

[9]   10 Geo II c 28. The Stage Licensing Act is given in Vincent J. Liesenfeld, *The Licensing Act of 1737* (Madison, WI: University of Wisconsin Press, 1984), pp. 191–3.

[10]   According to Matthew Kinservik, fitting a play to submit to the licenser meant that plays 'became cleaner and much less political'; see his *Disciplining Satire: The Censorship of Satiric Comedy on the Eighteenth-Century London Stage* (London: Bucknell University Press, 2002), p. 30. See also David Thomas, David Carlton and Anne Etienne, *Theatre Censorship: From Walpole to Wilson* (Oxford: Oxford University Press, 2007).

presence-effects developed by the performer and company rather than the author. Where playwrights might reassert their originating presence in a play was paradoxically in post-production. Published versions of the play were not subject to censorship applied to performance; hence, playwrights could restore their original versions in publication only a few days after first performance.

This change affords the novel an opportunity to take the place of the theatre as a site in which resistance to authority can be expressed through fictional hypothesised persons. We should not, however, overestimate the effects of the Licensing Act for the playwright after 1737. The plays of Eliza Haywood and Henry Fielding written and performed before that date are fully cognisant of the collaborative nature of presence in making theatre. However, after the Stage Licensing Act, the decline in overt political reference in new plays does bring theatre and novel closer to each other in terms of the kind of content they deal in as the stage steps away from partisan satire. *Both* modes of fiction tend to focus on domestic relations such as sexual and romantic intrigue and the pursuit of autonomy on the part of the young, poor, or oppressed. Even when they take as their topic significant historical figures in stage tragedy or historical narrative, the effect of the fiction is to provide an audience with the opportunity to experience the powerful emotions and cognitive dissonances of the past first-hand. Conflict is mediated through the affective presence of a suffering character rather than the representation of historical battles or the inner workings of government.

I have also selected these authors because their creations are in some ways *not* recognisable as what we would now expect to see in a novel or a stage play. The works discussed here are hybrid concoctions not apparently driven by the demand for cohesion and conclusion we now expect of our fictions. They demonstrate the openness of genre and form in the period. Nonetheless, one important distinction governs the ways in which the prose fictions and the stage plays manage their projections of presence: the awareness that writing for the stage always anticipates embodied presence in performance (even if the script is not brought to production).

In the case of each author, I consider a novel and a play or plays that were produced close in time and in what emerges as intermedial relationship: works in other words that were in some way 'present' to each other, produced in close synergy or proximity. In these works, and in their relationship to each other, we see each writer producing his or her presence at the time or site of the fiction's consumption – whether through the eyes of an audience in the theatre, or the eyes of a reader following the lines on the page of the printed novel or play. That production is a process of 'unconcealment' (a moment of revealing the author as 'being' and 'presence' more or less detached from the mimesis of the story) and 'withdrawal' (a consequent retreat or retirement of the authorial figure from the field of vision). It is in this dynamic of unconcealment and withdrawal that authorial presence is made.

Unconcealment is not the same as 'appearance'. It is itself a kind of fiction: the work produces the author and then the author apparently responds to that production by appearing as a person within or at the margins of the work. Authors unconceal through different means in different media. He or she is called upon or represented in a prologue to a play. A third-person narration shifts momentarily to the first person. In such acts of unconcealment the author also makes him or herself another 'person', apparently equivalent and existing on the same axis as other characters who feature in the work. Indeed, the fact that the author-persona *can* withdraw, conceal him or herself once more – that these moments tend to be brief, transitory, allusive – contributes to a disavowal of agency. Power, the power to produce a fiction of presence, is transferred to other persons. And yet this process completes the production of presence. Gumbrecht tells us that things are either 'present' or 'absent' to us, 'and, if they are present, they are either closer to or further away from our bodies'.[11] In what follows we see authors putting fictional(ised) versions of themselves in front of their characters and readers and imagining encounter and interaction. That interaction also takes place between the different generic modes of novel and theatre and in the author's movement from one to the other. Frequently, the author's agency is claimed to lie elsewhere – to have been established in his or her pedigree in another genre (the novel when writing for the theatre, the theatre when writing the novel): authorial presence is thus asserted through being elsewhere.

Authors fantasise that they can witness the reception of their creation, to 'be there' in the mind of the reader. Yet, paratextual and peritextual material – the prologue, the epilogue, the dedication, the preface – is most frequently premised on the absence of the author at the time of consumption. The author sends surrogates – actors and characters – to test an audience's response while he or she stands in the wings or is heard only at the margins of the text. Not only does each individual work stage this scene of imaginary co-presence (of author and audience) but, I suggest, novels and plays enter into conversation with each other about their respective capacities to make present an (invisible) authorial presence. And through the reworking of shared themes, contexts, allusions, they also produce an

---

[11]   Gumbrecht, *Production of Presence*, p. 17.

authorial 'signature' or 'function': a presence that inhabits the work as a whole and continues to do so. Playbills and novel title-pages rarely provide an author's name. It is the convention of the stage prologue in the eighteenth century that the actor clad in black appears as an envoy or surrogate for the author, pleading for attention but by reference to 'the author' rather than a named person.[12]

Presence is not, then, ownership or recognition through a printed or spoken name; it is more often produced through an allusive relationship to an onstage presence or a character in a narrative. Haywood appears as an actress in her own parts in plays that show women manipulating the expectations of their audience to engineer sexual and social freedoms. Fielding invites his audience to see the hack authors delivering vainglorious and empty farces, whom he satirises not only as versions of corrupt ministers mismanaging the state but also as versions of himself. Lennox's adaptation of her own novel into a play traces the dependent woman's struggle to find recognition of her intellectual and sociable talents in a hostile and competitive culture. The socially awkward heroes in Oliver Goldsmith's plays and his wildly successful only novel find acceptance within apparently adverse domestic and political environments – as did their author.

[12]   Diana Solomon, *Prologues and Epilogues of Restoration Theatre: Gender and Comedy, Performance and Print* (Newark, DE: University of Delaware Press, 2013), p. 44.

Chapter 2
Eliza Haywood: Authoring Adultery

See in the circle next Eliza plac'd
Two babes of love close clinging to her waste;
Fair as before her works she stands confess'd,
In flow'rs and pearls by bounteous Kirkall dress'd.[1]

Among the many writers presented as hacks and dunces in Alexander
Pope's *Dunciad*, Eliza Haywood (c.1693–1756), has the dubious privi-
lege of being one of only five women writers who appear in all the versions
Pope wrote and revised between 1728 and 1743.[2] She stands at the centre of
a circle on display as a prize in a competition between two publishers to see
who can urinate the greatest distance. This scene – of a woman competed
for by two men to 'own' her – is designed by Pope as a slur on a woman
writer he charged with 'profligate licentiousness' in the production of 'libellous Memoirs and Novels' that 'reveal the faults and misfortunes of both
sexes, to the ruin and disturbance, of publick fame or private happiness.'[3]
It takes the form of an act of counter-shaming, putting the writer who has
shamed others on display. But it also suggests a woman taken in adultery,
'confess'd' before her 'works' as a sinner is required to do: the products of
her shame two 'babes of love' or illegitimate children.

---

[1]   Alexander Pope, *The Dunciad Variorum* (1729), Book 2, lines 149–52, in *The Dunci-
      ad* (1728) & *The Dunciad Variorum* (1729), ed. Valerie Rumbold, vol. 3 of *The Poems
      of Alexander Pope*, Longman Annotated English Poets (London: Pearson Longman,
      2007), p. 232.
[2]   The major versions of the *Dunciad* are *The Dunciad* (1728), *The Dunciad Variorum*
      (1729) and *The Dunciad in Four Books* (1743). For an edition of the latter, see *The
      Dunciad: In Four Books*, ed. Valerie Rumbold, Longman Annotated Poets, 2nd ed.
      (Abingdon: Routledge, 2014). The other four women writers are Elizabeth Thomas,
      Lady Mary Wortley Montagu, Susanna Centlivre, Margaret Cavendish Duchess of
      Newcastle. See Valerie Rumbold, 'Cut the Caterwauling: Women Writers (Not) in
      Pope's Dunciads', *The Review of English Studies*, 52, no. 208 (2001), 524–39. Haywood
      appears in *Dunciad* (1728), book 2, lines 136–69; *Dunciad Variorum*, book 1, lines
      149–82 and *Dunciad in Four Books*, book 2, lines 157–60.
[3]   Pope, *The Dunciad*, book 2, note 149, Rumbold, ed., p. 232.

In fact, no children appear in the engraving to which Pope appears to be referring, nor pearls. There is a flower in the hair of the woman portrayed in head and shoulders who is looking directly from a circular frame at her readers, her dress loose and low cut. This engraving of Eliza Haywood was apparently printed as a frontispiece to the new (fifth) edition of Haywood's first novel, *Love in Excess* (1719–20), in 1724 and was not in fact by Elisha Kirkall as the note in the *Dunciad* asserts, but by George Vertue from a portrait by Jacques Parmentier. In the next two years, it appeared also as a frontispiece to two multi-volume collections of works, because apparently bound in with the fifth edition of *Love in Excess* to make the first volume of each. It was a bold move (for a relative newcomer to print and a woman) to see these named collections into the press: *Works of Mrs Eliza Haywood* (1724) and *Secret Histories, Novels and Poems* (1725).[4] The works before which Haywood stands confessed are not visible; whether children or libellous books they sit beneath or before or outside of the frame of the portrait to which the description refers. Haywood admitted to having two children and reported that she was obliged to work to support them; in a letter seeking patronage of 1729 she writes 'An unfortunate marriage has reduc'd me to the melancholy necessity of depending on my Pen for the support of myself and two children, the eldest of whom is no more than 7 years of age.'[5] If these circumstances were known, Pope chose to ignore them; his portrait of Haywood is not of a suffering wife but an adulterous one.

In attacking Haywood, Pope follows the pattern of 'unconcealing' and 'withdrawal' that we are investigating in the presence-effects of authorship in this period; he both puts a version of the author/Haywood on display and then conceals her, subsumes her; the booksellers 'own' her and it is their actions, their competition, that becomes the focus of the scene. Yet, Pope's satire unconceals and withdraws authors, he claims, for high ethical

---

4   Eliza Haywood, *The Works of Mrs Eliza Haywood*, 4 vols (London: D. Browne and S. Chapman, 1724) and *Secret Histories, Novels and Poems*. For discussion of this portrait and an overview of critical investigation into it, see Patrick Spedding, 'Imagining Eliza Haywood', *Eighteenth-Century Fiction*, 29, no. 3 (2017), 345–72.

5   BL Add. MS 4293, f.82. Quoted in Kathryn King, *A Political Biography of Eliza Haywood* (London: Pickering and Chatto, 2012), p. 61. Edmund Curll in his *A Compleat Key to the Dunciad* (London: A. Dodd, 1728) says that the two 'babes' were the 'Offspring of a Poet and a Bookseller'. These were the two works of scandal by Eliza Haywood that Pope cites in the footnote: 'those most scandalous books call'd *The Court of Carimania* [sic] and *The New Utopia*' (*Remarks* Ver. 157, *Dunciad Variorum*, book 2, p. 156). Jonathan Richardson the younger, friend of Pope, recorded on a copy of the 1736 *Dunciad Variorum* (now termed the Second Broglio) that 'She had 2 Bastards, other say Three' (Valerie Rumbold, note to book 2, line 138 of *The Dunciad. An Heroic Poem* (1728) in her ed., *The Dunciad* (1728) & *The Dunciad Variorum*, p. 57).

purpose – to expose wrongdoing – rather than for market profit. The pattern of unconcealing and withdrawal is especially marked among those who wrote both for the theatre and the 'new' market of the novel and it is a pattern that one might expect Pope – a writer who never produced works termed 'novels' – to characterise as a cheap marketing ploy. Nonetheless, Pope's presentation of Haywood does secrete some of the sympathy that we will see *she* expressed for wives subject to public display for adultery and it does so in similar terms to her own critique: that it is men who trade for their own profit in the sexual favours of women they 'own'. The unhappiness of wives, subject to the avarice of their husbands, is a recurrent theme in Haywood's works both theatrical and novelistic.

And stories of wives being pandered and abused by their husbands were also the common fodder of gossip about the theatre: one of the most notorious was the 1738 lawsuit taken by the obnoxious actor-manager Theophilus Cibber against his affluent lodger, William Sloper, for an adulterous sexual liaison (which it appears Theophilus himself had enabled) with Theophilus' actress wife, Susanna, in 1738. Susanna's impressive performances of the parts of wronged wives only gained added frisson from the scandal. Before he composed his *Dunciad*, Pope had collaborated with John Gay and Thomas Arbuthnot in his only play, *Three Hours After Marriage* (1717),[6] which sees two suitors ferociously pursue for sexual favours the beautiful young wife of an aged philosopher-scientist. Katherine Mannheimer observes that the play 'valorizes an improvisatory and performative mode of interpreting the world in addition to a more "reading"-based mode', a bastardised genre that mixes print and performance.[7] In this play, as in Pope's representation of Haywood in the *Dunciad*, the woman, Mrs Townley, is a co-conspirator with rival men, seeking her own sexual opportunity. Haywood, by contrast, gives us women who acknowledge their sexual and romantic attraction to men they should not admit to their beds and who strive to remain true to their duty and honour.

Eliza Haywood[8] appears to have begun her career in the arts as a stage actress: first at Smock Alley in Dublin in Thomas Shadwell's adaptation

---

6   John Gay, John Arbuthnot and Alexander Pope, *Three Hours After Marriage*, in *John Gay, Dramatic Works*, vol. 1, ed. John Fuller (Oxford: Clarendon Press, 1983).

7   Katherine Mannheimer, 'The Scriblerian Stage and Page: *Three Hours After Marriage*, Pope's "Minor" Poems, and the Problem of Genre-History', *Comparative Drama*, 43, no. 1 (2009), 63.

8   All information from Susan Brown, Patricia Clements and Isobel Grundy, ed., 'Eliza Haywood', in *Orlando: Women's Writing in the British Isles from the Beginnings to the Present* (Cambridge: Cambridge University Press Online, 2006), http://orlando.cambridge.org/ [accessed 20 February 2020].

of *Timon of Athens* in 1714 and later there is evidence that she was acting with a company in Nottingham. By 1719 she was living in London, with her debut novel *Love in Excess* published that year and a succession of short novels and collected works of fiction appearing in the 1720s. Nevertheless, she did not abandon acting nor her interest in the stage when she began writing fiction. She worked with Henry Fielding when he was an active playwright in the 1730s and acted in the troupe performing at the 'Little' Theatre at the Haymarket when he rented it between 1736 and 1737. She also wrote a companion to the plots of established (largely early-modern) plays for the English stage: *The Dramatic Historiographer; or, The British Theatre Delineated* (in 1734), in an attempt to revive the fortunes of Charles Fleetwood's flagging Drury Lane theatre.[9] Our focus in what follows is on two related works: a play (*A Wife to be Lett* of 1723) and a short novel (*The Fatal Secret* of 1724), which explore the damage done to women through nefarious incitement to, as well as (false) accusations of, adultery.

Haywood's authorial presence in both play and novel guides audience or reader to feel with the suffering wife, to stand in her shoes, and to reflect on what it is to be put into that position. As we shall see, these acts of imaginative projection are not just for Haywood a general means of social protest but also a way of making her ironic voice heard in relation to Robert Walpole's ministry and a very public scandal over the divorce of a libertine Whig minister of the Treasury, one William Yonge, from his estranged wife on grounds of discovered adultery. To be 'there' in this circumstance is to see fictions that deal with matter traditionally associated with women – domestic relations, the sufferings of women in marriage, the courtship plot – providing a means to occupy a place 'elsewhere' for women: the place of court, ministry and government. Moreover, the presence of Haywood – as actress, as author of other works, and as performer in different media – is felt in a cycle of unconcealment and withdrawal in both works which matches the similar serious play for survival of the female protagonists.

Haywood was a prolific writer of short fictions from 1719 onwards; there are only five plays attributed to her sole or partial authorship. Three are tragedies. *The Fair Captive* opened 4 March 1721 and was a reworking for John Rich at Lincoln's Inn Fields of a harem tragedy by Captain Hurst (Rich put on an additional benefit night for Haywood as second author,

---

[9]   Eliza Haywood, *The Dramatic Historiographer*, in *The Dramatic Historiographer and The Parrot*, ed. Christine Blouch, Alexander Pettit and Rebecca Sayers Hanson, in *Selected Works of Eliza Haywood*, gen. ed. Alexander Pettit, 6 vols, Set 2, vol. 1 (London: Pickering and Chatto, 2001).

which earned her the good sum of around £4.7s[10]). *Frederick, Duke of Brunswick-Lunenburgh* was a patriot heroic tragedy which debuted on 4 March 1729 at Lincoln's Inn Fields and ran for three nights turning £180 on its first two nights; the third night, Haywood's benefit, made £79.3s.6d of which she would have taken about £50 after costs.[11] *Arden of Feversham, An Historical Tragedy*, an adaptation of the sixteenth-century domestic tragedy *Arden of Faversham*, was staged at the Little Theatre, Haymarket on 21 January 1736 with Haywood in the lead part as the adulterous and murderous wife. One of her comedies was co-authored with the man who may have been her cohabiting lover, William Hatchett; *The Opera of Operas; or, Tom Thumb the Great* was a ballad-opera minimally changed from Henry Fielding's *The Tragedy of Tragedies*. It was performed at the Haymarket on 31 May 1733 with the text published the same day and sold at the theatre.[12]

The single-authored comedy on which we shall concentrate here, *A Wife to be Lett*, was first performed at Drury Lane on 12 August 1723. Haywood took the role of the virtuous wife, Mrs Graspall, who resists her undeserving husband's attempts to swell his coffers by pimping her to an attractive young aristocrat. The play was an adaptation of Aphra Behn's successful 1682 comedy *The Lucky Chance* in which the Whig city banker, Sir Cautious Fullbank, in order to meet a gambling debt, agrees to smuggle the ex-suitor of his wife Julia into her bedchamber.[13] Julia, like Susanna Graspall, resists being traded by her husband, but in Behn's source play, the marriage is undone rather than (however ambiguously) reformed. Behn's play offers the fantasy conclusion of 'the wife's excuse' found in other sex comedies of the period whereby the husband willingly divorces his wife and returns her estate leaving her free to be united with the man she prefers (a plot turn most familiar to modern audiences in George Farquhar's *The Beaux Stratagem* of 1707). Behn drew on contemporary scandals, including those well-known in theatrical circles. William Wycherley had been aggressively pursued by the married Countess of Drogheda and had married her when

[10] 'Eliza Haywood', in Philip H. Highfill, Kalman A. Burnim and Edward A. Langhans, *A Biographical Dictionary of Actors, Actresses, Musicians, Dancers, Managers and Other Stage Personnel in London, 1660–1800*, vol. 7 (Carbondale, IL: Southern Illinois University Press, 1982), p. 222.

[11] Spedding, *A Bibliography of Eliza Haywood* (London: Pickering and Chatto, 2004), p. 309.

[12] Highfill et al., 'Eliza Haywood', in *Biographical Dictionary*, vol. 7, p. 223.

[13] Earla Wilputte discusses both plays alongside Henry Fielding's *The Modern Husband* (1730). See 'Wife Pandering in Three Eighteenth-Century Plays', *Studies in English Literature, 1500–1900*, 38, no. 3 (1998), 447–64.

she was widowed in 1672, a poor bargain it turns out in that the union lost him the King's favour and the marriage was unhappy and debt-ridden.[14]

Haywood's reworking of Behn's play in the shape of a *Wife to be Lett* enjoyed considerable success in print as well as in performance, going through three London editions. The play opens with a prologue delivered by the actor and son of Colley Cibber (one of the Theatre Royal's three managers), Theophilus Cibber, who, at the tender age of eighteen, had taken on the management of the Drury Lane summer season. Prologues served as vehicles for the author through the voice of an actor to set out his or her wares and invite the tolerance of the audience, usually at the expense of 'critics'. Theophilus Cibber played the part of an obsequious fop called Toywell in the play itself.

The story goes that sudden illness on the part of another actress obliged Haywood to step into the lead part of the virtuous wife, Susanna Graspall, who foils her husband's plan to prostitute her to another man. Prologue and epilogue both advertised the unusual circumstance that the author of the play was also taking its lead role. The title page of the published play tells us the work was 'Written by Mrs. ELIZA HAYWOOD' and the 'Dramatis Personae' lists the part of Graspall as played by 'Mrs *Haywood*, the Author'. The Prologue delivered by Theophilus Cibber takes care to connect the actress and playwright to the already successful novelist.[15] He first compares the pomposity of the tragic muse with the familiarity of the comic and then introduces his female author, associating her with the latter. Haywood is characterised as, like the comic muse, able to criticise and correct folly and vice without resorting to the aggressive masculine railing of the class of critics. Her capacity to 'talk' well, the prologue asserts, has been established by her novel-writing. And indeed, by 1723, Haywood's narratorial persona was familiar: intimate, swift to anticipate her readers' responses to the passionate scenarios she depicted, inclined to generalise about the dangerous effects of feeling as well as the impossibility of resisting them.

> *Criticks! be dumb to-night—no Skill display;*
> *A dangerous* Woman-Poet *wrote the Play:*
> *One who not fears your Fury, tho prevailing,*

[14]   Ibid, p. 451.
[15]   Patrick Spedding notes that Haywood published almost half her works under her name either on publication or later, but especially during the early periods of her career in the 1720s: see Spedding, *Bibliography*, pp. 94, 65. By August 1723 she had seen into print several novels: three volumes of *Love in Excess* (January 1719 and February 1720); *Letters from a Lady of Quality to a Chevalier* (December 1720); *The British Recluse* (April 1722); *The Injur'd Husband* (December 1722); *Idalia* (April 1723).

More than your Match, in every thing, but Railing.
Give her fair Quarter, and whene'er she tries ye,
Safe in superior Spirit, *she defies ye:*
Measure her Force, by her known Novels, *writ*
With manly Vigour, and with Woman's Wit.
Then tremble, and depend, if ye beset her,
She, who can talk so well, may act yet better.[16]

Although the published play seems to have had some success, Haywood's acting – despite the ambitions of the prologue – did not receive great applause. The play met, according to David Erskine Baker, 'with but middling success; which might, however, in some measure, be owing to the season, and the small merit of the performers. The author herself maintained a principal part in it but met with little approbation.'[17] Nonetheless, the account of the performance does pay attention to the presence of the author playing a part in her own play. And this seems to have been Haywood's aim: or at least the aim of a theatre management looking to use the novelty of the circumstance to give its audience a sense of being present at a new experience.

The plot of the comedy itself concerned a theme always close to Haywood's interest in her prose fiction, her poetry, and her translations: adultery – whether reputed or real – and its consequences in terms of public shame for women. Adultery discovered is the act that makes women visible, makes their survival precarious. The play resolves the amatory concerns of four women. A merchant's niece, Marilla, has promised her dying father to marry John Toywell, a fop. Toywell is only interested in her money while Ned Courtly loves her honourably. Her cousin, Celemena Fairman, is promised by the merchant her father to a foolish, drunken, boorish man named Sneaksby, heir to the Widow Stately. When Charles Gaylove, Courtly's friend, meets Celemena he falls in love with her. Courtly and Gaylove trick Toywell into thinking Marilla's fortune has been lost by her banker so that he breaks with her. Toywell, meanwhile, is making unwanted advances to the lovely and virtuous wife, Susanna Graspall, who is warned by a mysterious young man against spending time with Sir Harry Beaumont, a charming young libertine. Mrs Graspall is appalled to discover that her mean husband, Tony Graspall, has – on discovering Beaumont's passion –

---

[16]   Eliza Haywood, 'Prologue', in *A Wife to be Lett, A Comedy* (London: Dan. Browne and Sam. Chapman, 1724), p. 5.

[17]   David Erskine Baker, *Biographia Dramatica, Or, A Companion to the Playhouse* (London: Longman et al., 1811), 4 vols, vol. 4, p. 409.

offered him a night with his wife in exchange for £2,000. Susanna discovers that the mysterious young man apparently protecting her virtue is in fact a disguised castoff mistress of Beaumont's whom he had promised to marry, Amadea. Susanna brings Beaumont to his senses by reintroducing him to Amadea which rekindles his passion for the latter along with his guilt.

In the final act when all the characters are gathered, and it is revealed that a footman has tricked the Widow Stately into marriage by pretending to be a knight (hence excluding Sneaksby from his inheritance), Susanna exposes her husband's meanness and cruelty. Beaumont enters duelling with the disguised Amadea whom he claims he discovered in bed with Mrs Graspall. The latter says that she has lost all sense of shame since her husband sought to prostitute her; Tony Graspall's repentance though is won somewhat ambiguously because Susanna tells her husband that she handed over the £2,000 to her lovely young suitor (Amadea) in payment for 'his' advances; finance remains Graspall's governing motive. The married couple are reconciled when he repents and she promises to be obedient. Only Toywell is left without a wife at the conclusion of the play.

Nonetheless, the play's message is clear: men's investment in women's chastity is more often driven by avarice than moral principle. Women need to be very clever indeed to protect themselves from private abuse and public calumny. While the plot is in many ways a familiar comedy of intrigue in this respect, there are added dimensions. These stem not only from the fact the lead female part was played by the play's author, but also that the play consistently reminds us of the other literary identity of that author: that of a successful amatory novelist whose books are a stimulus to readers' erotic visions. Emily Hodgson Anderson in her analysis of *A Wife to be Lett* observes this 'play' between on and offstage persona which afforded Haywood an opportunity for 'self-conscious performance' of an identity 'simultaneously mysterious and accessible to her public'.[18]

A relatively conventional scene gains new resonance when we contemplate Haywood's taking the part of Susanna Graspall. Susanna is discovered at her toilet reading a book and in soliloquy she complains:

> How small a Relief can Books afford us when the Mind's perplex'd? –
> The Subject that our Thoughts are bent upon, forms Characters
> more capital and swelling, than any these useless Pages can produce
> and 'tis no matter on what Theme the Author treats; we read it our
> own way, and see but with our Passions Eyes – *Beaumont* is here in

[18]   Emily Hodgson Anderson, *Eighteenth-Century Authorship and the Play of Fiction*, pp. 23, 29.

ev'ry Line – *Beaumont* in all the Volume – I'll look no more on't –
These Opticks too are Traytors, and conspire with Fancy to undo me –
To what shall I have recourse?
    Enter Beaumont.[19]

Haywood takes advantage of the stage opportunity. Imagining a character can conjure that person on to the stage. The fantasy in Susanna's mind is made solid. This is a fairly conventional piece of stage business. But complicating the scenario is the fact that – for an audience familiar with Haywood's amatory novels – the scene also makes solid, it gives physical voice and presence, to the narrator/authorial persona of that fiction. The scene recalls the warmest and most familiar episodes in Haywood's successful novel *Love in Excess* in which the virtuous Melliora inveighs against the softening effects of love in books, in front of the assembled company, but is found asleep over Ovid's *Epistles* by the man for whom she nurtures a secret and illicit passion: her married guardian D'Elmont. That night D'Elmont enters her room and is only prevented from fulfilling her somatic fantasy of seduction by him when he is interrupted by a knock at the door.[20] In the scene with Susanna Graspall, Haywood plays both principal character and narrator of her fiction. Not only does Susanna's behaviour recall that of Melliora (and many other Haywood heroines), but her speech and style imitate that of the fictional narrator of the works in which they appear.

The presence of the book reminds us that Haywood is an author (of novels and of this play) as well as an actress in role. And yet, Susanna's lines also remind us of a *lack* of authority; as a woman in the grip of a powerful sexual attraction, she cannot help but bring the image of her lover to whatever words she is reading on the page. The author who claims, as Haywood does, to *protect* her readers from the dangers of seduction and adultery here admits that it is *readers* who produce meaning and may wilfully ignore the moral authority asserted in the work in favour of indulging their own fantasies.

Haywood's signature style involves the play of authorial presence and absence in the depiction of the strong effects of feeling, especially amatory passion, on the reasoning self. See, for example, this passage from *Love in Excess*. In the dark confusion of the garden to which Melliora has been led by her friend and rival Melantha (the agent of the knock on the bedroom door), she finds herself entangled with the amorous D'Elmont once more.

[19] *A Wife to be Lett*, Act 2, p. 21.
[20] Eliza Haywood, *Love in Excess*, ed. David Oakleaf, 2nd ed. (Peterborough, ON: Broadview, 2000), pp.106–18.

In rendering the encounter, the narrator admits her lack of control over the language of representation, a disavowal that serves only to make the author's fiction of presence more manifest. Haywood's amorous sublime is evident here:

> Honour and virtue may distance bodies, but there is no power in either of those names, to stop the spring that with a rapid whirl transports us from our selves, and darts our solus into the bosom of the darling object. This may seem strange to many, even of those who call, and perhaps believe that they are lovers, but the few who have delicacy enough to feel what I but imperfectly attempt to speak, will acknowledge it for truth, and pity the distress of Melliora.[21]

To return to *A Wife to be Lett*, the author's presence is further underlined by the equation of wife, authoress and the use to which her 'books' can be put. Susanna refers to characters made more 'capital and swelling' by errant thoughts of a love object. Haywood's writing seems insistently to have attracted a characterisation as 'swelling'. In *The Authors of the Town* (1725), Richard Savage described Haywood satirically in a couplet that speaks of her stage ambitions following her success in romance fiction:

> Flush'd with Success, for Stage-Renown she pants,
> And melts, and swells, and pens luxurious Rants.[22]

In 1725 a poem of praise by James Sterling riffs on swelling again. Nature smiles as Haywood's pen composes:

> The charming page pale Envy's gloom beguiles
> She lowr's, she reads, forgets herself and smiles
> Proportion'd to the image, language swells,
> Both leave the mind suspended – which excels.[23]

Haywood's embodying of her authorial self in playing a character on stage prompts a strange optical effect where she is conceived of as a swelling

---

[21]   Ibid, p. 122. On the sublime in Haywood, see Kathryn R. King, 'New Contexts for Early Novels by Women: The Case of Eliza Haywood, Aaron Hill, and the Hillarians, 1719–1725', in *A Companion to the Eighteenth-Century Novel and Culture*, ed. Paula R. Backscheider and Catherine Ingrassia (Oxford: Blackwell, 2005), pp. 261–75.

[22]   Richard Savage, *The Authors of the Town: A Satire, Inscribed to the Author of the Universal Passion* (London: J. Roberts, 1725), n.p. In Eliza Haywood, *Love in Excess*, ed. David Oakleaf, p. 272.

[23]   James Sterling, 'To Mrs Haywood', in *Love in Excess*, ed. David Oakleaf, p. 277.

body, pregnant of course with her works, which are also the indicators of a potential unchastity (recalling Pope's representation of Haywood's presence in the *Dunciad*). But Haywood seems to have anticipated, indeed prompted, these equations by playing with the presence of books on stage as early in her career as *A Wife to be Lett*.

When Sir Harry Beaumont presses his suit after he has interrupted Susanna's reverie in the second act, she pushes him into a closet to prevent him being discovered in her chamber when someone else enters (again recalling in comic form the scene of Melliora's near-undoing in *Love in Excess*). The intruder turns out to be the foppish Toywell who himself begins to court her; in trying to fend off his kiss, she falls against the closet door revealing Sir Harry behind it. Harry is swift to think up an excuse; finding Mr Graspall not at home he retired to this closet 'which I knew to be well furnish'd with Books – designing no more than to amuse myself till he came home – I happen'd to meet with one which so agreeably entertain'd me, that till the opening of the Door, I had forgot where I was.'[24] Toywell is not fooled and takes the metaphor a stage further, implying that Susanna is a good book neglected by an elderly reader with weak eyesight: Mr Graspall, he says, 'has indeed an admirable Collection – but Age has somewhat impair'd his Eye-sight, poor Man! I believe he seldom reads – And I must own 'tis a great Conveniency for a Gentleman, who has not Books of his own, to have the liberty of so fine a Library.'[25] Offended, Susanna quits the room and Toywell only retracts his innuendo when Beaumont pulls out his sword and threatens him. The relatively familiar trope of woman as book, rehearsed in prose fiction romances, here acquires a peculiar embodied life of its own in the person of the author entering and leaving the stage in character.

In November 1725 Haywood sought to revive the play, placing an advert that again encouraged interest in the author's relation to her part: *Mist's Weekly Journal* of 6 November reads 'Mrs Graspal, who has been our Customer 2 years desires us to inform the Managers of Drury-Lane Play-House, that if they please to play the Comedy, called, *A Wife to be* Lett, within ten Days, they will oblige her and a great many of the Quality to whom she communicates her Design.'[26] Haywood may have been seeking to capitalise on an opportunity: the play's plot resonated with the recent scandalous divorce of the Whig grandee, William Yonge, from his wife, the former heiress Mary Heathcote, in the autumn of 1724. The scandal seems to have particularly gripped Haywood's imagination in her various publications

[24] Haywood, *A Wife to be Lett*, p. 24.
[25] Ibid., p. 24.
[26] Spedding, *Bibliography*, p. 128.

of 1724 and 1725. Between the summer of 1723 and the summer of 1724 Haywood had been feverishly fostering her career as a novelist, partly as a result of her growing alienation from the literary coterie of Aaron Hill from which she finally separated in September 1724.[27] A four-volume collection of her works had appeared as well as four separately published short novellas.[28] On 12 July 1724 she published two novels, *The Fatal Secret; or, Constancy in Distress*, dedicated to William Yonge, and *The Surprize; or, Constancy Rewarded*, dedicated to Sir Richard Steele, Whig playwright, MP and periodical author.

The Surprize concerns the machinations of two wealthy young women, Alinda and Euphemia, to engineer their marriages to the men they love. In so doing, they bring to heel one of the young men who had earlier pursued Euphemia but rejected her, because she was then poor, in favour of her friend Alinda. Haywood here reworks the plot of Richard Steele's successful play, *The Conscious Lovers* of 1722, putting the female protagonists at the centre in place of his male friends who act in concert in their love interests to their own mutual advantage.[29] Steele was himself known to have contracted a mercenary first marriage to a widow who left him wealthy on her death while he was still young, so the critique of men's mercenary motives in the novel could equally apply to that play's author.

Given the satirical tone of Haywood's dedication to Steele, her anti-Whig tendencies, and the fact that the companion work to *The Surprize*, *The Fatal Secret*, was advertised in May 1724 just before the commencement of the Yonge divorce trial, it seems likely that Haywood also had a satirical intent in her dedication of that novel to William Yonge. And here too, she seems to have decided to offer a woman's perspective on stories that celebrated male virtue and wit in the courtship-to-marriage plot. However, the plot of *The Fatal Secret* offers a much darker perspective on women's vulnerability to public shame than either her earlier comedy or Steele's. Haywood was not alone in feeling compelled to speak out about the usage of Mary

---

[27]   Christine Gerrard details the literary rivalry for Aaron Hill's favour between the writers Martha Fowke Sansom and Eliza Haywood which seems to have resulted in Haywood's eventual exclusion from his coterie. See Christine Gerrard, 'The Scorpion Haywood: The Breaking of the Hillarian Circle, 1723–1725', chapter 4 of her *Aaron Hill: The Muses' Projector, 1685–1750* (Oxford: Oxford University Press, 2003), pp. 81–101.

[28]   *The Works of Mrs Eliza Haywood*; *Lasselia* (October 1723), *The Rash Resolve* (December 1723), *The Masqueraders* (April 1724).

[29]   See Tiffany Potter, 'Introduction', to her ed. *The Masqueraders, or Fatal Curiosity, and the Surprize, or Constancy Rewarded* (Toronto: University of Toronto Press, 2015), pp. 44–6.

Yonge by her husband who was a man universally disliked even by his own chief minister. Another woman writer of a very different social class and aesthetic temperament, Lady Mary Wortley Montagu, wrote a poem which circulated widely in manuscript in the bitter voice of the suffering wife: 'An Epistle from Mrs Y___ to her Husband'.[30]

The facts of the Yonge divorce case were as follows. The former Mary Heathcote, heiress, had been living apart from Yonge. She was discovered 'in naked bed' with her lover.[31] Her husband divorced her by Act of Parliament, suing her lover Colonel Thomas Norton for adultery in June 1724 for £1,500, and obtaining control of her dowry and fortune of £12,000 as well as an agreement that he could remarry, which he swiftly did.[32]

Haywood's dedication to her novel drips with irony, reminding her reader of Yonge's evidently obnoxious personality by apparently praising his sweetness and excoriating his lack of pity for a wife humiliated in public and stripped of her financial independence:

> *THAT inimitable Affability; that unequall'd Sweetness of Disposition; that condescending goodness, which softning the Severity of your other Virtues, makes you as dear to the Generality of the World, as you are necessary to a Part of it:—It is from this Beneficence of Nature, that I alone can Hope a Pardon for the Presumption of my Zeal; and it is to this I offer the History of a Lady, whose greatest Misfortunes were occasioned by a Virtue not very common among Women, the* Gift of Secrecy. *If her Sufferings have any Pretence to your Pity, or the Relator of them to your Forgiveness, it will be a Favour which the whole study of my future Life can never acknowledge as I ought;—* [33]

In the novella itself, the heroine Anadea is discovered in bed on the information of servants (servants bore witness at the Yonge trial) with the man

[30] Mary Wortley Montagu, *Essays and Poems and Simplicity, A Comedy*, ed. Robert Halsband and Isobel Grundy (Oxford: Oxford University Press, 1977), pp. 230–2. For a discussion of the poem, see Lawrence I. Lipking, *Abandoned Women and Poetic Tradition* (Chicago, IL: University of Chicago Press, 1988), pp. 10–11.

[31] *Journal of the House of Lords* (27 November 1724), *Journal of the House of Lords: Volume 22, 1722–1726* (London, 1767–1830), pp. 343–61, p. 360. *British History Online*, www.british-history.ac.uk/lords-jrnl/vol22/pp343-361 [accessed 24 February 2020].

[32] H.T. Dickinson, 'Yonge, Sir William, Fourth Baronet (c. 1693–1755), Politician', *Oxford Dictionary of National Biography*, 23 September 2004; https://ezproxy-prd.bodleian.ox.ac.uk:3030/view/10.1093/ref:odnb/9780198614128.001.0001/odnb-9780198614128-e-30232 [accessed 20 February 2020].

[33] Eliza Haywood, *The Fatal Secret: or, Constancy in Distress* (1725); reprinted in *Secret Histories, Novels, and Poems*, vol. 3, pp. 207–54, pp. iiii–iv.

she has secretly married (the Count de Blessure), by a chevalier to whom her father has betrothed her. Blessure kills the chevalier in the ensuing fight and is imprisoned for his crime. Blessure's mercenary father obtains his son's freedom and wishes to force him to marry an heiress. Anadea remains true to her promise to keep the fact of their marriage secret. The father has his son abducted and removed to distant lands while Anadea retires shamed to the country. Here her path crosses with her father-in-law again. Unaware of their kinship and seized with lust, he drugs and rapes her. Meanwhile, Blessure has been making his way back to his bride, arriving the morning after the fateful rape. She wakes to find him by her bedside and her father-in-law standing nearby in his bedshirt. Anadea stabs herself with Blessure's sword, the father mad with penitence shoots himself, and Blessure dies of his grief a few years later.

In this story, then, Haywood makes the wife and – to a lesser extent – her lover-husband victims. Blessure's thoughts echo the speeches of Sir Harry Beaumont in *A Wife to be Lett*. Both men determine that the fact the women they love continue to give them access and listen to their suit is a sign that they will eventually give in to mutual desire. The French heroine, Anadea, thus bears close resemblance to Susanna Graspall. However, only one letter distinguishes her name from that of another character in *A Wife to be Lett*, the seduced Amadea who resorts to cross-dressing to pursue her seducer. Anadea and Amadea are amorous young women and both are treated with sympathy for their suffering. However, the lives of the novel heroine and the play heroine take very different courses. The novel heroine finds herself caught in a terrible tragedy due to an unwise secret marriage, whereas her namesake in the play wins herself the man she loves through her own witty and careful management of her opportunities. Nonetheless, Haywood indicates the thin line between these two outcomes in the closeness of their names.

Anadea also demonstrates traits that invite the reader to identify with her author, to see here also the borders of character and narrator blurred. She is identified early in the novel as intelligent and well-educated: 'Nor confin'd she her Studies to that Part of Education common to her own Sex, she had an extensive Genius, and emulated the other in their Search of Knowledge; she went a great way in the Mathematicks, understood several Languages perfectly well, and had she persever'd in Application, might have been as eminent for her Learning, as the celebrated Madam *Dacier*.'[34] In the novel's closing sequence, Anadea is still demonstrating the skills of an authoress. She turns herself into a character whose ethics can be debated

[34]   Ibid., p. 3.

with her father-in-law, speaking of herself in the third person and narrating her story as if it was that of another woman. When the latter courts her at her lodgings, she uses the occasion to challenge him about the treatment of his son, which has become common knowledge. Her arguments (or charms) are so persuasive that the father is forced to concede that – had the woman he thinks is his son's mistress the loveliness he finds in her – then he would not blame him for such stubborn loyalty. 'THESE Words,' comments the narrator, 'gave *Anadea* in the Character of a third Person sufficient room to plead her own Cause; which she did so effectually, that he had little to say to excuse his Severity.'[35] Haywood recalls the language and scenes known from her novels and alludes to her familiar stage role as a wife tempted by adultery. In the scene in which Anadea is raped by her husband's father, Anadea is drugged and Blessure's father climbs into bed with her; she dreams of her nights of union with her husband and responds in her dream state to the father's sexual advances until the 'real Warmth of those Caresses she receiv'd, making her Dreams more lively, she return'd his Ardors with an Extasy too potent for the dull God's Restraint. – Unbounded Rapture broke thro' the power of Art – all her Senses remain'd at once their Liberty, and she awoke, to sleep no more.'[36] In horror she cries, '*Adultery – Incest – Damnation.*'[37] Similarly, the heroine Melliora responds to D'Elmont's embraces while she sleeps and dreams of him, but reacts with alarm when she wakens to discover the embraces are real:

> [he] seized her with such a rapidity of transported hope-crowned passion, as immediately waked her from an imaginary felicity, to the approaches of a solid one. "Where have I been!" said she, just opening her eyes, where am I?" – And then coming more perfectly to her self, "Heaven! What is this?" – I am D'elmont," cried the orejoyed Count, "the happy D'elmont! the charming Melliora's D'Elmont."[38]

Melliora, of course, is truly attracted to the man who makes advances to her in her sleep but nonetheless pleads with him "forbear, I do conjure you, even by that love you plead, before my honour, I'll resign my life!"[39] It is only Melantha's knock on the door which prevents D'elmont from continuing; he flees to prevent their discovery together.

---

[35]   Ibid., p. 54.
[36]   Ibid., p. 55.
[37]   Ibid., p. 56.
[38]   Haywood, *Love in Excess*, p. 128.
[39]   Ibid., p. 128.

In later years, Haywood's stage appearances continue to reference her success as a popular novelist and to associate both with the suspicion of adultery. In 1730, actors played lifestyle puppets in a play by Henry Fielding called *The Author's Farce; and the Pleasures of the Town* presented at the Little Theatre in the Haymarket. The conceit is that a group of popular entertainers cross the River Styx and compete for the favour of the Goddess of Nonsense. The character of Mrs Novel was based, it seems, on Eliza Haywood's then well-established fame; daughter of the Goddess of Nonsense, she competes with her mother for the love of Signior Opera (a castrato) whom she (nonsensically) accuses of fathering her child. Of course, the union of opera and novel suggests the attraction rests on their mutual capacity for affective and meaningless noise. Haywood's biographer, Kathryn King, notes that this satirical representation of Eliza Haywood in the character of Mrs Novel was alternating in April 1730 with Haywood's own appearances at the Haymarket in the part of the passionate and charismatic castoff mistress, Briseis, to Achilles in *The Rival Father; or, the Death of Achilles*; the part of Achilles was taken by the play's author, William Hatchett, in his first produced play and his first role.[40] Hatchett was in his late twenties and Haywood in her mid-thirties.

The prologue to *Achilles* invites the audience to speculate that the pairing on-stage reflects one offstage and identifies Haywood as the partner with the power in the relationship:

> Our unskill'd Author too, who ne'er
> Before the Warrior's Truncheon graspt, nor Buskin wore,
> Your Favour for his first Attempt t'engage,
> Assumes, hard Task! Achilles on the Stage.
> To play Briseïs while *Eliza* deigns,
> All will be Real, that she only feigns.[41]

Hatchett relies, the prologue implies, on Haywood's presence to deliver his part. The pair continued to collaborate on plays and prose works through the 1730s and early 1740s: including translating together Crébillon fils' *Le Sopha* (1742), a new version of Henry Fielding's *Tragedy of Tragedies* as *The Opera of Operas* (1733) and an adaptation of *Arden of Faversham* (1736) in which Haywood played the adulterous wife, Alice Arden.

---

[40]   Kathryn King, 'Theatrical Thirties, 1729–1737', in *A Political Biography of Eliza Haywood*, pp. 55–72.

[41]   William Hatchett, 'Prologue, Written by A Friend', in *The Rival Father: or, the Death of Achilles* (London: William Mears and Thomas Corbett, 1730), n.p.

The habit of invoking Haywood's stage presence alongside her capacity as a prose fiction writer found more aggressive voice in the work of another man whom biographers have speculated may have had a sexual relationship with Eliza Haywood: Richard Savage. Savage was a poet who became infamous for his published claim to be the illegitimate child of Mrs Brett, Countess of Macclesfield, by Earl Rivers in *The Bastard* (1728).[42] He had also been part of the circle around Aaron Hill of the late 1710s but any friendship with Haywood turned sour when he appears to have sided with her rival, Martha Fowke Sansom; Haywood had presented him as Riverius, an unctuous pander to the sexual proclivities of Gloatitia (Sansom) in her *Memoirs of a Certain Island Adjacent to Utopia* (1724). Kathryn King makes short shrift of the flimsy evidence for the speculation that he may have fathered one of the children claimed to be Haywood's illegitimate offspring.[43]

Only two weeks after Pope had elaborated on Haywood's confessed sins in the footnotes to the *Dunciad Variorum* of 1729, Richard Savage (now known to have been one of the main Grub Street informants to Pope for the cast of the *Dunciad*) put Haywood centre stage in a prose work celebrating the art of the *Dunciad*. *An Author to be Lett* recalls Haywood's 1723 play in its title. It asserts that the author Iscariot Hackney found the manuscript now printed bound by a piece of greasy tape from 'Eliza's' hair ribbon or apron string. Among the other hacks who are advised to turn to alternative careers from their (bad) writing, Haywood is the only woman mentioned and she is mocked for her shortcomings as actress and novelist; the fact that she also wrote plays is not acknowledged. Savage suggests that when Haywood '*grew too homely for a* Strolling Actress' she might better '*tho'once a* Theatrical Queen' turn 'Washerwoman', and contemplate '*the sullied Linen growing white in her pretty red Hands, as an Emblem of her Soul, were it well scour'd by Repentance for the Sins of her Youth*'; but she '*rather chuses starving by writing Novels of Intrigue, to teach young Heiresses the Art of running away with Fortune-hunters, and scandalizing Persons of the highest Worth and Distinction*'.[44] Haywood also did not leave behind her acting and

---

42   Richard Savage, *The Bastard: A Poem, Inscribed with all Due Reverence to Mrs. Bret, once Countess of Macclesfield* (London: T. Worrall, 1728).

43   Kathryn King, 'Eliza Haywood, Savage Love, and Biographical Uncertainty', *The Review of English Studies*, new series, 59, no. 242 (2008), 722–39.

44   Richard Savage, 'The Publisher's Preface', in *An Author to Be Lett. Being a Proposal Humbly Address'd to the Consideration of the Knights, Esquires, Gentlemen, and other Worshipful and Weighty Members of the Solid and Ancient Society of the Bathos. By their Associate and Well-Wisher Iscariot Hackney* (London: Alexander Vint, 1729), n.p.

its association with the adulterous woman. On 21 January 1736, Haywood reprised the business of taking on the lead role of an unhappily married wife when she appeared in her own reworking of the sixteenth-century domestic tragedy *Arden of Faversham* as Alice Ardcn, a wife seduced by a lodger with whom she conspires to murder her husband.

Six years later, Haywood returned in her fiction to the insight she had provided in *A Wife to be Lett* into married women's vulnerability to a husband's avarice and the risks of public shame. The story she was handling was one covered in the newspapers and was a case of bigamy taken by Elizabeth Scrope against her cousin Thomas Cresswell whom she had married clandestinely in 1742. Two years later, he married an heiress Anne Warneford, who bore him two children. Meanwhile Elizabeth was courted by a rich neighbour, Lancelot Lee, and – when Cresswell refused to give up the estate he had promised her in marriage – she prosecuted Cresswell for bigamy. In the process of prosecution, it transpired that Cresswell had married a third woman prior to both of these marriages and hence his children with Warneford were deemed illegitimate. Letters in the *General Evening Post* defending themselves and accusing others appeared from Scrope, Cresswell and Lee. Cresswell and Scrope also published narratives accusing each other of hypocrisy and lying. Haywood published a novel in 1749 entitled *Dalinda: or, The Double Marriage* in which the cast of this scandal were entirely recognisable under the names of Malvolio (Cresswell), Dalinda (Scrope) and Leander (Lee).[45] As Earla Wilputte explains, it is a relatively even-handed treatment that does not reveal a secret truth about the guilt or innocence of parties, but rather critiques a marriage-market driven by money and the dangers of the public being duped by print media. Wilputte concludes that Haywood explores here 'not just how print has the power to lead readers astray, but how the public mistakenly regards print and the paper artifact as tangible evidence of a person's real character'.[46]

She also notes that Haywood is sceptical about contemporary claims that a written contract of marriage would provide more security for all parties than a verbal one (in fact the Scrope–Cresswell case was used to argue for Hardwicke's Marriage Act of 1752 by pointing out the plight of the wife left bigamous and her children illegitimate as a result of the prosecution). The authority of a husband, whether sealed through speech or writing, obliges women to submit: as Dalinda does in obedience to her vows to Malvolio

---

[45]   Eliza Haywood, *Dalinda: or, The Double Marriage* (London: C. Corbett and G. Woodfall, 1749).

[46]   Earla Wilputte, 'Haywood's Tabloid Journalism: *Dalinda: or, The Double Marriage* and the Cresswell Bigamy Case', *Journal for Early Modern Cultural Studies*, 14, no. 4 (2014), 131.

despite her discovery of his bigamy. In this last work, the presence of the stage figure of the wronged wife and the stage 'trick' of the 'wife's excuse' (the husband's agreement to divorce at the end of the play) have receded almost entirely from view. The form of the novel affords a means to counter the print fictions of newspaper journalism and the spoken performances of the law court. The incorporeality of an omniscient third-person narrator, unmarked by gender and wise to the rhetorical tricks of news and law court, stands surety for the promise that the book will instruct young women how to avoid Dalinda's fate.

In terms of the argument pursued here about the unconcealment and withdrawal of presence, *Dalinda* indicates a departure from Haywood's earlier authorial persona poised between theatre and novel. The version of authorial presence shaped in *Dalinda* is one that Haywood was to assert through her later career when she appears to have left behind a more ambivalent positioning between the corporeality of the playwright-per-former and the imaginative expansion of the amatory fiction-writer. The 'Preface to the Reader' asserts that:

> The Reader must ...expect no perfect Character – I have drawn my Heroes and Heroines, such as they really are, without any Illustra-tion, either of their Virtues, or their Defects. – Here are no poetical Descriptions, no Flights of Imagination, I have put no Rapsodies [*sic*] into their Mouths, and if I have not made them speak just as they did, I have at least made them speak as Persons in their Circumstances would naturally do.[47]

Novelistic prose now contains and manages the risks of a mode of empathy that was strengthened by a history of performance as well as representation.

Haywood's enemies and allies, from Savage and Pope to Fielding and Hatchett, repeatedly stage her in the figure of the wife attracted to adulter-ous liaisons. She is also cast as a woman subject to fantastical imaginings incarnated in forms without real substance such as the puppet Mrs Novel's impossible desire to reproduce with a dead castrato singer. Yet, the figure of the adulterous wife – whether actual or accused – seems to have provided Haywood with the opportunity to craft an authorial presence between the-atre and the novel. Her unusual status as actress as well as author added a particular frisson of embodiment (in actual performance or recalled in absentia through the voice of a print narrator) to these roles in both genres. However, that same figure often voices an anxiety about the power

---

[47]   Haywood, *Dalinda*, pp. vi–vii.

to control the mental images produced through the passions. Readers and audience are in most senses the author of the persons who appear on stage or in their minds as they read. No one in this sense 'owns' character. The act of adultery in a wife can be seen as a refusal of her husband's claim to ownership. And loyalty in a wife may not indicate submission to her husband's claim but rather an ongoing struggle to secure safety and happiness in the presence of a husband driven by jealousy, avarice or both. The play of unconcealment and withdrawal – between real contemporary scandal and fictional sources, between the elusive life of the author and the embodied lives of the characters she played on stage – constructs a presence-effect that extends beyond the single 'author'. The part of the 'wife' in the fictions performed by Haywood, written by Haywood and about Haywood produces a fiction of Being that eludes ownership while being closely identified with an authorial signature. That name becomes a name 'to be lett', open to being owned by others.[48]

---

[48]   Leah Orr argues that twenty-nine out of seventy-two works attributed to Haywood by Patrick Spedding in his *Bibliography* are based on unsatisfactory evidence. Leah Orr, 'The Basis for Attribution in the Canon of Eliza Haywood', *The Library*, 12, no. 4 (2011), 335–75.

Chapter 3
Henry Fielding: Ghost Writing

There can be no author of the eighteenth century whose presence as author was more determined by the changing fortunes of the theatre than Henry Fielding. Nor one more instrumental in translating, indeed transposing, the conventions of theatre to the new fictional vehicle of the novel. In the late 1730s and when Fielding himself was less than thirty years old – partly due to his own actions – the career he had made for himself writing for and managing theatre companies became too hot to handle. Henry Fielding turned to producing more of the partisan periodical writing he had already engaged in, alongside committing to two new professions in which his talent for fiction might thrive: the law and prose fiction.

Henry Fielding may be held partially responsible for the Licensing Act passed on 21 June 1737 which curtailed his career as manager of an acting company and prolific playwright. His modern biographers, Martin and Ruthe Batttestin, observe that in his stage career he 'broke too many windows and pulled down too many idols'.[1] He seems positively to have sought the intervention that meant, according to his contemporary Arthur Murphy, he 'left off writing for the stage when he ought to have begun'.[2] Rival playwright Colley Cibber, the target of so much of Fielding's satire, compared him to the ancient arsonist Herostratus who set fire to the second Temple of Artemis in Ephesus to establish his eternal fame, one 'who to make his poetical Fame immortal, like another Erostratus, set Fire to his Stage by writing up to an Act of Parliament to demolish it'.[3] On Monday 30 May 1737, the 'Little' theatre rented by the brilliant Henry Fielding at the Haymarket failed to open for its first night of two short farces that continued his satirical campaign against the government led by the prime

[1]   Martin C. Battestin and Ruthe R. Battestin, *Henry Fielding: A Life* (London: Rout-
      ledge, 1989), p. 233.
[2]   Arthur Murphy, 'The Life of the Author' (1762), in *The Works of Henry Fielding, Esq:
      With the Life of the Author*, 12 vols (London: W. Strahan, J. Rivington and Sons,
      1783), vol. 1, p. 42.
[3]   Colley Cibber, *An Apology for the Life of Colley Cibber: With an Historical View of
      the Stage During his Own Time*, ed. B.R.S. Fone (Ann Arbor, MI: University of Mich-
      igan Press, 1968), pp. 155–6.

minister, Robert Walpole. The landlord, John Potter, took down the scenery and filled the house with various forms of building material in order to prevent a performance he knew the government would disapprove.[4] Fielding was obliged to turn to other means of earning a living than the theatre for a period; despite the mercurial nature of his gifts, he was consistent in his merciless sending up of modish culture and popular appetites, while recognising that his own public and popular success rested on perilously proximate ground. His first experiments in the novel are parodies in line with these habits: his short satire of Samuel Richardson's *Pamela* entitled *Shamela* (1741) and the longer *Joseph Andrews* (1742), his 'comic Epic-Poem in Prose.'[5] This last – in its parodic mixing of high and low, comic and tragic – was itself a prose fictional re-rendering of the hybrid theatrical mock-forms for which he had become famous in the decade previous.

Henry Fielding's presence in his work – whether plays or novels – takes the form of a consistent spirit of mischief, a turbulent refusal to claim the moral high ground and a willingness to level his own career with those he condemns. Puppets and ghosts are Fielding's favoured devices, both on stage and page. They are used to figure the ghostly non-presence of authorial intention in a writing career he frequently characterises as a cycle of dispossession: an identity unable to create itself because it is (too) reliant on other 'hands'. Like the depictions of his *bêtes noires*, Prime Minister Robert Walpole and the theatre-manager John Rich, Fielding casts his authorial persona as a foolish puppetmaster pulling the strings of reluctant and crudely made instruments. Acts of virtue are more often the result of good impulse or accident than they are considered moral choices in Fielding's works.

The fiction of Fielding's presence was made in sequential and repetitive acts of unconcealment and withdrawal both within individual works and transmedially. I argue that it is best understood as a form of improvisation. Or rather a fiction of improvisation in acts of impersonation. This fiction – in both his plays and his novels – imbues his work with a sense of immediacy and creative risk: often manifest through the risky conflation of author with satiric target, when both are conjured into being in a flash of creative

4   See Thomas Lockwood, 'Introduction', in *The Historical Register for the Year 1736 and Eurydice Hiss'd*, in his ed., *The Plays, Vol. 3: 1734–42*, The Wesleyan Edition of the Works of Henry Fielding (Oxford: Oxford University Press, 2011), pp. 394–5. The two plays (of which no versions survive) were 'Macheath turn'd Pyrate: or, Polly in India' and 'The King and Titi'. Both titles indicated they were satirical (oppositional) treatments of Walpole's government.

5   Henry Fielding, 'Preface', in *Joseph Andrews*, ed. Martin Battestin, The Wesleyan Edition of the Works of Henry Fielding (Oxford: Oxford University Press, 1966), p. 3.

connection. The Latin 'improviso' denotes that which is 'unforeseen; not studied or prepared beforehand'; it is art – usually music, song, or speech – brought into being in the moment. As we know, gifted improvisers must rehearse their technique so as to be able to perform such acts of making in the moment. This fiction of improvisation provided a kind of tension between immersion and distance which supports the sense of immediacy.

Fielding specialised in particular in meta-theatre: the rehearsal play (*Pasquin*,1736), the play within the play (*The Author's Farce*, 1730, 1734, and *Eurydice*, 1737), indeed the play about the play (*Eurydice Hiss'd*, 1737). And the 'signature' style of his major novels (*Joseph Andrews* in 1742, *Tom Jones* in 1749 and *Amelia* in 1752) was metanarrative; readers become familiar with the presence of a narrator who travels with them, responding to events as they unfold, speculating on their likely reception and subverting expectations. We are as audience or reader intensely aware of the presence of the works' makers and the work (or lack of it) they put into its making: playwrights and authors fail to complete necessary revisions before or after rehearsal or performance or publication, actors fail to learn their lines. Contingency – family difficulties, debt, illness – intervenes not only to prevent completion but also to produce unexpected outcomes and unusual, 'novel', innovations. The author is often presented as a spectre at his own feast, present but without agency. Fielding's author takes the shape of a ghost in a variety of senses. He is unable to intervene in events and outcomes but able to make himself intermittently visible and to stir up controversy. He is helplessly dependent on the corporeality of others. He inhabits the bodies of others: actors, characters in fiction, the mortal enemies that have brought about his own demise.

See for instance, a telling scene in the Lucianic prose narrative, *A Journey from This World to the Next*, first published in the second volume of Fielding's three-volume *Miscellanies* of 1753. The spirit-author has arrived at the gates of Elysium where Minos decides whether to open the gates to hopeful candidates or send them back to live out another life and return with better prospects:

> a Spirit … told the Judge, he believed his Works should speak for him.—What works? answered *Minos*. –My Dramatic Works, replied the other, which have done so much Good in recommending Virtue and punishing Vice.—Very well, said the Judge, if you please to stand by, the first Person who passes the Gate, by your means, shall carry you in with him: but if you will take my Advice, I think, for Expedition sake, you had better return and live another Life upon Earth. The Bard grumbled at this, and replied, that besides his Poetical Works, he had

done some other good Things: for that he had once lent the whole Profits of a Benefit Night to a Friend, and by that Means had saved him and his Family from Destruction. Upon this, the Gate flew open, and *Minos* desired him to walk in, telling him, if he had mentioned this at first, he might have spared the Remembrance of his Plays. The Poet answered, he believed, if *Minos* had read his Works, he would set a higher Value on them.[6]

Fielding and Colley Cibber (the frequent target of Fielding's comedy in this and other works) were the only playwrights who had published collections with the title 'Dramatic Works' before the year that the *Miscellanies* were published. As elsewhere, in the *Miscellanies*, Fielding appears to have encouraged some conflation of his presence with that of Colley Cibber, leaving his reader unsure whether he is defending his own conduct or mocking that of a rival playwright and theatre manager whose career appeared to parallel his own.

A rival force is, then, overcome by an act of impersonation which both diminishes and appropriates. Henry Fielding used the technique to challenge those to whom he opposed himself aesthetically and politically such as Colley Cibber and Robert Walpole. Political and theatrical ascendancy are intimately associated as Stephen Greenblatt observed in his influential essay, the 'Improvisation of Power'. Greenblatt argues that Iago improvises a version of Othello's mind which Othello is then insensibly compelled to imitate. Iago designs a plot that defeats a competitor through an improvisatory power to imitate the 'other' in order to manipulate him or her.[7]

Fielding repeatedly locates this improvisational agency in non-human figures, especially the puppet and the ghost. Ghosts from the spirit world were also commonly represented in Fielding's plays as puppets. Most eccentrically, his 1730 play *The Author's Farce*, in which Eliza Haywood was lampooned as Mrs Novel, saw the ghosts of nonsensical forms of popular entertainment portrayed by actors playing puppets. With squeaky voices and mechanical movements, actors communicated the shallow aesthetics of modern culture and its forms of entertainment: opera, Methodistical sermonising, pantomime, novel. Puppets, like ghosts, are presences that

---

[6]   Henry Fielding, 'A Journey from This World to the Next', in *Miscellanies by Henry Fielding, Esq: Vol 2*, ed. Bertrand A. Goldgar and Hugh Amory, The Wesleyan Edition of the Works of Henry Fielding (Oxford: Oxford University Press, 1993), book 1, chapter 7, pp. 32–3.

[7]   Stephen Greenblatt, 'The Improvisation of Power', chapter 6 of *Renaissance Self-Fashioning: From More to Shakespeare* (Chicago, IL: Chicago University Press, 1980), pp. 222–54.

represent death-in-life. That they are played on stage by real live bodies adds to the comedy of the satire for Fielding.

In book 12, chapter 5, Tom's tutor Partridge persuades Tom to attend a puppet theatre performance of the Vanbrugh/Cibber play *The Provok'd Husband* of 1728 (see Chapter 8). The show they see treats only the serious and moral main plot of the play concerning the reform of a society woman, Lady Townly, who renounces her late-night pleasure-seeking in gaming and society to save her marriage. The company watching the show agree that it promotes good behaviour among the young and impressionable but Tom dissents, expressing his preference for Punch and Judy (in the spring of 1748 Fielding had set up a puppet theatre under the name of 'Madame de la Nash' to perform '*the Comical Humours of* PUNCH *and his wife* JOAN').[8] Tom and Partridge find their landlady the next morning cuffing her maid, Grace, whom she has discovered 'on the Puppetshow Stage in Company with the Merry Andrew, and in a Situation not very proper to be described'.[9] The 'Merry Andrew' is the clown in an entertainment troupe and it is left ambiguous whether the reference here is to the clown puppet or a clown who accompanies the puppetmaster. Regardless, the maid Grace (who shares her name with the exemplary sister-in-law of Lady Townly in *The Provok'd Husband*) has been found on the stage substituting her lewd performance for the exemplary one performed by the puppets earlier. Here too, then, living bodies substitute for, but perform as, puppets on a stage. Fielding's stage plays and novels, the stages in the novels, and the novelties performed on his stages-within-stages, invite confusion between the dead and the living, the corporal and the machine.[10]

In this chapter, I concentrate on one volume of the three-volume work Fielding embarked upon after the Licensing Act of 1737 with the ambition to restore his fortunes as a writer: his *Miscellanies*. He had enjoyed considerable success as a playwright, more than any other of the 1730s; of his

---

8 Battestin, *Henry Fielding*, p. 435. See pp. 435–9 for more detailed discussion of the puppet wars between Colley Cibber, Henry Fielding and Samuel Foote in the spring of 1748.

9 Henry Fielding, *The History of Tom Jones: A Foundling: Vol. 2*, ed. F. Bowers and M.C. Battestin, The Wesleyan Edition of the Works of Henry Fielding (Oxford: Oxford University Press, 1974), p. 461.

10 See Joseph Drury, 'Realisms Ghosts: Science and Spectacle in *Tom Jones*', in *Novel Machines: Technology and Narrative Form in Enlightenment Britain* (Oxford: Oxford University Press, 2017), pp. 84–107, p. 105. Marcie Frank also discusses this scene in *Tom Jones*; she sees it as illustrative of Fielding's ironic treatment of the theory of aesthetic response as imitation that had prompted the reform of the 'rakish' stage in the 1690s; Grace imitates behaviour she has *not* seen on stage (Frank, *Novel Stage*, p. 103).

twenty-nine plays many enjoyed long runs and revivals. Thomas Keymer totals that over three nights from 27 to 29 April 1736, seven different plays could be seen across four venues in a total of nine stagings.[11] However, Fielding came from a large family in straitened circumstances, was famously improvident and expensive in his appetites, and now had his own young family to support. He appears to have begun organising materials early in 1741, exhausted from running two careers as a hack-writer and student of law, but still in urgent need of income. The *Miscellanies* were to be published by subscription with a price to subscribers of one guinea, one half at the time of subscription and the other at delivery, and hence more likely to provide an income to compete with that of the playwright rather than the piece rates from publishers that occasional publication could provide. A list of 427 subscribers was published with the *Miscellanies* on 7 April 1743.

He had already seen into print novels and plays written after the Licensing Act: *Shamela* (April 1741) and *Joseph Andrews* (February 1742) were ephemeral and experimental novels in response to Samuel Richardson's *Pamela* (November 1740). In May 1742, Fielding had also helped to write a play in collaboration with David Garrick, *Miss Lucy in the Town*. And on 17 February 1743, a new play, *The Wedding-Day*, opened for Garrick's first season at Drury Lane. Alongside these works in the genres of theatre and novel, he was working on the *Miscellanies* which can be seen as an important – if improvised – work of intermediality *between* theatre and novel. As with most improvisation, the causes were contingent. Fielding found it difficult to gather sufficient material for the three-volume work and was obliged to announce a series of delays to the planned date of publication, as well as repurpose works to meet the promised substance in the eventual work.[12]

The first volume was given over to short pieces and occasional works, including the relatively small amount of poetry Fielding produced. It showcased his ethics, his principles and his skills as a translator, and it included poems and essays in verse, a translation from the Olynthiac orations of Demosthenes, some brief satires and sketches in imitation of Lucian as

---

[11]   Thomas Keymer, 'Henry Fielding's Theatrical Career', in *The Cambridge Companion to Henry Fielding*, ed. Claude Rawson (Cambridge: Cambridge University Press, 2007), p. 19.

[12]   *Miscellanies* was originally advertised in *The Daily Post* of 5 June 1742 to appear by 25 December 1742 which noted that 'The Publication of these Volumes hath been hitherto retarded by the Author's Indisposition last Winter, and a Train of melancholy Accidents scarce to be parallell'd' ('General Introduction', in *Miscellanies by Henry Fielding, Esq. Vol. 1*, ed. Henry Knight Miller (Oxford: Clarendon Press, 1972), p. xlvi).

well as some prose essays. The third was given over entirely to his fictional version of the life of Jonathan Wild, the notorious thief whose career was presented in a far-from-implicit parallel with that of the now retired prime minister, Robert Walpole. The second was always intended to contain his Lucianic fiction, *A Journey from This World to the Next*, but was also provided with 'filling' in the shape of the publication of two unsuccessful plays: *Eurydice* and *The Wedding Day*, neither of which were mentioned in the original 'Proposals' for publication of 5 June 1742. Both the plays had seen publication shortly after their first performance, *Eurydice* considerably earlier in 1737 but *The Wedding Day* had been performed as recently as February 1743 and had been printed while it was still in performance in a short run at Drury Lane.

The second volume of *Miscellanies* might then seem to be a work of improvisation, put together virtually on the spot to complete a long-advertised work that was running into difficulties with an ever-extending deadline. Yet, it acquires a coherence that the other volumes lack, the first a compendium of many short pieces and the third containing only one work – a criminal biography – that sat oddly with the claim to miscellaneity. The second volume moves from a Lucianic journey to heaven, to the earthly ground of the London comedy of intrigue in *The Wedding-Day*, to katabasis, a visit to the underworld. I follow this journey to observe the improvisational play with authorial presence (as ghost or spirit) in each of these spaces and times. The second volume of the *Miscellanies* provides us with a sequence of unconcealments and withdrawals that look back to a performed past to construct a present in print.

The second volume of *Miscellanies* concludes with a version of the myth of Orpheus in the shape of the one act farce, *Eurydice*. In the classical myth, Orpheus takes a journey to the underworld to retrieve his much-loved wife, Eurydice. He is granted his wish if he succeeds in crossing back to life from the underworld without looking back at his wife as she follows, a proviso he fails to keep. Joseph Roach describes 'performance' itself as Orphic. Performance is Orphic because, as in the story of Orpheus, it cannot help but look back even as it looks forward. While performance is always just a beat ahead of its anticipated reception by an audience, it is always haunted or ghosted by past performances successful or failed. Improvisation as performance is a heightened version of this tension between an absent past and an imminently-to-be-realised future. It rests on contingency, the future event or circumstance which is possible but cannot be predicted with certainty. To successfully improvise you must draw on past knowledges and performances, but you must also break free from them. To look back can be to cripple a future:

The action that the Orphic plot imitates—moving forward while glancing back—recapitulates the risky act of performance itself, for the performer typically feels the urge to look back, despite the prohibitions and costs, because performance always seems to be authorized by something prior, even when it isn't.[13]

As Roach points out, performance involves surrogation: a performer represents a part or person from a past, a new actor takes a part known from a previous performance. So too, the Orphic myth is one of surrogation. Eurydice is after all punished *for* and *in place of* Orpheus; it is he who looks back, she who must remain. Performance is a repetitive, imitative behaviour which looks 'back' to past performances and is punished for it – locked in a perpetual present. However, Eurydice's absence or loss is also the ground for an artistic presence, an artistic life. Orpheus must fill her absence with compensatory song.

Loss is both the impediment to and the reason for the *Miscellanies* and seems especially resonant in this second volume: there is explicit reference to the loss of Henry and Charlotte Fielding's oldest child, five-year-old Charlotte, who died early in March 1742. When the narrator of *A Journey* enters into Elysium, he is reunited, to his 'extatic Joy,'[14] with his 'little Daughter, whom I had lost several Years before.'[15] In the fantastic space of Elysium, a re-union, a restoration of the lost thing, can be imagined. Absence and presence, loss, substitution and repletion, are distributed across the forms of play and novel in the shared print space of a volume which appears to be the product of contingency and improvisation. In what follows, I look at each work in turn, pointing out the ways in which they rehearse preoccupations with lost pasts and imagine new futures. A vision of an intermedial future (between theatre and novel) is made present in futures and spaces that move between and across different worlds.

The world of the stage is never far from the Lucianic print fantasy of *A Journey.* The Spirit who narrates his journey to Elysium and the other spirits he encounters there, is meant to be recognised as a version of Fielding himself through reference to his fame as a playwright. The Spirit, for example, has a comical, friendly encounter with the spirit of the diminutive hero

---

[13] Joseph Roach, 'Performance: The Blunders of Orpheus', *Periodical of the Modern Languages of America (PMLA)*, Special Topic: Literary Criticism for the Twenty-First century, 125, no. 4 (October 2010), 1078–86.

[14] Fielding, *Miscellanies Vol 2*, book 1, chapter 8, p. 37.

[15] Ibid., p. 36.

Thomas Thumb, whom Fielding had immortalised in his burlesque play *Tom Thumb* (1730) and its adaptation as *The Tragedy of Tragedies* (1731).[16]

Minos, the keeper of the gate to the Elysian fields, either lets applicants through or requires them to go back to earth to transmigrate into another life and hope to earn entrance again on its completion. This system looks like nothing so much as that of a stage manager casting his company; the unsuccessful actor plays one part and no more. In the Lucianic tale, unworthy spirits are obliged to take further parts until they prove sufficient virtue to enter. Hence Julian the Apostate (Flavius Claudius Julianus, AD 331–63, a Roman emperor who converted to paganism), we discover, was obliged to be reborn as Archbishop Latimer, the Protestant martyr burned at the stake in 1655. This, we are told, was the last manifestation of many. He:

> had been denied Admittance, and forced to undergo several Pilgrimages on Earth and to act in the different Characters of a Slave, a Jew, a General, an Heir, a Carpenter, a Beau, a Monk, a Fidler, a wise Man, a King, a Fool a Beggar, a Prince, a Statesman, a Soldier, a Taylor, an Alderman, a Poet, a Knight, a Dancing-Master, and three times a Bishop, before his Martyrdom, together with his other Behaviour in this last Character, satisfied the Judge, and procured him a Passage to the blessed Regions.[17]

Fielding's spirit-author asks Julian for a 'Recital' of his transmigratory adventures and – like the proficient actor required to maintain a huge range of repertory parts in his mind – Julian says 'he perfectly recollected every Circumstance.'[18]

The bulk of *The Journey* (chapters ten to twenty-five) consists of Julian's first-person narration of his different rebirths; the author-spirit sits with the spirit of his dead daughter on a flowery bank and Julian commences his tale with 'the Time I acted the Part of the Emperor *Julian*.'[19] After each life, Julian returns to Minos who considers him to have insufficiently demonstrated the necessary goodness for successful entry. Julian conceives of himself as an actor it seems, slipping into a series of parts and often struggling to shake off the character he adopted even though he has now retired to a state of passionless detachment. In chapter xxii, when describing his life as a tailor, he finds that his past adopted persona continues to infect his

---

[16]　Ibid, book 1, chapter 9, pp. 41–2.
[17]　Ibid., book 1, chapter 10, pp. 45–6.
[18]　Ibid., p. 46.
[19]　Ibid., p. 46.

present narrating self: 'In several of the Characters which I have related to you, I apprehend, I have sometimes forgot my self, and considered my self as really interested, as when I personated them on Earth. I have just now caught my self in the Fact: for I have complained to you as bitterly of my Customers as I formerly used to do, when I was a Taylor.'[20]

Where does the author sit in this ethical economy of manager/judge and actor(s)? Fielding's authorial spirit does not gain admittance on the basis of his aesthetic achievements; their ethical influence cannot be proved, as we have seen. It is on other grounds – his benevolent use of his earnings to alleviate the sufferings of a friend – that he wins entry.

When the narrator does gain entry to Elysium, however, he encounters a number of other writers (Homer, Virgil, Milton): all of whom are very resistant to providing him with answers to his questions about the meanings of their work. Theatrical characters, such as Tom Thumb, and the actors who play their parts, prove much more forthcoming than this group of authors. Shakespeare, for instance, is impatient with a debate vigorously disputed between Barton Booth and Thomas Betterton about how to interpret the emphasis in a line from *Othello*.[21] Fittingly, the line is delivered as Othello sends Desdemona to the next world: 'Put out the light, and then put out the Light.' Fielding-spirit cannot help but weigh in with his own reworking. The dispute is about how the actor might render the line. Betterton argues for even emphasis, Booth wants the emphasis on the second 'the', Fielding suggests 'thy' in the place of the second 'the', an unnamed fourth disputant suggests the 'very *sophisticated* in my Opinion' 'thee Light', and a fifth wants to alter the last word to make the final words of the line 'thy Sight'.[22] After all of this contention, Betterton, originally an advocate of an even reading, now says if they are to disturb the text in this way, they might as well convert 'thy Sight' to 'thy Eyes'.[23] When the disputants attempt to refer the decision to Shakespeare, he answers:

> 'Faith, Gentlemen, it is so long since I wrote the Line, I have forgot my Meaning. This I know, could I have dreamt so much Nonsense would have been talked, and writ about it, I would have blotted it out of my Works; for I am sure, if any of these be my Meaning, it doth me very little Honour.'[24]

---

[20]   Ibid., book 1, chapter 20, p. 99.
[21]   Ibid., book 1, chapter 7, pp. 39–40.
[22]   Ibid., p. 39.
[23]   Ibid., p. 40.
[24]   Ibid.

Shakespeare as author here acknowledges a lack of control over the 'meaning-effect' of his works and the power of 'presence-effect'; the actor's interpretation presents itself as though it were the embodiment of the author's intention. The author himself, though, rather than asserting ownership of meaning when he is given the opportunity, simply disavows it. Meaning is improvisatory and in the moment, not a manifestation of an intention that can be affirmed, owned and reasserted by reference to its apparent maker.

Further, the printed editions of the works of celebrated authors only further undermine the only effect that Shakespeare is prepared to own (up to): that of plain meaning. Shakespeare refers the disputants to Lewis Theobald's *The Works of Shakespeare* (1733) and the 'three or four more new Editions of his Plays' but is surprised at their search for 'obscure Beauties' in lines rather than admiration for the beauty of the 'plainest and most striking' meanings.[25] There is, of course, a delicious irony in the fact that all the 'author' and 'actor' speakers are spirits separated from the earthly bodies that wrote the play-text or delivered the words on stage. Their non-presence is what makes possible this meeting of minds from different temporalities and geographies. For Fielding the joke lies in the *lack* of insight that this supposed union provides. Indeed, the very insubstantiality of the spirit world – its lack of real presence – makes impossible the interpretive singularity of the embodied performance: which at least contingently fixes meaning in one performance or the selection of a preferred editorial variant.

In this prose fiction, Fielding turns the tables on his practice as a comic playwright. Fielding's Lucianic and rehearsal comedies are peopled with actors playing the parts of spirits, ghosts and puppets. Comedy derives from the fact that their material bodies are frequently a hindrance to the symbolic meanings these roles are designed to convey. In *A Journey from This World to the Next*, disembodied spirits are paradoxically given an emetic 'which immediately purged us of all our earthly Passions'. It seems that self-hood cannot be thought beyond or outside of bodily presence. Comically, at the opening of his account, the author-spirit describes his struggle to find a method of egress from his own body finally emerging from his nostrils and – once liberated – is dismayed to find that he cannot, as he hoped, fly; hopping provides a serviceable but far less attractive alternative means of self-transportation.[26]

For Fielding it is arguable that, even in life, the author is already closer to a state of disembodied vulnerability to co-option by other selves who

[25]   Ibid.
[26]   Ibid., book 1, chapter 1, p. 8.

enjoy more sway through their physical presence in the institutions in which he works: the actor, the theatre manager, the minister of state, the licenser, even the audience member. Authorial presence manifests in written script and is subject to reworking in rehearsal, licensing, performance, in response to audience. Some insight into the self-conscious instability of Fielding's control of authorial selfhood perhaps lies in the playful inclusion of a manuscript 'fragment' at the end of the *Journey*. Seventeen other books, we are told, have been lost and all that remains as conclusion is a first-person narration by the spirit of Anna Boleyn of her life.

The character of Anne Boleyn was one of the best-known roles in she-tragedy due to the continuing popularity of John Banks' *Vertue Betray'd: or, Anna Bullen* (1682).[27] The treatment of Anna Boleyn in *The Journey* is a departure from her characterisation in Banks' Protestant hagiography: she acknowledges that she was blinded by the attractions of the crown and is frank about her worldly education in manipulating men as a teenager at the French court. Nonetheless, she is an object of pity in her tragic wrong choice – in keeping with the theme of the *Miscellanies* that goodness is incompatible with the (fruitless) pursuit of greatness. The author-spirit of Henry Fielding wilfully silences itself or subjects itself to the resonant tones of celebrated actors, Julian and Anna.

We have seen that the *Journey* primarily refers to the author-spirit's writing as dramatic and brings him into contact with his fictional stage inventions such as Tom Thumb. 'The Introduction' plays with the conceit that his prose fiction characters are embodied members of the book-trade world. The editor of the *Journey* is given the work by Mr Robert Powney, Stationer (Powney did business at the Ship and Star close to that of Fielding's publisher, Andrew Millar) because of the editor's capacity to decipher near illegible script. He takes on the task of preparing it for print and shows the manuscript to his friend, Parson Abraham Adams 'who after a long and careful Perusal, returned it me with his Opinion, that there was more in it than first appeared' and that the Author 'seemed not entirely unacquainted' with the writings of Plato. The moral of the *Journey* is, like that of *Joseph Andrews*, that the aspiration to goodness and benevolence is more important than either its fulfilment in practice or historical greatness. Parson Adams is the embodiment of this moral in *Joseph Andrews*, and the same principle was a recurrent theme of Fielding's political propaganda (the basis of his attack on Robert Walpole, the Great Man, and the failing with which he charges his previous Opposition Patriot allies in the early 1740s).

[27] John Banks, *Vertue Betray'd: or, Anna Bullen* (London: R. Bentley and M. Magnes, 1682).

It seems also to have been a moral that the author Henry Fielding seems obliged to have frequently reminded himself in his own career.

If the topic of *The Journey* is an account of the struggle to achieve elevation to Elysium, the two dramatic works with which it was published in the second volume of the *Miscellanies* – despite Fielding's repudiation of any unity of design in the collection[28] – appear to have covered the two other regions. *Eurydice* offers katabasis, a journey into the underworld, while *The Wedding Day* (first performed 17 February 1743 at Drury Lane) is firmly grounded in the everyday world of fashionable London. Like those in *A Journey*, *Eurydice*'s characters (with the exception of the framing author and a critic who sit on stage to observe the play) are ghosts.

In publishing these two plays with *The Journey* Fielding may have been seeking to provide them with afterlives due to the failure of both works in performance to maintain an embodied life on stage. *The Wedding Day* was not performed until 1743 but Fielding describes it in the 'Preface' to the *Miscellanies* as the third dramatic work he wrote which dates its first composition to 1729–30.[29] The play had been separately published before the *Miscellanies* appeared in April 1743; Fielding's publisher Andrew Millar produced an overambitious run of 3,000 copies a week after the first performance of Fielding's first play on the London stage after the Licensing Act; the play however only ran for six nights and the two author benefits were especially poorly attended.[30] *Eurydice; or, the Devil Henpeck'd* was performed at Drury Lane on 19 February 1737 as an afterpiece to Addison's celebrated tragedy, *Cato*, but did not win approval for a second night. Fielding swiftly turned the death of his play into a very successful political satirical interlude, *Eurydice Hiss'd*, first performed at the 'Little' Theatre in the Haymarket he was renting on 13 April 1737; *Eurydice Hiss'd* paralleled the unsuccessful play hissed off stage to the unpopular Excise Act of Robert Walpole hissed out of the Commons in 1733. It was Fielding's last production before the Licensing Act closed down his company at the Haymarket; fittingly 23 May 1737 saw a benefit night for Eliza Haywood where she performed in the mainpiece *The Historical Register for the Year 1736* as well as

---

[28] The opening sentence of the Preface to the first volume of the Miscellanies asserts 'The Volumes I now present the Public, consist, as their Title indicates, of various Matter; treating of Subjects which bear not the least Relation to each other', *Miscellanies by Henry Fielding, Esq, Vol. 1*, ed. Henry Knight Miller, The Wesleyan Edition of the Works of Henry Fielding (Oxford: Oxford University Press, 1972), p. 3.

[29] Ibid., pp. 4–5. If it was his third work, then it was composed after *Love in Several Masques* (1728) and *Don Quixote in England* (written 1728–9).

[30] Hugh Amory, 'General Introduction', in *Miscellanies: Vol 2*, p. xlvi.

the afterpiece *Eurydice Hiss'd.*[31] *Eurydice* was not printed until it was added to the *Miscellanies* with the changed title of *Eurydice, A Farce. As it was d-mned at the Theatre-Royal in Drury Lane.*

In both works the 'author' features as a character invoked both on and offstage and the author's capacity to control the interpretation and reception is consistently mocked. The danger throughout is that the satirical target may become the author rather than the forms of superficial and unethical behaviour his work is designed to put on stage for mockery. Both plays are satires on fashionable married life, but *Eurydice* is in the mould of the mock-heroic conventions found at the height of Fielding's opposition output in the later 1730s. A gulf divides *Eurydice* and *Eurydice Hiss'd* from the direction he took after the 1737 Licensing Act when he turned to writing playscripts and novels representing the contemporary social world and its vices.

Fielding was practised in the mock-heroic style of the rehearsal or performance play which he preferred in his plays of the 1730s (*Tumble-Down Dick, The Author's Farce, Pasquin*). Here, the audience watches either a rehearsal or performance take place observed by the creator, whether author or manager, and critics. In *Eurydice*, the author and a critic settle down to watch a play. First on are actors playing the ghosts of two beaus, a soldier and a courtier. They refer to the presence in Hades of Signior Orpheo, a parodic treatment of the popular castrato opera singer, Farinelli (Carlo Maria Michelangelo Nicola Broschi); he seeks out the ghost of his wife, Eurydice, who – it transpires – is indifferent to her husband given that he is ill-equipped to provide her with the pleasure she seeks in the bedroom rather than through her ears (in his lovely singing voice). The allusion in this afterpiece to Fielding's three-act play, *The Author's Farce* (first performed 1730), is evident: in that play, the hero Harry Luckwood seeks to make his fortune through a puppet theatre. Adult actors took the part of puppets crossing the River Styx and seeking the patronage of the Goddess Nonsense. Mrs Novel (intended to be recognised as a comical treatment of Eliza Haywood) seeks reunion with her estranged lover, Signior Opera, whose (improbable) child she claims to have died giving birth to. Her mother, the Goddess Nonsense, falls in love with Signior Opera when he delivers an aria about the pleasures of money. Here then novel and opera are mutually derided as nonsensical vehicles for affect – they stimulate the senses without making sense.

---

[31]   Philip H. Highfill et al., *A Biographical Dictionary of Actors, Actresses*, vol. 7, p. 224. Haywood played a Lady and Mrs Screen in the mainpiece and the Muse in the afterpiece.

In *Eurydice*, Pluto, against the advice of his wife and moved by Orpheus's singing, agrees to the unusual exemption of allowing a dead person to return to earth. Proserpine responds to Eurydice's covert attempts to escape this new doom by saying that should Orpheus look back in the course of the journey then Eurydice can return to Hades. When he does turn at Eurydice's cries for help, the two dispute whether she purposefully cried out or he purposefully turned since neither is convinced of the other's passion. The play concludes back at Pluto's court, with Eurydice happily re-ensconced, a dance, and Pluto's assertion that man's earthly vices become their perpetual punishment when they come to his kingdom. Proserpine, though, has the last word with a more prosaic piece of advice that husbands would do best to give in to their wives' wills if they are to live an easy life.

The moral that the author-character draws from the play differs from those fielded by his characters of Pluto and Proserpine. The author declares that he wrote the play with the intention of exposing the moral and aesthetic poverty of the Italian opera for which there is a popular craze. Thus at the conclusion of *Eurydice*, when the Critic observes that Orpheus can only sing when he is out of his senses, the Author responds:

> Why, Sir, for an *English* people to support an extravagant *Italian* Opera, of which they understand nor relish neither the Sense nor the Sound, as heartily as ridiculous and much of a piece with an Eunuch's keeping a Mistress: nor do I know whether his Ability is more despised by his Mistress, or our Taste by our Singers.[32]

Mocking opera had been a preoccupation in Fielding's other plays; we have observed it in his 1730 *Author's Farce*. But we need not assume that the author-character is simply a substitute for Fielding; Fielding, as is his wont, may be mocking the practice of such mocking, the poor work of those playwrights who deride it (and *Eurydice* is not his finest hour as a play), and indeed his own well-known style(s). Nonetheless, creating a character called an 'author' who voices a similar position to that expressed elsewhere by the playwright and is played by an actor presents authorship with absence alongside presence; he is a ghost or spirit who inhabits another body at the scene of representation. Never slow to wrest every *double entendre* and paradox from his box of writing tricks, Fielding reminds his audience of this fact. *Eurydice* opens with the stage direction: '*Enter the* Author *in a Hurry. A* Critick *following.*'[33] The author complains that the

---

[32] 'Eurydice', in *Miscellanies Vol. 2*, p. 148.
[33] Ibid., p. 131.

actor who plays the Devil is not dressed and asks the prompter not to start the overture yet. 'Well, Sir, how do you find yourself? In what State are your Spirits?', asks the Critic.[34] The author's 'spirits' may be his own attitude to his creation and its performance or the reference may be to those actors he ostensibly 'owns' as they play the parts he has written for them. This is the familiar commonplace from William Shakespeare's *Tempest* where actors are described as spirits temporarily conjured up for the performance of a play. These, Prospero declares:

> As I foretold you, were all spirits, and
> Are melted into air, into thin air.[35]

However, Prospero is only associated with his author, Shakespeare, through analogy. Fielding invites a stronger association with his presence: here, as in *A Journey*, author-spirit appears to be a version of the author himself (like Fielding, this author has an animus toward opera). And yet, we cannot help but be reminded that he is himself present only in a 'spirit' form: the actor speaks his lines or represents a version of him. Fielding does not play himself.

Where, indeed, does an author find himself on the London stage? Here, the answer appears to be in the body of an actor who, like the reluctant Eurydice, may not be coupled easily with the author's spirit. Authors frequently complained that their plays have failed because of the inadequacies of the actors' performances. Indeed, part of the failure of the other play included in Fielding's second volume of *Miscellanies*, *The Wedding Day*, on its first production from 19 February 1743, may have lain at the door of casting. Fielding's favourite, the comic actress Kitty Clive, refused to take the part of the bawd, Mrs Useful (purportedly because she felt she should have taken the role of a virtuous heroine)[36] and it went instead to Macklin's

---

[34] Ibid., p. 132.

[35] William Shakespeare, *The Tempest*, Act 4, scene I, lines 148–50, *Modern Critical Edition*, ed. G. Taylor, J. Jowett, T. Bourus and G. Egan, The New Oxford Shakespeare (Oxford: Oxford University Press, 2016). Oxford Scholarly Editions Online, doi:10.1093/actrade/9780199591152.book.1 [accessed 20 February 2020].

[36] Fielding's friend, Charles Hanbury Williams, printed a comic poem about the spat. The first five lines again give the author a speaking part:

> 'A bawd! A bawd! – where is the scoundrel poet?
> Fine work, indeed, by G_d the town shall know it'
> Fielding, who heard and saw her passion rise,
> Thus answer'd calmly, 'Prithee Clive be wise,
> The part will fit your humour, taste, and size.'–
> (quoted Amory, 'Introduction', in *Miscellanies*, p. xlvi).

wife. In fact, Fielding hoped his own failings as an author would be compensated for by the presence of a consummate acting talent: that of David Garrick. Fielding admitted he was not 'warm' in pitching the play and only agreed to adapt it for performance due to Garrick's importunity for a role that would keep him, Garrick, on stage for a long time. Indeed, the rakish hero Millamour is on stage for most of the five acts. Even this could not compensate for the many faults Fielding admitted were in the play. Due to the serious illness of his wife in the week he had before submitting the script for a licence, he failed to correct it.[37]

In the end the spirit that kept the production afloat seems to have been neither Garrick's performance nor the author's talent as a playwright but the author's newfound reputation as a novelist. Any success it did have was thought to have been the result not of his reputation as a playwright but stemmed from curiosity about a new work by the author of the latest hit as a novel, *Joseph Andrews*. As in the case of *A Journey* discussed earlier, it is Parson Adams who stands surety. On the third day of the first production at Drury Lane, Mrs Russell observes:

> Fielding's Play had a fair hearing last night, first and second Acts tolerable but from thence every one grew worse to the End, but his friends will support it to a third night to which I hear of many going for the sake of Joseph Andrews.[38]

The author is present in spirit at *The Wedding Day* and emphatically so in terms of his new profile as a novelist. A prologue delivered and written by Charles Macklin was not apparently submitted to the Licenser but was made available in printed versions of the play. It is only another twist of irony (possibly purposeful) that Macklin's prologue only appears to have been available in print since it rests on the conceit that the author is present in the theatre to be called up and called upon by one of his actors. It is a prologue that rests heavily on the imagined presence of author and actors at the opening of a new play easily recognised by an audience familiar with their embodied appearances. Macklin opens by explaining why the prologue is not delivered by the lead actor, Garrick, who is so overwhelmed by the copiousness of his part that he cannot come onstage to deliver the Prologue. Macklin took the relatively small part of Mr Stedfast, the too-old prospective husband of Millamour's love-interest, Charlotte (the part Clive had wanted to take but was played by Peg Woffington); Mr Stedfast learns

---

[37]   See Fielding, 'Preface', in *Miscellanies, Vol. 1*, pp. 6–7.
[38]   Amory, 'Introduction', *Miscellanies Vol. 2*, p. xlvi.

in the nick of time that he is about to marry his illegitimate daughter by the bawd Mrs Useful which leaves Charlotte free to be claimed by Millamour.

Macklin reports in his prologue that the Author has told him not to bother with a Prologue but changed his mind when Macklin warned the audience will damn the play without it. The Author then asks Macklin to give a Prologue because he has a *'good long, dismal, Mercy-begging Face'*.[39] Rather than taking on this role of surrogate, Macklin points out the author in the audience and indeed invites comparison between his dismal face and the inappropriate merriment of that of the author (given that he faces a likely critical panning). Fielding has been lifting his 'spirits' through alcoholic spirits:

> *'Sir, your humble Servant: You're very merry.' 'Yes,' says he; 'I've been drinking*
> *To raise my Spirits; for, by Jupiter! I found 'em sinking.'*
> *So away he went to see the Play; O! there he sits:*
> *Smoke him, smoke the Author, you laughing Crits.*[40]

In a further attempt to divert a potential disaster, Macklin gestures to another absent (and entirely fictional) character, rather than his own in the Prologue or those staged in the play, and one he says looks more likely to gain applause from the author: Parson Adams in *Joseph Andrews*. Macklin speaks directly to the author in the audience inviting a comparison of their faces:

> *What think you now? Whose Face looks worst, yours or mine?*
> *Ah! thou foolish Follower of the ragged Nine,*
> *You'd better stuck to honest* Abram Adams, *by half:*
> *He, in spight of Critics, can make your Readers laugh.*[41]

Fielding's powers as an author are here represented as exhausted and under threat. He can no longer ask actors to stand in his place and defend him from criticism, but his experiments, improvisations or impersonations in novelistic character – especially the foolish, learned, virtuous Adams – may protect him. As in *A Journey* and *Eurydice*, Fielding's characters come to have more energy and power than the authors who are imagined as co-present with them at a variety of scenes: Tom Thumb, Parson Adams,

---

[39]   Charles Macklin, 'Prologue', in *The Wedding-Day*, in *Miscellanies Vol. 2*, p. 155.
[40]   Ibid., p. 155.
[41]   Ibid.

Anna Bullen, have more robust presence and confidence in their agency than their 'creators'.

Authorship emerges in Fielding's work as something 'improvised' in performance. The author anticipates his or her own presence in the mind of the consumer of the art work; to make that presence visible may not be to secure authority but rather to destabilise and decentre it. *Eurydice* again provides the cue. The author is himself impersonated or improvised by an actor in the opening scene of *Eurydice*. But the apparent abdication of such authority can also be a means of mocking those forms that appear to challenge it on stage: the sensory power of song substituting for sense, women's preference for sexual pleasure over aesthetic experience as expressed by Eurydice and Proserpine. Fielding improvises improvisation: he writes a performance play in which the anticipated narrative is not completed (neither Eurydice nor Orpheus want to be reunited) and in which those who make the stage play (author, prompt, critic, actors, even audience) also threaten to undermine its anticipated effect. But in doing so he enacts a process of control: he staves off or rather incorporates predictive uncertainty within the economy of theatre. He does so of course at a point when government threatened (and indeed succeeded in) introducing external controls. The Licensing Act was passed in May 1737, *Eurydice* was performed for one night in February and Fielding's satire *Eurydice Hiss'd* was performed in April.

In *Eurydice Hiss'd*, Fielding returns to the scene of the disgrace of his *Eurydice*. It was hissed off the stage. Fielding parallels his failure as author to the political failure of his arch-antagonist, Horace Walpole, the prime minister. Walpole's attempt to pass an Excise Act was hissed out of the House of Commons in 1733. Fielding's *Eurydice Hiss'd* was the final provocation for Walpole who then introduced a restrictive act against the stage. So here, Fielding plays the part of the improvisatory Iago to Walpole's Othello, improvising his enemy's part in order to manipulate him and subject him to the improviser's narrative. Fielding suggests that – in anticipating and neutralising the insurgent tendencies of the stage – the stage can be relied on to regulate itself. It does not require state intervention. The case of Fielding's *Eurydice* suggests that in the end it is the audience that determine the fate of the art work and can be relied upon to regulate extremes and restore aesthetic values. Neither author nor government need take on this role.

When Fielding embedded *Eurydice* in a print volume with two other works, one a work of prose fiction and the other a play, he invited readers to speculate about the kind of regulation the medium of print could afford by comparison with the stage. Not subject to licensing, print forms could

restore lost versions of plays (and the manuscript of *The Wedding Day* submitted to the Licenser on 19 January was much annotated by him to exclude
lewd passages[42]), provide paratextual accounts in dedications and prefaces
of performance history. Authorial *Miscellanies* simultaneously restored or
created a fiction of authorial presence and agency in that they are organised
around a single author[43] and revealed the contingent imperatives that were
often the very basis of miscellaneity. And this was an even more evident
tension in subscription miscellanies. Authors had to seize what was to hand
to meet commitments made in print to their subscribers; the work had to
speak of a presence and an aesthetic achievement beyond the incidental,
coincidental or collaborative success organised around the 'person' of an
author worth collecting with a likely posterity.

Henry Fielding had built his 'person' before that date on an impression of
the ephemeral and the improvisatory, indeed on a capacity to impersonate
others, to encourage a conflation between his person and his satiric target.
A surrogate actor could stand both for the author and the man he sought
to derogate (Robert Walpole, John Rich, Colley Cibber). In his fiction, nar-
rators have a facility of impersonation: Shamela improvises a version of
Pamela, Mr Wilson in *Joseph Andrews* tells Henry Fielding's life-story as
his own. And Henry Fielding's improvisatory techniques could accommodate the voices of others within his work: his sister Sarah Fielding provides
the letter from Leonora to Horatio in *Joseph Andrews*, completes the story
of Anne Boleyn in *The Journey*. And Henry Fielding returns the favour in
the shape of a Preface and five 'ill-assorted letters' (XL–XLIV) in Sarah's
Familiar Letters between the Principal Characters in David Simple (1747).
There are as many instances of dispersal of person as there are of aggrega-
tion. Equally, person repeatedly transforms into states of being other than
the human: the ghost, the puppet. Acts of unconcealment and withdrawal
add up, paradoxically, to an extraordinary mastery of authorial presence
and one that was to provide a model for many of – and especially – those
later novelists who sought to annexe the living energies of the stage for the
novel: William Makepeace Thackeray, Charles Dickens and George Eliot.[44]

---

[42]   See Battestin, *Fielding. A Life*, p. 361.
[43]   See Carly Watson, *Miscellanies, Poetry, and Authorship, 1680–1800*, Palgrave Studies
in Enlightenment, Romanticism, and the Cultures of Print (London: Palgrave Macmillan, 2020).
[44]   See David Kurnick, *Empty Houses*.

Chapter 4
Charlotte Lennox:
(In)dependent Authorship

Charlotte Lennox chose to adapt only one of her novels for the stage: *Henrietta* (1758). Her five-act comedy entitled *The Sister* opened on 18 February 1769 at George Colman the Elder's Haymarket theatre over a decade after *Henrietta* was first published. A novel by the writer who was the subject of our previous chapter, Henry Fielding, provided a source for the opening chapter of *Henrietta*. The reader meets the eponymous heroine pleading to join the company in a crowded stagecoach. The scene is a conscious imitation of that in the twelfth chapter of Henry Fielding's *The History of the Adventures of Joseph Andrews and of his Friend Mr. Abraham Adams* (1742). Henrietta Courtenay's fate is less severe than that of Joseph Andrews: Joseph is beaten, robbed and thrown into a ditch, while Henrietta is only introduced to two admirers, a predatory male rake and a silly 'whimsical' romance reader, both of whom are to prove dangerous to her later in the story. The latter, Miss Woodby, swiftly dubs Henrietta 'Clelia' to her 'Celinda' and recommends her to lodgings with a respectable milliner in London; in error, Henrietta is delivered to the door of the disreputable Mrs Eccles rather than that of the exemplary Mrs Egret.

The measure of Mrs Eccles's unsuitability is revealed in the milliner landlady's collection of 'novels and plays', among which Henrietta finally lights on a copy of *Joseph Andrews* 'one of the most exquisite pieces of humour in our language' having rejected Delarivier Manley's *New Atalantis* and a collection of 'Novels' by Eliza Haywood, these last warmly recommended by Mrs Eccles as the 'finest love-sick, passionate stories'.[1] From its opening scenes, then, *Henrietta* sets its moral compass according to the contemporary scene of narrative prose fiction: Miss Woodby's addiction to the seventeenth-century French romance indicates her Quixotic cast of mind, Mrs Eccles to Eliza Haywood her dissolute one, and Henrietta's fondness

---

[1] Charlotte Lennox, *Henrietta*, ed. Ruth Perry and Susan Carlisle, Eighteenth-Century Novels by Women series (Lexington, KY: University Press of Kentucky, 2008), vol. 1, book 6, pp. 22, 23.

for *Joseph Andrews* her powers of aesthetic discrimination regardless of her ignorance of the world. This early allusion to Henry Fielding's exquisite humour also indicates the kind of style and authorial presence that the author of *Henrietta* sought to emulate.

Henry Fielding as we have seen, turned his style as a playwright into a 'new' kind of composition, the comic novel, when he could no longer earn a living from the stage. The same could be said for Charlotte Lennox, who turned from a failed career as an actor to that of a novelist and took up writing for the stage when her reputation as a novelist was established, partly through the vigorous promotion of literary influencers in eighteenth-century London including Samuel Johnson, David Garrick, Joshua Reynolds. The daughter of an army officer, Charlotte Ramsay spent her childhood in Albany, New York where her father was colonel of the British fort. She came to London unaccompanied at the age of fourteen to stay with an elderly aunt in Essex who could not in the end support her. The young Charlotte, undaunted, secured the patronage of two aristocratic women, Lady Cecilia Isabella Finch, first lady of the bedchamber to the royal princesses, and Lady Mary, the Marchioness of Rockingham. At seventeen, she appeared in the part of Lavinia in Nicholas Rowe's *The Fair Penitent* at Drury Lane (1746): a substantial role portraying a virtuous and intelligent wife. The following year she saw through the press her *Poems on Several Occasions* only one month after her marriage on 6 October 1747 to Alexander Lennox who may have been the assistant to her publisher William Strahan. In 1748 she appeared in private theatricals at Richmond and in February 1749 she took the role of Almeria, the lead role, in Congreve's tragedy of *The Mourning Bride* at the 'Little' theatre, Haymarket.

Her first novel *The Life of Harriot Stuart* was published in 1751 and included a satirical portrait of her one-time patron, Lady Finch. It was swiftly followed by the two works for which she is now best known: the novel *The Female Quixote* (1752) and a three-volume work of criticism *Shakespear Illustrated* (1753–54). She continued to publish drama in the shape of an unperformed dramatic pastoral *Philander* in 1758 and a comedy *Old City Manners* adapted from Ben Jonson, Chapman and Masters' *Eastward Hoe* which was performed and published in 1775. Three more novels appeared in print including *Henrietta* in 1758, *Sophia* in 1762, and *Euphemia* in 1790. She was also a talented translator, accomplished poet and had some success as a writer and editor of a periodical entitled *The Lady's Museum* (March 1760–February 1761). There is an edition by Norbert Schürer of Lennox's letters which reveals the extent of her network among London theatrical and literary influencers and the precarity of her existence as a jobbing writer.[2] And a biography by Susan Carlile which martials new evidence to demonstrate that Lennox had 'not only a startlingly astute but also a thoroughly independent mind'.[3] Lennox, like her model Fielding (although she does not seem to have shared Fielding's improvidence), seems to have struggled to have made a living from her artistic gifts, and was obliged in her last years from 1790 until her death in 1804 to apply to funds for her support from the Royal Literary Fund.[4]

In this chapter, I argue that Lennox's authorial presence was narrated through her career as a process of unconcealment and withdrawal that rested on an often aggressive critique of dependency. In this process, independence is not easily or obviously achieved through acts of surrogacy, particularly acts of substitution of one woman for another, which prove more likely to defer or displace than undo dependencies. We have seen already how the bed trick of stage drama (in which an unchaste woman is substituted for a chaste one in the bed of a lover or husband), was used to preserve Susanna Graspall's (reputation for) chastity and reform the rake in Haywood's *A Wife to be Lett*; the already seduced Amadea takes Susanna's place in the bed of her seducer/the man who has 'rented' Susanna from her husband. One way to understand stage adaptation from and to novels is as a form of rhetorical 'bed trick' in which the new media substitutes 'novel' characters for theatrical ones and vice versa. In translating from stage to novel, techniques of diegesis must substitute for mimetic corporeality; in translating from novel to stage, diegetic techniques substitute for mimetic corporeality. One way of representing the troubled complexity of power relations in acts of substitution (between genres, between authors and patrons, between friends) was in terms of the dynamic of Quixotism: a dynamic which had at its heart the mutual dependence of Quixote and servant and one that was equally compelling for Lennox as for Fielding.

---

[2]   Norbert Schürer, 'Introduction', in *Charlotte Lennox: Correspondence and Miscellaneous Documents* (Lewisburg, PA: Bucknell University Press, 2012).

[3]   Susan Carlile, *Charlotte Lennox: An Independent Mind* (Toronto and London: University of Toronto Press, 2018), p. 5. For a further biographical source, see Hugh Amory, 'Lennox, (Barbara) Charlotte (1730/31?–1804)', in *Oxford Dictionary of National Biography* (Oxford: Oxford University Press, 2004); online edn, May 2009, http://ezproxy-prd.bodleian.ox.ac.uk:2167/view/article/16454 [accessed 20 February 2020].

[4]   Jennie Batchelor, 'Women Writers, the Popular Press and the Literary Fund, 1790–1830', chapter 4 of *Women's Work: Labour, Gender and Authorship, 1750–1830* (Manchester: Manchester University Press, 2014).

For both Lennox and Fielding, Quixotism was an enduring preoccupation whether writing for the stage or the page.[5] Fielding's versions of Don Quixote and Sancho Panza in Parson Adams and Joseph Andrews, Tom Jones and Partridge, are only the best known of many such comic pairings in his work. Quixotism might be understood to be a kind of dependence, a form of creativity derived from the imitation of a mode of outworn fiction-making. Aaron Hanlon suggests we reconsider this characterisation of Quixotism, however. Quixotism is deeply engaged in the present and the modern through its own coherent, indeed relentless, logic of exceptionalism, a logic so powerful it promotes imitation in others and makes them speak in its terms. Quixotes he reminds us are 'adept reasoners and manipulative rhetoricians',[6] who render themselves exceptions to rules. Female Quixotism is particularly invested, he argues, in forms of surrogation (or 'kyriarchy') in which domestic servants stand in or act as surrogates for their mistresses, compelled by the force of the mistress's logic to comply with or imitate it.[7]

Lennox's best-known heroine, Arabella in *The Female Quixote; or, the Adventures of Arabella* (1752), has such a relationship with her kind and admiring maid, Lucy; she treats Lucy as though she were a companion (as well born as her) such as the heroines of seventeenth-century romance fiction enjoy. Lucy, however, has neither the intellectual and sensible capacity nor the opportunity to undergo the conversion to 'right-thinking' (away from the romance and to the novel as a model for designing a life) her mistress achieves. That process of conversion in her mistress is kick-started by a different female surrogate who takes the part of acting 'for' the heroine. Arabella's conniving suitor, Sir George, hires an actress to impersonate a romance princess named Gynecia. Had Arabella spent her time reading the English romance by Philip Sidney, *Arcadia*, rather than the seventeenth-century French romances she is so fond of, she would

---

[5]   Henry Fielding's play *Don Quixote in England* was the second play he began to write but it was not finished nor produced until 1734. On Quixotism in eighteenth-century culture, see Gillian Brown, 'The Quixotic Fallacy', *NOVEL: A Forum on Fiction*, 32, no. 2 (1999), 250–73; Susan Staves, 'Don Quixote in Eighteenth-Century England', *Comparative Literature*, 24, no. 3 (1972), 193–215; Ronald Paulson, *Don Quixote in England: The Aesthetics of Laughter* (Baltimore, MD: Johns Hopkins University Press, 1998); and Wendy Motooka, *The Age of Reasons: Quixotism, Sentimentalism, and Political Economy in Eighteenth-Century Britain* (London: Routledge, 1998).

[6]   Aaron Hanlon, *A World of Disorderly Notions: Quixote and the Logic of Exceptionalism* (Charlottesville, VA and London: University of Virginia Press, 2019), p. 13.

[7]   Aaron Hanlon, 'Maids, Mistresses, and "Monstrous Doubles": Gender-Class Kyriarchy in the *The Female Quixote* and *Female Quixotism*', *The Eighteenth Century*, 55, no. 1 (2014), 77–96.

have recognised that the character of Gynecia is that of a faithless wife. The actress persuades Arabella that she is fleeing an unwanted suitor and Arabella loses sight of her as she runs through Richmond Park. Arabella casts herself into the Thames in an attempt to escape the rumoured ravishers in imitation of the heroic action by Madeleine de Scudéry's romance heroine, Clelia, who leaps into the Tiber in similar circumstances. On her recovery from life-threatening illness due to this folly, Arabella receives counselling from a wise, well-read tutor so that she arrives at a stable position where she can admire the worthy qualities of literary precedents without depending on them.[8]

In particular, Arabella transfers her reading loyalty from romances to the modern novel. One way that she arrives at this new position and set of loyalties is that she learns to stop expecting to find physical embodiments in the real world of the fictional constructions she responds to so powerfully on the page. Here too the actress is an important vehicle to mediate that understanding; the folly of her mistake and the severe illness Arabella suffers as a result of her foolish plunge motivates her to adopt a new way of life and to reject her romance reading in favour of a new kind of fiction accommodating to a more pragmatic ethics: the novel. As so often in the story of the novel's challenge to the theatre, romance and performance are closely aligned, sometimes equated; both romance and theatrical performance provide – according to this narrative – sensational pleasures without a sound ethical underpinning.

By the late 1750s, when she composed and saw into print *Henrietta*, Lennox's reputation as a novelist was relatively well-established and her career as an actor was apparently over, although she retained good and enabling connections to the licensed stages. In *Henrietta* the heroine is both protagonist and surrogate, in that she chooses to take on work as a dependent, rather than submit to tyrannous domestic authority. In this, the heroine of *Henrietta* appears to the biographer to be a surrogate for her author, working out a fantasy of achieving freedom from enforced dependence by choosing to submit to it elsewhere.

This process was not simply a personal one. Lennox was evidently seeking to establish a productive emulatory relationship with her immediate literary predecessors and models: especially Fielding and Haywood, two authors who had also built their careers between the theatre and the novel. Despite the apparent repudiation of Haywood in *Henrietta*, Lennox's career bore close resemblance to that of her female predecessor. Like Haywood,

---

[8]   Charlotte Lennox, *The Female Quixote: or, the Adventures of Arabella*, ed. Margaret Dalziel (Oxford: Oxford University Press, 2008).

Lennox sought throughout her life to subsist through a combination of acting, translating, composing prose fiction, periodicals for women, stage criticism, a smattering of poetry and some playwrighting. Like Haywood, she appears to have struggled to do so despite evident talent and some recognition from her male contemporaries. Jennie Batchelor nuances our understanding of Henriettta's choice from the bookshelves; she suggests that the choice 'is not so much a badge of honor, but a sign of the heroine's naïvety'; Henrietta fails to recognise the signs that she may be staying with a bawd.[9] The seduction fictions of Manley and Haywood could have provided clear warning to a more savvy reader about the precarity of women's honour. Despite her three previous readings of *Joseph Andrews*, Henrietta appears to have missed its ironic content and indeed its debts to those earlier works of fiction by women. Henrietta is not, however, seduced and betrayed as are the heroines of Haywood's fiction; she retains her honour and her robust chastity, securing herself a brilliant match despite the adversities she faces. Her stubborn, seemingly Quixotic, refusal to see herself as conforming to rules that apply to other unprotected women is vindicated. Of course, the sway of the Quixote is such that the plot of the novel comes to conform to just this exceptional view the Quixote holds.

Lennox's experiments between stage and page in fiction are preoccupied with the navigation of relations of dependence by her protagonists. Lennox was keenly aware of the dependent nature of authorship. While the act of authorship is imagined as a means of achieving independence (from unhelpful literary models, from personal debt, from a difficult husband), it is frequently revealed to be a new form of dependence: whether on a literary inheritance that is already compromised, on a public that is not always welcoming, patrons that require too much obeisance, or industries that are indifferent to anything but profit. Norbert Schürer concludes that 'Lennox conceived of herself not so much as an independent author creating autonomous works of art, but as a labourer in the literary marketplace trying to make a living as easily and profitably as possible.'[10]

We concentrate here on a particular incident of dependency, however, that between source and adaptation. In 1766, Lennox adapted one of her novels for the stage; to be precise, she converted one incident from a novel into a play. The play did not survive a night due to the unruliness

---

[9]   Jennie Batchelor, 'The "Latent Seeds of Coquetry": Amatory Fiction and the 1750s Novel', in *Masters of the Marketplace: British Women Novelists of the 1750s*, ed. Susan Carlile (Bethlehem, PA: Lehigh University Press, 2011), p. 149.

[10]   Norbert Schürer, 'Introduction', in *Charlotte Lennox: Correspondence and Miscellaneous Documents* (Lewisburg, PA: Bucknell University Press, 2012), p. xxxvii.

of the audience attending,[11] but it subsequently enjoyed considerable success in print. In this sense, the 'novel' has a variety of dramatic and print afterlives: *Henrietta* was carefully and fairly substantially revised by its author between the first and second edition, turned into a play called *The Sister* performed for one night over a decade after the novel's first publication, on 18 February 1769 at Covent Garden theatre, and this play was published twice in the same year in London and Dublin. To be independent is not to be free of any kind of relationship to what has gone before or currently exists. Lennox's works are consistently interrelated but have an independent life. One especially vivid illustration of this is in the co-dependence and independence of these two works: the novel and the play she adapted from it.

Lennox was well-versed in the frustrations as well as opportunities of dependence before the 1760s. And she did not take kindly to it. Norma Clarke observes, 'Throughout her life she either bit the hand that fed her or contemptuously disdained to eat the crumbs.'[12] Close to home was another literary work by a woman which anatomised the experience of dependency and turned the temptation to bite back into literary form. Lennox sent the manuscript of *The Female Quixote* in 1751 to Samuel Richardson and he helped her to secure a publisher in Andrew Millar who also published Henry Fielding's *Joseph Andrews* and his subsequent novels.[13] Jane Collier, intimate friend of Henry's sister Sarah Fielding and member of Samuel Richardson's circle (who is also thought to have lived in his household for a period), had published in 1753 a satirical work that may have informed Lennox's scathing representation of the misery of dependency in affluent domestic households for indigent women: *An Essay on the Art of Ingeniously Tormenting* provides advice to those in positions of power on how to maximise the physical and emotional distress for those dependent on them.[14] Important to the aesthetic effect of the work is a poise of distance and classical restraint as the best foil for the communication of an idea of intense suffering. The precision of the carefully applied torture of the mistress of the house is countered by the arts of the (hidden) author. Jane Collier had experience, like Charlotte Lennox, of living as a genteel dependent

[11] Norbert Schürer comments that the disruption was 'apparently planned by individuals who objected to Lennox's stance on Shakespeare' (p. xxxviiii).

[12] Norma Clarke, *Dr Johnson's Women* (London: Random House, 2011), p. 76.

[13] See Carlile, *Charlotte Lennox*, pp. 85–7.

[14] Jane Collier, *An Essay on the Art of Ingeniously Tormenting*, ed. Audrey Bilger, Broadview Literary Texts (Peterborough, ON: Broadview, 2003).

in the homes of others and she, like Charlotte, deployed surrogate voices to provide her readers with an insight into being there.[15]

Lennox may have seen the stage as an opportunity to escape a career as an unhappy dependent. She certainly tried her hand as a stage actress. She may not have been as poor an actress as Horace Walpole judged (he described her as 'a poetess, and deplorable actress' in 1748); after all, she enjoyed a benefit as Almeria in *The Mourning Bride* at the Haymarket on 22 February 1750.[16] Her knowledge of the stage was not limited to her acting. The same year as she saw *Henrietta* into publication, Lennox composed a dramatic pastoral opera entitled *Philander* which did not get to the stage but was published in London. Between the first and second editions of *Henrietta*, Lennox had also seen into print her translation, with the assistance of a number of other hands, of an important French Jesuit work about the stage: *The Greek Theater of Father Brumoy* (1760).[17] Lennox's plots consistently critique Catholic orthodoxy and *Henrietta* includes among its cast of character a villainous Jesuit priest who prejudices Henrietta's guardian aunt against her stoutly Protestant ward. However, she nonetheless subscribed to the principles of using narrative, especially in drama, to train the passions along the lines advocated by Jesuit thinkers such as Brumoy.

Central to Pierre Brumoy's account of the Greek stage is the argument that moral education requires bringing to life past examples before the audience's eyes. Immersion through embodied experience leads to new moral understanding. This appears to be what Brumoy understood to be the essence of 'theatre' whether or not it took the form of a story represented on a stage by actors. John Boyle, fifth earl of Orrery, stalwart promoter of

[15] See Ros Ballaster, 'Passing Judgement: The Place of the Aesthetic in Feminist Literary History', in *Women's Writing, 1660–1830. Feminisms and Futures*, ed. Jennie Batchelor and Gillian Dow (London: Palgrave Macmillan, 2016), pp. 11–32.

[16] Horace Walpole, letter to George Montagu (3 September 1748), in *The Yale Edition of Horace Walpole's Correspondence*, 48 vols, ed. W.S. Lewis (London: Oxford University Press, 1937–83), vol. 9, p. 74. It has been assumed that Walpole saw Lennox perform in a private theatrical he attended, but the wording in the letter is ambiguous: 'I am just come from a play at Richmond, where ... we had a new actress, a Miss Clough; .... Garrick is to produce her next winter, and a Miss Charlotte Ramsay, a poetess, and deplorable actress. Garrick, Barry, and some more of the players were there to see these new comedians; it is to be their seminary.'

[17] Pierre Brumoy, *The Greek Theatre of Father Brumoy*, trans. and ed. Charlotte Lennox (London: Millar et al., 1760), 3 vols. Carlile describes Lennox as a 'project manager' securing a team of learned men to work with her on the translation including John Boyle, Earl of Orrery and Cork, Dr James Grainger, Dr Gregory Sharpe, John Barryau, and Samuel Johnson (*Charlotte Lennox*, p. 162). George, Prince of Wales was the work's dedicatee.

Lennox, provided translations for the three prefatory essays to Lennox's three-volume edition of Brumoy's work into English. These essays move fluidly between epic poetry, stage tragedy and 'novels' for their examples of the power of 'theatre'. Boyle explicitly refers to Lennox's novels as imitating the capacity of French fiction to promote this sense of embodied experience of a real humanity:

> Their novels are inimitable; they represent the times, the manners, the disposition of the whole nation; while we, to say the truth, are at once the constant detractors and imitators of our adversaries, and wandering from nature and probability, attempt only to represent persons who never existed even in imagination, faultless monsters, or aukward fine gentlemen. This appears to be the general distinction between the French novels and our own. If particulars may claim an exception to this general remark, *The Female Quixote* and *Henrietta*, I hope may lay some claim to that exception.[18]

Boyle marks out Lennox's two novels as exceptional in the field of English fiction of the 1750s and implies that this may be due to her good acquaintance with French models. Lennox may have selected Brumoy for translation because she shared his aesthetics or she may have ensured that the three volumes she saw into translation stressed these aspects of his aesthetics in order to promote her own. Either way, she consistently characterised aesthetic judgement as a matter of providing this kind of 'enlivening representation' whatever form its mediation took. The aim of art is to make its consumer feel 'there' for Lennox as for Brumoy. This is equally true of translation itself, an art on which Lennox depended for her living. Boyle in his translation of the first essay, 'A Discourse upon the Theatre of the Greeks', translated Brumoy's description of the act of translation thus: 'A cold translation is a face of wax. It bears a resemblance in some manner, but every feature is frozen and dead.'[19] This sense that translation must bring to life a source is central to Lennox's conception of her own authorship. Impassioned expression, rather than argumentative exposition, was the test for presence for Lennox and she seems to have found it easier to recognise and perform in the shape of prose fiction than in writing for the stage. And this is especially evident when we compare *Henrietta* with its stage adaptation.

---

[18]   Brumoy, vol. 1, pp. iv–v.
[19]   Ibid., p. xv.

Henrietta was not only reworked for the stage by its author but it was also revised by her as a novel between the first edition of 28 January 1758 and the second of Spring 1761. The changes, its modern editors observe, tend toward making the second edition more polished. The theme of a struggle to escape the precarity of dependence was consistent throughout however. The heroine, Henrietta Courtenay, is orphaned and her younger brother is abroad in France. He is unaware of her predicament when her dogmatic aunt Meadows, under the influence of a scheming Roman Catholic private priest Danvers, attempts to force her into an unsuitable match with an ageing aristocrat. Henrietta flees when she is warned that she may be made to join a convent if she continues to refuse. She now embarks on a series of attempts to find protection. We have already met Henrietta befriended by romance enthusiast Miss Woodby and (mis)directed to lodgings. Miss Woodby is flattered into confiding Henrietta's history to a beau who is also lodging with the less-than-respectable milliner Mrs Eccles. When the beau hides himself in her room, Henrietta once again acts decisively to flee and accepts the protection of the son of her absent guardian, Mr Damer. She is lodged with a virtuous woman named Mrs Willis who warns her that the newly married Mr Damer also has designs on Henrietta as a mistress.

Henrietta now takes a series of jobs as a servant, expressing her preference for honest service over the dependence of being a 'companion'. Her employment with vulgar but wealthy Miss Cordwain goes disastrously wrong when the former's fiancée is revealed to be the love-struck beau who pursued Henrietta at the milliner's, one Lord B__. Lord B__ attempts to arrange a marriage with her rather than Miss Cordwain and he presses Henrietta (much to her contempt) to appear to comply with her aunt's demand for conversion to Catholicism in order to lay hands on her inheritance. To escape his pursuit, Henrietta moves on to several weeks' employment with an aged coquette Mrs Autumn, but this too proves unsuitable and Henrietta takes new employment under the name of Miss Benson with the melancholy Miss Belmour who is enamoured of a married man. Henrietta persuades Miss Belmour to leave England to try and break the connection and on the way to Dover they encounter two young men, tutor and pupil, who go by the names of Mr Freeman and Mr Melvil. Melvil and Henrietta are instantly attracted and the gentlemen accompany the women to Paris. Here, Freeman attempts to disengage his young charge from his passion for Henrietta knowing that Melvil's wealthy and aristocratic father will disapprove of so unsuitable a match. When the attachment proves deep, Freeman resorts to trying to persuade Henrietta to admit the besotted young man as a lover, but when he discovers her real identity, he recognises that she is in fact his long-lost sister. The remainder of the novel sees Freeman (now known by his real name of Courtenay) endeavour to reconcile his aunt (now free of the influence of the malign priest) to his sister, Henrietta. The impulsive young marquis, previously known as Melvil, continues to try and seek out Henrietta as she complies with her brother's demand that she avoid his importunities. Eventually, Courtenay secures a sufficient inheritance for Henrietta from the aunt and her now-returned guardian, the trader Damer, to satisfy the marquis' father and the two are married. Their happy union is contrasted with the many unhappy alliances made by Henrietta's onetime friends, protectors and employers: apart from her brother Courtenay who is rewarded for his (eventually) proven virtue by a love match with an heiress.

Henrietta is a sparky heroine, witty and determined. Lennox skilfully uses free indirect discourse both to focalise the majority of the story through Henrietta but also to provide moments of critical distance, in which the heroine reflects on the nature of dependency and freedom. This is especially evident in the scenes in the novel when Henrietta decides to embark on a career in service. After her escape from her first risky lodgings, she finds a home with a new landlady, Mrs Willis, who, on discovery of Henrietta's plight, invites Henrietta to live with her and share her meagre income. Their exchange is freighted with complexity concerning the meaning of service. Mrs Willis seeks to 'serve' Henrietta by providing her with a home, while Henrietta will not burden Mrs Willis with her dependence and seeks a life of paid service elsewhere:

> "Tell me, how can I serve you? O! that you would honour me so far as to let this house be your asylum till fortune does justice to your merit. Condescend to live with me, my dear miss, and share my little income."
>
> "You are very kind, dear Mrs. Willis," replied Henrietta, "but my circumstances will not permit me to continue your boarder, and no distress shall oblige me to be burdensome to a friend. I have already resolved how to dispose of myself, and in the scheme I have formed, I shall need your assistance."
>
> "Tell me, my dear," cried Mrs. Willis, eagerly, "how can I be of any use to you!"
>
> "You must," replied Henrietta, blushing a little: "you must get me a service, my dear Mrs. Willis."[20]

---

[20]   *Henrietta*, vol. 2, book 3, chapter 4, pp. 133–4.

Mrs Willis is true to her promise and puts out enquiries with a relative enjoying great success as a high fashion mantua-maker. The latter quickly finds Henrietta employment as a servant to Miss Cordwain, the daughter of a wealthy merchant.

At the close of her interview with the haughty, silly Miss Cordwain, Henrietta reveals her own tendency to Quixotic imaginings, but also brings them swiftly in check:

> Henrietta, whose imagination was naturally lively, and not wholly free from those romantic notions which persons of her age readily admit, began to consider transformation from the niece of Lady Meadows, and a presumptive heiress, into the waiting-maid as a cit, as one of those caprices of fate which never fail to produce surprising effects. She could not help fancying herself the future heroine of some affecting tale, whose life would be varied with surprising vicissitudes of fortune; and that she would at last be raised to a rank as much above her hopes, as the station she was now entering upon was below all that her ears had ever suggested.
>
> But these reflections were succeeded by others more reasonable and which indeed afforded her a more solid satisfaction: she was going to refute the censures of an injurious world; to make that innocence which had been so vilely traduced manifest, in her cheerful submission to poverty and servitude, at a time when a shining fortune was offered to purchase a change in her religious principles, and when perhaps a little dissimulation, or a temporary compliance with her aunt's proposals, might restore her to a rank in life suitable to her birth.[21]

Of course, the denouement Henrietta is given is closer to her Quixotic imaginings than the virtuous destiny to which her second thoughts turn her. Here, Lennox suggests her own ironic turn. It is more likely that fate will bring about a sudden reversal of fortune through unlikely accident (meeting her brother and his affluent pupil as she travels impulsively to Dover) than the world will consider virtue proved through submitting to servitude and holding to religious principle in private.

The world of imagination and reflection – the private world of weighing behaviour and outcomes – is the world of prose fiction. That of the drama by contrast is one in which character is tested through the encounter with others. In comedy, the unfolding of mistakes and errors of judgement is the vehicle for proving the real truth and virtue of character(s). Instead of

---

[21]   Ibid., vol. 2, book 3, chapter 5, pp. 138–9.

the presence of protagonists' thoughts in the readers' mind, the audience is present at the representation of a series of actions and responses.

There is no equivalent in Lennox's stage adaptation of her novel to the robust – if sometimes compromised – reflections of the novel's heroine in the source *Henrietta*. Indeed, all of Henrietta's independence appears to have been translated into that of her vibrant coquettish friend, Miss Autumn, who plays a major part in the stage play. With one exception. The play reproduces a moment of considerable political independence on the heroine's part. Harriot (the play version of Henrietta) also expresses contempt for her brother's failure to protect female honour in general. Contrast Henrietta's speech in the novel and Harriot's in the play, in response to Courtenay's changed perspective when he discovers that the woman he is trying to persuade to accept a role as mistress is in fact his sister: '"Oh! that my brother," replied Henrietta, "would be taught by this accident never more to form designs against innocence, and in cases like mine, to consider every virtuous young woman as a sister."'[22] If anything, the play is even more robust. Harriot exclaims: 'Oh! that my brother may be taught by this adventure, never more to insult distress and innocence and to consider every virtuous, unprotected young woman as a sister.'[23] Susan Carlile notes that, paradoxically, the novel's more expansive social range than its version as a play makes Henrietta's comment consistent with a number of sharp observations about failures on the part of those with public responsibility to act to defend those who are virtuous and, through no fault, dependent. By contrast, the stage adaptation makes this a matter of private and kin relationships. Although the stage is the more public genre, *Henrietta* does not give her young female character a public role in her play. Paradoxically, Henrietta functions far more publicly in the genre known for its privateness, the novel. Thus, in the play Harriot is scornful of her brother only in private familial settings; whereas Henrietta, in the novel, speaks out to illustrate larger societal problems that are the result of a male-dominated society.[24]

Some of the play's inadequacies may be ascribed to Lennox's lack of experience as a playwright when she turned to her adaptation. Nonetheless, *The Sister* was clearly a serious attempt to find ways of adapting novel fiction for the stage. Lennox did not attempt to retell the picaresque series of encounters in the novel. She designed rather a dramatic rendering of

---

[22] Ibid., vol. 2, book 5, chapter 4, p. 222.
[23] *The Sister*, Act 2, p. 28.
[24] Susan Carlile, '*Henrietta* on Page and Stage', in *Masters of the Marketplace: British Women Novelists of the 1750s*, ed. Susan Carlile, p. 134.

the last book only: the business of Henrietta's romance and reconciliation with her brother in Paris. She transferred the action, in accordance with the conventions of English city comedy, to a location in England, that of Windsor (the site of the home of Henrietta's aunt Meadow in the novel) and she revived the character of Mrs Autumn. The comedy is a conventional 'double' courtship in which, the sober couple of Harriot and Clairville are contrasted with the gay couple. Freeman/Courtenay is in love with Miss Autumn, stepdaughter to the ridiculous widow, Lady Autumn, who mistakes his interest in her daughter as amorous passion for her own person.

Lady Autumn is a fine comic creation, in the mould of many lascivious ageing coquettes. And her presence carries on the theme of the novel – the critique of dependence. If the mark of Lennox's authorial presence had become the presence of surrogates, *The Sister* does not disappoint. Henrietta's dislike of the role of companion and confidante is put in the mouth of another servant, Lady Autumn's woman, Simple.

> LADY AUTUMN. ... I am resolved to make you my confidant.
> SIMPLE. Confidant! I thank you, Madam – but, but – I had rather keep the place I was hired for, Madam.
> LADY AUTUMN. Yes, I am determined to deposite all my secrets in your breast.[25]

The secret deposited is Lady Autumn's passion for the young Freeman. And she reports the birth of that passion to her maid servant in terms familiar to those acquainted with Quixotism. Lady Autumn casts herself as a heroine of pastoral romance saved by a young hero:

> LADY AUTUMN. One morning, when I was sauntering in the forest, habited in a loose white sack, with my walking-crook in my hand – poor Lord Autumn used to say I looked like a nymph in this dress – I found myself fatigued, and was obliged to rest under a tree. – Here I sat, or rather reclined, in a pensive attitude, when I was roused by the sight of a monstrous snake, that had fastened on my arm –
> SIMPLE. Lord bless me! Madam, what did you do? –
> LADY AUTUMN. Do! I screamed so loud, that two young gentlemen, who were walking at a little distance, came running to me: – both were eager to assist me; – but Mr. Freeman's assiduity was so animated, so languishing – so – so – in short, the blow was struck: I perceived immediately that I had made a violent impression.

[25]   *The Sister*, Act 1, p. 16.

SIMPLE. But pray, Madam, if I may be so bold, how did your Ladyship get rid of the snake?
LADY AUTUMN. The snake!—O, I was mistaken: it was only a cater-pillar, which my fears had magnified into a snake.[26]

The scene is a familiar one from Lennox's other works. Simple, like Lucy in *The Female Quixote*, is unfamiliar with the generic tradition on which Lady Autumn draws to narrate her fictional romance. She reads it literally while her mistress is tangled in the language of pastoral 'fall' (the snake and the tree) into amorous desire, enjoying the figurative opportunities of the 'blow' which dispenses with the 'snake' to point to the mutual striking of hearts with love. The comedy lies in Lady Autumn's depositing of a secret in the breast of a confidante (and here she turns a servant into a confidante where the heroine of the novel Henrietta turns herself from confidante to servant) which only puts on display her own dependence on the tired cli-chés of an outworn form: the romance.

The history of the play's conception illuminates the relationship between the two works. Despite the decade between novel publication and play pro-duction, the play was clearly thought of soon after the novel's first edition. On 29 May 1759, David Garrick wrote to Lennox commenting 'Henrietta pleas'd me much, & wants, I think, only some little alterations to compleat it. – I am much flatter'd that the Author approves of the little hints I gave.'[27] Since the novel was already in its first edition, Garrick must have been referring to a stage play well under way in composition and, at that stage, sharing the same title as the novel from which it was derived, since Lennox had already introduced some alterations suggested by him. However, it did not get to the stage that year. On 26 October 1768, Lennox wrote again to Garrick and reminded him of the earlier existence of a playscript suggest-ing that the recent successes of other women playwrights (Norbert Schürer suggests Elizabeth Griffith and Frances Sheridan) has emboldened her to return to the plan:

The success which has lately attended Writers for the Stage, and some of them too, of my own Sex, has encouraged me to write a comedy, which I beg you will read with your usual candor [*sic*], and that indul-gence you have always shown for my writings. You will find that I have pursued a hint you gave me some years ago, which has furnishd [*sic*] me with one of the most interesting incidents in the whole piece: You

---

[26] Ibid., pp. 17–18.
[27] Schürer, ed., *Correspondence*, p. 104.

may depend upon it that every alteration, and amendment which you judge necessary, will be readily, and thankfully admitted....[28]

Since Garrick's 'hint' is lost to us we cannot know what incident it was he supplied – and certainly there are many differences between the play and the novel on which it draws – but in any case, it is clear he did turn it down. It was George Colman who accepted it for Covent Garden theatre instead.

Colman also provided the play with an unusual prologue, one which sought to call attention to the play's novelistic pedigree, indeed the dependence of its reception on a previous success in novel form. It was unusual in that it was delivered by a woman, the actress Isabella Mattocks (1746–1826). Mattocks did not have a role in the five-act mainpiece. The actress opened by declaring a break with the convention of a dark-coated male actor speaking on behalf of the author. And she closed with the conceit that she served as the sunny female figure of the weathervane by comparison with the dark umbrella-clutching male counterpart, inviting applause and merriment in place of gloom. Prologues were conventionally delivered by actors who acted as surrogates for the playwright, clad in a black cloak to signal precisely the kind of absent presence of the writer in the stage performance, as well as vouch for the playwright's sobriety and authority. Colman plays with that convention by suggesting a parallel between the absent black-clad actor and the mannequin figure of the weathervane in dark clothes and holding an umbrella that will act as a screen from harsh 'weather'. In their absence, a brightly dressed actress speaks. Conventionally, actresses delivered epilogues seeking to encourage the audience to clap for a future performance and indeed Mattocks had acquired a name for delivering epilogues of this kind.[29] Here the world is turned topsy-turvy – Quixote like – with the actress appearing to introduce the play, confident and independent. Indeed, Isabella Mattocks appears to be only another in the chain of female surrogates or substitutes we have observed in Lennox's work, along the lines of the Sancho figure of Lucy the servant in *The Female Quixote*. She explicitly declares herself the 'servant', the 'Sancho' of the play's absent author.

Colman has the actress make explicit reference to Lennox's great success with a work of fiction in the previous decade, her *Female Quixote*:

---

[28] Ibid., p. 115.

[29] Diana Solomon, *Prologues and Epilogues of Restoration Theatre. Gender and Comedy, Performance and Print* (Newark, DE: University of Delaware Press, 2013), pp. 44–8.

Boast not your gallant deeds, romantic men!
To-night a Female Quixote draws the pen.
Arm'd by the Comic Muse, these lists she enters,
And sallies forth – in quest of strange adventures!
War, open war, 'gainst recreant knights declares,
Nor Giant-Vice nor Windmill-Folly spares:
Side-saddles Pegasus, and courts Apollo,
While I, (you see!) her female Sancho, follow.
    Ye that in this enchanted castle sit,
Dames, squires, and dark magicians of the pit,
Smile on our fair knight-errantry to-day,
And raise no spells to blast a female play.
    Oft has our Author, upon other ground,
Courted your smiles, and oft indulgence found.
Read in the closet, you approv'd her page;
Yet still she dreads the perils of the stage.
Reader with Writer due proportion keeps,
And if the Poet nods, the Critic sleeps!
If lethargied by dullness here you sit,
Sonorous catcalls rouse the sleeping pit. [30]

This seems a conventional appeal for the novelist to be given favour in her maiden entry to the stage, but the author of the prologue, Colman, already had a reputation for stage satire of women's novel reading. His farce, *Polly Honeycombe*, was a staple afterpiece since its first performance in 1760, in which a lively novel-reading heroine insists on living out the plots of her favourite reading matter. Polly bears some resemblance to Charlotte Lennox's Arabella in many respects, albeit it she is an addict of the quick and more everyday pleasures of novelistic intrigue rather than the idealistic virtuous romance.

With regard to the specific context of Lennox's debut adaptation of her novel to the stage, however, Colman draws attention to very different contexts of reception. Reading fiction positively enables moments of inattentive reverie whereas if a play fails to keep its audience attentions it is catcalled into silence. This was in fact the fate of *The Sister*. Newspapers reported that a concerted and successful effort was made by the first night audience to see the play off the stage on its first night; a letter from Colman to Lennox of 20 February 1769 expresses his regret that she was forced

---

[30] George Colman, 'Prologue', in Charlotte Lennox, *The Sister* (London: J. Dodsley and T. Davies, 1769), p. A2.

to withdraw the play from further performances insisting 'I thought I had never read a play that was more certain of comanding [*sic*] a patient hearing.'[31] Colman warmly endorses her plan to publish the play to try and make some profit from it. Certainly, one newspaper was not persuaded that the play itself deserved such treatment and applauded the attempt to translate what was attractive about the novel to a new reading audience to the stage:

> On Saturday last was *half*-acted at this Theatre, a new comedy called *The Sister*, written by the truely [*sic*] ingenious Author of the Female Quixote, and partly founded on another of her Productions, called Henrietta. In an age so favourable to Sentimental Comedy, and Novels in Dialogue, we cannot help thinking the censure on the fair Author rather severe. As far as we are capable of judging from so interrupted an Exhibition, the Piece is neither deficient in Interest, Sentiment, or Diction.[32]

Colman's characterisation of the female speaker of *The Sister*'s prologue as a Sancho to her author's Quixote invites us to think of the relation of dependent on master, adaptation or surrogate on source, dramatic adaptation on original novel, as a form of manifesting rather than undermining authorial presence. Here, the actress acts as surrogate or servant to an absent author, one among a number of guarantors that include her other and better known work (*The Female Quixote*) and the patrons male and female such as George Colman who have made her reputation as a literary celebrity but also in so doing made her dependent on their patronage. Charlotte Lennox, like her heroine Henrietta, not only positions other women 'in front of' her reputation (like the intermittently visible figures of the weathervane), but also alternates her own positions, between that of servant and 'dependent'. It is precisely in displacements and acts of surrogation – acts that were familiar from the world of theatre – that a 'novel' presence is shaped. In Lennox's fictional worlds authorial presence is always dependent on the presence of others: especially those in positions of servitude and dependence. Their presence casts into relief as well as casting into doubt the creative autonomy of an author whose person is impersonated or substituted for by a central female protagonist.

---

[31] Schürer, ed., *Correspondence*, p. 125. Schürer's notes to this letter reconstruct with care the context of the play's one-night reception (pp. 127–30).

[32] 'Theatrical Intelligence', *St James' Chronicle*, 18–21 February 1769, 1245, p. 4, quoted in Lennox, *Correspondence*, p. 127.

In fact, the print version of *The Sister* proved a satisfactory substitute for the play which ran only for one night. Lennox had sought to publish it by subscription without success but it thrived in print nonetheless. Booksellers Dodsley and Davies published the play two weeks after its one performance, required a second edition two weeks later and in total 1,500 copies were printed. The publisher of *Henrietta*, Thomas Lowndes, sought to capitalise on the play adaptation's success in print by advertising *Henrietta* from March 1769 through June 1770.[33] The play itself had proved no earning slouch. The *Covent Garden Theatre Ledger* shows that the single Saturday night to a packed house at Covent Garden on 18 February, despite being hissed off stage, earned 234 pounds 5 shillings, making it one of the five highest-grossing plays of thirty-seven performed that month.[34] This kind of intermedial playing off print publication and performance between theatre and novel maximised earnings as well as fostering a sense of extended authorial 'presence'.

The Sister attracted the attention of another author whose precarious existence in mid-century London depended on versatile positioning between the stage and prose fiction, and someone who also enjoyed promotion by the same media influencers as Lennox in the circle of Samuel Johnson. Oliver Goldsmith provided an epilogue to Lennox's *The Sister*, delivered by Mary Bulkley (1747/48–92), the actress who had played the lively Miss Autumn and was to take on the part of Kate Hardcastle in the first production of Goldsmith's *She Stoops to Conquer* in March 1773. Goldsmith's epilogue expressed impatience with the sentimental style that preached reward for virtuous suffering. Bulkley chastises the authoress for '*five long acts – all to make us wiser*'. Apparent contrast secretes similarity as Lennox amply demonstrates in shaping her (in)dependent authorial presence. Consistently, in his own compositions for the stage and in the novel, Goldsmith also dramatised the struggle to 'keep' and 'own' authorial character, which he simultaneously revealed and withdrew in a repertoire of character-surrogates. Goldsmith's epilogue gives the last word to a character apparently designed to play second fiddle to the sentimental heroine. The actor stays in role to insist that the play would have fared better if it had in fact depended on her:

> *What! Five long acts and all to make us wiser!*
> *Our authoress sure has wanted an adviser.*

---

[33] Carlile, *Charlotte Lennox*, p. 237.
[34] Ibid., p. 223. Carlile cites *Covent Garden Theatre Ledger*, British Library Egerton MS 2274.

> *Had she consulted me, she should have made*
> *Her moral play a speaking masquerade.*
> *Warm'd up each bustlng scene, and in her rage*
> *Have emptied all the Green-room on the stage.*
> *My life on't, this had kept her play from sinking,*
> *Have pleas'd our eyes, and sav'd the pain of thinking.*[35]

The actress here chastises the novelist for requiring thought from an audience, from filling her play with plot rather than drawing on the corporeal potential of the stage play to provide an audience with a 'speaking masquerade'. While she argues for the attractions of performative wit, she also discloses its shallowness (it pleases the eyes without exercising the mind). As we shall see, Goldsmith maintained this ambivalence in his career, ostensibly complaining about the tedium of a novelised stage given over to sentiment while sceptical about the capacity of the stage, even when it returned to the satiric wit of the comedy of intrigue, to compete with the claims of prose fiction 'novels' to make present self-reflexive properties of mind.

---

[35] Colman, 'Prologue', *The Sister*, p. 76.

Chapter 5
Oliver Goldsmith:
Keeping Up Authorial Appearances

Oliver Goldsmith turned to the stage relatively late in a precarious career. Most of his major works did bring Goldsmith money and success but he was as prodigal with his earnings as he was with his gifts, never managing to balance his books. Unlike Charlotte Lennox, he did manage to secure lasting patronage; from 1764, his earnings from publication were enlarged by support from Sir Robert Nugent, Member of Parliament and fellow Irishman. Goldsmith's first play, *The Good Natur'd Man*, held its opening night at Covent Garden Theatre on Friday 29 January 1768, just over a decade after he began writing periodical essays and translations for Grub Street. It was also his first work for the stage after the runaway success of his short novel, *The Vicar of Wakefield* (1766), which went into five editions within a year of publication. The story Samuel Johnson told, of rushing to secure a sixty pound payment from the bookseller John Newberry for the manuscript of the novel so that Goldsmith could meet his rental obligations to a furious landlady, indicates the hand-to-mouth existence Goldsmith led as an author.[1] And a version of the story Goldsmith knew so well of the author's struggle to earn money through literature, letters and the patronage of others is given to George Primrose, the Vicar's son in *The Vicar of Wakefield* who sets off to try and repair the family's fortune when his engagement to Arabella Wilmot is called off because of their sudden poverty. George is reunited with his father and still-devoted fiancée when they find him working as a strolling player in a barn performance of Nicholas Rowe's pathetic she-tragedy, *The Fair Penitent*.

The title of chapter 21 (George Primrose's story) is 'The history of a philosophic vagabond, pursuing novelty, but losing content'.[2] The title invites us to recognise the hidden 'novel' in 'novelty', a term poised in the

[1]   James Boswell, *Life of Johnson*, ed. G.B. Hill and L.F. Powell, 6 vols (Oxford: Oxford University Press, 1934–50), vol. 1, pp. 415–16.

[2]   Oliver Goldsmith, *The Vicar of Wakefield*, in *Collected Works of Oliver Goldsmith*, ed. Arthur Friedman, 5 vols (Oxford: Clarendon Press, 1966), vol. 4, p. 16.

mid-century between an open association with anything that was new and apparently did not conform to the narrative expectations of established genres, and the more modern denotation as a form of short prose narrative. George's story is an inset novel within the larger one of his family. So too 'content' has a double meaning: 'content' is both narrative material and personal equilibrium. We might also recognise that the title suggests that George's story of growing discontent with his life and its opportunities is also one that rather inclines us to 'lose' the thread of the main 'content': the story of the Vicar and his family. It transpires by the end of the novel that the work of the villain Thornhill to undermine the contented family life of the Vicar was also present in this apparent digression from the main story: it is Thornhill who works to bring about the separation of George from Arabella in his own pursuit of the latter for a wife.

The story George tells his father of his adventures after he left the family home was easily recognised as a version of the life of his author, Oliver Goldsmith.[3] It is both tragic and picaresque, detailing a sequence of failed attempts to make ends meet – writing essays on demand for the periodical press in London, travelling to Holland to teach English to the Dutch and Louvain to teach Greek, playing his flute across Europe, employment as a travelling tutor to a young gentleman on the grand tour. On his return to England, he joins the company of strolling players and recounts that:

> The company seemed not much to disapprove of me for an associate. They all, however, apprized me of the importance of the task at which I aimed; that the public was a many headed monster, and that only such as had very good heads could please it; that acting was not learnt in a day; and that without some traditional shrugs, which had been on the stage, and only on the stage, these hundred years, I could never pretend to please. The next difficulty was in fitting me with parts, as almost every character was in keeping. I was driven for some time from one character to another, till at last Horatio was fixed upon....[4]

George acquires a part to keep. Actors 'kept' parts or characters that they played again and again: even when they no longer bore any resemblance to the type they portrayed. This was necessary for the large turnover of plays

[3]   See Norma Clarke, *Brothers of the Quill: Oliver Goldsmith in Grub Street* (London and Cambridge, MA: Harvard University Press, 2016), pp. 17–18.

[4]   *Vicar*, chapter 20, p. 122. Johnson's story is likely not true or may only refer to the usual advance of £20 for a third of the copyright on an unfinished manuscript. See A. Lytton Sells, *Oliver Goldsmith: His Life and Works* (London: George Allen and Unwin, 1974), p. 252.

in the repertory to be maintained. Felicity Nussbaum refers us to what she terms 'performative property':

> Performative property was located in possessing a role of one's own, and yet also becoming representative of a property that was abstracted from the real in that its actuation was realized in a unique performance that could never be exactly replicated.[5]

When George joins the troupe he not only lacks worldly experience, the shrugs or 'knocks' that develop character, he also lacks a part to be fitted with since most are already in keeping with others. He has to make do with occupying the role of Horatio, the loyal friend and husband who seeks to make his innocent friend Altamont recognise the infidelity of the woman Altamont passionately loves, the fair penitent of the play's title, Calista. *The Fair Penitent* was a touchstone throughout the eighteenth century of extravagant feeling and violent catastrophe (Calista's lover, Lothario, spends the majority of the last act dead at the centre of the stage while she and her father debate their different versions of Roman virtue).

There are parallels between the tragic plot of *The Fair Penitent* and *The Vicar of Wakefield* – a virtuous woman (Calista/the vicar's daughter Olivia) is lured into a secret sexual liaison with a lothario (Lothario/the local landowner young Thornhill), a noble father suffers inordinately at the hands of an unjust senate (Sciolto/the Vicar is treated roughly by legal and penal systems). The story also had resonances with Goldsmith's family history. The third of five children to an Anglican vicar who took up a curacy in Kilkenny West, Goldsmith had to enter Trinity College, Dublin as a sizar, a low class of student supported by doing menial tasks for wealthier ones, because his father had committed to pay his older sister Catherine £400 in dowry after she eloped with the son of a wealthy neighbour, Daniel Hodson, who had been studying with Oliver's older brother Henry, curate and teacher; the father Charles Goldsmith, like Charles Primrose in *The Vicar of Wakefield*, was anxious to prove his integrity and to dispel the rumours that the family were angling for an advantageous match.[6]

Beyond immediate biographical parallels, there is a wider sense of the distribution of roles and the testing of character in *The Vicar of Wakefield*.

---

5   Felicity Nussbaum, 'Owning Identity: The Eighteenth-Century Actress and Theatrical Property', in *Mediating Identities in Eighteenth-Century England*: Public Negotiations, Literary Discourses, Topography, ed. Isabel Karremann and Anja Müller (London: Routledge, 2016), p. 73.
6   See *The Letters of Oliver Goldsmith*, ed. Michael J. Griffin and David O'Shaughnessey (Cambridge: Cambridge University Press, 2018), p. 3.

A dramatic understanding of the distribution and keeping of character informs the way that the novel insistently debates the terms of individual and relational identity. The ethics of Goldsmith's novel – a Christian stoical argument for intrafamilial loyalty, the maintenance of community through personal integrity, the argument that feeling for and with others is necessary to social flourishing – are a challenge to the notion of character being something that belongs to or is kept by a single individual. Character is, as it is in a troupe of actors, something that is distributed among thinking and feeling persons. Particular attitudes ('shrugs') encode emotional states to the audience and to one's fellow actors. The way that his fellow actors present it to George, the company's maintenance of the balance of its parts is a matching and counterforce to the 'many-headed' audience, also a form of community. As in Primrose's family, the village community that embraces and tries to defend them when they move to a new parish, and even the ragtag members of the gaol that Primrose spends six days bringing to a state of penitence through his teaching and preaching, the community finds its strength in numbers.

But character in *The Vicar of Wakefield* is a quality that can be hard to sustain, to keep up and in. Not least because sentimental character is produced through feeling with others, those repetitive acts of imaginative identification with strong feelings, especially suffering. Of course, this giving of the self is also a form of taking from others to make being. Adam Smith, in his *Theory of Moral Sentiments* (1759), acknowledges that we can only feel for another suffering being by imagining what it would feel like to be in that situation ourselves:

> By the imagination we place ourselves in his situation... His agonies, when they are thus brought home to ourselves, when we have thus adopted and made them our own, begin at last to affect us, and we then tremble and shudder at the thought of what he feels.[7]

In this chapter, I characterise the authorial 'presence-effect' of Oliver Goldsmith, achieved through a process of 'unconcealment and withdrawal', in terms of a distribution of a cast of characters he 'kept' that were promoted as more or less 'close' to that of their 'author'. That closeness was represented and experienced by the audiences of the plays he wrote and the readers of the novels he wrote as a kind of reluctant but necessary system of

---

[7]   Adam Smith, 'Of Sympathy', in *The Theory of Moral Sentiments*, ed. D.D. Raphael and A.L. Macfie, vol. 1 of the *Glasgow Edition of the Works and Correspondence of Adam Smith* (Indianapolis, IN: Liberty Fund, 1982), section 1, chapter 1, p. 60.

extended kinship. Family traits are shared, distributed, imitated, passed on. Family is necessary to maintaining or 'keeping up' a character – rallying to defence when persons run into dangerous disrepute – but also, and more intimately, required to maintain 'being'. 'Being' then always lies elsewhere, in others.

In *The Vicar of Wakefield*, pronoun shifting is a giveaway of the process of 'unconcealment and withdrawal' we have charted elsewhere as productive of an effect of authorial presence. The enigmatic Mr Burchell attaches himself early to the Primrose family; he appears to be simply the village eccentric given to acts of impulsive generosity to relieve the poor, but he proves disloyal to the family when he writes a letter to prevent the two Primrose daughters from taking an opportunity to encounter fashionable society in London. At the close of the novel it is discovered that Mr Burchell is in fact the older Sir William Thornhill, 'one of the most generous, yet whimsical, men in the kingdom',[8] and that he has been acting throughout to protect the Primrose family and especially the reserved and gentle second daughter, Sophia, whom he offers to marry. It is Burchell who tells Charles Primrose as they walk beside the family on horseback to their new home on the Thornhill estate about the eccentric Sir William who has left the estate to the governance of his nephew, the villainous younger Thornhill. It appears that Burchell is another version, not only of Charles Primrose, but also of his author, Goldsmith, a 'philosophic vagabond' who 'in his own whimsical manner... travelled through Europe on foot'.[9] In telling his own life story in the third person, Burchell's choice of pronouns threaten to give him away. Sir William Thornhill, Burchill tells Charles Primrose, has come to despise his own sensibility and attendant generosity; he attracts a crowd of dependents whom he must inevitably disappoint and they are resentful when he attempts to mete out advice.

> He now therefore found that such friends as benefits had gathered round him, were little estimable: he now found that a man's own heart must be ever given to gain that of another. I now found, that—that—I forget what I was going to observe: in short, sir, he resolved to respect himself, and laid down a plan of restoring his falling fortune.[10]

Burchell (nearly) gives himself away at the point that he is complaining that a man must give his own heart away to win the hearts of others. And

---

8   *Vicar*, chapter 3, p. 29.
9   Ibid., chapter 3, p. 30.
10 Ibid., chapter 3, p. 3.

he stumbles on his words as he appears to recognise his own act of disclosure. If Charles Primrose noticed this failure to maintain character, he
does not admit to it in his account. And this not because he is any sense
distracted from attending to Burchell's story. In fact, he acknowledges that
his 'attention was so much taken up'[11] with Mr Burchell's account that he
failed to notice that Sophia has been thrown from her horse into a rapid
stream. Burchell – inevitably – saves her. Those familiar with romance narrative and with stage comedies would recognise that the man who saves the
heroine from drowning is always the one marked out to be her suitor and
spouse. Charles Primrose is, however, characterised as a man whose learning extends to sermons and to classical history rather than stage plays and
fiction. His lack of familiarity with the cues of the plots in these works may
also explain his lack of interpretive attention to Burchill's telling and the
slippage from third to first person that gives away his identity. Something
is disclosed in this conscious act of unconcealment which associates the
person of the author with his characters but also disperses him across lines
of kin (George and Charles Primrose) and not kin or to-be kin (Burchill).

Goldsmith admitted to similar faults to those he gave Burchell/Sir
William Thornhill, writing to his brother Henry c.13 January 1759 to communicate advice to Henry's infant son, also called Henry.[12] In particular,
Goldsmith complains of a family resemblance: 'Whence this romantic turn
that all our family are possessed with, whence this love for every place and
every country but that in which we reside?'[13] To warn young Henry off such
diffusion of his energies and presence, the result of that desire always to be
absent from the place you reside, Goldsmith tells his brother:

> Let his poor wandering uncles example be plac'd in his eyes. I had
> learn'd from books to love virtue, before I was taught from experience
> the necessity of being selfish. I had contracted the habits and notions of
> a Philosopher, while I was exposing myself to the insidious approaches
> of cunning; and often, by being even from my narrow finances charita-
> ble to excess, I forgot the rules of justice, and placd [*sic*] myself in the
> very situation of the wretch who thank'd my bounty.[14]

In his private correspondence, his published and performed works, Goldsmith cultivated this version of his character, indeed kept and maintained

[11]   Ibid.
[12]   'To the Reverend Henry Goldsmith', in *The Letters of Oliver Goldsmith*, pp. 40–7, p.
       42.
[13]   Goldsmith, *Letters*, p. 42.
[14]   Ibid., p. 43.

it, to the extent that it is not clear whether the works reflect a set of traits or forged them as a convenient and effective form of identity (for an author) apparently formed through responsiveness to the presence of others.

In that same letter to his older brother, and not unrelated to his theme of the compulsion always to be elsewhere than one is, Oliver Goldsmith spoke of the dangerous attractions of prose fiction and its capacity to convey a sense of presence more compelling than experience itself. He advises Henry to ensure his son 'understands perfectly well Latin, French, Arithmetic and the Principles of the civil law, and can write a fine hand' but:

> Above all things let him never touch a romance, or novel, those paint beauty in colours more charming than nature, and describe happiness that man never tastes. How delusive, how destructive therefore are those pictures of consummate bliss, they teach the youthful mind to sigh after beauty and happiness which never existed, to despise the little good which fortune has mixed in our cup, and by expecting more than she ever gave.[15]

The sense-experience that fiction provides is communicated in particular by Oliver Goldsmith's injunction not to 'touch' a romance or a novel. Simple contact – the sense of touch – is enough to conjure an entire world of illusion. Reading print fiction is a tactile as well as visual, experience which opens a world of sensation (including that sense of 'tasting' something not possible in the 'real' world). In composing *The Vicar of Wakefield*, Oliver Goldsmith seems to have put together a novel that is determinedly *not* one, or at least not 'that' kind of novel he describes here: this 'novelty' is episodic and discontented. And its conclusion owes more to the evident artifice of the stage comedy and tragicomedy, much more easily recognised through the experience of visuality and co-presence with an audience as a 'fiction' designed only to bring an entertainment to its end than to reflect or mirror a real world. Burchill reveals himself as Lord Thornhill, rescues Olivia and reveals that her marriage to his nephew the younger Thornhill is legitimate. Charles Primrose is freed from gaol and the novel concludes with a double wedding of George and Arabella, Sophia and Lord Thornhill, only slightly marred by some aggravation among the brides as to who should have priority at the wedding ceremony and the wedding table.

The pleasures of family life which confer a place on each of its members – albeit always contested with sharp elbows as the humorous conclusion of the *Vicar* implies – are consistently presented as lost or illusory

---

[15] Ibid., p. 43.

for Oliver Goldsmith. And yet, Goldsmith's letter to his brother exposes a central paradox: that presence is conferred always in absence. It is conjured in the act of writing to an absent relative, in describing a place of origin left behind, or in the encounter with another person in conversation or a dramatic scene. The author makes presence-effects from the encounter with another person. In particular, for Goldsmith, his presence is both unconcealed and withdrawn in the multiple displacements of space and place between genres, media and persons that are nonetheless drawn from a restricted repertoire of family traits. In writing his letter, Goldsmith creates connection to family and kin that he perceived himself to have lost: complaining of his own prematurely aged and gaunt appearance, he says to Henry: 'I conceive you as grown fat sleek and healthy, passing many an happy day among your own children or those who knew you a child. Since I knew what it was to be a man this is a pleasure I have not known.'[16] The conception of Henry births Oliver's capacity to conceive of himself.

And this reliance on kin to conceive of a self is also charted in *The Vicar of Wakefield*. The pronominal slippage we have seen in Burchill is also a feature of the third character in *The Vicar of Wakefield* through whom Goldsmith presents a fiction of his own biography, Charles Primrose himself.[17] The first chapter indicates early that singular identity is a fantasy, and that identity is always the product of social and especially kin relationship. Hence, Primrose opens with the assertion 'I was ever of opinion, that the honest man who married and brought up a large family, did more service than he who continued single, and only talked of population.'[18] Primrose's first person 'I', his assertion of his opinion, is already pressed into the service of a principle of the advantage of plurality. Identity is made through procreation, dissemination and community. Primrose finds himself a wife and by the second paragraph he has already settled into a first-person plural. 'However, we loved each other tenderly, and our fondness increased as we grew old.'[19] The Primrose parents and their six children form a 'little circle'[20] which comes under threat from a merchant who absconds with the family wealth, a predatory landowner, a fairground trickster and thief, the natural disaster of a fire. There is room for individuation in this circle: Mrs Primrose is given to worldly vanity and is swift to judge, her husband is more temperate, soft-hearted, inclined to fail to live up to his stoical

[16]   Goldsmith, *Letters*, p. 41.
[17]   See Maureen Harkin, 'Goldsmith on Authorship in *The Vicar of Wakefield*', *Eighteenth-Century Fiction*, 14, nos. 3–4 (April–July 2002), 325–44.
[18]   *Vicar of Wakefield*, chapter 1, p. 18.
[19]   Ibid.
[20]   Ibid., p. 19.

principles, their older daughter Olivia is vain, the younger Sophia measured and virtuous, the second son Moses an innocent like his father while the older son George has more independence and boldness.

Like characters in a play, however, there is little room for these persons to develop or act against type. And, as James Carson points out, the nostalgic politics of the family republic cannot resist the pressure of commercial society and luxurious pursuit of pleasures, confirming Goldsmith's conservative politics.[21] Charles' dominant trait – his capacity to feel for others in their suffering to the extent that he risks losing his own capacity to judge – is one to which Goldsmith returned in his fictions for the stage and page. In the case of *The Vicar of Wakefield*, the reader is encouraged both to feel with the family as they experience a series of troubles, and also to retain an ironic distance from them, recognising their faults and failings without blaming them. Goldsmith mocks a sentimental cast of mind that can only feel and not judge. Burchell talks of the dangers of a 'sickly sensibility of the miseries of others' which leads to what is ultimately a selfish attempt at cure through charitable giving.[22] Goldsmith assumes one character – that of the gullible, innocent vicar who wears his good nature as a badge of honour – to enable another to be expressed: an angry critique of exploitation by the powerful of the weak and a family life far removed from Goldsmith's own unhappy experience as the son of the vicar of Kilkenny West.[23]

A further necessary leaven to the sickliness of sentiment is the lively, mocking wit Goldsmith tended to associate with the earlier comedic playwrights of the Restoration and that he sought to emulate. One of the earliest references to this theme is found in an exchange between Charles Primrose and the strolling player he meets before his reunion with his son, George. The player says that audiences are not happy with the tragedies of John Dryden and Nicholas Rowe and show a strong preference for 'Fletcher, Ben Jonson, and all the plays of Shakespear'.[24] He admits, however, that the success of the plays rests not on the talent of the authors but rather the attitudinising of the actors. Indeed, often the plays are pantomimes 'under the sanction of Jonson's or Shakespears name'[25] far distant from their originals. He concludes:

---

[21] James P. Carson, '"The Little Republic" of the Family: Goldsmith's Politics of Nostalgia', *Eighteenth-Century Fiction*, 16, no. 2 (January 2004), 173–96.
[22] *Vicar of Wakefield*, chapter 3, p. 29.
[23] See Norma Clarke, *Brothers of the Quill*, p. 251.
[24] *Vicar of Wakefield*, chapter 18, p. 96.
[25] Ibid.

> it is not the composition of the piece, but the number of starts and
> attitudes that may be introduced into it that elicits applause…. No, Sir,
> the works of Congreve and Farquhar have too much wit in them for
> the present taste; our modern dialect is much more natural.[26]

When Goldsmith turned to playwriting for his next attempt to make a
profit from his writing (despite its relative success, he did not write another
novel after *The Vicar of Wakefield*), he claimed to imitate those early eighteenth-century (Irish) wits, William Congreve and George Farquhar, who
achieved that balance between a generosity of spirit (a form of sentimentalism) and ironic distance that the *Vicar* promotes to its readers. This balance is required to avoid the loss of character, the dissipation of self in the
suffering of others, that is the effect of sentiment, and also to prevent falling
into the opposite behaviour, the assertion of self in the cynical exploitation of others for one's own gratification (the role played by the libertine
nephew Thornhill in the novel).

The critique of theatrical sentiment through the deployment of comic
irony was a feature of Goldsmith's writing. It recurs in his *Citizen of the
World* (1760), where Goldsmith has his Chinese letter-writer describe the
two licensed stages to his correspondent at Pekin as two armies at war.
The letter was originally published as the seventy-ninth of a series in the
Public Ledger, before Goldsmith published the series as an epistolary novel
in 1762. Lien Chi Altangi's letter was published Tuesday 30 September, ten
days after the opening of Drury Lane for the season on Saturday 20 September (Covent Garden followed on Monday 22 September). Like other
characters before and after him, Lien Chi Altangi, the Chinese informant,
is a first time visitor to the theatres, but far from being entranced by the
magic of the stage and the authenticity of the performance, he finds the
noise on and offstage distracting: 'If I enter the house with any sentiments
in my head, I am sure to have none going away, the whole mind being filled
with a dead march, a funeral procession, a cat-call, a jig, or a tempest.'[27]

Lien Chi Altangi next turns to his observations about the kind of talent
required of an author for the contemporary stage. And in particular he
deduces that authorial presence depends on an ability to cater to the performance of actors:

> One player shines in an exclamation, another in a groan, a third in an
> horror, a fourth in a start, a fifth in a smile, a sixth faints, and a seventh

[26] Ibid.
[27] Oliver Goldsmith, Letter 79, *The Citizen of the World*, in *Collected Works*, ed. Arthur
Friedman, vol. 5, pp. 324–5.

figets [*sic*] round the stage with peculiar vivacity; that piece therefore will succeed best where each has a proper opportunity of shining; the actors business is not so much to adapt himself to the poet, as the poet's to adapt himself to the actor.[28]

There is, it appears, no cognitive agency in the theatre at all. Knowing actors is the same as knowing the stage set and its instruments, and the author's job is to write to provide opportunities for the actor to deliver the mechanical rehearsed tricks of face and body in performance. The author's presence is seen only in the actor's gesture. Lien Chi Altangi mentions tragedy as a particularly noisy, mechanical and affectless affair; audiences' applaud and weep over meaningless physical contortions ('theatrical *ah*'s and '*oh's*') and 'a whining scene must strike most forcibly'.[29]

What he described in his prose fictions, Goldsmith sought to perform in his plays: a sentimental affect suitably distanced by techniques of comic irony. Goldsmith's first play, a comedy called *The Good-Natur'd Man*, was, according to the preface its author wrote to accompany its publication seven days after its first performance, written in imitation of 'the poets of the last age':

> The term, *genteel comedy*, was then unknown amongst us, and little more was desired by an audience, than nature and humor, in whatever walks of life they were most conspicuous. The author of the following scenes never imagined that more would be expected of him, and therefore to delineate character has been his principal aim.[30]

A studied resistance to gentility in favour of low humour is associated with these poets of the last age, despite their aristocratic and libertine values. Most famously, the essay he published to prepare his audience for the hit comedy, *She Stoops to Conquer* (debuted 15 March 1773), the *Essay on the Theatre: Or, A Comparison between Sentimental and Laughing Comedy* asks, 'which deserves the preference,--the weeping sentimental comedy so much in fashion at present, or the laughing, and even low comedy, which seems to have been last exhibited by Vanbrugh and Cibber?'[31]

Robert D. Hume sees Goldsmith's complaint about the prevalence of sentimental comedy as alarmist and demonstrates that the sentimental

---

[28] Ibid., p. 325.
[29] Ibid.
[30] Oliver Goldsmith, *The Good-Natur'd Man*, in *Collected Works of Oliver Goldsmith*, ed. Arthur Friedman, vol. 5, p. 13.
[31] Oliver Goldsmith, *Collected Works*, vol. 3, p. 210.

comedy had much less purchase and ubiquity on the Georgian stage than Goldsmith claimed.[32] The *Essay* may have been designed to vindicate Goldsmith's last play as much as prepare his audience for his next. If so, there is a touch of the familiar irony about his own authorship. In the *Essay*, he complains of the lack of comedic skill required of authors who sought success through writing sentimental comedies, the only apprenticeship required being that of hack novel-writing. 'Those abilities that can hammer out a Novel, are fully sufficient for the production of a Sentimental Comedy.'[33] By 1773, Goldsmith was recognised as one of the most celebrated practitioners of the sentimental novel. The essay, then, may have been an attempt to vindicate his 1768 play *The Good-Natur'd Man* which was in direct competition with Hugh Kelly's more polite and sensitive comedy, *False Delicacy*, mounted at David Garrick's Drury Lane in January 1768 just before *The Good-Natur'd Man*.

Garrick was likely choosing between the two plays, both of which offer a critique of oversensitivity. In Hugh Kelly's play, a comic wit named Cecil, with the aid of a lively widow Mrs Harley, succeeds in untangling a series of misalliances and securing three marriages between parties who, as Mrs Harley puts it, 'plague one another... heartily with their delicacy.'[34] By 19 July 1767, Goldsmith had tired of Garrick's objections to the script and sent it to George Colman at the rival Covent Garden. Colman appears to have delayed opening *The Good-Natur'd Man* so it could rival (and mock) Hugh Kelly's play then settled in the repertory. Finally, the *Essay* might also make more sense as an attack on the market for published fiction and a rueful backward glance at the circumstances that led Goldsmith himself to 'hammer out' a novel to support himself in straitened circumstances.

Certainly, audience members who knew the novel *The Vicar of Wakefield* would have recognised elements of that novel in the stage play of *The Good-Natur'd Man*: in particular, the character type of the hero who wastes his feelings and his finances on others. Goldsmith's biographer, A. Lytton

---

[32] Robert D. Hume, 'Goldsmith and Sheridan and the Supposed Revolution of "Laughing" against Sentimental Comedy' (1972), rpt in his *The Rakish Stage: Studies in English Drama, 1660-1800* (Carbondale, IL: Southern Illinois University Press, 1983), pp. 312–55. Between 1746 and 1776, no more than 10 per cent of mainpieces with an inclusive definition of the term could be counted as 'sentimental' comedies according to George Winchester Jnr in his ed., *The London Stage 1660–1800: Part Four 1746–1777*, 3 vols (Carbondale, IL: Southern Illinois University Press, 1962), vol. 1, pp. clxii–clxv.

[33] Oliver Goldsmith, *Collected Works*, vol. 3, p. 213.

[34] Hugh Kelly, *False Delicacy* (London: Baldwin, Johnston and Kearsly, 1768), Act 3, p. 58.

Sells, describes the play as a 'dramatic variation' of *The Vicar of Wakefield.*[35] It concerns young Honeywood – 'strange good natur'd, foolish, open hearted'[36] – who has ruined his fortune by giving it away to all and every petitioner and cannot offer marriage to the woman he loves, the heiress Miss Richland. She generously pays off his bailiffs and struggles to evade the plan of her guardian, the doleful pessimist Croaker, to marry her to his son, Leontine. Young Honeywood adds insult to injury when he tries to persuade her to accept the proposals of the absurdly pretentious Mr Lofty, who claims to have influence with the mighty which he is supposed to be exerting to release a portion of Miss Richland's fortune. Leontine in turn has returned from Paris with an heiress in tow whom he is passing off to his parents as their daughter, Olivia, sent to be educated abroad by an aunt at a young age. All is resolved at the Talbot Inn from which the false Olivia and Leontine plan to elope to Scotland when it is discovered that young Honeywood's father, Sir William Honeywood, has returned from abroad and sought to correct his son's follies by remaining disguised and having him imprisoned for debt. Sir William reveals the emptiness of Lofty's claims and the way is now clear for both pairs of marriages. Young Honeywood concludes by asserting, 'I now too plainly perceive my errors. My vanity, in attempting to please all, by fearing to offend any. My meanness in approving folly, lest fools should disapprove. Henceforth, therefore, it shall be my study to reserve my pity for real distress; my friendship for true merit, and my love for her, who first taught me what it is to be happy.'[37] Honeywood is another in a succession of feeling heroes in Goldsmith who foolishly expend themselves in feeling for others.

The most direct predecessor and namesake for Goldsmith's hero was a character in Goldsmith's *The Life of Richard Nash* of 1762. One of the lovers of a Miss Sylvia is S___:

> the celebrated S___, who, at that time, went by the name of *the good-natured man.* This gentleman, with talents that might have done honour to humanity, suffered himself to fall at length into the lowest state of debasement. He followed the dictates of every newest passion, his love, his pity, his generosity, and even his friendships were all in excess....[38]

---

[35] A. Lytton Sells, *Oliver Goldsmith: His Life and Works* (London: Allen & Unwin, 1974), p. 329.

[36] *The Good-Natur'd Man*, Act 1, p. 20.

[37] *The Good-Natur'd Man*, Act 5, p. 81.

[38] Quoted in Arthur Friedman, 'Introduction', in *Collected Works of Oliver Goldsmith*, vol. 5, p. 4.

Sylvia, like Miss Richland, discharges her suitor's debts. Young Honeywood also has features of George Primrose and Burchell/Thornhill. Like George, he steps away from the woman he loves leaving her vulnerable to the advances of much less deserving suitors. George tells his father that he employed his skill in disputation to make his way across Europe, arguing cases for different sides as he travels. So too, young Honeywood too often sees both sides in a case and abdicates his own powers of judgement. Like Burchell/Sir William Thornhill he is overgenerous. Unlike Burchell however, he fails to be an active enabler of resolution in the plot; the character of the older Honeywood, who shares the title Sir William, takes on this role. And young Honeywood also has affinity with Charles Primrose in that he contemplates a solitary retreat from kinship ties as a fitting punishment for his foolish generosity to the world at large: 'How have I sunk by too great an assiduity to please! How have I overtax'd all my abilities, lest the approbation of a single fool should escape me! But all is now over; I have survived my reputation, my fortune, my friendships, and nothing remains henceforward for me but solitude and repentance.'[39]

There are, however, important distinctions between stage performance and the reception of the play in a printed form. The problems with the stage play that hindered its success seem to have been to do with bringing characters on stage, embodying them in performance. The play opened on the Friday and did not play a second night, but it returned for all six nights of the next week and the first three nights of the week following (8–10 February), providing the author with two benefits. By its second performance, the play had been revised in response to the audience's negative reaction to one scene in particular which had been excised: a scene in which young Honeywood kits out a pair of bailiffs in his own suits of clothes to pass them off as gentlemanly company but they expose themselves through their vulgarity to Miss Richland. On the play's publication the scene was restored in print, leading a critic in *The Monthly Review* to comment:

> An agreeable play to *read*. – It is not every dramatic production that will *act well*; to borrow a phrase used by players and play-going people. Of this, Mr. G's comedy is a proof, – in respect to some of its scenes, particularly: though it must be allowed that the capital part of the old, whimsical, ill-boding *Croaker*, was even improved by Mr. Shuter's exquisitely droll and humorous performance. On the other

---

[39]   *Good-Natur'd Man*, Act 5, pp. 75–6.

hand, the bailiff and his black-guard follower appeared intolerable on the stage; yet we are not disgusted with them in the perusal.[40]

Goldsmith's next play succeeded where *The Good-Natur'd Man* seems to have failed; it managed the balance between lettered individual genius and ensemble performance, the distribution of character to produce an effective whole in performance, and a reference to the 'novelistic' and the 'novel' which enhances rather than undermines the experience of being present at the play.

The plot of *She Stoops to Conquer* (1773) hinges on the issue of whether 'character' is maintained in order to promote social harmony and reform vice or to cause mischief and disorder. Goldsmith, however, abandons in this work the stock types of an over-feeling hero and a predatory or exploitative rogue, whether of the upper or lower classes. Charles Marlowe and Tony Lumpkin, true to form, display traits known to be shared with their author: Marlowe shares Goldsmith's social awkwardness and Lumpkin his rustic genius. But they also depart from their shadowy forebears in *The Vicar of Wakefield*, the predatory Squire Thornhill and the thief, Jenkinson. Marlowe is confident in pursuit of women below his class and tongue-tied in the presence of a woman who is his social equal; he has some of the sensibility of the modern feeling hero but a libertine cast that recalls the predatory rakes of the comedies of the early part of the eighteenth century that Goldsmith admired. Tony Lumpkin's mischievous trickster actions also contribute to bringing about a happy conclusion in the eventual marriage of his cousin Constance and her lover, Marlowe's friend, George Hastings. It is however the heroine, Kate Hardcastle, who demonstrates the capacity to 'keep' a character in order to win a husband fit for her purposes: she keeps up the role of the innocent chambermaid. She herself acknowledges a dramatic model when, having donned her disguise, she asks her maid 'Don't you think I look something like Cherry in the Beaux Strategem?'[41] Cherry is the barmaid in Farquhar's comedy of 1707 who is pursued by the young rakes who come to her inn. However, a novel-reading audience would also recognise the presence in Kate's performance of the characteristic resilience and wit of the maid, Pamela, of Samuel Richardson's novel of 1740. Kate in her role as maid wins a proposal of marriage from her rakish suitor, as does Pamela. Marlowe proposes marriage in very similar terms to those used by *Pamela*'s Mr B, insisting that what he first saw as

[40] *The Monthly Review* 38 (February 1768), Art. 44, pp. 159–60.
[41] Oliver Goldsmith, *She Stoops to Conquer*, *Collected Works*, 5, pp. 99–217; Act 3, p. 186.

affectation and performance he now recognises as signs of virtue: 'What at first seem'd rustic plainness, now appears refin'd simplicity. What seem'd forward assurance, now strikes me as the result of courageous innocence, and conscious virtue.'[42] Kate turns the tables on her lover when she reveals her true identity as the daughter of Mr Hardcastle, accusing him of adopting a 'character':

> In which of your characters, Sir, will you give us leave to address you. As the faultering gentleman, with looks on the ground, that speaks just to be heard, and hates hypocrisy: or the loud confident creature, that keeps it up with Mrs. Mantrap, and old Miss Biddy Buckskin, till three in the morning; ha, ha, ha.[43]

The audience is well aware of the distinction between Kate's assuming her character of the chambermaid in order to test and reform her suitor and Marlowe's divided identity which is not apparently within his control to put on and take off as she suggests.

In this last play, Goldsmith appears to have achieved distance from the authorial character he had sustained up to that point: the overly benevolent and gullible fool. While versions of the identity he peddled still circulate in *She Stoops to Conquer*, the leaky subjectivity of the sensitive man, formed only in and through response to the strong feelings of others, is no longer the subject of reform. And that distance from a spendthrift authorial subjectivity is also marked in the play's new attitude to the novel as rival and presence on the eighteenth stage. Nonetheless, the history of the composition of the play we now know as *She Stoops to Conquer* remained connected with Goldsmith's earlier two works about the dangers of a too-benevolent heart, *The Good-Natur'd Man* and *The Vicar of Wakefield*. Francis Newbery the publisher had apparently commissioned a novel from Goldsmith in the early 1770s and paid him an advance of two to three hundred pounds. The manuscript he received was though no more than a reworking of the plot of *The Good-Natur'd Man* and he refused it; the always improvident Goldsmith signed over the copyright of another play he was composing in place of return of the advance.[44] It appears that the play with the 'lost' subtitle of

---

[42]   Ibid., Act 5, p. 210.
[43]   Ibid., Act 5, p. 213.
[44]   See A. Lytton-Sells, *Oliver Goldsmith*, pp. 383–96, p. 155 and 'Appendix 1', pp. 383–96. 'The History of Francis Wills and the Mystery of Goldsmith's Lost Novel' explores the possibility than an anonymous two volume work published by Vernor and Chator in two volumes in 1772 may have been this novel turned down by Newbery.

'novel' may be connected to a lost novel which Goldsmith was composing alongside it.

The reader searching for *She Stoops* among the manuscripts submitted to the licenser, John Larpent, might be surprised to discover it submitted to the licenser under the title 'The Novel: or, Mistakes of a Night'.[45] Indeed, the evidence suggests that the title may even have been 'The Novel of a night' given that 'Mistakes of' is an insertion in a different pen; more likely, however, this is a correction of the professional copyist's error in transcription which he has corrected since it is in the same hand. A different hand from this is responsible for the two notes, the first above the title 'It was subsequently called She Stoops to Conquer', and below it (and very faint) '– note Dr Johnson in Boswell's Life – of the difficulty of finding a title for (?) this –'. These are probably the notes of John Payne Collier who bought the Larpent collection of manuscripts (with Thomas Amyot) in 1832 and annotated many of them. A third hand has inserted the words 'Covent Garden', the theatre for which the licence is being requested.[46]

In titling his work 'The Novel', Goldsmith may be invoking an earlier and more descriptive use of the word 'novel' dating from the early eighteenth century to refer to anything 'new': stories without an original in another published source or referring to recent events, secret histories, gossip or scandal. Stories in other words that do not play out as expected through conventional formulae. The play is not 'novel' in its main plot: the drama of a well-born woman passing herself off as a serving maid to a prospective suitor brought to her father's house was a relatively familiar one, best known from Pierre Marivaux's 1730 play *Le Jeu de l'Amour et du Hazard*. However, Tony Lumpkin's inventions that his stepfather's house is an inn and his trick driving his mother around the countryside are both 'new', and the suggestion of this short-lived title is there in a Covent Garden playbill for the ninth night of Arthur Murphy's *Alzuma* of Saturday 13 March 1773 which announced 'On Monday, (Never Performed), a New Comedy call'd The Mistakes of a Night'. On Sunday 14 March, Joseph Younger informed Goldsmith in a letter that he had complied with Goldsmith's request to order the playbills with the revised title of *She Stoops to Conquer; or, Mistakes of a Night*.[47]

---

[45]   235 Oliver Goldsmith, *The Novel; or, Mistakes of a Night*, The Huntington Library, San Marino, California, LA349, p. 4.

[46]   For fuller discussion and a full list of variants between Larpent and the first edition, see Coleman O. Parsons, 'Textual Variations in a Manuscript of "She Stoops to Conquer"', *Modern Philology*, 40, no. 1 (1942), 57–69.

[47]   *The Collected Letters of Oliver Goldsmith*, ed. K.C. Balderston (Cambridge: Cambridge University Press, 1928), p. xlvii). For further discussion of the term 'novel'

By the end of the play we find Goldsmith using the word 'novel' in the more familiar sense of a prose fiction work of tiresome sentimentality. George Hastings returns from a rash attempt to elope with Constance Neville, and the two plead for tenderness from Mr Hardcastle despite the cruelty of Constance's rapacious aunt. Constance arrogates the title reference to herself in her closing lines in this fifth act when she complains that since the death of her father, who had agreed to her marriage to Hastings:

> ... I have been obliged to stoop to dissimulation to avoid oppression. In an hour of levity, I was ready even to give up my Fortune to secure my choice. But I'm now recover'd from the delusion, and hope from your tenderness what is denied me from a nearer connexion.

Mrs Hardcastle cuts in with a contemptuous 'Pshaw, pshaw this is all but the whining end of a modern Novel.'[48] We note that Goldsmith's Chinese letter-writer, Lien Chi Altangi, also used the term 'whining' to complain about the sentimental histrionics of the plays being written for the modern stage. Here, though, the play seems to be once more marking its *distance* from the novel. It is not going to end like a sentimental novel with tearful reconciliations. Or Goldsmith is not going to import the whining style of modern fiction into his brisk, witty comedy. However, the fact that it is Mrs Hardcastle, tasteless addict of the modern, who dismisses Constance's plea also suggests the play's sympathy with the ethical force of sentimental narrative. And it is Mr Hardcastle, the resolute loyalist of old values, who brings about their marriage by inviting his wife's preferred suitor, her own son Tony Lumpkin, to repudiate the offer of Constance's hand. Mrs Hardcastle is firmly excluded from a happy resolution in which the four young lovers are able to indulge their true feelings in happy unions. Goldsmith appears to be using the different and changing meanings of the word 'novel' to indicate his play's capacity to accommodate the old (the satirical, the scandalous, the mocking Restoration culture) with the new (ethical, feeling, sentimental Georgian culture). Goldsmith implies that the 'novel' and its associations with a particular capacity for sentimental affect could, when properly harnessed, rejuvenate a theatre he saw as declining into decadence.

Goldsmith invests the presence-effects of theatre with the power to absorb the rival energies of the novel. What is novel is re-contained within a theatre which recalls the past: the comedy of intrigue in which wit could

---

in the title, see K.C. Balderston, 'A Manuscript Version of *She Stoops to Conquer*', *Modern Language Notes*, 45 (1930), 84–5.
[48]   *She Stoops to Conquer, Collected Works*, Act 5, p. 215.

bring about reform. It is worth recalling however that it was Goldsmith's robust resistance to the authority of his theatrical manager that brought the play to the stage and secured its success. George Colman the elder dithered about accepting the play for Covent Garden and, when he did accept it, made public his concerns (possibly founded on the poor reception of the low scenes in the *Good Natur'd Man*). Goldsmith refused to adopt any of the changes Colman recommended. The manager was widely ridiculed in the press when the play proved wildly successful on its first performance on 15 March 1773. Goldsmith had completed a complete draft of the play by September 1771.[49] Goldsmith was too nervous to attend the first night and took a walk in St James' Park. His receipts though for the play in profits from the third, sixth and ninth nights totalled £502 18s 6d.[50]

The printed play included two epilogues and we conclude this chapter with some thoughts about what the complex history of the different epilogues to *She Stoops* reveals about Goldsmith's authorial presence-effects. As with *The Vicar of Wakefield*, this is a story in which the company (in this case of Covent Garden actors) and a community (in this case of fellow authors and theatre folk) prove ultimately to be the kin which confirms the author's Being; but not without threatening to dissipate and displace his powers. Four epilogues were in circulation and Goldsmith turned the story of their adventures into an emollient letter to the composer of one of them, Joseph Cradock, to whom he wrote after the first performance on 15 March but before the first benefit night of 18 March.

In this history of competing voices and media (playwrights Arthur Murphy and George Colman, actresses Mary Bulkley and Anne Catley, newspapers, performance, manuscript drafts), we can hear Goldsmith's presence being shaped out of a sequence of acts of unconcealment and withdrawal. His letter to Cradock, letting him down gently because the epilogue Cradock had composed for the character of Tony Lumpkin did not arrive in time to be spoken, is a small 'novel' in its own right. Here, the adventures of the epilogue act as surrogate for the troubled history of bringing his play to performance:

My dear Sir,

The play has met with a success much beyond your expectations or mine. The news papers are now abusing Colman to some purpose. I thank you sincerely for your Epilogue which however could not be

[49]   *Letters of Oliver Goldsmith*, p. 111.
[50]   Ibid, p. 115.

used, but with your permission shall be printed. The story in short is this; Murphy sent me rather the outline of an Epilogue than an Epilogue, which was to be sung by Mrs. Catley, and which she approved. Mrs. Bulkley hearing this insisted on throwing up her part unless according to the custom of the theatre she were permitted to speak the Epilogue. In this embarrassment I thought of making a quarrelling Epilogue between Catley and her debating who should speak the Epilogue, but then Mrs. Catley refused after I had taken the trouble of drawing it out. I was then at a loss indeed, an Epilogue was to be made and for none but Mrs. Bulkley. I made one, and Colman thought it too bad to be spoken, I was therefore obliged to try a fourth time, for nobody would think of letting Quick speak the Epilogue, and I made a very mawkish thing as you'l shortly see. Such is the history of my stage adventures, and which I have at last done with. I cannot help saying that I am very sick of the stage, and tho I believe I shall get three tolerable benefits yet I shal[l] upon the whole be a loser, even in a pecuniary light. My ease and comfort I certainly lost while it was in agitation.[51]

The jostling for position in the wedding scenes at the end of *The Vicar* seems to be being rehearsed among the theatrical kin of the Covent Garden stage in these rival epilogues, and rival actors, and rival authors, all fielded as possibilities for the epilogues of *She Stoops*. Where *The Vicar* turned to stage conventions to undercut a realism in the novel that, for Goldsmith, only served to promote delusionary ideals, here the novelistic flavour of his account of the fortunes of the epilogues reinforces the conclusion that Being, especially public recognition of authorial Being, is made through, not despite, alliances of kin and kind.

[51]   *Letters of Oliver Goldsmith*, pp. 114–15.

Chapter 6
From Author to Character

The first part of this book has focused on the various ways in which authors made their presence felt when working between and across the fictional forms of novel and theatre. The author-character has emerged as a distinctive presence. Speakers of prologues and epilogues are author surrogates as are, on occasion, those *dramatis personae* that resemble known characteristics of the author (Goldsmith), were performed by the author him or herself (Haywood), or put an actor on stage in the play as a version of the author (Fielding). In turn novels draw on conventions from the stage to announce the presence of a narrator (asides, shrugs, keeping character), and shape versions of the author's biography through analogy with the biographies of their characters. Consistently and anxiously, authors return to the struggle to represent their own presence in their works. This process itself reveals the extent to which authorial 'identity' is a function of the presence of audience, whether in the shape of those in the physical auditorium or in the novelistic sensorium of the reader's mind.

I have argued that it is the play of unconcealment and withdrawal that organises authorial presence. I have explored the different ways in which this process plays out in specific cases of four authors whose careers were distributed between writing novels and writing for the theatre. While we can identify moments of conscious fictionalising of themselves as authors, a concentration on works in both media that are produced together close in time (and often in relation to each other) allows us to see not so much the intention of the author as the combination of forces and elements that go to construct fictions of presence where a kind of authorial signature or mark is provided. While these are examples specific to authors and take individual shape and patterns, they are also the result of a shared experience and positioning. I have often termed this *between* novel and theatre and have taken particular interest in those hybrid works that appear to bridge both media: the play that has more success as a published 'novelised' fiction, the prose fiction populated with characters from a play or allusion to a stage-play world. However, that *between* might suggest too comfortable a passage from one media to another or capacity to integrate both in one space or performance. The process of unconcealment and withdrawal requires incompleteness and tension. What emerges is a pattern whereby the attempt to bring an author into being forces the recognition that Being lies elsewhere: in another genre, in an audience, in a performance by another actor, another writer, both rival and kin.

We have seen this process of unconcealment and withdrawal play out in different ways for each author and combination of their works under discussion. In each case authorial intention is hard to disentangle from the determinations of genre and gender, of circumstance and contingency. Eliza Haywood's authorial presence rests on a pattern of owning and disowning. Owning for women becomes 'owning up', putting oneself on display, and that display in itself is understood to be a form of confession. Haywood turns her own visibility, especially on stage, into a means of speaking about and representing the exploitation of women's bodies especially by those who own them: husbands and fathers.

Henry Fielding's authorial presence is marked by recurrent acts of ghosting and puppetry. Comedy is made out of the paradox that spirit, ghost or absence embodied (the ghost in *Hamlet*, the transmigration of a spirit in *A Journey*) always manifests as failure for the author, not only in the financial sense (failing to make a living as a writer), but in the sense of producing a convincing effect of presence. In a strange act of reversal, in these acts of translating spirit to body/person, Fielding brings versions of himself perilously and purposefully close to the objects of his satire, thereby abdicating authorial presence itself.

Charlotte Lennox's authorial presence uses forms of surrogation to resist the unhappiness of dependency. Novels and plays act as surrogates for each other, while revealing the impossibility of a fantasy of independence as an expression of presence. Characters, like their author, alternate between the roles of Quixote and servant, blurring the distinction between original and surrogate. Genre and media-switching in Lennox's career –and especially in her adaptation of a novel into a play – reveal that attempts to assert independence only confirm a network of dependencies.

Oliver Goldsmith's authorial presence is found in a pattern of keeping and letting go. Authorial character, by analogy with the actor's part, is something it is hard to maintain and keep up; it is prone in Goldsmith's work to dispersal and distribution along lines of kin and kind. The authorial mark of signature of 'giving' the self – in attention to others – is also a form of taking from others to make Being. Goldsmith's fiction of presence is serially manifest in parts on the stage and the page that construct a version of his character always invested in imagining itself elsewhere.

Authors seek to live through their writing. Not only by supporting themselves through their writing. But also, in the sense that the writing *is* a form of life. In interacting with the book, with the stage, and the mutual audience of both, writing comes to life and gives an impression of a life 'behind' or 'beyond' the written word. Indeed, it may be that the very need, the urgency of earning through this labour, is what produces the impression of energetic being. The knowledge of, and first-hand experience of, working with and on Georgian stages, informs the experimental approach these authors brought to the novel.

In their dependence on their profession, the writers under discussion here find affinity more often with actors than with other human agents in their chosen industries. So too, like an actor, the author achieves what Joseph Roach refers to as an 'interiority effect' by associating him or herself with a particular part or role.[1] Both Haywood and Lennox were actors, and their acting contributed to the portfolio careers they struggled to sustain. According to Felicity Nussbaum, the eighteenth century sees the emergence of what she terms 'performative property', a property acquired by the actor, especially the female actor, as a star performer. Nussbaum observes that performative property has a particular value for women – who therefore become adept at cultivating it – because of their exclusion from ownership of other forms of property in their own right in this period.[2] The assertion of 'ownership' of a play, a part, a work, is something women writers often made or maintained with more assiduity than their male contemporaries. Fielding and Goldsmith could, despite their own precariousness financially, still afford to give away or appear to be careless with their reputation and their claim to 'presence' than Haywood and Lennox.

It is the corporeal presence of the actor that differentiates the audience's experience of character from the printed type that renders character in the novel or the playscript. 'Character' might be seen as the category that connects and mediates the different kind of persons and the different ways in which each person manifests between theatre and novel. Actors play characters, own characters, step out of character. Authors invent characters who act as surrogates for their own biographies or – we might also speculate – invent versions of their biographies by invoking and inviting readers to see similarities between the persons in the work(s) and the person imagined to be 'behind' them. Accordingly, the next section of this book turns from authorial presence to the presence of other kinds of character in the novel and on the stage.

---

[1] Joseph Roach, *It* (Ann Arbor, MI: University of Michigan Press, 2007), p. 3.
[2] Felicity Nussbaum, *Rival Queens*, p. 3.

PART 2

Characters: Occupying Space

Chapter 7
Introducing Characters

The actor, Charles Macklin, is reported to have responded to the question 'what is character?' with the answer: 'the alphabet will tell you. It is that which is distinguished by its own marks from every other thing of its kind.'[1] Macklin alludes here to the primary meaning of the word: the external mark or sign by which something is recognised (and differentiated from other marks or signs). The Greek *kharakter* (Χαρακτηρ) refers to an instrument for creating or stamping a distinctive mark: the term swiftly moves from tool to the mark itself.[2] Macklin refers to the marks constituting the characters of the alphabet that serve this purpose of distinguishing one element from another. Together alphabetical marks constitute a system, put together in different combinations and sequences they form different meanings. So too the characters of the repertory theatre have places in a system, an economy, of possible combinations according to genre and type.

Stage 'character' clearly worked this way in that the *dramatis personae* was made up of a familiar set of types – the blustering father, the witty daughter and the rakish suitor of comedy; or the tyrant, the virgin and the sexual predator of tragedy – put together to deliver a plot with some variation through combination and complexity. This was a requisite of a repertory theatre where actors had their own 'lines of business', kept even when the performers' physical presence spoke violently against type: heavily pregnant women played virgins, elderly men played young rakes. When actors played against their 'type' they were criticised for 'stepping out of line'. They could also step out of character when they 'pointed', directing a speech with gesture directly to the audience. Audiences did not come to the theatre to be surprised by what characters did, but to be impressed by the quality of the actors' technique in delivering their business.[3]

---

[1]   J.T. Kirkman, *Memoirs of the Life of Charles Macklin*, 2 vols (London: Lackington & Co., 1799), vol. 1, p. 66.

[2]   See John Frow, *Character and Person* (Oxford: Oxford University Press, 2014), p. 7.

[3]   See Lisa Freeman, *Character's Theatre: Genre and Identity on the Eighteenth-Century English Stage* (Philadelphia, PA: University of Pennsylvania Press, 2002), pp. 28, 31.

The places eighteenth-century stage characters occupy are best under-stood, theatre historians know, by attending a production. The confusion of alphabetical and semantic proximity in the naming of play characters on the comic stage, in particular, disappears when bodies perform roles. Millamant and Mirabell, Witwoud and Wilful and Waitwell (all charac-ters in William Congreve's 1700 play, *The Way of the World*), consist of different bodies blocked on a stage that has a distinct topography and hierarchy. Certainly, the naming conveys meaning, including the meaning that it can be hard to discriminate between persons of virtue and vice in a highly-mannered society. But corporeality – presence in the theatre with the actors' bodies in performance – enables an understanding that does not require the work of interpretation. Further, Gumbrecht suggests, in a 'presence culture' such as the eighteenth-century theatre, humans 'don't see themselves as eccentric in relation to the world but as being part of the world (they are indeed in-the-world in a spatial and physical way)'. In this section of the book, we explore the ways in which the character system(s) of presence culture in theatre inform the shaping of character in print in the novel. And the ways in which characters from and in novels become, or are imagined to be, embodied in other forms of media, par-ticularly theatrical ones. In so doing, I draw on Gumbrecht's description of the vertical dimension of 'Being's movement in space', which he says is associated with its 'emergence into being there and with occupying a space'.[4] Character occupies space. Not in ways that confine it, but rather in ways that allow character to move, to expand: in this instance, beyond and between the media of theatre and novel. Characters occupy their audience on the page and the stage in the sense that they keep them busy, reacting to and anticipating potential futures in the context of a more-or-less known set of possibilities. They also, and frequently, occupy the narratives they act in, turning attention *away* from the unfolding of plot. They can impede the progress of story in their moments of self-reflexive dilation, of mental preoccupation.

Through the course of the eighteenth century the more modern and qualitative sense of character, the 'estimate formed of a person's moral qualities' as Elaine McGirr describes it,[5] comes to gain purchase and to sit alongside the quantitative alphabetical definition Macklin invokes. And these new associations, if they cannot be said to be caused by the rise of the novel as a genre, were at least claimed by novel writers (and

---

4   Ibid., pp. 68, 69.
5   Elaine McGirr, *Eighteenth-Century Characters: A Guide to the Character of the Age* (Basingstoke: Palgrave Macmillan, 2007), p. 1.

those that puffed and promoted their work) as the ambition and *raison d'être* of the genre.

Deidre Shauna Lynch proposes that the 'ethical' sense of character starts to emerge in a mid-eighteenth-century booming culture of trade. As everything starts to become property to be alienated for profit, the argument for an 'interior' property of special and unmarketable value must be imagined into being. To give someone a character is to provide them with a letter that stands surety for their integrity as a recipient of 'credit'. People, Lynch asserts, 'used characters... to renegotiate social relations in their changed, commercialized world'.[6]

The printed world of new 'types' found in the novel is the primary mediator of this sense of being. Here, the letter carries the credit of one person to another; it stands as a form of surety for that person's ethical integrity or at least their capacity to meet a debt. The novel acquires increasing legitimacy, its entertainment offering a kind of ethical surety, through this claim to underwrite the shaping of a good character in its reader. Attacks on the novel treat as suspect and hypocritical the claim to stand surety for the good behaviour of a reader. In Lynch's formulation, the novel is the quintessential product of the market precisely in its claim to traffic in an 'inner meaning', a precious set of individual and interior qualities beyond what can be bought and sold in everyday life. It acquires thereby an 'aura' of distinction and it distinguishes its readers' individual taste and discernment from that of the masses engaged in more transparent forms of social and market exchange.

It is in the treatment of character that the stage and the novel are most often seen to diverge. Indeed, one story of the changing nature of literature in the eighteenth century is that of the novel's cuckoo-like usurpation of the stage's monopoly on the delivery of character. The novel's development of techniques that deliver a simulation of interiority displaces the drama's traditional contest of performances and surfaces between different beings, set in conflict on a single stage. Anti-theatrical language had long complained not only that embodied performance was dangerously seductive by comparison with the freedom of mental exploration of 'being' through reading, but also that the body of the actor was a poor instrument to communicate the true greatness and complexity of a larger sense of being – especially of the divine or transcendent. Hence, by 1811, in an essay first published in *The Reflector*, Charles Lamb concludes that Shakespeare's genius is not best served by the dramatic performance of his plays. Performed drama

---

[6]   Deirdre Shauna Lynch, *The Economy of Character: Novels, Markets, and the Business of Inner Meaning* (Chicago, IL: University of Chicago Press, 1998), p. 4.

is for the workaday author, and there is a quality in the written text that is changed and impoverished when it is put into performance for Lamb:

> What we see upon a stage is body and bodily action; what we are conscious of in reading is almost exclusively the mind, and its movements; and this, I think, may sufficiently account for the very different sort of delight with which the same play so often affects us in the reading and the seeing.[7]

The presence of the actor is of course what distinguishes the rendering of character in stage fiction from that of print fiction. John Frow reminds us that 'the actor is simultaneously herself and another, imaginary person, the two fused into a single yet, paradoxically, divided entity'.[8] For Charles Lamb the actor's performance obscures the true character not only of the part he or she plays but the creative genius who first conjured the part into being, the author:

> But such is the instantaneous nature of the impressions which we take in at the eye and ear at a playhouse, compared with the slow apprehension oftentimes of the understanding in reading, that we are apt not only to sink the play-writer in the consideration which we pay to the actor, but even to identify in our minds in a perverse manner, the actor with the character which he represents.[9]

Lamb complains that we substitute the impoverished imagination of an actor trained only in gesture and repetition for that of the creator of the work.

Lamb's essay expresses a concern about the overemphasis on the actor as the mediator of character and sets the author's genius and the consumer's experience of and with the text at odds with the engrossing force of the actor's person, personality and talent. Lamb was born a year before David Garrick retired from the stage (1775) and was a child while Sarah Siddons and Siddons-mania preoccupied the London stage. He writes in the wake of the emergence of celebrity culture to complain that the actor has come to eclipse character and role, to have occupied the place of both entirely.

---

[7] Charles Lamb, 'On the Tragedies of Shakespeare Considered with Reference to Their Fitness for Stage Representation', *The Reflector: A Quarterly Magazine, on Subjects of Philosophy, Politics, and the Liberal Arts*, 2, no. 4 (1811), 298–313, p. 310.
[8] Frow, *Character and Person*, p. 290.
[9] Lamb, 'On the Tragedies of Shakespeare', pp. 299–300.

Julia Fawcett illuminates the nature of new theatrical celebrity, closely related to what I identify in this book as a process of unconcealment and withdrawal in the making of presence. Fawcett provides a series of case studies of 'overexpression' among theatrical celebrities: a means of both making a version of the self public and shielding it from public view. She describes the 'unique but related strategies [celebrities] developed to paralyze their publics' attempts to decipher their private selves'.[10] Overexpression, an 'unskilled or overwrought attempt at self-definition',[11] is a means of obscuring apparent legibility, a form of putting on display that also withdraws the performer from being seen or discovered.

Fawcett, as I do, finds this technique of performance adopted in print works that render versions of 'real' selves: her cases include male actors (David Garrick, Colley Cibber) and female (Mary Robinson, George Anne Bellamy, Charlotte Charke), and a male author who did not perform on the London stages (Laurence Sterne). However, her interest in character only extends to the ways in which roles become attached to persons who are managing their public performances through overexpression. My own study in this section begins with the character as the case and charts the recurring presence of individual characters across works of drama and prose fiction. This process is necessarily more contingent and less open to interpretation as intentional than Fawcett's analysis, or my own in relation to the authorial presences discussed in the first section of this book.

Lisa Freeman sees the theatre and the novel of the eighteenth century as two competing and distinctive ways of characterising modernity, each equally concerned with the question of how to present being in fiction:

> While the production of identity in the novel relied upon the process of developing a psychological conjunction between being and behaving, figured through the presentation of an individual mind capable of taking itself as an object, the stage eschewed such self-consciousness and, throughout the representation of identity as a contingent effect of character, concerned itself with cultural anxieties about the psychology of knowing.[12]

Freeman's distinction hinges on whether the character 'knows' itself as object (the novel) or can be 'known' as object (villain or virtue) through presentation (the drama). Think here of the Surface brothers in Richard

---

[10] Julia H. Fawcett, *Spectacular Disappearances: Celebrity and Privacy, 1696–1801* (Ann Arbor, MI: University of Michigan Press, 2016), p. 3.

[11] Ibid., p. 3.

[12] Freeman, *Character's Theatre*, p. 27.

Sheridan's famous *School for Scandal* (1777): although Charles is virtuous behind the veneer of rakeliness, and Joseph vicious behind a performance of devout reserve, nonetheless both brothers are still rendered through 'surface' and indeed the conflict between the two is played out as 'staged contests between interpretable surfaces'.[13]

The chapters in this second section of *Fictions of Presence* aim to move away from any simple dichotomy between stage character and novelistic character, to demonstrate rather how the interaction between the two modes worked to generate a sense of 'being there' or 'being with' characters who had lives beyond, between, across and indeed outside their fictional performance. Put simply, certain 'characters' of mid-eighteenth-century culture acquired a status and a mobility – across genres and time – that moved beyond 'type': often despite rather than because of their self-confessed self-consciousness about their own eccentricity.

Our concern here lies not in measuring the different capacity of the media of theatre and novel to deliver character, but rather in the ways that character appears to escape the confines of media, to gain an independent being beyond the determinants of genre and mediation. This is not to say that the mediation of 'character' is insignificant to its effect: indeed, translation from one media to another, from one genre to another, often amplifies or redirects some aspect of characterological presentation. In other words, it amplifies the character's presence to a modern audience. David Brewer understands the afterlife of fictional characters in the eighteenth century as evidence of an imaginative exercise of 'common' possession, a fantasy of infinite generative abundance, by contrast with the narrow literary property of authorship and publication.[14] Discussion in this book does not only address the representation of a fictional character's afterlife; it explores a network of repetitions and allusions associated with individual characters across the media of stage and page. Fictional characters, here, generously afford further repetition and allusion. Repetitions seek to deliver to an audience a sense of encounter with living being. Re-presentation achieves presence.

The characters I examine in this section acquire what is perhaps best described as 'personality' through the layering of actors, authors and fictional persons. Even if they do not do so self-consciously, these characters release an intense reflection on the quality of their 'being' for an audience.

---

13   Ibid.
14   David A. Brewer, 'Cottagers upon the Textual Commons: An Introduction', in *The Afterlife of Character, 1726–1825* (Philadelphia, PA: University of Pennsylvania Press, 2011), pp. 1–24.

They are consistently conjured up across a variety of media and moments and have a particular resonance, a capacity to 'hail' their audience, even when (and maybe even because) they are not characters invested with any exceptional intellect or psychological complexity. In her chapter 'What Hails Us?', Blakey Vermeule notes the extreme portability of character by comparison with other elements in literature (plot or allusion) and asserts that '[s]ince the eighteenth century, literary characters have had a tremendous power to circulate, to give people shared stories, and to sponsor discussion about personal and collective values.'[15] In the following chapters we look at four characters with just such portability that seems consistently to hail or interpellate an audience: two who begin their life as *dramatis personae*, and two who are first brought into being in novels.

This is not a rehearsal of E.M. Forster's famous differentiation between 'flat' and 'round' characters. For Forster, there is a distinction between a character with one consistent trait (the flat) and a character who can convincingly display more than one: 'The test of a round character is whether it is capable of surprising in a convincing way. If it never surprises, it is flat. If it does not convince, it is a flat pretending to be round.'[16] By these lights, the characters we discuss here *lack* depth and interiority: they engage consistently with surfaces and with their presence as surface. Stage and page come to gain an uncanny resemblance simply as a platform from which to project a fictional person. Such characters seem to reach out beyond the page or the stage to seize the imagination of their audience and readers as strange, magnetic, persistently present beings.

These characters were not the only ones to have significant afterlives and mobility across genres. Nevertheless, they do as a group, however various and strange, offer some comprehensivity of type: protagonist and antagonist, male and female, town and country. We consider in turn: Lady Townly in the play *The Provok'd Husband* (1728), Samuel Richardson's Pamela of the novel *Pamela; or Virtue Rewarded* (1740), Ranger, the part made famous by David Garrick in Benjamin Hoadly's *The Suspicious Husband* (1747), and Tristram in Sterne's *Tristram Shandy* (1759–67).

It may not be surprising that two of the characters under discussion (Ranger and Tristram Shandy) were invented by clergymen and one by an actor (Townly). Clergymen and actors were familiar with the demands of performance in their delivery of sermons and of stage business. In 1753 the Scottish Presbyterian minister, James Fordyce, who had attracted large

---

[15]   Blakey Vermeule, *Why Do We Care about Literary Characters?* (Baltimore, MD: Johns Hopkins University Press, 2010), p. 51.

[16]   E.M. Forster, *Aspects of the Novel* (London: Harcourt Brace, 1927), p. 48.

crowds of admirers (among them David Garrick and Samuel Johnson) when he came to London and preached, published *An Essay on the Action Proper for the Pulpit*; he expresses particular admiration for Garrick's capacity as an actor to steer the feelings of his audience. Garrick, Fordyce comments, 'seems... upon the stage to have a kind of despotic Empire over the Human Passions, not over those alone of the most *refined* Hearers, but those too of the most *Vulgar*'.[17] Fordyce characterises the audience for the stage as hearers, perhaps because of Garrick's famously attractive voice, but also because this brings stage acting closer to the action of sermonising. When the actor steps 'out of line' he speaks directly to the audience and uses his body and voice to impress the lines directly on their consciousness. It may be that Trim's sermon in book 2, chapter 17 of *Tristram Shandy* – designed to parody Fordyce's exact descriptions of the preacher's physical posture and an act where a servant conspicuously steps out of line – carries the trace of the sermon as actor's performance. So too Richardson explicitly connects the performances required of pulpit and stage in Mr B's famous oscillation between admiration for Pamela as a commanding preacher of virtuous sermons and condemnation of her as a consummate actress.

Two new forms of writing about acting contribute to the shaping of eighteenth-century ideas of character: the guide to acting and the memoir of the actor's life. Cibber was one of the first and best-known autobiographers in the latter mould with his *An Apology for the Life of Mr. Colley Cibber* (1740). Virtually every major actor of the period provided or was provided with such a memoir, history or 'apology'.[18] These works gave an insight into the formation of the actor's character through the experience of the repertory or strolling company, which formed extended kin and kind as well as insight into their practices on stage of promoting and shaping character.

Cibber's errant daughter, Charlotte Charke, reminds us of the ever-present association of the stage 'character' with the print 'character'. She describes the 'Extacy of Heart' she felt 'on seeing the Character I was to appear in the Bills', but also her concern – as she takes on more significant roles – as to whether she can measure up to the great contemporary actresses who have taken them on. 'I solemnly declare', she confesses, 'that

17   James Fordyce, *An Essay on the Action Proper for the Pulpit* (London: R. and J. Dodsley, 1753), p. 16.
18   See Michael Caines et al., *Lives of Shakespearian Actors*, series editor Gail Marshall (London: Pickering and Chatto, 2012–15), 2 parts, 5 vols; Sharon Setzer, ed., *Women's Theatrical Memoirs. Part 1*, 5 vols (London: Pickering and Chatto, 2007); and Sue McPherson and Julia Swindells, ed., *Women's Theatrical Memoirs Part. 2*, 10 vols (London: Pickering and Chatto, 2008).

I expected to make an odd Figure in the Bills of Mortality – DIED ONE, OF CAPITAL CHARACTERS.'[19] As she marks out her own character – and distinguishes it from her more famous and estranged father, and his own autobiographical writings – Charke draws attention to the ways in which character circulates in print. She capitalises her own reference to character and admits the stage fright that attaches to taking those 'capital' or 'principal' characters. She hints too at a third source of professional 'death' relating to the capital and its character; a considerable portion of Charke's memoir also describes her experience as a strolling player outside the capital of London, excluded from taking on those major roles by her estrangement from her father and family. Characters are, then, both opportunities and hazards for actors. As Charke recognises, the playbill, like the bill of mortality, also 'levels' the person, counting him or her as one of a number who have occupied the same place. Marked out by capitals on the page as a number or a role, the person paradoxically loses personality and individuation.[20]

In this sense, the new genre of the guide to acting confirmed the idea that the actor as a vehicle for character was legible through a process of standardisation. Guides to acting were focused, however, not on the character of the actor who took the role but rather on the means effectively to communicate character to an audience on stage. The first and most influential author of a print guide to Georgian acting, Aaron Hill, understood the profession in terms of the demand to perform the 'character' of the different passions. He concluded that there were six primary passions – joy, sorrow, fear, scorn, anger and amazement; he then advises:

> There are many other *auxiliary Passions*, which cannot, in their own simple Character, be impress'd upon the *Countenance*. Yet may be well enough represented, by a *Mixture*, or Two, or more, of the *Six Capital Dramatics* – Such are JEALOUSY, REVENGE, LOVE, PITY...[21]

---

[19] Charlotte Charke, *A Narrative of the Life of Mrs. Charlotte Charke*, p. 32.

[20] See Julia Fawcett's contrast between Charke's expression of her body as a blank that resists gender assignment by contrast with her father's over-expression of his gender as 'both-at-once', exaggerated masculinity and effeminacy. In Julia Fawcett, 'The Growth of Celebrity Culture: Colley Cibber, Charlotte Charke, and the Overexpression of Gender', *Spectacular Disappearances*, pp. 61–97.

[21] Aaron Hill, *The Prompter* 66 (27 June 1735), 84. The essays published in the periodical were gathered together as an *Essay on the Art of Acting* (London: J. Osborn, 1746). See also Lisa Zunshine, ed., *Acting Theory and the English Stage, 1700–1830*, 5 vols (London: Pickering and Chatto, 2009).

Here, then, character lies in the elemental passion that is represented on stage, rather than in the whole complex mixture of those passions that constitutes 'person'. Guides to acting and actors' life-writings may appear to enrich and deepen the insight into character in the period. They also, however, remind their readers of character outside or beyond the stage in prose forms that render character through print forms rather than embodied action. The language of character in these forms is self-conscious and reflective in ways that are usually proscribed in stage performance. Even when a stage character steps out of a line, he or she does so in 'role'. This action is one of acknowledging the presence of the audience rather than the presence of the actor in the part.

The four characters we discuss have a distinctive kinship as well as individual resonance. The short period 1740 to 1741 saw three interrelated cultural sensations in the history of character on stage and page. First, Colley Cibber's *Apology* was published on 7 April 1740. Cibber, co-author of *The Provok'd Husband*, introduced the genre of actor's memoir, the account of theatre history intermingled with a single life. Sterne's *Tristram Shandy* alluded to Cibber's memoir in its title, parodied and played with its style and sentiment in its pages.[22] Second, Samuel Richardson's *Pamela* appeared on 6 November of the same year. Richardson invented the dramatic rendering of experience close to the moment in Pamela's letter-journal technique. Both Cibber's and Richardson's works sought to prove the virtue, integrity and cultural sway of relatively low-born characters and both innovated in terms of form and style. Third, a young actor in his mid-twenties, David Garrick, debuted on the London stage in October 1741 taking the title role in Colley Cibber's adaptation of *Richard III* at Goodman's Fields Theatre, London. He was an immediate success and a source of fascination to his audience, celebrated for introducing a new naturalism to the art of acting. Garrick was to dominate the stage into the 1770s.

Pamela, Garrick, Cibber, Sterne are significant figures in the creation of what we have now come to recognise as a celebrity culture.[23] The London theatres were at the centre of this burgeoning culture, and character (the

---

[22]   See Julia Fawcett, 'The Canon of Print: Laurence Sterne and the Overexpression of Character', chapter 3 of *Spectacular Disappearances*, pp. 98–135.

[23]   See Julia Fawcett, *Spectacular Disappearances*. Also Joseph Roach, *It*; Sharon Marcus, *The Drama of Celebrity* (Princeton, NJ: Princeton University Press, 2019); Claire Brock, *News, Biography, and Eighteenth-Century Celebrity* (Oxford: Oxford University Press, 2016); Cheryl Wanko, *Roles of Authority: Thespian Biography and Celebrity in Eighteenth-Century Britain* (Lubbock, TX: Texas Tech University Press, 2003); Mary Luckhurst and Jane Moody, eds, *Theatre and Celebrity in Britain, 1660–2000* (Basingstoke: Palgrave Macmillan, 2005); Emrys Jones and Victoria Joule, ed.,

extension, extravagance, enigma of character) was its stock in trade. The novel needed to make its way on to that stage or to appropriate conventions from the stage if it were to thrive in the market. Tracing the portability of character across stage and page allows us to see the ways in which apparent rivalry also served mutually to extend the reach of both theatre and novel: from metropolitan centre to the provinces, from one kind of audience to another. In what follows, I identify four different ways in which character extends to achieve celebrity beyond a specific or single performance or genre: 'outdoing' (Lady Townly), 'sway' (Pamela), 'expansion' (Ranger), 'play' (Tristram).

Intimacy and Celebrity in Eighteenth-Century Literary Culture: Public Interiors (Basingstoke: Palgrave Macmillan, 2018).

Chapter 8
Outdoing Character: Lady Townly

Character is mediated by the body of an actor. Yet, that mediation is most successful aesthetically when the audience is persuaded that the character exceeds their immediate experience of it. Some characters are *so* powerfully present that they appear to have a life beyond the instance of their mediation: the body of the actor, the performed play, or the written text. Colley Cibber, in his preface to *The Provok'd Husband* (1728), communicates this sense even as he acknowledges the contribution of the actors to the success of the play. His compliment to Anne Oldfield, the actress who took the part of Lady Townly, was to attract particular attention:

> But there is no doing Right to Mrs. *Oldfield*, without putting People in mind of what others, of great Merit, have wanted to come near her – 'Tis not enough to say she *Here Out-did* her usual *Out-doing*. I might therefore justly leave her to the constant Admiration of those Spectators, who have the Pleasure of living while She is an Actress.[1]

Cibber's phrase seeks to capture the excess that attaches to the 'presence-effect' of character when performed by a remarkable actress. Here, there is a marriage of character and actress: both exceed the expectation of a familiar role. In 'doing' a character, Anne Oldfield manages to move 'out' of it.

Alexander Pope, never slow to mock Cibber, parodied Cibber's ridiculous formulation in the sixteenth chapter of his satirical instructional work, *Peri Bathous: or the Art of Sinking in Poetry* (1728), in which the instructor praises the stage managers-actors of Drury Lane – Robert Wilks, Barton Booth and Colley Cibber – with the phrase: 'to this present day they continue to *Out-do* even their *own Out-doings*'.[2] Pope's parody recasts Cibber's

1   Colley Cibber, 'Preface', in *The Provok'd Husband; or a Journey to London. A Comedy, as It Is Acted at the Theatre-Royal by His Majesty's Servants. Written by the Late Sir John Vanburgh, and Mr. Cibber* (London: J. Watts, 1728), n.p.
2   Alexander Pope, 'A Project for the Advancement of the Stage', in *Peri Bathous: or the Art of Sinking in Poetry*, in *Miscellanies in Prose and Verse. In Two Volumes. By Jonathan Swift, D.D. and Alexander Pope, Esq.* (London, 1732), vol. 2, p. 136.

over-excitable repetition of 'outdoing' as effluence and waste. Though Cibber was not to be promoted by Pope to the role of King Dunce until the version of the *Dunciad* that was published in 1743, he is here cast in the same mould as the dull poets who feature in the 1728 *Dunciad* and *Peri Bathous*, parasitic cannibalisers of their own waste products, which they ingest and recirculate repetitively. In applying the same phrase that the manager, playwright and actor Cibber had used for the actress Anne Oldfield's 'character' to Cibber himself, Pope also suggests that character is a piece of stage business designed to secure the profits of the stage industry.

Cibber recognised the awkwardness of the phrase and characterised it as his own act of 'outdoing', going too far and being carried away by the moment. In his *Apology for the Life of Colley Cibber*, he admits that the phrase was 'A most vile Jingle, I grant it!' and confesses that 'like a Lover in the Fulness of his Content, by endeavouring to be floridly grateful, I talk'd Nonsense'.[3] In the edition of *The Provok'd Husband* printed on 28 January 1729, one year later, he changed the phrasing to say that Oldfield '*outdid* her usual *excellence*'.[4]

Cibber confesses to an act of what we can now recognise as 'overexpression', a phrase Julia Fawcett helpfully coins to describe that celebrity-making strategy of the eighteenth century which both invites the audience to recognise the person of the actor in the character played and serves simultaneously to deny access to that person. His own action is not unrelated, I suggest, to the role of Lady Townly that contributed to Anne Oldfield's considerable celebrity. Lady Townly appears to have commanded just this response of fascination in its long history on the stage and off it: in newspaper accounts of performances, biographies of actresses, and a long and meaningful afterlife in prose fiction. This is not because Townly is a wholly original character: she is in fact a familiar stock type. The society woman given over to gambling and social pleasures and risking her reputation was a familiar one and had been played by Anne Oldfield in her early career. However, her expression in Cibber's reworking of Vanbrugh was an apotheosis of that type and served to propel the type into the manifestation of 'person' in a variety of other subsequent media and textual manifestations.

[3] Colley Cibber, *An Apology for the Life of Colley Cibber*, p. 34.
[4] Colley Cibber, 'To the Reader', in John Vanbrugh and Colley Cibber, *The Provok'd Husband*, ed. Peter Dixon, Regents Restoration Drama Series (London: Edward Arnold, 1974), p. 7. The edition of 28 January 1729 was given as the 'second' edition, but in fact a revised version of the first printed edition (31 January 1728) had been published without advertisement between the two but presumably before Pope's mockery in *Peri Bathous* (published 8 March 1728) since Cibber did not change his 'outdoing' phrase (see Dixon, pp. xiii–xxvi).

The part of Lady Townly was one of twelve that Cibber wrote for Anne Oldfield[5] and she was given fifty guineas as a gift by the Drury Lane management in acknowledgement of her contribution to the play's huge success of twenty-eight performances on an opening run, and a profit of over £140. *The Provok'd Husband* opened Drury Lane for the following two seasons and was a staple of the repertory of both licensed companies through to the early nineteenth century. The story of Lady Townly's character in the eighteenth century is one that apparently shadows the story of her character in the play in which she first appeared. Always popular, she travels to new genres and media and yet, that expansion into and occupation of new spaces, also results in growing confinement to domestic and private spaces, to private theatricals and to a bit part in a series of prose fictions that promote private and sentimental virtues in women.

At the heart of the play is the contrast between the ways in which different women respond to the attractions of the town: the urban sophisticate, Lady Townly, married too young and without apparent inclination to her husband, and 'immoderate in her pursuit of pleasures'[6] such as gambling, theatricals, assemblies, masquerades; Lady Grace, sister to Lord Townly, a paragon of the virtues, but temperate and sympathetic in responding to the excesses of her sister-in-law; Lady Wronghead, a silly wife swift to waste her husband's dwindling fortune on shopping; and her daughter, Jenny Wronghead, 'pert and forward'[7] who is the prey of Count Basset, a gamester. Myrtilla, niece to the landlady Mrs Motherly, conspires with Lord Townly's friend, Mr Manly, to prevent disaster falling on the Wrongheads. Myrtilla acts as a double agent against the man who has seduced her, Lord Basset, in promising to aid him to a marriage with Jenny in exchange for entrapping Jenny's booby brother, Richard. In the final act all parties come together at a masquerade in Lord Townly's house, Count Basset's perfidy is exposed to Sir Francis, and Lady Townly repents of her behaviour when her husband acts on his threat to order that she leave their home. The Townlys are – with sentimental expressiveness – reconciled while Grace accepts Manly's proposal. So popular was the Townlys' reconciliation scene, that performances most often placed it *after* the masquerade scene to bring the comedy to a fitting close. In *The Provok'd Husband*, Colley Cibber and his daughter-in-law, Jane Cibber, first wife of Theophilus, played Sir Francis Wronghead and his daughter Jenny. Cibber had taken the part of Lord

5   Elaine McGirr identifies eight comedies and four tragedies Cibber wrote around Oldfield. Elaine McGirr, *Partial Histories: A Reappraisal of Colley Cibber* (London: Palgrave Macmillan, 2016), p. 179.
6   'Dramatis Personae', *Provok'd Husband*, ed. Dixon, p. 11.
7   Ibid.

Brute opposite Anne Oldfield's Lady Brute in the version of *The Provok'd Wife* that Vanbrugh revised (largely making more polite) for a production at Drury Lane on 11 January 1726. Cibber clearly sought in choosing the title of *The Provok'd Husband* to make this work a companion to *The Provok'd Wife*.

The play opens on the famously explosive line delivered by Lord Townly, 'Why did I marry?'[8] Townly proceeds to explain that his wife's sexual purity seems to act as her alibi to indulge every other vice of the town. When Lady Townly enters, after complaints about her absenteeism and late hours, he solicits a serious response to his question as to why she married him. Lady Townly answers, with surprising modernity and honesty: 'I think – I married – to take off the restraint that lay upon my pleasures while I was a single woman.'[9] She details the public freedoms that her wifely status gives her to enjoy the pleasures of the town:

> To begin then, in the morning: a married woman may have men at her toilet, invite them to dinner, appoint them a party in a stage box at the play, engross the conversation there, call 'em by their Christian names, talk louder than the players; from thence jaunt into the City, take a frolicsome supper from an India-house, perhaps (in her *gaieté de coeur*) toast a pretty fellow, then clatter again to this end of town, break with the morning into an assembly, crowd to the hazard table, throw a familiar levant upon some sharp lurching man of quality, and if he demands his money, turn it off with a loud laugh, and cry – you'll owe it him, to vex him. Ha, ha!'[10]

Lady Townly's liberties are those of noise and specifically of voice, the special currency of the eighteenth-century actress. She invites, appoints, engrosses conversation, talks loudly over actors, toasts, laughs and shouts out.

From the first scene, a conflict is established between husband and wife for command of the space of the stage and the dialogue: a battle over which partner holds most sway. Lady Townly secures £500 from her husband by chopping logic with him about whether he seeks to win her trust or curtail her activity by denying her money. In a telling aside, Lady Townly confides in the audience her determination to maintain the upper hand and her insecurity in the venture: 'Now am I convinced, were I weak

8   Ibid., Act 1, scene 1, p. 13.
9   Ibid., Act 1, lines 74–6, p. 16.
10 Ibid., Act 1, lines 83–95, pp. 16–17.

enough to love this man I should never get a single guinea from him.'[11] In the third act, husband and wife lock horns again and she mocks him for his early hours, which she condemns as those of a 'plodding mechanic'[12] by comparison with her own 'active, spirited three in the morning' return, which has 'the air of a woman of quality'.[13] He threatens to lock her out if she does not return before midnight and leaves her puzzling over what she sees as this latest stratagem: 'There's something that I don't see at the bottom of all this.'[14]

Lady Grace, Lord Townly's sister, acknowledges Lady Townly's attractive charm even in speeches that admit to her bad behaviour. Toward the denouement of the conflict between husband and wife, Grace informs her suitor, Manly, that Lady Townly returned at 5 a.m., by which time her husband had retired to another chamber in high dudgeon. Nonetheless, she admits the charm of Lady Townly's speech:

> though she has lost every shilling she had in the world, and stretched her credit even to breaking, she rallied her own follies with such vivacity, and painted the penance she knows she must undergo for them in such ridiculous lights, that had not my concern for a brother been too strong for her wit, she had almost disarmed my anger.[15]

Lord Townly and his wife next confront each other, and the husband asserts that since his wife's heart is lost to pleasures he cannot share, they must separate. He will maintain her in a separate establishment at her aunt Lovemore's on a modest means without luxury. He acquits her of any suspicion with regard to the honour of his bed. Lady Townly now admits her faults and puts them down to the indulgence of her father, the world and Lord Townly himself: 'It added strength to my habitual failings, and in a heart thus worn in wild unthinking life, no wonder if the gentler sense of love was lost.'[16] She submits to her punishment and concedes that it will take time and proof of her good conduct to win the pardon she hopes for from him. Lord Townly is however swift to forgive: 'Your errors thus renounced, this instant are forgotten. So deep, so due a sense of them has made you – what my utmost wishes formed, and all my heart has sighed for.'[17] He rec-

---

[11]   Ibid., Act 1, lines 142–4, pp. 18–19.
[12]   Ibid., Act 3, line 315, p. 82.
[13]   Ibid., Act 3, line 314, p. 82.
[14]   Ibid., Act 3, lines 375–6, p. 84.
[15]   Ibid., Act 5, scene 1, lines 57–60, p. 122.
[16]   Ibid., Act 5, scene 2, lines 316–19, p. 142.
[17]   Ibid., Act 5, scene 2, lines 338–41, p. 142.

ommends, and Lady Townly willingly embraces, that she model herself on his sister Grace's behaviour and he gives permission for Grace to become Manly's wife.

The fascination of Lady Townly lies not only in the character's wit but also in her *lack* of self-knowledge. The success of the play hinged on Lady Townly's sudden reformation, and the requirement that it appear sincere rather than a strategic survival ploy at the point where all that gives her pleasure in life threatens to be taken from her grasp. Her husband, after all, not only asserts they will separate but that he will not provide her with the financial support she needs to indulge her tastes. The characterisation of Lady Townly invites a sense of a troubled undertow, a craving for love and recognition, which can make sense of the final reconciliation scene as one where both husband and wife finally manage to recognise the other's 'heart'. Lord Townly says aside to Manly after Lady Townly has confessed the errors of her upbringing: 'Oh Manly, where has this creature's heart been buried?' To which Manly responds 'If yet recoverable – how vast a treasure!'[18]

Cibber put the success of the part down in great measure to Anne Oldfield's performance. By 1728 Anne Oldfield was a mature actress in her forties, well-established in the Drury Lane company with an assured income of 300 guineas a year and a benefit that brought her twice that sum according to Cibber's estimate. She was the established mistress of Charles Churchill, illegitimate nephew of the first Duke of Marlborough, and mother to his son, as well as having a son by her first lover (Sir Arthur Mainwaring who passed away in 1712).[19]

Cibber observes in his *Apology* that:

> the last new Character she shone in (*Lady Townly*) was a Proof that she was still able to do more, if more could have been done for *her*. She had one Mark of good Sense, rarely known, in any Actor of either Sex, but herself.... To the last Year of her Life, she never undertook any Part

[18] Ibid., Act 5, scene 2, line 320, p. 142.
[19] Jane Milling, 'Oldfield, Anne (1683–1730), Actress', *Oxford Dictionary of National Biography*, 23 September 2004, https://ezproxy-prd.bodleian.ox.ac.uk:3030/view/10.1093/ref:odnb/9780198614128.001.0001/odnb-9780198614128-e-20677 [accessed 29 February 2020]. Oldfield moved in aristocratic circles, accepted as though she were the wife of Churchill. She was one of the first of a long line of actresses who, in taking the part of Lady Townly, were situated ambiguously in public reputation: either the part seemed to confer a convincing status of 'fine lady', or actresses with some access to that status appeared to confer it on the part.

she lik'd, without being importunately desirous of having all the Helps in it, that another could possibly give her.[20]

Like Lady Townly, Anne Oldfield proves open to improvement, to seeking the help of others, to reform. Her character is then both fixed (she always seeks assistance in improving her parts) and impressionable (it responds to the contributions it seeks from others in its formation). And it is also – and tellingly – always capable of doing 'more' (a rephrasing of her capacity to 'outdo' herself). The capacity to go beyond presence is also one that asserts the dominance of the actor's performance on the stage. However, it also relies on the support of others: Anne Oldfield is always assiduous to gain assistance from the others who are present at the making of (the centrality of) her character.

Distinctive to the role of Lady Townly was the sense that the actress had to appear *not* to be acting, to leaven the implied tragedy of the role with a measure of wit while making her repentance convincing. It was recognised as a role that required maturity on the part of the actress but Lady Townly's wit had not to appear to be cynicism. A 1787 review of Frances Abington's performance in the part which she owned for many years indicates the kind of expert poise between tragedy and comedy expected of the actress in the final reconciliation scene between the Townlys. The *Public Advertiser* of 27 January 1787 commented of Abington's performance at Covent Garden the preceding night (significantly this was her first role of the season): 'Mrs Abington's reconciliation scene was particularly fine – no declamation – no attempt at tragedizing – it… carried the full proof of conviction and repentance.'

The greatest tragic actress of the later eighteenth century was especially celebrated for her delivery of this comic part. It also appears to have served as proof of her capacity to attract the admiration of the very highest members of society. Sarah Siddons was invited to deliver scenes from *The Provok'd Husband* at a private reading for George III, his queen, and a select group at court. Mrs Mary Delany (née Granville), a paper artist and pensioner of George III and Queen Charlotte at Windsor, in a letter of 19 May 1785 dictated to Mrs Frances Hamilton (Delany was in her eighties), records an invitation on 9 May to hear Mrs Siddons read from the play. In attendance were the king and queen, their five daughters and Prince Edward along with a number of aristocrats (largely female) seated in two rows of chairs the length of the room:

---

[20] Cibber, *Apology*, chapter 9, p. 168.

> Mrs. Siddons read standing, and had a desk with candles before her: she behaved with great propriety, and read two acts of "The Provoked Husband," which was abridged, by leaving out Sir Francis and Lady Wronghead's parts, &c. But she introduced John Moody's account of the journey, and read it admirably. The part of Lord and Lady Townly's reconciliation, she worked up finely, and made it very affecting. She also read Queen Katherine's last speech in King Henry 8th.[21]

Siddons was demonstrating her range as an actress; the speech by John Moody, Sir Francis' butler and bailiff, is a comic set piece to be delivered with a Yorkshire accent by a silly retainer describing the comic and absurd entry of the Wrongheads with their country servants and accoutrements piled high in the coach-and-six drawn by two additional cart horses. However, the fact that she read the reconciliation scene and followed it with Katherine of Aragon's last speech from William Shakespeare's *Henry VIII* indicates that the majority of the performance concerned acts of wifely submission to powerful men. Siddons seems to have selected speeches that were ambiguous about women's blame in marriage conflict. And certainly parts that showcased the charismatic attraction of the wife who simultaneously resists and submits to a husband's autocratic governance. In their acts of noble submission and assertion of domestic loyalty, Lady Townly and Queen Katherine outshine their husbands both in their suffering and their charisma. These are also speaking parts to select for a performance dominated by the presence of women and especially Queen Charlotte and her many daughters. Charlotte also enjoyed a reputation for wifely loyalty and maternal devotion.

The selection of the part of Queen Katherine may have seemed an obvious compliment to Queen Charlotte, if complicated by the fact that Katherine is a cast-off wife demonstrating her continuing loyalty to both monarch and husband. That of Lady Townly serves rather to compliment those wifely skills on which Charlotte prided herself and for which she was celebrated. It is the uncertainty of the role of Lady Townly, its poising *between* tragedy and comedy, *between* authentic and strategic performance of submission that makes it a part of such special resonance.

Given the popularity of both part and performers, it is unsurprising that the character of the brittle, disenchanted town lady swiftly entered the world of the novel and was consistently associated with acting and performance.

---

[21]   Mary Delany, *The Autobiography and Correspondence of Mary Granville, Mrs. Delany: with interesting reminiscences of King George the third and Queen Charlotte*, ed. Augusta Llanover, second series, 3 vols (London: R. Bentley, 1862), vol. 3, p. 255.

Most memorably in the shape of Maria Edgeworth's unhappy society wife, Lady Delacour in her 1801 novel, *Belinda*, a work which quickly made both character and author famous and fascinating. Lady Delacour was recognised to be modelled on real-life society women. On 11 November 1801 William Drennan writes to his sister Martha McTier: 'By the bye, we began a novel yesterday called Belinda by Miss Edgeworth in which there are portraits drawn with a masterly hand, as far as we have gone – Lady Delacour (perhaps Lady Clare) is done in high style.'[22]

The troubled Lady Delacour, the hostess to the young heroine Belinda in London, is portrayed as being in restless pursuit of immoderate town pleasures and neglectful of her domestic duties. This character was not only thought to be a version of Anne Fitzgibbon, Countess of Clare – Anglo-Irish leader of fashion at odds with her husband's politics (he orchestrated the passing of the Acts of Union in 1800 and opposed Catholic relief) – but was also seen as a caricature of the Whig political activist and fashionista, Georgiana, Duchess of Devonshire (married young to a boorish husband who was notoriously unfaithful).[23] Maria Edgeworth herself seems to have been inclined to see the character of Lady Delacour as indebted to the real-life actresses she knew and admired. She cut out the title pages and got her aunt Margaret Ruxton to read the novel out loud to her, pretending the work was by the notorious actress and feminist, Mary Robinson, former mistress of the Prince of Wales.[24] Lady Delacour's secret – her diseased breast which she thinks is a cancer but proves to be an unhealed wound from a foolish duel into which she was persuaded by her radical friend, Harriet Freke – might also have been associated with Mary Robinson's lower-limb paralysis which left her disabled. However, another actress – and one who according to Maria Edgeworth had been spectacularly successful in translating the presence of the stage into the field of the novel – also remained uppermost in Edgeworth's mind as she continued to rework *Belinda*: Elizabeth Inchbald. In the 'Advertisement' composed 20 April 1801, for the first edition of *Belinda*, Edgeworth terms the work:

> a Moral Tale – the author not wishing to acknowledge a Novel. Were all novels like those of Madame de Crousaz, Mrs. Inchbald, miss Burney or Dr Moore, she would adopt the name of novel with delight:

[22]   William Drennan and Samuel McTier, *The Drennan-McTier Letters 1776–1819*, ed. Jean Agnew, 2 vols (Dublin: The Women's History Project, 1999), vol. 2, p. 737.

[23]   See Siobhán Kilfeather, 'Introduction', *Belinda*, vol. 2 of *The Novels and Selected Works of Maria Edgeworth*, general ed. Marilyn Butler and Mitzi Myers (London: Pickering and Chatto, 2003), pp. xiv–xv.

[24]   Ibid., p. vii.

but so much folly, errour and vice are disseminated in books classed under this denomination, that it is hoped the wish to assume another title will be attributed to feelings that are laudable, and not fastidious.[25]

However, Inchbald's pre-eminence for Edgeworth was not confined to her transparently moral intention but also in her capacity to bring character to life, to convince readers that they are present at a scene performed before their eyes. In a letter to Elizabeth Inchbald of 14 January 1810, Maria Edgeworth waxed lyrical about *A Simple Story*'s reality effects: 'I believed all to be real, and was affected as I should be by the real scenes as if they had passed before my eyes.'[26]

In 1809, Inchbald's novel was again before her eyes. Maria Edgeworth was correcting *Belinda* for inclusion in Anna Letitia Barbauld's *The British Novelists*.[27] As so often in the Lady Townly tradition, the role seems to have been paired with another 'wife', in this case Edgeworth's satirical *The Modern Griselda*; in this work a modern fashionable wife behaves in ways directly counter to the virtuous and long-suffering Griselda of medieval fairy tale.[28] Edgeworth reports to her cousin Harriet Ruxton in a letter of December 1809 that she is rereading for the fourth time Inchbald's novel *A Simple Story* at the same time as she is correcting *Belinda* for Mrs Barbauld's collection. She admires in particular Inchbald's capacity to disappear and make fully present only her characters: 'I was totally incapable of thinking of Mrs. Inchbald or of anything but Miss Milner and Dorriforth, who appeared to me real persons whom I saw and heard, and who had such power to interest me, that I cried my eyes almost out before I came to the end of the story: I think it is the most pathetic and the most powerfully interesting tale I ever read.' She bemoans the lifelessness of her own heroine by comparison: 'I really was so provoked with the cold tameness of that

---

[25]   Ibid, p. 5.
[26]   Maria Edgeworth, letter to Mrs Inchbald, 14 January 1810, quoted in James Boaden, *Memoirs of Mrs. Inchbald*, 2 vols (London: Richard Bentley, 1833), vol. 2, p. 152.
[27]   Anna Letitia Barbauld, *The British Novelists*, 50 vols (London: F.C. and J. Rivington, 1810).
[28]   I use here Maria Edgeworth, *Belinda*, ed. Kathryn J. Kirkpatrick (Oxford: Oxford University Press, 1994). The Oxford University Press takes as copy-text the 1802 corrected and improved second edition (first edition was 1801). A version of 1810 revised by Edgeworth is the basis of Joseph Johnson's third edition of 1811 which is taken as copy-text for Siobhán Kilfeather, ed., *Belinda*, Pickering Masters volume 2 of *The Novels and Selected Works of Maria Edgeworth* (London: Pickering and Chatto, 2003). The 1802 text seems to me a version closer to the Townly tradition than the later work both in terms of chronology and style.

stick or stone Belinda, that I could have torn the pages to pieces: and really, I have not the least heart or patience to correct her.'[29]

Edgeworth imagines doing away with the page that somehow inhibits rather than enables access to the character-in-performance. The choice of the verb 'provoke' may even suggest the presence of *The Provok'd Husband* in the author's thoughts and the recollection that Lady Grace's sobriety may have been more provoking than Lady Townly's vivacity to her audience. And it is the flawed, troubled, ambivalent society town lady, as opposed to her prudential countrified counterpart, who seems to have a special capacity to live beyond the page, or rather to bring to the page the animated complexity of the actress in performance that Inchbald knew so well from her own career.[30]

Lady Delacour is consistently, indeed insistently, associated with the stage. We are first introduced to her as though she were a stage actress, 'spoiled' out of having any character when not on the stage:

> Abroad, and at home, lady Delacour was two different persons. Abroad she appeared all life, spirit, and good humour – at home, listless, fretful, and melancholy; she seemed like a spoiled actress off the stage, over stimulated by applause, and exhausted by the exertions of supporting a fictitious character.[31]

The novel famously concludes with Lady Delacour in her drawing room positioning the principal characters, duly coupled up and reconciled, in 'proper attitudes for stage effect' before instructing herself to come forward 'to address the audience with a moral' in a suitably enigmatic couplet as though she were the lead actress at the end of an epilogue:

> Our *tale* contains a *moral*, and no doubt,
> You all have wit enough to find it out.[32]

[29]   *Memoirs of Richard Lovell Edgeworth, esq. begun by himself and concluded by his daughter, Maria Edgeworth* (London: R. Hunter, 1820), vol. 1, pp. 229–30.
[30]   For a related argument that the style and convention of stage melodrama stems from a hybrid experimentation between stage and novel such as is found in Inchbald's *A Simple Story*, see Marcie Frank, 'Melodrama and the Politics of Literary Form in Elizabeth Inchbald's Works', *Eighteenth-Century Fiction*, 27, nos. 3–4 (Spring–Summer 2015), 707–30.
[31]   Kirkpatrick, ed., *Belinda*, pp. 10–11.
[32]   Ibid, p. 478.

Lady Delacour's closing words appear to chime with the opening lines of the 'Advertisement'. The work is a moral tale not a novel. However, it also troubles that claim – the claim to reform – by refusing to make explicit the nature of the moral. Rather it is the 'wit' of the audience that must find out the moral. Lady Delacour will not herself speak it. Here, as in the ambivalence of the apparent 'reform' of the society wife at the close of *The Provok'd Husband*, the charisma of female performance appears to deflect rather than confirm the capacity to represent convincing 'reform'.

There are a series of allusions to the 'Provok'd' plays of Vanbrugh/Cibber in *Belinda*. The heroine, Belinda, shares her name with the niece in *The Provok'd Wife*, the more sober accomplice to Lady Brute's gay, society adventures. Lady Delacour explicitly cites a 'provocation' as the engine behind her actions. Because her preferred suitor, Henry Percival, will not love her for her faults, she accepts in a fit of pique the proposal of the unsuitable gambler, Lord Delacour. 'I was provoked, and I married, in hopes of provoking the man I loved. The worst of it was, I did not provoke him as much as I expected. Six months afterward, I heard of his marriage with a very amiable woman.'[33]

By chapter nine ('Advice'), Belinda has discovered that Lady Anne Percival is providing a happy family home and environment for Lady Delacour's neglected and sensitive twelve-year-old daughter, Helena. When Helena writes to Lady Delacour, the latter's attempts to seem unconcerned about her daughter's apparent preference for the tender domestic care of Lady Anne only reveal unhappiness and jealousy to Belinda. Their conversation seems to be routed through allusion to *The Provok'd Husband* and its prologue-moral's call to husbands to govern their wives with common sense:

> '... I do believe I did provoke Percival by marrying Lord Delacour. I cannot tell you how much this idea delights me. I am sure that the man has a lively remembrance of me, or else he would never make his wife take so much notice of my daughter.'
>
> 'Surely your ladyship does not think,' said Belinda, 'that a wife is a being whose actions are necessarily governed by a husband.'
>
> 'Not necessarily – but accidentally. When a lady accidentally sets up for being a good wife, she must of course love, honour, and obey. Now, you understand, I am not in the least obliged to lady Anne for her kindness to Helena; because it all goes under the head of obedience, in my imagination – and her ladyship is paid for it by an accession of

---

[33] Ibid., p. 37.

character – she has the reward of having it said, "O, lady Anne Percival is the best wife in the world," "O, lady Anne Percival is quite a pattern woman!" I hate pattern women, – I hope I may never see lady Anne, for I'm sure I should detest her beyond all things living…'[34]

Lady Delacour pits her 'character' (her wit and vivacity) against Lady Anne's 'character', a public endorsement or witness of her model femaleness (demonstrated through her obedience to her husband). She turns Lady Anne's generosity into an act of servitude, a pride in obedience to a husband still so attached to his first love that he obliges his wife to host the daughter who (Lady Delacour imagines) strongly resembles this other woman. Of course, in speaking in these terms Lady Delacour only gives away her own insecurity and personal misery, her sense of loss of both lover and child to another woman. She gives herself away in the admission that hers is an 'idea', an act of 'imagination'. Belinda's quiet correction is to indicate that Lady Anne might not be an enemy and rival but rather an agent of reform (like Lady Grace in *The Provok'd Husband*).

As in *The Provok'd Husband*, it appears that the reform of the society wife is not the result of a husband's assertion of his authority but rather of the sympathetic influence of a virtuous woman who is not yet married and yet displays great powers of sobriety and prudence: Lady Grace and Belinda. It is their courtship-to-marriage plots that drive the action and yet they are repeatedly eclipsed by the troubled presence-effects of the society women they counterpose. Indeed, pose and counterpose give way to the sheer force of character in ways that Belinda herself cannot but acknowledge.

By chapter five, Belinda has sufficient evidence of Lady Delacour's real unhappiness to begin to learn to reason for herself rather than from appearances: 'for the first time in her life she reasoned for herself upon what she saw and felt. It is sometimes safer for young people to see, than to hear of certain characters. At a distance, Lady Delacour had appeared to miss Portman the happiest person in the world; upon a nearer view, she discovered that her ladyship was one of the most miserable of human beings.'[35] It is this kind of nearer view that the fiction of domestic courtship promises to extend to its reader. Edgeworth's deft use of free indirect discourse renders Belinda through her own idiom (her youthful hyperbole swiftly designates Lady Delacour 'the most miserable of human beings') while also overlaying a mature narrator's perspective ('for the first time in her life') not available to the heroine herself. Edgeworth was keenly aware that prose fiction, if it

[34] Kirkpatrick, ed., *Belinda*, chapter 9, p. 121.
[35] Kirkpatrick, ed., *Belinda*, chapter 5, p. 69.

was to convince its readers of the reality that it invented (and for Edgeworth only such a conviction could cause moral reform in the reader), could not do so if characters were conscious of the presence of an audience:

> Writers of inferior genius waste their words in describing feeling; in making those who pretend to be agitated by passion describe the effects of that passion, and talk of the rending of their hearts, &c. A gross blunder! … for the heart cannot feel, and describe its own feelings, at the same moment.[36]

The very means of narration makes possible a kind of insight or access which does not undermine the presence-effect Edgeworth prioritises in her development of realism. Like the reader, Belinda develops powers of moral reflection without seeking them or being self-conscious about their acquisition as a modern 'art': 'the very means, which Mrs Stanhope had taken to make a fine lady of her niece, tended to produce an effect diametrically opposite to what might have been expected'. Belinda, then, resolves to 'profit by her bad example; but this resolution it was more easy to form than to keep. Her ladyship, when she wished to please or to govern, had fascinating manners, and could alternately use the sarcastic powers of wit, and the fond tone of persuasion, to accomplish her purposes'.[37] Emily Hodgson Anderson shrewdly observes that Edgeworth here, as elsewhere in her fiction, sees performance as requiring the mediation of didacticism (facilitated by novelistic narration) which can ethically stabilise dramatic expressivity.[38]

Like Lady Townly, Lady Delacour has powers of fascination that put at risk the reformatory purpose she serves within the fictional plot in which she is expected to play a particular part: she outdoes her role. There is a containing force in a prose narration that maintains a watchful invisible control over the performative inventiveness of the characters it has created. Here then, Edgeworth presents us with a revival of the part of Lady Townly in the figure of Lady Delacour, but one that imagines a sophisticated and ethically self-conscious narration as a means to manage or correct a vivacity that the proximity of stage to the physical sway of character can*not* achieve. Character in this novel is not so much antithetical to character on stage as a means of rehearsing, replaying and reviving character, reanimating it.

---

[36]   Maria Edgeworth, letter to Elizabeth Inchbald, in James Boaden, *Memoirs of Mrs. Inchbald*, vol. 2, p. 153.

[37]   Kirkpatrick, ed., *Belinda*, p. 70.

[38]   Emily Hodgson Anderson, 'Pedagogical Performance: Maria Edgeworth's Didactic Approach to Fiction', in *Eighteenth-Century Authorship*, pp. 107–32.

Terry Robinson correctly concludes in her reading of the importance of stage conceptions of character to *Belinda*'s new brand of realism '[r]ather than define itself against the theatre, then, *Belinda*'s narrative is intertwined with the stuff of the stage'.[39]

The promise of Edgeworth's didactic vision for fiction – that it would be instrumental in the reform of the vices that are the product of the attractions of fashionable life – is that it will contain, while it acknowledges, the energies of theatrical character. However, as we have seen in the account of Belinda's struggles to stick by her resolution, the town lady's own restless and complex performance threatens always to overcome her function as vehicle for an ethical as well as realistic perspective on the true nature of metropolitan identity. In the hands of a novel writer with less aesthetic command than Edgeworth, the Lady Townly role tends either to fall into empty caricature or entirely drown out the less visible charms of her counterpart/counterpoise (the Lady Grace role). However, one example of this problem can also serve to illustrate the point that other readers of Edgeworth who sought fame through the medium of the novel appear to have connected *Belinda* with the characters of *The Provok'd Husband*.

Medora Gordon Byron published in 1809 a novel entitled *Celia In Search of a Husband*.[40] The choice of the names of the contrasting country and city sister, Celia Delacour and Lady Townly, suggest that the heroines of *The Provok'd Husband* and *Belinda* were both present in the author's mind. And Celia proves to be as much a 'stick' and a 'stone' as the heroine-character

---

[39] Terry F. Robinson, '"Life is a Tragicomedy!": Maria Edgeworth's *Belinda* and the Staging of the Realist Novel', *Nineteenth-Century Literature*, 67, no. 2 (September 2012), 146.

[40] *Celia In Search of a Husband* (London, 1809), 2 vols. She shares her first name with the daughter (born 1814) of Lord Byron, thought to be his illegitimate offspring by his sister Augusta Leigh. Anthony Ashfield has suggested that the novelist Miss Byron must be Julia Maria Byron (1782–1858), first cousin to the poet Byron. Julia Maria had literary interests, and she married in 1817, after the last 'Miss Byron' novel appeared. She died as Mrs Heath in 1858. Susan Brown et al., ed., 'Medora Gordon Byron', in *Orlando*, http://orlando.cambridge.org/ [accessed 20 February 2020]. Ostensibly, *Celia* is an imitation and female version of Hannah More's hugely successful *Coelebs in Search of a Wife* (1809). The author signs herself 'a modern antique' in her preface and the fiction aims to show how a female protagonist arrives at a meeting of true minds in marriage as More's hero did. Like Coelebs, Celia espouses country values and is unimpressed by London mores and manners. Unlike him, however, Celia is explicit that she has not come to the metropolis to find a husband; rather, she has rushed to her sister's side on the death of the latter's young son seeking to console her. When she arrives, she finds her sister, Lady Fanny Townly, neglectful of her domestic duties, unappreciative of their potential pleasures and indulging herself in a round of public entertainments.

that so frustrated Edgeworth in her attempts at rewriting the earlier novel. In this she also resembles Lady Grace, the sister-in-law whose repetitive use of the adverb 'soberly' in her description of the married life she imagines for herself split between town and country was often mocked.[41] Celia is given to disquisitions to her sister on the need to pay attention to her young daughter, Rachel's, values and virtues. Celia brings her sister to a sense of the dangers of neglecting her daughter just as Belinda does Lady Delacour with regard to her daughter, Helena. Unlike Lady Delacour, however, Lady Townly in *Celia* is attached to a virtuous husband and one who is much more long-suffering than the original Lord Townly of *The Provok'd Husband*. Like his original, however, Gordon Byron's Lord Townly hopes that the sister (Lady Grace/Celia) will demonstrate true wifely virtues and act as an example to the errant but ultimately intelligent and ethical woman he knows lies hidden behind the superficial character. Lady Fanny Townly has much of the vitality and ambiguous poise between tragedy and comedy of her original. Gordon Byron's narrator diagnoses her behaviour in psychological terms – it is a lack of self-confidence that produces her nervous pursuit of pleasures, her tendency to choose impulsively one path and regret it (she leaves her sick son fearing to contract his illness and instantly longs to return to his side; she torments her husband with attempts to minister to him and weeps at his indifference when he is genuinely ill):

> Now this was the moment in which Lady Townly *ought* to have reflected, and it was precisely *that* in which she could not bring herself to think; like every being who wants *self-confidence*, she found it necessary to support her spirits, because she felt her unworthiness; yet when no immediate cause for regret existed, she looked *back*, and wondered how she had ever been so remiss.[42]

Philanthropic Mrs Welgrave chides Lady Townly for her lack of pockets when the latter expresses a desire to give to charity but has nothing about her: 'I consider *you* as possessing a very good heart, but you sometimes suffer it to slumber.'[43] We learn through the character of Lady Townly that superficiality, the pursuit of surface, as in the case of Lady Delacour, hides

---

[41]   Grace imagines her country months 'taking a dish of tea, or a game at cards, soberly; managing my family, looking into its accounts, playing with my children (if I had any), or in a thousand other amusements – soberly!', *The Provok'd Husband*, ed. Dixon, Act 3, lines 520–3, pp. 89–90.

[42]   *Celia*, vol. 1, chapter 8, pp. 134–5.

[43]   Ibid., vol. 1, chapter 10, p. 166.

an absence, a lack, and a longing to be fulfilled in the tender love of another person.

This technique which enables a character (Lady Townly) to make something visible to an audience or reader not otherwise apparent to her fellow stage-characters nor to herself was exploited by a more significant and talented woman novelist than Medora Gordon Byron, Frances Burney. Frances Burney played parts in private theatricals – most well-known is her taking the role of the neglected wife Mrs Lovemore in Arthur Murphy's two-act farce, *The Way to Keep Him*, in 1802.[44] She does not seem to have been especially accomplished as an actress but she certainly understood well the business of the public stage; she tried her hand at playwriting producing seven plays between 1779 and 1801, one of which – the verse tragedy *Edwy and Elgiva* (composed 1790) was produced at Drury Lane, 21 March 1795.[45]

However, it is as an observer, a member of the audience – and the translation of that observational position in all the intensity of its projection of being into stage character – that Frances Burney clearly found her model for the novelistic rendering of character. *The Provok'd Husband* was a consistent and recurrent touchstone in her novel-writing. Marcie Frank notes that the word 'provoke' and its variants appears forty times in *Evelina*; for Frank, the reforming power of provocation translates into a powerful ethics of shame in Burney's novels manifest in her capacity to engineer perspectival shifts in her readers that are always attendant on and associated with theatricality.[46] I turn to a different history of the presence of *The Provok'd Husband* in Burney, especially the figure of Lady Townly who functions as a gateway to a meditation on the portability of character – the ways in which characters from the stage can be used to interpret the 'hidden' nature of characters in the print fiction. But it also serves as a way of reflecting on the power of affect, and the ambition to produce the intensity of feeling for and with a stage female performer in the techniques of the novel. Burney is most fascinated by the effect of acting on her audience. Interestingly, her novels often carry an implied assessment of the different forms of affect experienced through 'closet' reading (whether of the novel or plays) or of attending a play.

---

[44]   Frances Burney, *Early Journals and Letters: Vol. V 1782–1783*, ed. Lars E. Troide and Stewart J. Cooke (Oxford: Oxford University Press, 1988), vol. 5, p. 210.

[45]   See Francesca Saggini, *Backstage in the Novel: Frances Burney and the Theater Arts*, trans. Laura Kopp (Charlottesville, VA and London: University of Virginia Press, 2012).

[46]   Frank, 'The Promise of Embarrassment: Frances Burney's Theatre of Shame', chapter 4 of *The Novel Stage*, pp. 97–124.

We know that Burney experimented in an earlier draft of *Camilla* with an extended narrative around amateur theatricals. A draft section of manuscript in the Bodleian Library[47] has the young protagonists rehearse *The Provok'd Husband* under the direction of a Mrs Solea or Mrs Solen who was the prototype for Mrs Arblery. Tybalt (the prototype for Lionel) was cast as Lady Wronghead and Ariella (Camilla) as Jenny, her foolish and pert country daughter. There is relevance to the casting. Lionel has Lady Wronghead's extravagant tastes that risk running his entire family into debt. Jenny is, like Camilla, innocent and tempted by the attractions of metropolitan society. Cyrill (the Edgar prototype) thinks Ariella should rather play Lady Grace (indicating the moral seriousness of the main female protagonist) but she is content to play Jenny, 'earnest only to belong to a scheme she thought so delightful, [she] accepted it without hesitation.'[48]

In her final novel, *The Wanderer, or Female Difficulties* (1814), Burney returned to the idea of staging *The Provok'd Husband* in an amateur performance at a private house and performance of the role of Lady Townly now takes centre stage. Here too, we come to a better understanding of the dynamics between central protagonists in terms of the casting and performance of the play. A strange young woman (much later in the novel named as Juliet Granville), apparently a destitute émigré from the turmoil of the French Revolution, is being reluctantly accommodated in a country house in Lewes by the penny-pinching martinet, Mrs Maple. The choice of play is first dictated by Miss Arbe, a young lady admired in the neighbourhood for her performances at private theatres who has offered 'her services for the character' of Lady Townly in *The Provok'd Husband* and 'would study no other.'[49] Mr Maple's radical niece, Elinor Jodrel, rival with the unnamed 'Incognita' for the affections of Mr Harleigh, casts the rest of the play. Elinor gives herself the part of the foolish country aristocrat, Lady Wronghead, although she is disappointed that she cannot enjoy scenes of romantic reconciliation with Harleigh who takes the part of Lord Townly.

As with the shenanigans around the private theatricals in Jane Austen's *Mansfield Park*, published in the same year as *The Wanderer*, the concern about amateur dramatics is less about young people engaging in a

---

[47]   Undated Camilla manuscript, Egerton 3696 fols 27–73, British Library, London.
[48]   'Appendix VI', of Burney, *The Wanderer, or Female Difficulties*, ed. Margaret Doody (Oxford: Oxford University Press, 2001), p. 904. For further discussion, see Hilary Havens, 'Omitting Lady Grace: *The Provok'd Husband* in Frances Burney's *Camilla* and *The Wanderer*', *Journal for Eighteenth-Century Studies*, 38, no. 3 (2015), 413–24. The manuscript hand is hard to read; Doody transcribes the name as Solen and Havens as Solea.
[49]   Burney, *The Wanderer*, vol. 1, chapter 9, p. 70.

disgraceful public art than that the choice of play and the casting will allow illicit romance to blossom under cover of performance. When Miss Arbe suddenly pulls out of her obligations, Elinor plans to take over the role but finds it impossible to learn Lady Townly's many lines and the 'stranger' (who has come to be termed 'Ellis' because of the initials 'L.S.' on a piece of her correspondence) is forced to take the part. Ellis/Juliet is the only one with this capacity since she has not only acted as prompter in rehearsals but diligently transcribed the whole part for Miss Arbe after the latter's copy of the script was spoilt. And her performance as well as her behaviour – by contrast with the bad behaviour of the other players – wins Harleigh's admiration and increasing affection.

Ellis/Juliet's taking of the part of Lady Townly anticipates her eventual union with Harleigh, her Lord Townly. However, it also invites the reader conversant with the play – and it was still at the end of the eighteenth century a popular feature of the repertory – to speculate as to the true nature of the enigmatic stranger. It transpires that Juliet/Ellis is indeed already married, like the woman she played, and even more unhappily; her marriage to Harleigh is only made possible when her husband is executed as a spy. Moreover, we might go further in paralleling the character of the novelistic protagonist and the stage role she takes on: we question whether we are to see Ellis/Juliet as a vulnerable woman or a natural actress. Harleigh after all listens carefully to her growing confidence as prompter and observes that 'her voice, from seeming feeble and monotonous, became clear and penetrating: it was varied, with the nicest discrimination, for the expression of each character, changing its modulation from tones of softest sensibility, to those of archest humour; and from reasoning severity, to those of uncultured rusticity'.[50]

Burney asks us as readers to do more than note how plots map on to each other, and to embrace or reject correspondences between dramatic roles and the characters in the novel. She asks us also to think about our own response to the responses of others and stimulates 'affect'. Ellis/Juliet's performance in the first scene is hesitant and unremarkable, 'But her second scene exhibited her in another point of view' and 'From this time, her performance acquired a wholly new character'.[51] Of her performance, the narrator reports:

> Every feature of her face spoke her discrimination of every word; while the spirit which gave a charm to the whole, was chastened by a taste

---

[50] Burney, *The Wanderer*, vol. 1, chapter 9, p. 80.
[51] Ibid., chapter 11, p. 94.

the most correct; and while though modest she was never awkward; though frightened, never ungraceful.

A performance such as this, in a person young, beautiful, and wholly new, created a surprize so powerful, and a delight so unexpected, that the play seemed soon to have no other object than Lady Townly, and the audience to think that no other were worth hearing or beholding; for though the politeness exacted by a private representation, secured to every one an apparent attention, all seemed vapid and without merit in which she was not concerned; while all wore an air of interest in which she bore the smallest part; and she soon never spoke, looked, nor moved, but to excite pleasure, admiration, and applause, amounting to rapture.

Whether this excellence were the result of practice and instruction, or a sudden emanation of general genius, accidentally directed to a particular point, was disputed by the critics amongst the audience; and disputed, as usual, with the greater vehemence, from the impossibility of obtaining documents to decide, or direct opinion. But that which was regarded as the highest refinement of her acting, was a certain air of inquietude, which was discernible through the utmost gaiety of her exertions, and which, with the occasional absence and sadness, that had their source in her own disturbance, was attributed to deep research into the latent subjects of uneasiness belonging to the situation of Lady Townly. This, however, was nature, which would not be repressed; not art, that strove to be displayed.[52]

The peculiar power of Burney's novel – to centre our fascination on a woman and her performance, indeed to render the novel almost wholly from the point of view of that woman, while withholding from the audience an understanding of her origins – is acted out in this early vignette in the novel. We, like the audience of *The Provok'd Husband* in the drawing room at Lewes, feel with Ellis/Juliet – we are convinced of her authenticity, but the narrator refuses to allow us insight into the nature of her quest, and the likely outcome of her romantic attraction to and for the hero Harleigh.

By the second decade of the nineteenth century, then, Lady Townly had acquired the status of an independent character of immense attraction. She was also a perpetual enigma, a byword for undecidability. An actress could choose to deliver the famous reconciliation scene with self-conscious irony (as many in the present day do the wifely submission scene at the conclusion of Shakespeare's *Taming of the Shrew*). This interpretation makes the

---

[52]   Burney, *The Wanderer*, vol. 1, chapter 11, pp. 94–5.

audience complicit in an act of strategic submission – but it also under-mines the indeterminacy on which the performance rests. Lady Townly's 'reform' is authentic in the sense that it was a tragic necessity of plot. If it is a necessary act because the pleasures of town life will now be closed to her whether or not her husband separates from her, it also extends the possibil-ity of a new interiority: that the evident void in Lady Townly's psyche will be filled with genuine and affectionate relationship not only with her husband but with her sister-in-law, Lady Grace. It is perhaps inevitable that the next step in presenting Lady Townly was to reform her from maternal errancy. Edgeworth and Byron both concentrate their renderings of the Townly plot on the story of the reform of a mother who neglects her daughter. In so doing they both fulfil the character's destiny as it was first imagined by the actress for whom the part was written: Anne Oldfield outdoes herself in relying on the assistance of others. It is in interrelationship and mutual dependency that Lady Townly becomes herself: the daughter novelists pro-vided her with is a means to 'outdo', to do something for another beyond herself. The reform of the Lady Townly character provides her with ways of relating 'outside' of herself within the domestic space rather than beyond it. So too the novel 'outdoes' the theatre or at least stakes a claim to do so: it brings the theatre into a domestic space and in so doing reforms its character. This was the achievement of the female character often proposed as the antithesis of the society lady: Samuel Richardson's Pamela, who con-sistently converts theatrical performance into (novelistic) identity and in so doing reforms others rather than herself.

Chapter 9
The Sway of Character: Pamela

We turn now to a character who appears in every way the opposite of Lady Townly. Indeed, she may have been a character composed to answer back to another conventional stage type: not the town lady, but the shrewd country maidservant swift to exploit the predatory instincts of the young men in the household she serves. In Samuel Richardson's novel, *Pamela: or, Virtue Rewarded*, first published on 6 November 1740, a fifteen-year-old servant girl stoutly resists her young master, Mr B, in his attempts to seduce her. Mr B, his sister Lady Davers, the servants who abet his endeavours, all finally acknowledge Pamela's virtue and the capacity of her writing, the letter-memoir she writes recording her persecution, to bring others to virtue. Mr B persecutes Pamela, abducts her to his remote country estate, but finally sets her free; Pamela returns of her own volition to him and he offers her honourable marriage. The novel was an instant hit, enabling its printer-author to expand his London premises behind Salisbury Court in 1741. He published a continuation on 7 December 1741. Both parts were printed together in the sixth edition on 8 May 1742.[1]

Responses to *Pamela* are legion and proliferate across media – from William Hogarth's expensive engravings, to a fan illustrating scenes from the novel, to verse rejoinders, to earnest works of criticism.[2] Samuel Richardson's *Pamela* also, however, swiftly attracted satirical re-presentation, which recast the heroine's virtuous resistance to Mr B's advances as a strategic manipulation to secure her best future advantage. In this respect – a scepticism informing the reception by audiences of their marital settlements – there is an affinity between the fine lady who reforms herself (Lady

---

[1] See Albert Rivero, 'Publication and Early Reception', 'General Introduction', in *Pamela; or, Virtue Rewarded*, ed. Albert Rivero, The Cambridge Edition of the Works and Correspondence of Samuel Richardson, vol. 2 (Cambridge: Cambridge University Press, 2011), pp. xlviii–lxiv.

[2] The print responses are gathered in Thomas Keymer and Peter Sabor, ed., *The Pamela Controversy: Criticisms and Adaptations of Samuel Richardson's* Pamela *1740–1750*, 6 vols (London: Pickering and Chatto, 2001).

Townly) under threat of punishment, and the country girl who reforms others (Pamela) through her own virtuous example.

Pamela as character has, I suggest, 'sway'. Gumbrecht glosses sway as occupying space in a vertical dimension: sway is 'emergence and its result: being there'.[3] It is a bodily presence that exerts influence by virtue of that occupation. Both the book and character of Pamela are in the eighteenth century recognised as 'novel', as birthing a new kind of fiction from the romance and novel forms that pre-existed it. Pamela is, in every sense, an upright character: not only in terms of her ethical integrity, but in terms of the presentation of her embodiment. She stands firm before her assailants. Mr B repeatedly seizes her body and she resists his attempts to fondle and kiss her. Once their reconciliation is underway and he is reading the letters and diary notes she has kept, he recognises her virtue. The couple revisit the dreadful scene of her not-executed attempt at suicide in the pond at the Lincolnshire estate where he has kept her prisoner and Mr B has been reading her account of it. He concedes, 'I see you have been us'd too roughly; and it is a Mercy you stood Proof in that fatal Moment'.[4] Pamela stands proof: as witness of her own persecution and as a body that is resistant to assault and defeat. We should note also that verticality is best maintained when it has some sway or give, as in the architectural design of tall buildings. Pamela's soft body absorbs while repelling the unwanted attempts of others to breach it. She repeatedly kneels before her master both before and after his assaults, pleading with him to show mercy but without conceding to his advances. She bends then without submitting. And indeed her body is the vehicle that both incites desire and communicates her resistance. Her presence-effect is presented as corporeal. Pamela's body is what creates desire, what is desired and what resists desire. In this respect she embodies the *phusis* Gumbrecht associates with the vertical dimension of presence (from the Greek 'to grow' and denoting 'nature').

Pamela is, moreover, a (fictional) being who brings into being a presence-effect that resonates not only in the text that first creates her, but across a wide range of media and cultural objects. Her *phusis* (natural influence) births other forms in her image. She touches others (she moves them sentimentally) as they touch her, not only in those moments where characters convert to sympathy for her when they touch her in the story, but those metatextual encounters with her writing and her person: in reading her letters, in touching the book and reading the book in which she features. Critics have increasingly come to speak of *Pamela* not as a single-authored

---

[3]   Gumbrecht, *Production of Presence*, p. 68.
[4]   Richardson, *Pamela*, ed. Rivero, vol. 2, p. 223.

text or being, but as a 'media-event', presented/re-presented in art from popular to high image, artefacts, performance and print.⁵ Thomas Keymer and Peter Sabor brand the many and swift print responses to *Pamela* 'a Grubstreet gabfest'.⁶ Examples of Pamela's sway abound and in particular her capacity to capture her readers and compel imitation of her idiom. One enthusiastic reader self-styled as 'PhiloPamela' writes to Richardson in March 1742 telling him that he is 'so delighted & affected by this Book that my Friends tell me I talk in no other language than Pamela's'.⁷

Pamela's 'sway' over her readers is both an intradiegetic and extradiegetic effect; indeed, the text's presence lies in the capacity of Pamela as character to capture and infect every being she encounters, however hostile. Pamela touches and converts others within the text. James Grantham Turner points out the repetitive lexis of hands and touching (the writing hand, the invasive hand of seduction, the touch that completes a scene or painting) in *Pamela* the 'original' publication, its sequels, imitations and critiques.⁸ Pamela is a powerful body in the imagination of her readers. Although Pamela's bodily presence is often characterised in terms of the dramatic scene, as equivalent to the actor's embodied capacity to move an audience through impassioned gesture, it is also profoundly *anti*-theatrical. Physical attraction (deep, powerful and moving as it is understood to be in *Pamela*) is converted into romantic and spousal love through the medium of a surrogate for physical presence: the letter. Pamela's sway as character originates partly from her exclusive command of the writing act and all written accounts of the action of the novel. The (fictional) hand that shapes the alphabetical characters of the letters that constitute *Pamela* renders all characters, all the *dramatis personae* of the scene of action. This is especially meaningful (indeed ironic) given the character's social position and profession, which relies on the 'giving' of character by others. Pamela records in her third letter that her dead employer's daughter and sister to

---

⁵ See William B. Warner, 'The *Pamela* Media Event', in *Licensing Entertainment: The Elevation of Novel Reading in Britain, 1684–1750* (Berkeley and Los Angeles, CA: University of California Press, 1998), pp. 176–230; Richard Gooding, '*Pamela, Shamela*, and the Politics of the *Pamela* Vogue', *Eighteenth-Century Fiction*, 7, no. 2 (1995), 109–30.

⁶ Thomas Keymer and Peter Sabor, *Pamela in the Marketplace: Literary Controversy and Print Culture in Eighteenth-Century Britain and Ireland* (Cambridge: Cambridge University Press, 2005), p. 2.

⁷ Quoted Albert Rivero, 'General Introduction', in *Pamela in her Exalted Condition*, The Cambridge Edition of the Works and Correspondence of Samuel Richardson, vol. 3 (Cambridge: Cambridge University Press, 2012), p. lxi.

⁸ James Grantham Turner, 'Novel Panic: Picture and Performance in the Reception of Richardson's Pamela', *Representations*, 48 (1994), 73.

Mr B, the married aristocrat Lady Davers, has been living in the household for a month and 'she told me I was a very pretty Wench, and that every body gave me a very good Character, and lov'd me.'[9]

The word 'character' in *Pamela* is used to refer to a public reputation of identity, the fulfilling of an anticipated role. Ten instances are found of the word's usage in the two volumes of the first edition of *Pamela* and all relate to character as something that is given out to endorse or describe a person's behaviour (ranging from the sense of an employer's recommendation to a public perception of a person's virtues or vices). Hence when Pamela reports to her now-husband that his sister Lady Davers – convinced that Pamela has been debauched rather than legitimately married – has ordered her to serve dinner as a servant would do, Mr B responds 'if you did, and knew not what belong'd to your Character, as my Wife, I shall be very angry with you.'[10] And only three paragraphs later, Pamela reports that the guests Mr B has brought from Stamford to the Darnfords' house for supper have all been given by the Darnfords 'such a Character of me, that they said they were impatient to see me.'[11]

It is striking that there is little reference to theatrical 'character' in *Pamela*, and none before her marriage. Indeed, although Pamela is accused of playing a part it is that of the heroine of a romance rather than an explicit accusation that she is acting or an actress. Pamela herself tends to draw on the tradition of instruction in animal fable, casting herself as prey to the predators Mr B and Mrs Jewkes.[12] It is not until very late in the novel that she is paralleled with a character from drama: when taunted by Lady Davers, who calls her 'young Lady *Wou'd-be*', the vain, ignorant wife of Sir Politic Wou'd-be who apes the manners of Venetian courtesans in Ben Jonson's *Volpone*.[13] Lady Davers bears more than a passing resemblance to Lady Townly in her quick passions and well-hidden good nature, and Pamela's pertness might have suggested to her readers a link to the forwardness of a Jenny Wronghead who is nearly tricked herself into a sham marriage. However, explicit parallels with dramatic plots in the text of *Pamela* are carefully avoided. The conceit of the letter-journal is that Pamela is the witness and it is just feasible that allusions to dramatic characters are not recorded because Pamela, as a country-raised young girl who has only worked in the

---

[9] Richardson, *Pamela*, ed. Rivero, vol. 1, p. 13.
[10] Richardson, *Pamela*, ed. Rivero, vol. 2, p. 369.
[11] Ibid., p. 369.
[12] See Thomas Keymer, 'Pamela's Fables: Aesopian Writing and Political Implication in Samuel Richardson and Sir Roger l'Estrange', Bulletin de la Société d'Etudes Anglo-Américaines des XVIIe et XVIIIe Siècles, 41, no .1 (1995), 81–101.
[13] Richardson, *Pamela*, ed. Rivero, vol. 2, p. 355.

private house of a Bedfordshire widow, would not be familiar with them. Certainly, it is not until he penned his own sequel that Samuel Richardson took his heroine to the theatre. The more likely explanation, though, is that Richardson is (mis)directing his readers toward the reforming intention of his work with regard to the dangerous pleasures of prose fiction, which are referred to in the prefatory material and within the novel repeatedly.

Pamela elevates low sensational prose fiction into high ethical enter-tainment on paper. The novel's silence about drama's capacity to do this work is an effective means of quietly excluding novelist Richardson's more powerful competitor from the debate. However, the work's very silence may have served as an invitation; those who satirised his work were swift to make parallels with the wrongheadedness and duplicity of familiar charac-ter types from the playhouses, and they were themselves authors who had fallen on hard times as a result of a Licensing Act passed in 1737: Henry Fielding, John Kelly, Eliza Haywood.

I suggest here that Richardson's first published novel sought to sway audiences away from the embodied influence associated with theatrical rendering of character and win their loyalty to the 'new' form of render-ing character it claimed for the novel. It did so by a strategic disavowal of theatrical sway. Richardson claimed rather to be moralising the novel than the theatre: to aim to moralise theatre would be to acknowledge its presence and sway in the history of making fiction. More often than not, as we shall see, 'romance' stands as the surrogate for theatrical performance in *Pamela*. The romance is represented as a form of prose fiction wedded to abstraction and unable to provide the presence-effect of bodily sensation, the touch, which the novel as form arrives to provide. In this history of genre, the theatre is quietly erased. Much of the work of erasure is per-formed by Pamela herself, whose textual life claims a novel authority, a vertical sway, of its own making repudiating the presence of theatre in her history and character. We have too often read *Pamela* as a reforming agent for the novel where we might better understand it as a work geared toward establishing prose fiction/the novel as *the* medium of reformed character.

Richardson was unusual as a novelist who had no direct engagement with the theatre as an author of plays, printer of plays or dramatic criticism. His 1740 *Pamela* does not so much 'take' its character from the familiar conventions of the stage, as shape a new kind of 'presentness' of character particular to prose fiction. The device of the letters and journals, which cap-ture the action only just after it passes, provides an effect of presence rival-ling that of the theatre (to bring to life past actions in a present moment).

And here too (as with the case of Lady Townly), Pamela's presence and sway as character lies not in an especially complex interiority so much as the presentness of person to audience: a proximity and intimacy in the now that is compelling. Indeed, Pamela is not a person of depth – albeit she is, we are consistently reminded, one of exceptional virtue. She arrives at insights of some depth, but these are not ascribed to a formidable intellect, exceptional imagination or spiritual rigour. Her exemplarity seems also to lie in her ordinariness. For example, her thoughts on the temporal eva-nescence of earthly happiness after she has enjoyed a poem written to her flowery beauty by her husband are abruptly ended by her comment: 'But I shall get out of my Depth; my shallow Mind cannot comprehend, as it ought, these weighty Subjects.'[14]

Pamela's original sway and ethical authority is increasingly diminished in her dramatic and novelistic afterlives. It is in her original 'form' – the maidservant whose reforming power stems entirely from the integrity of her character and the power of her aesthetic affect – that Pamela is the perfect 'fit' for the new cultural norms ushered in with the licensed stage: she is a moralised and reformed version of a familiar stage type (the pert maid), who ushers in a new kind of being (the robustly ethical bourgeois heroine of the novel) that will revitalise a stage perceived to have fallen into licentiousness.[15]

Certainly, Richardson conceived of 'character' as a kind of property of the author. His concerns about the sequel by Hugh Kelly – discussed with him by the publisher Richard Chandler and Kelly's first volume published on 28 May 1741 as *Pamela's Conduct in High Life* – hinged on what he saw as likely abuses of 'Plan' and 'Character'. In August 1741 he writes to James Leake, his brother in law and fellow printer, that he would advertise against continuations 'rather than my Plan should be basely ravished out of my Hands, and, probably, my Characters depreciated and debased.'[16] Here, Richardson returns to the insistent reference to 'hands' in his first two volumes: Mr B's hands demonstrate gallant affection rather than under-take predatory seizure by the end of the novel. Pamela's hand records her

[14]   Richardson, *Pamela*, ed. Rivero, vol. 2, p. 455.
[15]   Richard Gooding observes that whether parodying or promoting Richardson's *Pamela*, later versions tended to neutralise and obscure the radicalism of the poli-tics in the original work' ('*Pamela, Shamela,* and the Politics of the *Pamela* Vogue', p. 125). On Richardson and the stage, see also Jocelyn Harris, 'Introduction', in *Richardson's Published Commentary on Clarissa 1747–1765. Volume 1 Prefaces, Post-scripts and Related Writings*, ed. Thomas Keymer (London: Pickering and Chatto, 1998), pp. xi, xxxv. Mark Kinkead-Weakes is more concerned to explore the ways in which Richardson sought to make his novels give a sense of the dramatic present-ness of performance. See *Samuel Richardson: Dramatic Novelist* (London: Methuen and Co., 1973).
[16]   Albert J. Rivero, 'General Introduction', in *Pamela in her Exalted Condition*, p. xxviii.

experiences in writing; it comments on the 'huge Hand'[17] of the odious Mrs Jewkes; it sews the embroidery on her master's waistcoat, her country clothing, her papers into the lining of her undercoat to conceal them from the prying hands of others. The hand that writes character takes over that character and should hand it on with responsible fidelity (just as a character reference recommends a person from one employment to another). But it can equally traduce and misrepresent.

Pamela the character is insistently equated with *Pamela* the novel, handled with chivalry by her editor to her proper course into marriage to Mr B. Her retouching by another hand is a form of abduction, an act of ravishment. The coupling of 'character' and 'hand' indicates Richardson's project to elevate the novel to ethical and epistemological authority over forms that mediate 'character' in ways that conceal the writing hand: drama and performance. Stage adaptations of *Pamela* and the stage sources from which her character derived rely on hands as instruments of gesture and point, in common with all the other stage performers. An embodied Pamela, paradoxically, cannot have the upper hand as informant; her scribbling hand could not be dramatically interesting to a theatre audience whereas it has command and priority in our experience as readers of her tale in print. The process of elevating the 'novel' as ethical medium through the presentness of virtuous character is effected through the effacing of the theatre's claim to this role.

Richardson's *Pamela* certainly drew on the plots of plays for its material. Ira Konigsberg identifies a number of dramatic sources that involved servant girls and country maidens pursued by city libertines whom they eventually reform:[18] a subplot in Thomas Brewer's *The Countrie Girl* (1646) was turned into the main focus of John Leanerd's *The Country Innocence: or, The Chamber-Maid Turn'd Quaker* (1677).[19] Charles Johnson's *The Country Lasses, or, The Custom of the Manor* (which was performed four times in the same year that *Pamela* was published in 1740) has two young gentlemen divert themselves in the country in the pursuit of innocent maidens.[20] Flora stoutly resists Heartwell and wins a proposal only to disclose that

[17] Richardson, *Pamela*, ed. Rivero, vol. 1, p. 105.

[18] Ira Konigsberg, 'The Dramatic Background of Richardson's Plots and Characters', *PMLA*, 83, no. 1 (1968), 42–53. See also Ira Konigsberg, *Samuel Richardson and the Dramatic Novel* (Lexington, KY: University of Kentucky Press, 1968).

[19] Anthony Brewer (Thomas), *The Countrie Girl* (London: A.R., 1646); Leanerd, John, *The Country Innocence: or, The Chamber-Maid Turn'd Quaker* (London: Charles Harper, 1677).

[20] Charles Johnson, *The Country Lasses, or, The Custom of the Manor* (Dublin: S. Powell, 1727).

she is really a wealthy noblewoman. George Lillo's first work for the stage was a ballad-opera called *Silvia; or, The Country Burial* (1730); Silvia resists the advances of a country squire named Welford who is aided by wicked servants.[21]

If sources from the stage are a hidden presence in *Pamela*, stage-writers were the first to seek to re-form Pamela's character in later novels and plays. The earliest responses to *Pamela* were from authors whose careers were deeply bound up with the stage and who had been forced to turn (back) to prose fiction with the introduction of licensing and its attendant radical shrinking of new writing (since it was only new writing that required a licence). Moreover, these respondents recognised Richardson's attempt at an aesthetic *coup*, supplanting the power of drama to bring being to life in the imagination of an audience with that of the novel. Henry Fielding published his *An Apology for the Life of Mrs. Shamela Andrews* on 2 April 1741 and Eliza Haywood her *Anti-Pamela* on 16 June 1741;[22] both these works rewrite Pamela's character as that of the actress, carefully staging her innocence in order to secure a marriage that will lift her out of labour into leisure (the path of the stage actress who becomes a kept mistress).

The stories of Fielding's Shamela and Haywood's Syrena unfold differently to that of Pamela because these characters lack her integrity: Shamela is a denizen of Drury Lane who has engaged in an unwise flirtation with Parson Williams and – under the tutelage of her mother and bawd, Henrietta Maria Honora Andrews – adopts the name Pamela to put herself in the way of a booby country squire and thus repair her fortunes. Syrena Tricksy is also taught her arts by a cunning mother. Both girls threaten to fail to follow parental guidance and risk losing their prey (Syrena falls pregnant because she gives in to a lover against her mother's advice). In some ways these actress-characters under the sway of maternal instruction prove Pamela's extraordinariness rather than necessarily undermine her authority. Pamela, after all, acts without guidance; her parents' letters stop reaching her early in the novel and those few letters she does read consist largely in reminding her of her intrinsic value and the importance of virtuous principle rather than managing her behaviour. And it may also be that Fielding and Haywood were conceding the ground he sought to Richardson: Syrena and Shamela are *not* Pamela, nor are they the secret truth of Pamela; they are different women who show that – usually – women's lives pan out differently from hers.

---

[21] George Lillo, *Silvia; or, The Country Burial* (Dublin: S. Powell, 1730).
[22] Catherine Ingrassia, ed., *Shamela and Anti-Pamela* (Peterborough, ON: Broadview Press, 2004). Facsimiles of both works are available in Keymer and Sabor, eds, *The Pamela Controversy*, vol. 3.

Attempts to convert Pamela into theatrical character, tended also not to challenge the exceptionalism and sway of Richardson's character. Rather they rewrote the story to locate that ethical sway elsewhere. On 23 September 1741 (seven months after the first publication of *Pamela*) rehearsals for Henry Giffard's *Pamela, A Comedy* began at Goodman's Fields Theatre. This theatre had been the target of a parliamentary bill introduced by Sir John Barnard in 1735 for a Stage Licensing Act, which Richardson's pamphlet *A Seasonable Examination of the Pleas and Pretensions of the Proprietors of, and Subscribers to, Play-houses, Erected in Defiance of Royal License* (1735) was published to support.[23] Barnard's bill had failed due to lack of support from the prime minister Sir Robert Walpole, who only returned to the plan to limit the number of playhouses and censor playscripts in 1737 when Henry Fielding's Haymarket political parodies became intolerable to him.

In this adaptation, Pamela – albeit armed with book, pen and writing paper – lacks energy and the magnetic sway of her novel original. The props of writing in a novel translate into a prose that brings character to life; on the stage they more often hinder corporeal performance and point to a character's life elsewhere than that present moment. This was not the only reason that Pamela's character is subdued and suppressed in favour of other characters in Giffard's adaptation. The parts of Mr B and Pamela were taken by Giffard and his wife, then forty-seven and thirty-four in age respectively (Mr B is twenty-five and Pamela fifteen). It is perhaps unsurprising given this casting, regardless of the unremarkable nature of the script, that the attractions of the play lay elsewhere. It is the two young and contrasting secondary male protagonists who take centre stage: Jack Smatter (played by David Garrick) and Parson Williams (played by Giffard's son, William). Belvile (Giffard's version of Mr B) is not converted by Pamela's virtue but rather by the robust chivalry of Parson Williams. At the end of the fourth act, it is Williams whose words sway the amorous squire to offer virtuous marriage. Williams is advised by John Arnold of a wicked plot between Mrs Jewkes and Colebrand (now a cunning French valet rather than a brutal Swiss enforcer) to marry Pamela to Colebrand and then sell her on to the Squire. Belvile comes to Pamela's bedroom intent on seducing her; when he seizes Pamela and she struggles, Williams interposes, *his* verbal agency, physical presence and sway substituting for Pamela's. He reveals the plot to Belvile and restores his sense of virtue. Belvile acknowledges Williams'

---

[23] Richardson's pamphlet in support of an unsuccessful 1735 attempt to introduce a Stage Licensing Act was published in April 1735. *A Seasonable Examination of the Pleas and Pretensions of the Proprietors of, and Subscribers to, Play-Houses*, in *Early Works*, ed. Alexander Pettit, The Cambridge Edition of the Works and Correspondence of Samuel Richardson, vol. 1 (Cambridge: Cambridge University Press, 2012).

sway. 'Thou excellent Man! What do I owe thee for thy honest Help? Not less than if you snatcht me from the Hands of Death—Nay, I was dead to Virtue—but thus recover'd, I must repent—'.[24]

If Williams takes over Pamela's role in converting Mr B, Jack Smatter (a relatively minor figure in Richardson's original) demonstrates the wit and humour that Pamela (at least in her first incarnation at Richardson's hand) demonstrated. Unlike the other actors, David Garrick, who took the part of Jack Smatter in the play, was not listed by his name in the 'Dramatis Personae'. The play opened on 9 November 1741, less than three weeks after Garrick's hugely successful stage debut as Richard III. Garrick was billed in fact as the 'Gentleman who acted King Richard'. Smatter was the first newly written part the white-hot talent had taken. Garrick's presence engrossed the fifth act, especially in a *tour de force* where Jack Smatter reads out a letter (composed by Garrick himself) from Colebrand to Mrs Jewkes. Here, Colebrand in broken Frankish English, reveals to his new 'bride', Mrs Jewkes, that he has absconded with her money to return to his wife and thirteen children in his own country. In an adaptation of a novel composed entirely of letters – the majority of them in one hand only, that of Pamela – the only lively stage business with a letter has nothing to do with the main plot concerning the heroine. And everything to do with the glamour and wit of a sensational new actor given space in a fifth act to show his versatility.

It is noticeable that the theatrical renderings of *Pamela*, unlike their prose fictional contemporaries such as Hugh Kelly's *Pamela's Conduct in High Life* (the second volume of which was published only thirteen days before Giffard's *Pamela* opened at Goodman's Fields), were not interested in continuing Pamela's story after marriage. Stage adaptations relied on recycling the scenes of most dramatic interest in the novel: Pamela's attractive appearance in her country dress; Mr B gaining access to her bed by disguising himself as the maid Nan (sleeping off drink in a chair with an apron over 'her' head); Pamela's throwing her clothes into the pond and contemplating suicide when escape proves impossible.

Giffard's version seems to have been the only one that enjoyed success on the London stage in the immediate afterglow of the craze for the novel *Pamela*. A number of printed editions of play-adaptations of the work survive, but scant records of performances. On 16 November 1741 a new stage adaptation, *Pamela; or Virtue Triumphant*, 'intended to be Acted at the Theatre-Royal in *Drury-Lane*', possibly by a young actor named James

---

[24]   Henry Giffard, *Pamela. A Comedy* (London: J. Robinson, 1742), vol. 6 of Keymer and Sabor, ed., *The Pamela Controversy*, Act 4, p. 51.

Dance, was published but there is no mention of a production.[25] Here too it is the male character who proves more interesting, and whose visible conflict between honour and attraction takes centre stage. In Act 1, Scene 2, Squire Beaulove comments aside as Pamela kneels and weeps before him:

> this Girl alarms me, and allures me at the same Time, I burn for her with the most ardent Desire, but her steady Virtue, as she calls it, or rather Pride, throws Water on the rising Flame and damps its Force, I have conquer'd several e'er this, but never met with so obstinate a Pride; if I leave off here she triumphs over me, and publishes her Victory. – 'Sdeath what Mortals we are? – A Man whose modest Address would not suffer him to desist from Gallantries at the Frown of a first Dutchess, shall be awed into less than manhood at the affecting Prudery of a Chambermaid.[26]

Stage adaptations enjoyed more success when they were produced at some distance in time from the original publication of the novel; when, in other words, Pamela's immediate sway as novel heroine had somewhat abated. Hence, a lively burlesque comedy, *Mock-Pamela*, had a single performance at Smock-Alley in Dublin on 14 May 1750 as an afterpiece to Shakespeare's *Henry IV Part 2* at a benefit for Theophilus Cibber, Colley's son. It was revived as an afterpiece to a performance of *The Provok'd Husband* (1728) at the Richmond Theatre, Surrey, on 4 August 1750.

It is interesting to speculate about the likely effect of seeing these two plays side by side. The device of the mother of an unvirtuous serving-woman plotting for her daughter to draw a foolish squire into marriage also features in Cibber's play (Motherly, Myrtilla and Squire Richard Wronghead). In *Mock-Pamela*, the servant Blossom is swiftly revealed to be the illegitimate daughter of the housekeeper Mistress Stock and the steward Mr Root, at the household of Squire Gudgeon and his mother. *Mock-Pamela* is one of the earliest plays to provide a heroine who enters, novel in hand, declaring her pleasure in the work and her intention to follow its precepts.[27]

---

[25]   In Keymer and Sabor, ed., *The Pamela Controversy*, vol. 6. They question the attribution of authorship to Richard Dance in their 'Introduction', pp. xv–xvi.

[26]   *Pamela; or Virtue Triumphant* (London: Samuel Lyne, 1741), Act 1, scene 2, Keymer and Sabor, ed., *The Pamela Controversy*, vol. 1, p. 20.

[27]   *Mock-Pamela* (1750), facsimile in vol. 6, Keymer and Sabor, ed. *Pamela Controversy*, vol. 6. George Colman's *Polly Honeycomb* (1760) also opens with a heroine reading a novel. See Ros Ballaster, 'Rivals for the Repertory: Theatre and Novel in Georgian London', *Restoration and Eighteenth-Century Theatre Research*, 27, no. 1 (Summer 2012), 5–24; and 'Enter the Novel: Prose Fiction in the Georgian Theatre',

Pamela was a good fit for a comic opera. The sway Pamela exerts over everyone she meets in Richardson's novel could be conveyed by the sweet delivery and fine tone on the part of a singer-actress wielded on stage. The earliest operatic version of *Pamela* was printed but not performed in Newcastle in 1742. It is an adaptation of Giffard's play by one 'Mr Edge', now identified as Joseph Dorman; the concentration of the work is on humour, song and bawdiness (Jack Smatter and Colebrand play no part in the action).²⁸ The most successful adaptation of *Pamela* to the English stage was Isaac Bickerstaff's comic opera (with music by Samuel Arnold) of 1765, *The Maid of the Mill*. This hugely popular work saw twenty-nine performances in its first season at Covent Garden and sold almost as many copies in ten years as the first print run of *Pamela* (20,000).²⁹ Its original plot derives from a 1618 play by Francis Beaumont and John Fletcher; the Renaissance work ended with the disclosure that the country heroine is in fact the lost daughter of a nobleman adopted by a kind mill-owner. Bickerstaff substituted the *Pamela* plot for this device, keeping his heroine country and low born but as remarkable for her taste and virtue as her model.³⁰

---

in *Eighteenth Century Drama: Censorship, Society and the Stage* (Marlborough: Adam Matthew, 2016), www.eighteenthcenturydrama.amdigital.co.uk/Explore/Essays/Ballaster [accessed 20 February 2020]. No country innocent, Blossom has already entertained the advances of Squire Gudgeon's valet, Perch, and has been sent her 'little angelical-guide, *Pamela*', by an aunt (Branch), tire-woman at Goodman's Fields, who raised her in the heart of the London acting trade. Like Shamela and Syrena, then, Blossom, is under instruction by an experienced maternal figure to trick a foolish country squire into marriage. Her plot is foiled by the jealous Perch and the upright Lady Gudgeon, but not with great hardship since her quick-thinking father Root has ensured the squire signs a deed promising that should he breach the marriage promise he will pay her two thousand pounds. *Mock-Pamela* was on its first performance, and unusually, printed as a book and sold at the theatre as a souvenir. Its music was credited to the composer John Frederick Lampe, whose wife Isabella played Blossom and sang four of the songs in the play.

²⁸ See Keymer and Sabor, 'Introduction', in *The Pamela Controversy*, vol. 6, pp. xvii–xviii. A facsimile of *Pamela: or, Virtue Rewarded. An Opera* (Newcastle: John White, 1742) is found in the same volume.

²⁹ See Keymer and Sabor, *Pamela in the Marketplace*, p. 130.

³⁰ Isaac Bickerstaff, *The Maid of the Mill* (London: Newbery and others, 1765). Bickerstaff comments in his preface on Pamela's success as a stage play in other languages, particularly by Goldoni in Italian and Voltaire in French. The most successful French translation was Voltaire's *Nanine, ou le préjugé vaincu* first performed 16 June 1749 at the Comédie Française, Paris and translated into English in 1763; Goldoni's comedy *Pamela Nubile* was first performed in Mantua in spring 1750, later in Venice in November and printed as a bilingual edition by John Nourse in 1756. See Keymer and Sabor, 'Introduction', in *Pamela Controversy*, vol. 6, pp. xxii–xxiii.

Pamela and Mr B are recast as Patty and Lord Aimworth, who enjoy a chaste attraction that finally surmounts their social distinction. This follows closely the arguments Mr B comes to adopt for his own marriage in Richardson's original novel: the exceptional virtue of his choice, her capacity to make him happy, her submission to his authority. Patty is first seen reading a book at a window while her father and brother sing about the pleasures of hard work. The oafish brother, Ralph, is revealed to be jealous of the 'refinement and leisure of "Suster Pat"', acquired through her service in Lady Aimworth's household, and he complains that in returning to the miller's household he thought 'she was to have been of some use in the house; but instead of that, she sits there all day, reading outlandish books, dressed like a fine madumasel, and the never a word you says to she'.[31]

The rivalry between brother and sister may have informed a later play with evident debts to *Pamela*, Oliver Goldsmith's *She Stoops to Conquer*, first performed at Covent Garden in 1773. Kate Hardcastle's courtship of the awkward Marlowe in her servant dress evidently recalls *Pamela*, but the sibling rivalry between Kate and her stepbrother, Tony Lumpkin, may have found its origins in this earlier work. Only one month before the premiere of *She Stoops*, Samuel Foote had put on a puppet show farce, a one-act Anti-Pamelist work entitled *The Handsome Housemaid, or Piety in Pattens* (its first night was at the Haymarket on 15 February 1773) based on and mocking *The Maid of the Mill*. Squire Turniptop rivals Thomas the Butler for the attentions of the unkind and ignorant Polly.[32]

Richardson's fiction was often praised as a form of 'dramatic' representation. In one of his Prefaces to the second edition of *Pamela* (published 14 February 1741), Richardson's friend Aaron Hill praised the work for its dramatic quality:

> One of the best-judg'd *Peculiars*, of the Plan, is, that These Instructions being convey'd, as in a kind of Dramatical Representation, by those beautiful *Scenes*, her own Letters and Journals, who acts the most moving and suffering *Part*, we feel the Force in a threefold Effect,—from the Motive, the Act, and the Consequence.[33]

---

[31] Isaac Bickerstaff, *The Maid of the Mill* (London: Newbery and others, 1765), Act 1, p. 2.

[32] *Samuel Foote's Primitive Puppet-shew, Featuring Piety in Pattens; a Critical Edition*, ed. Samuel N. Bogorad (Pittsburgh, PA: University of Pittsburgh Press, 1973).

[33] Aaron Hill, 'Preface' (dated 17 December 1740), in Richardson, *Pamela*, ed. Rivero, p. 465.

In this concluding section we return to consider the ways in which Richardson himself responded to appropriations of his work. Here, we see a direct engagement with the issue of the stage's rival powers of characterisation. If the first part of *Pamela* silences and represses theatrical reference, the second part invokes it repeatedly to claim the superiority of the novel form and especially the presence of novel character as able to appropriate and displace the power of the actress. Richardson's sequel to *Pamela, Pamela in Her Exalted Condition*, makes a passionate case for character as the provenance of the novel and sets up theatre as its competition. The novel heroine must be differentiated from the stage queen in order for her character to, as Gumbrecht terms it, stand-there-on-itself, to sway.

Certainly, Richardson seems to have been more concerned in publishing his own sequel to reassert his intellectual and editorial property in his character of Pamela than in answering the 'anti-Pamelists'. *Pamela in her Exalted Condition* appeared with an advertisement clearly directed at Hugh Kelly's prose fiction continuation, which had been published in two volumes on 28 May 1741 with the title *Pamela's Conduct in High Life*. In the account Richardson gave to his brother-in-law and fellow publisher, James Leake, as to the circumstances that led him to write and see into print his own two-volume sequel on 7 December 1741, he seems especially exercised by the fact that the author Hugh Kelly was (in Richardson's opinion) a failed playwright: 'a Bookseller's Hackney, who never wrote any thing that was tolerably receiv'd, and had several of his Performances refused by the Stage'.[34]

It may be that Richardson was especially tender on the suggestion that he might have been seen, as he saw Kelly, as a failed playwright rather than the originator of a new form of fiction that had all the capacity of the stage to move, yet none of its immoral and licentious potential. So too, in the course of the sequel we see Pamela temporarily identify her history and circumstances with those found in stage performances and then swiftly distance herself from such collocations. Pamela takes a position of orthodoxy on the London stage; recent criticism has noted that the 1737 Licensing Act might be seen less as a repressive act of Walpole's administration weary of incendiary political satire than a response to a felt popular demand for regulation and control of stage content.[35] Pamela pontificates precisely in that vein:

[34]   The letter is transcribed (from a manuscript in the Victoria and Albert Museum FM xvi, I, fols 55–6) by Albert Rivero in the 'General Introduction', in *Pamela in her Exalted Condition*, p. xxxviii.

[35]   See Matthew Kinservik, 'Reconsidering Theatrical Regulation in the Long Eighteenth Century', in *Players, Playwrights, Playhouses: Investigating Performance,*

I think the stage, by proper Regulations, might be made a profitable Amusement. But nothing more convinces one, than these Representations, of the Truth of the common Observation, That the best Things, corrupted, may prove the worst. The Terror and Compunction for evil Deeds, the Compassion for a just Distress, and the general Beneficence which those lively Exhibitions are so capable of raising in the human Mind, may be of great Service, when directed to right Ends, and induced by proper Motives.[36]

The stage's capacity to stimulate feeling in its audience is, however, too often given to the representation of raging love, complains Pamela. Here, as elsewhere, we see the novel acknowledging the 'liveness' of the stage exhibition. Pamela's liveness, her writing to the moment, her turning of her immediate present into novelistic performance, seeks to match that power while evidencing a transparent motive for virtue often questioned and challenged in the equally lively anti-theatrical debates that preceded the Licensing Act.[37] Stage comedy had, of course, been subject to extensive moralising and sentimentalising (Cibber's *Provok'd Husband* was part of that process) in the wake of decades of campaigning from the 1690s onwards.[38] However, the advocacy of *Pamela* lies in insisting on the ethical value of the medium itself: correspondence-turned-novel preserves the lively character of dramatic performance, but contains it and measures its effect more surely in the smaller domestic familiar environments which it imagines to be the site of its own reception. Hence, Pamela insistently delivers her reforming acts of character in domestic spaces and within the bordered confines of the letter page.

Pamela describes three London performances she attends on her first visit to the metropolis after her marriage. Unsurprisingly Pamela's relationship to the stage is mediated by her writing, by text. She undertakes to write a little book for Lady Davers commenting on all the plays she has seen with the aid of the marginal notes she took in a printed collection of plays. The plays remain largely 'off' the stage of Pamela's own 'dramatic scenes', then, with only two representative examples discussed. The plays she selects are

---

1660–1800, ed. Michael Cordner and Peter Holland (Basingstoke: Palgrave Macmillan, 2007), pp. 152–74.

[36] Richardson, *Pamela in Her Exalted Condition*, ed. Rivero, letter 14, p. 341.

[37] See Lisa A. Freeman, *Anti-Theatricality and the Body Public* (Philadelphia, PA: University of Pennsylvania Press, 2016).

[38] See Aparna Gollapudi, *Moral Reform in Comedy and Culture, 1696–1747* (Farnham: Ashgate, 2011).

particularly relevant examples speaking to her own circumstances and the reforming logic of her novelistic sway.

Diana Solomon writes perceptively about Pamela's response to the first play she discusses, a production of Ambrose Philips' tragedy, *The Distressed Mother* (first produced and printed in 1712, an adaptation of Racine's *Andromaque*).[39] Pamela takes particular exception to the prologue written for Anne Oldfield in which the sprightly actress guys ironically to imply that the heroine's decision to marry again after the death of a much-loved husband – and to her husband's enemy, in order to protect her son – was made in bad faith and is in fact an act of sexual opportunism to obtain sexual satisfaction with a new husband. Pamela explains in her own distress that it was:

> An Epilogue spoken by Mrs. *Oldfield* in the Character of *Andromache*, that was more shocking to me, than the most terrible Parts of the Play; as by lewd, and even senseless *Double Entendres*, it could be calculated only to efface all the tender, all the virtuous Sentiments, which the Tragedy was design'd to raise.[40]

Mr B is both amused and impressed by his new wife's sensitivity to the bathos of the epilogue. He admits that he too has always found it to have spoilt the tragic effect of the play, but he advises her that she may take as a moral from seeing the epilogue an understanding of 'what a Character that of an Actor and Actress is, and how capable they are to personate any thing for a sorry Subsistence.'[41] Pamela is swift to divert this line of argument, which might to the cynical reader suggest further parallels. After all, if Pamela were play-acting through the period of her courtship her performance was sustained enough to win her more than a 'sorry Subsistence'; she has secured a marriage to a wealthy and loving man. Pamela quickly returns to her own purpose, the territory where she has sway: that of moralising rather than monetarising performance.

> Well, but, Sir, said I, are there not, think you, extravagant Scenes and Characters enough in most Plays, to justify the Censures of the

[39]   Diana Solomon, 'Tragic Play, Bawdy Epilogue', in Daniel J. Ennis and Judith Bailey Slagle, *Prologues, Epilogues, Curtain-Raisers, and Afterpieces: The Rest of the Eighteenth-Century London Stage* (Newark, DE: University of Delaware Press, 2007), pp. 155–78.
[40]   Richardson, *Pamela in Her Exalted Condition*, ed. Rivero, letter 14, pp. 353–4.
[41]   Ibid., p. 354.

Virtuous upon them, that the wicked Friend of the Author[42] must crown the Work in an Epilogue, for fear the Audience should go away improv'd by the Representation.[43]

Pamela's circumstances to some extent mirror those of the tragic heroine she discusses, and she runs the very real risk of being seen as a consummate actress rather than a virtuous innocent. *Pamela in Her Exalted Condition* might be seen as a form of epilogue to *Pamela*, an epilogue in which a sexually knowing married woman nods to a reader who suspects that she was less than innocent in her earlier attempts to flee a sexual aggressor. Pamela seeks to put some distance between herself and this reading in her critique of Oldfield's epilogue. Here, as elsewhere, Pamela associates the breaking of plausibility and consistency in character (the 'realism' of narrative performance) with a failure to sustain a moral purpose: arguably the ethical and aesthetic project of her own eponymous construction. Pamela embodies the novel.

If Pamela might be seen as an accomplished actress, her husband might well be characterised as an accomplished fool. And Pamela's next letter turns from her responses to tragedy to a discussion of a comedy, a performance of Richard Steele's *The Tender Husband; or, the Accomplished Fools*. Steele's play (which included two scenes penned by Joseph Addison, his co-founder of the celebrated periodical, *The Spectator*) concerns the tricking of two errant women: one married and obsessed with French fashions, whose husband Clerimont Senior engages his friend Fainlove in a plot to court her in order to correct her folly; and the other a merchant's niece, obsessed with romances and unhappy at the union arranged for her with a country clodhopper who is persuaded into a clandestine marriage by a needy aristocrat passing himself off as a romance suitor, Clerimont Junior. Steele's play was first titled 'The City Nymph; or, the Accomplish'd Fools' suggesting the emphasis was on the plot concerning Biddy Tipkin, the unmarried bourgeois romance fantasist, rather than that of the husband's 'tender' chastisement of a fashionable wife. The play was first performed at Drury Lane on 23 April 1705 with a new title but the same subtitle.[44]

Pamela is equally dissatisfied with this play especially as she had anticipated enjoying it because the script had been penned by the much-admired

---

[42]   Pamela alludes here to the author of the Epilogue, Eustace Budgell.

[43]   Richardson, *Pamela in Her Exalted Condition*, ed. Rivero, letter 14, p. 354.

[44]   Two scenes (Act 3, scene 1 and Act 5, scene 1) and the prologue were written by Joseph Addison, Steele's collaborator on both *The Tatler* and *The Spectator*. See Shirley Strum Kenny, 'Two Scenes by Addison in Steele's "Tender Husband"', *Studies in Bibliography*, 19 (1996), 217–26.

authors of *The Spectator*. The coupling of ethical and aesthetic virtue displayed on the printed pages of a periodical is not matched on the stage:

> There seems to me... to be a great deal of Wit and Satire in the Play:
> But, upon my word, I was grievously disappointed as to the Morality
> of it: Nor, in some places, is *Probability* preserved; and there are divers
> Speeches so very free, that I could not have expected to meet with
> such from the Names I mentioned.[45]

She takes particular exception to a scene in which Clerimont Junior is introduced to Biddy as a painter preparing her picture for her wedding. Biddy
wants to be portrayed as a romance heroine with a white palfrey drawn by
a dwarf; Clerimont tells her a 'story' of a noble lover who disguises himself
as a painter to gain access to the woman he adores. Readers of *Pamela*
of course know that the heroine takes her name from one of the pastoral
princesses in Philip Sidney's *Arcadia*, but the hugely successful first part of
the novel took pains to insist that this Pamela is not a princess in disguise
as a country innocent (as she is in *Arcadia*), and that her idiolect is that of
simple piety not the romancing with which Mr B persistently charges her.
Anne Oldfield took the part of Biddy Tipkin, alternating in repertory with
that of Andromache at Drury Lane. Biddy was a part in which Oldfield
distinguished herself; her last appearance in the role was 20 April 1730,
only eight days before her death. Pamela here too appears to recognise an
affinity and insist on a distinction – she is not an actress taking the part
of a foolish girl. Her speech is not that of a knowing woman who delivers
double entendre with a nod and a wink to her audience when she gives a
virgin's ignorant innocent lines. Equally, Pamela has to avoid association
with the part Oldfield played: Pamela is not a version of Biddy, a silly female
Quixote deluded by romance fantasies.

Pamela promotes her own brand of novelistic virtue by dismissing
romance in the same terms as she does the plays she writes about to Lady
Davers. And here she converts the domestic space of her own home into a
theatre for the performance of novelised virtue. In the sixty-third letter of
Pamela in Her Exalted Condition, Pamela – now a well-travelled mother
with a large young family – describes to her friend, Lady G, a conversation
with two mature women, Mrs Towers and Lady Arthur, and four young
ladies brought to her for instruction by the father of one of them. Eighteen-
year-old Miss Stapylton is 'over-run with the Love of Poetry and Romance'.

[45] Richardson, *Pamela in Her Exalted Condition*, ed. Rivero, letter 15, p. 355.

Pamela tells them about her own teenage reading under the guidance of Mr B's mother:

> there were very few Novels and Romances, that my Lady would permit me to read; and those I did, gave me no great Pleasure; for either they dealt so much in the *Marvellous* and *Improbable*, or were so unnaturally *inflaming* to the *Passions*, and so full of *Love* and *Intrigue*, that hardly any of them but seem'd calculated to *fire* the *Imagination*, rather than to *inform* the *Judgment*.[46]

Once more, Pamela's reforming novelistic agency is set against the dangerous illicit attractions of another form of prose fiction, the romance. But it is also a staged form of instruction to an audience explicitly addicted to plays and play-acting (Miss Stapylton is prone to reading plays out loud and 'when she reads a Play, she will put herself into a Sweat... distorting very agreeable Features'[47]). It is important that Pamela delivers this speech alone to an 'audience'. Her criticism of both tragedy and comedy discussed above hinges on the complaint that the playwrights were overly swayed by a 'friend' to corrupt the high purpose of the genre and should have sought to curb his exuberance. Pamela's robust individualism in all her appearances requires that she arrive at her judgement alone and express it in the face of others' cynicism (Mr B) or admiration (the young ladies whom she instructs). Pamela exercises sway and is not herself swayed by others. In this respect, too, despite her derogatory reference to the novel in the same breath as the romance, Pamela is the bearer of the values of novelisation, turning theatrical elements and information into narrative prose distanced from the space and place of the theatre itself.

Bethany Wong rightly diagnoses Pamela's one significant action in the novel as 'remediation', when a new form of media (the novel) absorbs that of an old (theatre). In letter thirty-five to Lady Davers, Pamela gives an account of the 'trial' she has staged in her closet before an audience of one, Mr B, apparently putting herself in the dock (she stands behind a row of chairs) inviting him to judge the virtue of her behaviour in the face of his suspected infidelity with the lively widowed Countess (who has pursued him since they met and flirted at the masquerade). Unlike Oldfield, Pamela stays firmly in character and her tragic effect on her audience has sway. Mr B admits 'there is Eloquence in your Eyes I cannot resist; but in your present solemn Air, and affecting Sentences, you mould me to every Purpose of

---

[46]   Ibid., p. 582.
[47]   Ibid, p. 569.

your Heart; so that I am a mere Machine, a passive Instrument, to be play'd upon at your Pleasure'.[48] Wong concludes that the 'process of remediation articulates how a traumatic confrontation in the playhouse helps Pamela to become a virtuous actress in the home'.[49]

Pamela's tragic maternity properly staged to her private audience (her spouse) overcomes the comic sprightliness of her rival queen, the Countess, proving the possibility of 'virtuous theatricality'. And moreover, with the relentless logic of Pamela's sway in Richardson's rendering of her character, the Countess too is brought into line. Her fascination with Mr B is converted into admiration for Pamela herself, through whom all future relationship with Mr B (he administers the Countess' estate while she heals her heart by an extended tour of Italy) is managed.

Pamela's appearances across all the four volumes that Richardson wrote are domestic stagings in which her mere presence teaches an audience how to behave virtuously. Unlike the actress, Pamela is not, of course, playing a part, but in some respects she might be seen as the kind of 'actress' Richardson's vision of the reforming sway of the novel imagines: she is an instrument for the growth of virtue to others, a model of natural virtue. In the second part, *Pamela in Her Exalted Condition*, Pamela's staged performances increasingly bring together the two forms of knowledge she studies in her little books: John Locke's theory of education and the stage play. The last letter of the sequel (letter sixty-four) has Pamela describe to Lady G a scene in the nursery in which her children are carefully placed about her, listening to her nursery tales in which good children are rewarded and naughty ones punished. The younger children are sent to bed leaving Pamela with her adopted daughter, Mr B's illegitimate offspring Miss Goodwin, now a teenager. Pamela tells Miss Goodwin a story about the varying fates of four pretty ladies (recalling perhaps the four young women we saw her instruct in the preceding letter): Coquetilla, Prudiana, Profusiana and Prudentia. Miss Goodwin swiftly recognises the virtuous fourth girl, Prudentia, as a version of Pamela and pledges to imitate her:

> O Madam! Madam; said the dear Creature, smothering me with her even clamorous Kisses, PRUDENTIA is YOU!—Is YOU indeed!—It *can* be nobody else! –O teach me, good GOD! to follow *your* Example, and I shall be a SECOND PRUDENTIA—Indeed I shall![50]

---

[48]   Ibid., *Pamela in Her Exalted Condition*, p. 423.
[49]   Bethany Wong, 'Pamela, Part ii: Richardson's Trial by Theatre', *Eighteenth-Century Fiction*, 29, no. 2 (Winter 2016–17), 182.
[50]   Richardson, *Pamela in her Exalted Condition*, ed. Rivero, p. 600.

There is irony here. Pamela has earlier acknowledged that Miss Goodwin has faults like those of her father (haughtiness and hastiness).[51] The story is designed to reform those faults just as the instructional scene with the four young ladies in the previous letter did. Pamela's behaviour is to be imitated but it must be learnt by young readers with faults, where Pamela needed no instruction. We have already seen a potential repetition of the story of her own courtship founder, when Pamela's serving maid Polly Barlow gives in to a dalliance with Lady Davers' nephew, Jackey. Polly is not Pamela. Pamela is *in*imitable. And in this staged scene of cautionary education, Richardson once again asserts his own creative property over the character he invented. Richardson remediates Pamela as Pamela remediates drama (under guise of romance) as novel. Pamela reforms others through the sway of a remediated storytelling; she converts romance and stage drama into novelistic affect, which reorients her audience to virtue.

---

[51] Pamela acknowledges to Lady Davers that she has concealed Miss Goodwin's faults in describing her to her biological mother in Jamaica. She 'is a sweet pretty Dear; but permit me to say, has a little of her Papa's Spirit; hasty, yet generous and acknowledging, when she is convinc'd of her Fault' (letter 48, p. 487).

Chapter 10
The Expanse of Character: Ranger

The unreformed rake, Jackey, of Samuel Richardson's *Pamela* was played in Giffard's dramatic adaptation (opened 9 November 1741 at Goodman's Fields) by a young actor, one David Garrick. Garrick fever had taken off less than three weeks earlier with the twenty-four-year-old actor's subversive transformation of the part of Richard III: the one tragic part for which Colley Cibber – co-author of *The Provok'd Husband* and of a memoir of his own life which had enjoyed double-billing with *Pamela* as the publishing sensation of 1740 – had been celebrated. Jackey was the first newly written part Garrick took, and it set the terms for a comic type with which he continued to be associated: the flamboyant, energetic rake, more camp than predatory.

Garrick's *tour de force* in the part was Jackey's reading out of a letter in *Franglais* (that Garrick had himself composed) from a Swiss villain named Colebrand to Mrs Jewkes, revealing Colebrand's bigamous turpitude. In 1747 Garrick extended his rakish repertoire further when he played this type in two different incarnations at Covent Garden: on 17 January he debuted as the fashion-addict effeminate suitor Fribble in a farcical two-act afterpiece of his own composition, *Miss in Her Teens*,[1] and the play ran for forty nights in that one season. And on 12 February he assumed the role of the rakish Ranger in a new five-act comedy *The Suspicious Husband* by Benjamin Hoadly at Covent Garden. It was a role he was to play more than 120 times over the next thirty years, the part he performed most often from his huge repertory.[2]

The name of this stage rake signifies a debt to and departure from earlier versions of the type (and throughout his career as playwright and actor Garrick aimed to revisit, revise, adapt older parts and plays). The rake by definition is an invader of other's space, breaking into polite homes,

---

[1] Garrick, David, *Miss in Her Teens; or the Medley of Lovers* (Dublin: S. Powell, 1747).
[2] Peter Thomson, 'Garrick, David (1717–1779), Actor and Playwright', in *Oxford Dictionary of National Biography*, 23 September 2004, https://ezproxy-prd. bodleian.ox.ac.uk:3030/view/10.1093/ref:odnb/9780198614128.001.0001/od-nb-9780198614128-e-10408 [accessed 29 February 2020].

penetrating the bodies of women. Aphra Behn's rake is a rover (Willmore of the 1677 *The Rover*), Hoadly's a ranger. However, Willmore is a drunk, a boor, a potential rapist, who trails mayhem in his greedy wake. Ranger, as his name implies (a ranger polices the borders and behaviour of an estate or park), moves around the stage and enters the (domestic) space of others driven by selfish but guileless sexual opportunism, but his witness eventually restores reputations, justice and right feeling. By April 1747 Garrick had manoeuvred himself into a position to take possession of the space he seems to have coveted for some time: the actor-manager of Drury Lane theatre sharing the patent with James Lacy. In role and in life, Garrick perfected the art of occupation.

If Pamela is a figure who consistently subjects other characters and discourses to her sway, drawing them into the domestic space that she theatricalises while disavowing her performances as an 'act' or a kind of 'acting', Ranger offers us an illustration of another, avowedly theatrical kind of character in the eighteenth century: one that depends on the association between the actor's body and the role s/he plays. Such characters often occupy and colonise spaces and places. In other words, they take themselves into territory and populate it with their own parts and props. Cormac Power identifies the charisma of the actor as a form of 'having presence', an 'auratic' effect.[3] And it appears that David Garrick's performance of Ranger was to have this kind of presence at first appearance on stage and in the character's relatively extensive afterlife in theatrical and other media. The part of Ranger, although it was taken by other actors in the course of its stage life, does not appear to have been conceived of in terms that excluded Garrick's presence. The memory of Garrick travelled with the part long after Garrick ceased to play it, in other performances of the role by other actors, and in Ranger's rich afterlife in other media.

Ranger's 'aura' is not that of the ritual or the sacred (an important feature of the auratic modernist theatre of Artaud and others). This was a part of intense and particular, positively eccentric, energy that came to encapsulate Garrick's stage character/presence. It rested in particular on corporeality: stage drunkenness requires a display of athleticism. And Ranger is a part associated with a different kind of verticality from Pamela's stalwart resistance to the attacks of other bodies. Ranger was most famous for shinning up a rope ladder on stage and appearing at the highest point of the stage looking out from a window stage to the boxes and galleries of the Covent Garden Theatre Royal. In the third act, Ranger has the stage to himself

---

[3]   See Cormac Power, chapter 2, 'Having Presence: The Auratic Mode of Presence', in *Presence in Play*, pp. 47–86.

and stumbles across the ladder. Ranger is evidently physically energetic and mentally agile, if to farcical effect:

> *Rang.* Hark!—Was not the Noise this Way—No—There is no Game stirring. This same Goddess, *Diana*, shines so bright with her Chastity, that egad! I believe the Wenches are asham'd to look her in the Face. Now I am in an admirable Mood for a Frolick! I have Wine in my Head, and Money in my Pocket, and so am furnish'd out for the cannonading any Countess in Christendom! Ha! What have we here! a Ladder! This cannot be placed here for nothing—and a Window open!—Is it Love, or Mischief now that is going on within?—I care not which—I am in a right Cue for either—Up I go—Stay—Do I not run a greater Chance of spoiling Sport than I do of making any? That I hate as much as I love the other—There can be no harm in seeing how the Land lies—I'll up (*Goes up softly*)—All is hush—Ha! a Light, and a Woman, by all that's lucky, neither old, nor crooked—I'll in—Ha! she is gone again! I will after her, (*Gets in at the Window.*) And for fear of the Squawls of Virtue, and the Pursuit of the Family, I will make sure of the Ladder. Now, Fortune, be my Guide.
> (*Exit with the Ladder.*)[4]

The part of the rake Ranger is characterised by Garrick's invasive actions – his occupation becomes one of occupying space. With no love-plot of his own, he invades those of others, causing confusion. His physical performance, his corporeality, occupies the attention of the play's audience at the expense of the numerous other performances around him. The retitling of the play attempts to step down Ranger in the hierarchy of stage character: the decision to title the play after the 'husband' seems to have been a relatively late decision in the work's conception and rehearsal. The manuscript was submitted to the Licenser as required ten days before first performance under the title 'The Rake'.[5] As elsewhere, the fiction of being is made through a process of unconcealment and withdrawal: Ranger occupies spaces, reveals himself (at windows, from closets, through side doors), causes disruption, and then retreats.

Contemporary biographers represented David Garrick in similar terms: as an expansive character in his verbal loquacity and his physical ubiquity, his stage busy-ness. Indeed, that characterisation may have been brought

---

4   *The Suspicious Husband* (London: J. and R. Tonson and S. Draper, 1747), Act 3, scene 1, pp. 34–5.
5   *The [[Rake]]*, LA63, The Huntington Library, San Marino, California.

into being through his success in the part of Ranger. In *The Life of David Garrick* (1801), Arthur Murphy concludes that '*Ranger*, as Garrick presented him, was the most sprightly, gay, frolicksome young rake that had ever been seen on the stage.'[6] The play's astounding first run only came to an end after twelve nights (it ran 12–25 February 1747) when Garrick fell ill.

Garrick's invasive occupation of roles that had previously belonged to others, and his usurpatory 'succession' to Colley Cibber in particular, was often commented upon.[7] In Hoadly's play he found a vehicle for this kind of action. Arthur Murphy remarks on the unacknowledged excellence of *Miss in Her Teens* and adds: 'To this piece succeeded in the month of February 1747, the *Suspicious Husband*, a comedy by Dr. Hoadley. This was the first good comedy from the time of the *Provoked Husband* in 1727; a long and dreary interval.'[8] Hoadly's play was surely invoking Cibber's earlier success as well as suggesting a new kind of 'reformed' comedy after the Licensing Act of 1737. In this play, it is the husband who reforms rather than the wife and in this play it is not the town that is at fault: the suspicious husband of the title, Mr Strictland, must learn to be less strict and to trust to the intrinsic virtue of his wife who moves in fashionable circles with civility, politeness and unquestionable loyalty to her marriage.

The craze for Garrick followed fast on the heels of that for Pamela in the early 1740s. Both were associated with the other literary *cause célèbre* of the time, Cibber's published memoirs of 1740. However, the supposed first-person writings of characters with charisma and sway (Cibber and Pamela) were also to some extent challenged – possibly even eclipsed – by the energetic presence of the new young actor commanding the London stage.[9] Quicksilver, comic, self-deprecating Ranger was the star attraction of Hoadly's play and Garrick's star turn.

Garrick and Ranger seem to have shaped each other's being. The physician Benjamin Hoadly was, along with his brother the Reverend John

---

[6] Arthur Murphy, *The Life of David Garrick*, 2 vols (London: J. Wright, 1801), vol. 1, p. 124.

[7] See Julia Fawcett, 'The Fate of Overexpression in the Age of Sentiment: David Garrick, George Anne Bellamy, and the Paradox of the Actor', chapter 4 of *Spectacular Disappearances*, pp. 136–72. Fawcett comments that Garrick's early performances aped the 'overexpressive disguises' of Cibber.

[8] Murphy, *Life of Garrick*, vol. 1, pp. 118–19.

[9] Hoadly's play was an adaptation of Ben Jonson's *Every Man in His Humour*. As Lorna Hutson observes, Hoadly's play defuses and suppresses the homosocial, potentially homo-erotic charge, between the two young men who are the heroes of the Jonson play. See Lorna Hutson, 'Liking Men: Ben Jonson's Closet Opened', *English Literary History*, 71, no. 4 (2004), 1065–96, p. 1088.

Hoadly, a close friend of Garrick's and both had aspirations to playwriting. Garrick reports to John in a letter of 19 August 1746 from Chelmsford:

> I had ye Pleasure of ye Doctor's Company to supper at My Lodgings the Night before, I set out for this Place; we talk'd about Ranger, but whether he will appear next Winter or Sleep for ever in ye Scritore, is not yet determin'd: tis pity faith—I am drinking the Waters Here as an Anti-Scorbutick—the Place is very dull, & I shall return soon to Town.[10]

Here, Garrick imagines his own being occupied by the part of Ranger as a means of waking him from illness and dullness. Putting Ranger on stage will both wake up the actor and the part (Ranger currently 'sleeps' in the playscript in the writer's desk). Ranger's life circumstances and his idiom bear close resemblance to what we know of the actor who played him. The part was clearly written with Garrick in mind; in the meeting between Hoadly and Garrick at Garrick's lodgings it is not clear whether discussion is about the part of Ranger or the play as a whole referred to by its (then) lead character and this is surely the point. Ranger is the play and the play is Ranger. Or at least in an ambitious young actor's imagination. But it is also the case that the playwright may have drawn on Garrick's own history to give his character the backstory that drives him to action in the play.

The play opens in Ranger's chambers, where he has returned after a hard night's revelling in order to resume his legal studies. The young David Garrick abandoned the legal career his father planned for him when his father died suddenly in March 1737, only days after David had been enrolled at Lincoln's Inn Fields. The text Ranger is studying turns out to be a love poem by William Congreve referred to by Ranger as 'a Man after my own Heart'.[11] Ranger paces the stage sending his servant Simon for news from the coffee house, reading a letter from his cousin Clarinda, flirting with a pretty milliner who brings him goods, and greeting his friend Bellamy. Whenever Ranger appears on stage he acts as a catalyst to the action and is consistently aware of his own aspiration to break in and enter (conversations, domestic spaces, the bodies of attractive women). He inclines to speak of himself in the third person, especially in announcing his own entrances. In the second act he interrupts a conversation between his two friends, Bellamy and Frankly, as they confess to each other that they are both in love:

---

[10]   David Garrick, 'To the Reverend John Hoadly', in *The Letters of David Garrick*, ed. David M. Little and George M. Kahrl, 3 vols (London: Oxford University Press, 1963), vol. 1, p. 84.

[11]   *Suspicious Husband*, Act 1, scene 1, p. 2.

Bella. Pshaw! *Ranger* here!
Rang. Yes, *Ranger* is here, and perhaps does not come so impertinently as you may imagine. Faith! I think I have the knack of finding out Secrets.[17]

Later, he uses the third person to persuade himself to perform the part of the rake when he finds himself with an opportunity to make advances to a young single woman in a bedchamber:

Rang. By Heaven she comes! ah, honest *Ranger*, I never knew thee fail!—
Jacin. Pray, Sir, where did you leave this Hat?[13]

When Ranger realises her innocence, distress and commitment to his friend Bellamy he discontinues his pursuit and aids Jacintha in making her escape in male disguise from the house to elope with her lover. More often than not Ranger confounds rather than confirms the character type of the rake. Luckily, other characters have little difficulty in recognising him – nor his failure to conform to the type of the predatory rake he affects to assume. In the fourth act, Ranger is still dialoguing with his rakish persona, this time in the second person. His cousin Clarinda hides her real identity behind a mask and teases him by encouraging some flirtation. Ranger comments aside: 'By her Forwardness, this should be a Whore of Quality. My Boy *Ranger*, thou art in luck to-day.'[14] Clarinda tells him that she has no trouble identifying him through a set of distinctive mannerisms: 'The pretty Stagger in your Gait, that happy Disposition of your Wig, the genteel Negligence of your whole Person, and those pretty Flowers of modish Gallantry made it impossible to mistake you, my sweet Cuz.'[15]

In his development of the role of Ranger, Garrick refined his portrayal of effeminate rakes explicitly identified as heterosexual in their orientation (from Fribble in his comic interlude *Miss in Her Teens* of 1747 onward). He promoted a kind of gentrified manliness by mocking the ineffectual sexuality of men who displayed feminine manners (such as Ranger), while declaring a predatory interest in women. In so doing he contributed to attempts to counter the perception of an increased effeminacy in British masculinity (complained about after the near-defeat at the hands of Jacobites in the

---

[12]　Benjamin Hoadly, *The Suspicious Husband*, Act 2, scene 4, p. 27.
[13]　Ibid., Act 3, scene 3, p. 43.
[14]　Ibid., Act 4, scene 4, p. 57.
[15]　Ibid., Act 4, scene 4, p. 58.

rebellion of 1745). Garrick's brand of manliness also stressed the symbolic and political capital of a modern politeness – as opposed to what was seen as an outdated militarised masculine aggression, or exclusive interaction between men in heterosocial exchange, such as that represented in the play's source: Jonson's *Every Man*.[16]

Ranger's frenzied but unproductive stage activity tends to impede and complicate the plans of his friends and his cousin Clarinda. Bellamy is courting Mrs Strictland's ward, Jacintha, but Mr Strictland refuses the match. It transpires that the woman with whom Frankly has fallen madly in love at Bath is a friend of Mrs Strictland's, the very same Clarinda. On a drunken night out, Ranger scales the rope ladder which has been thrown out of the window of the Strictlands' home to enable the escape of Jacintha who has donned male clothing. He encounters Mrs Strictland at her toilet and makes advances to her before hiding when Mr Strictland enters having retrieved Jacintha. Jacintha covers for Mrs Strictland when Ranger's discarded hat is spotted, claiming it as part of her own male disguise. When Jacintha is left alone, Ranger tries his hand with her, but on realising her identity he produces the ladder and aids her escape, conducting her to the house of his friend Jack Meggot in order to reunite her with Bellamy. Confusion of identities leads Frankly and Bellamy to challenge each other to a duel. Mr Strictland casts his wife out of the house convinced of her infidelity and she gains refuge with Clarinda. Clarinda and Ranger engineer a meeting at Meggot's house of all the parties. The two young couples are united and Ranger testifies to Mrs Strictland's innocence, procuring her husband's apologies to her and Strictland's promise not to indulge his jealousy in future.

Garrick's invasive presence in the part of Ranger was a matter for comment in a celebrity-obsessed press. In 1759 a pamphlet characterised Garrick as such a ubiquitous and mesmerising performer that no other actor was visible to the audience; the part of Ranger served as the most striking example. The play is in fact rather overcrowded with rake figures: Jack Meggot was also much admired for his foolish, rakish cosmopolitanism, but after a strong entrance confabulating with the two young suitors, Frankly and Bellamy, in the second act he disappears until the final act, apparently out-raked by Ranger. The pamphlet author complains that

---

[16] On the figure of the 'fribble' as a sign of gender and national anxiety in mid-century British culture manifested in 'effeminophobia', see Declan Kavanagh, "'Of Neuter Gender, tho' of *Irish* Growth": Charles Churchill's Fribble', *Irish University Review*, 43, no. 1 (2013), 119–30; and Declan Kavanagh, *Effeminate Years: Literature, Politics, and Aesthetics in Mid-Eighteenth-Century Britain* (Lewisburg, PA: Bucknell University Press, 2017).

Garrick's performance as Ranger eclipses those of the other male parts he knows from this reading of the part:

> when I go to see the *Suspicious Husband,* there I see Mr. *Garrick* in the part of *Ranger*; and sure no man will deny, but that he plays that part, better than any other man in the world; But will any person be so hardy as to tell me, I shall part with my money, to see *honest Ranger* only; I want to see *Frankly* and *Bellamy* and ratling *Jack Meggot*; I would willingly see Mr. *Strictland*; the character, who gives title to the Comedy, yet am I herein debarred, by Mr. *Garrick's* intrusion, for when he appears on the stage, I am so blinded, either by prejudice or admiration, that I can see no body else; I can hear no body else; I can bear no body else.[17]

Garrick's capacity to occupy every spectator's line of vision was not unconnected to his dexterity with the two props of such significance in his breaking and entering: the rope ladder and the hat. Character in this instance is marked by accessories. Interior truth or sincerity – and the good heart that beats behind Ranger's raffish exterior is of course essential to the success of this new sentimental drama – is not what makes this character distinctive: it is rather his association with and deft handling of stage props. Most celebrated was the business and bustle with a rope ladder which physically raised Garrick vertically in the audience's line of sight as well as providing him with a heightened view of and out from the stage.

That Garrick continued to play a part requiring an athletic sprint up a rope ladder became the subject of some humour as he aged. Reverend Williams asks Garrick:

> you come out often in Don Felix, Ranger, Archer, etc.—what can this mean? Do you think you are not growing old?... In Ranger, you mount the ladder fast enough; too fast; perhaps from a desire of appearing active. Yet if there were not an inch of your face to be seen, I should guess nearly at your age.—But your face: —I am sorry to look into it, when you personate the tender and amorous youth. *Your wrinkled visage and lack-lustre eye*, should never be held out on such occasions.[18]

---

[17] *Reasons why David Garrick, Esq. should not appear on the Stage, In a Letter to John Rich, Esq.* (London: J. Cooke, 1759), pp. 10–11.

[18] David Williams, *A letter to David Garrick, Esq. On his conduct as Principal Manager and Actor at Drury-Lane* (London: S. Bladon, 1772), pp. 32–3.

Garrick is trying too hard it appears; his athleticism is forced rather than natural. If his legs do not give him away by failing him, his face does, a face exposed when he leaves his hat on the table for the young breeches-dressed Jacintha to claim as her own. Paradoxically, an ageing Garrick playing Ranger might be seen to be fulfilling the demands of the role rather than failing them. Ranger plays the part of a rake but he is indeed all mouth and no trousers. He gains entry to the Strictlands' house, yet does not act on the sexual threat he presents to the women within. Indeed, he proves relatively gallant. Ranger's occupations of theatrical space, the sight and minds of his audience, remain superficial and none the less attractive for that – just as his character is signalled through the props he handles and that decorate the surface of his body. As we have seen with Pamela, the projection of a depth or sophistication of mind is not a requirement in the making of fictional presence-effect and its concentration in a single fictional person who occupies multiple spaces and subject-positions in both mimetic and diegetic telling.

Julia Fawcett also recognises this quality in Garrick's performances and sees parallels with the novel heroine, Pamela, whose novelty in the 1740s similarly rests on a claim to earnestness, a new sincerity or naturalism. However, Fawcett points out that Garrick manages the risks and exposure of celebrity by making character all surface and role. She notes that young actors imitated his superficial energy, but at a point when it had already become hackneyed and overfamiliar. In 1757 *The Theatrical Examiner* reports on this phenomenon: 'You observe all the young actors start, jump, and Garrickize, which is the true reason there is none of them tolerable, and that the public so soon let them fall from the pinnacle they are at first set on.'[19] It seems that the precarious mounting of Ranger's ladder infects this account of the risky mountings of his imitators. To Garrickize, Fawcett concludes, is to present 'performances that allow the body to avoid scrutiny by seeming to bare all.'[20]

Despite the mockery of his failure to live up to his own character as he aged, it was the part of Ranger that Garrick chose for his two retirement performances in 1776. And it is one of these performances that Evelina attends in Frances Burney's comic epistolary novel of 1778.[21] Reference to attending plays, to playhouses and to performances plays an important

[19]   *Theatrical Examiner: An Enquiry into the Merits and Demerits of the Present English Performers in General* (London: J. Doughty, 1757), p. 31.
[20]   Julia Fawcett, *Spectacular Disappearances*, p. 163.
[21]   See Paula Backscheider, 'Shadowing Theatrical Change', in *Players, Playwrights, Playhouses: Investigating Performance, 1660–1800* (Basingstoke: Palgrave Macmillan, 2007), pp. 78–101, pp. 81–3.

part, as it does here, in constructing the naturalistic reality-effects of contemporary fiction. Shortly after arriving in London, the country ingénue Evelina Villars is beside herself with excitement about attending a performance of David Garrick as Ranger at Drury Lane. She writes from Queen Anne Street on Saturday 2 April to her guardian the Reverend Villars:

> This moment arrived. Just going to the Drury-Lane theatre. The celebrated Mr. Garrick performs Ranger. I am quite in extacy. So is Miss Mirvan. How fortunate, that he should happen to play! We would not let Mrs. Mirvan rest till she consented to go; her chief objection was to our dress, for we have had no time to *Londonize* ourselves; but we teized her into compliance, and so we are to sit in some obscure place, that she may not be seen. As to me, I should be alike unknown in the most conspicuous or most private part of the house.[22]

On her return that evening, Evelina cannot wait to record her excitement:

> O my dear Sir, in what raptures am I returned! Well may Mr. Garrick be so celebrated, so universally admired – I had not any idea of so great a performer.
>
> Such ease! such vivacity in his manner! such grace in his motions! Such fire and meaning in his eyes! – I could hardly believe he had studied a written part, for every word seemed to be uttered from the impulse of the moment.
>
> His action – at once so graceful and so free! – his voice – so clear, so melodious, yet so wonderfully various in its tones – such animation! – every look *speaks*!
>
> I would have given the world to have had the whole play acted over again. And when he danced – O how I envied Clarinda! I almost wished to have jumped on the stage and joined them.
>
> I am afraid you will think me mad, so I won't say any more; yet I really believe Mr. Garrick would make you mad too, if you could see him. I intend to ask Mrs. Mirvan to go to the play every night while we stay in town.[23]

---

[22]   Frances Burney, *Evelina, or a Young Lady's Entrance into the World* (1778), ed. Susan Kubica Howard, Broadview Literary Texts (Peterborough, ON: Broadview Press, 2000), letter 10, p. 116.

[23]   Ibid., pp. 116–17.

Evelina is seized by Garrick-mania. Like Partridge before her, the response to Garrick is a somatic and imitative one. Evelina finds herself yearning to leap into action, to move and dance like Garrick himself, while she apparently longs to take the place of his dancing partner. Clarinda in fact dances with her suitor Frankly while Ranger takes the hand of Mrs Strictland at the conclusion of the play. It may have been that Burney was adding a small compliment to her friend the actress Jane Barsanti, who took the sprightly comic part of Clarinda on a number of occasions. At Crow Street Theatre, Dublin on 21 May 1778 Barsanti took the part of Clarinda at a benefit of *The Suspicious Husband* on her behalf and delivered a farewell epilogue.[24] More importantly, however, in this scene, Burney, the young female author of a debut novel – a transformative experiment in a new naturalism, which was itself to acquire cult status – seeks connection to the celebrity of an ageing actor on the point of retirement. She does so through apparent affinity with the body of the actress he dances with. But, in a bold move, Burney substitutes the name of the part taken by her close friend and actress for that of the established actress who took the part of Mrs Strictland. And she also signals in this move the supremacy of the comic feminine mode in her own novel over the tragic styles of the sentimental heroines of earlier fiction.

The epistolary mode of *Evelina*'s telling offers an entirely different means of rendering character from the stage performances she refers to in this letter. Evelina is in public awkward, mute. Indeed, Lord Orville suspects she may be simple. Her observational wit, her quick intelligence, and her true virtue is visible to the readers of her letters. This version of interiority, the delivery of character through a first-person epistolary communication evidently designed on that of Pamela, is (as we have seen in the case of *Pamela*) profoundly anti-theatrical. This novel heroine, like Pamela, wins the love of a high-born gentleman through her integrity and wins the hearts of her audience not through a public performance – whether of sentiment or wit – but through the circulation of a 'private' correspondence that proves her virtue while preserving her physical modesty. In this account of Evelina's (restrained) longing to jump on stage and dance with the charismatic actors, Frances Burney both invokes a connection with stage conventions of character and marks the distance of her own work from those

---

[24] John Genest, *Some Account of the English Stage, from the Restoration in 1660 to 1830*, 10 vols (Bath: H.E. Carrington, 1832), vol. 5, p. 591. On Burney and Barsanti, see Gillian Skinner, "'An Unsullied Reputation in the Midst of Danger": Barsanti, Propriety and Performance in Burney's Early Journals and Letters', *Women's Writing*, 19, no. 4 (2012), 525–43.

conventions.[25] Here, Ranger's range and reach seem to be arrested and he gives way to a 'novel' kind of character. So too, the rakes of Evelina prove to be empty stagey figures (Mr Lovel, Sir Clement Willoughby, Lord Merton) who prove no real threat to the integrity of the virtuous heroine. They are the afterlife of an exhausted Ranger in the new world of the novel, a world governed (invisibly and offstage) by women.

Ranger had a life in fictions of less distinction and subtlety than Frances Burney's *Evelina*. In these works, paradoxically it might seem, his hybrid vigour as a fictional character who could stray easily between page and stage, between role and actor, was the very ground of the work's fabrications, rather than one among a number of other effects that add realist texture to a work of polite and sentimental fiction such as *Evelina*.

Works by two male writers in the mid-1750s (at the height of Garrick's success) exploit the ranging reputation of Garrick's *Ranger*, making him the central character in a series of ramblings. Both the periodical eidolon and the picaresque hero have close kinship with the strolling player, and their ramblings in metropolitan and rural environments frequently venture into the stage-play world.[26] A young Irish banker, Arthur Murphy, embarked on a career writing for London periodicals before he took to the stage as actor and author at the end of the decade. After a series of contributions to the *Craftsman*, Murphy launched a single-authored weekly periodical on 29 September 1753. The fictional author, Charles Ranger, speaks as one already known to the public (through the *Craftsman* essays we presume, but perhaps also through the histrionic associations of his name). He is apprehensive of 'my new form of Appearance' which is 'sitting about me like a new Fashion'; the flamboyant effeminate stage rake is recalled here, not least in the fact that this writer is also a lawyer-in-training who promises to expose the 'Vices, Follies, and Foibles' of his Gray's-Inn world.[27]

Like Garrick in his, Ranger aims to clean up his profession: he will not include adverts 'only fit for an Hospital or a Brothel' and aims 'to promote useful Mirth and good Humour'.[28] Like his namesake, this Ranger has a habit of entering the parlours and dressing rooms of women; in his second

---

[25] See James Evan's discussion of *Evelina's* treatment of a different actor, Frances Abington, in the role of Miss Prue: '*Evelina*, the Rustic Girls of Congreve and Abington, and Surrogation in the 1770s', *The Eighteenth Century*, 52, no. 2 (Spring 2011), 157–71.

[26] On the periodical eidolon, see Manushag Powell, *Performing Authorship in Eighteenth-Century Periodicals* (Lewisburg, PA: Bucknell University Press, 2012).

[27] Arthur Murphy, *The Gray's Inn Journal, by Charles Ranger, Esq.* (London: W. Faden and J. Bouquet, 1753), no. 1, p. 2.

[28] Ibid., p. 4.

number, he asks female readers to dismiss their servants and mantua-makers and make room for him (his paper):

> I am aware that the Ladies will be alarmed at the Thought of being alone with *Ranger*, but the Reason of my desiring this Dismission of so many Favorites, is, because I profess the very same Art, to which that Class of People have always aspired, that of heightening the Charms of Female Beauty.[29]

This Rambler cannot resist venturing into the world of the stage, writing papers about acting (number four), Macbeth (number eight), King Lear (numbers sixteen and seventeen), the vindication of Shakespeare in a letter to Voltaire (number twelve), pantomime (number twenty-eight), tragedy (number forty-eight), comedy (number forty-nine). Like the stage Ranger, this paper Ranger has a habit of addressing himself in the third person. The eleventh number (8 December 1753) finds Ranger in a conversation with his Soul, which is rendered on the page as a playscript. Ranger warns his Soul that people are complaining: 'you are too fond of mentioning Players' and the Soul admits that 'there is a Performer on the Stage, who has upon many occasions surprized me with new Lights in Passages that were before obscure, and who has often had an irresistible Power over my Passions': David Garrick no doubt.[30]

In the fourth number (20 October 1753), the 'Intelligencer' letters and reports that are appended to his regular essay include one from a Charlotte Ramble who writes: 'Pray, Sir, are you any Relation to *Ranger* on the Stage; he's a dear man, and I shall love you the better for his Sake.'[31] 'Charles Ranger' answers:

MADAM,

> If you mean *Harlequin Ranger*, let what will be the Consequence, I must disown the Kindred; but if you intend Mr. Garrick's *Ranger*, it is with pleasure I inform you, that we are nearly related; and to shew you how desirous I am of your Esteem, I wish it were in my Power to make as striking a Figure in my Province, as that Gentleman does in his; and so, Madam, as my Cousin says, "My Service to your Monkey".[32]

---

[29] Ibid., no. 2 (6 October 1753), p. 7.
[30] Ibid., p. 64.
[31] Arthur Murphy, *The Gray's Inn Journal*, p. 23.
[32] Ibid., no. 4, 20 October 1753, p. 24.

Charles Ranger here quotes his 'kindred' predecessor's parting quip to his friend Jack Meggot in Hoadly's play. Ranger, Frankly and Bellamy part from each other at the end of the first scene of the fourth act, Frankly and Bellamy to seek out the women they love and Ranger to seek attention from some 'kind Wench or other'. Ranger's parting shot to the fourth man, Meggot, is the immortal line 'My Service to your Monkey', suggesting Meggot's lack of success with or lack of interest in women (a pet monkey is his source of pleasure and dalliance). The line is also another mark of Ranger's capacity to blunder mistakenly with ignorance into sensitive territory, since Meggot has earlier reported the sad death of his monkey, Otho, to the other young men about town but Ranger the 'Rattlepate' has not taken note of the news.[33] The line also, however, suggests an affinity between Meggot's monkey and Ranger himself: physically deft and mischief-making but without powers of reflection or anticipation.

In playing the very physical part of Ranger, Garrick brought himself close to the non-verbal and clowning elements of pantomime he often criticised. In the previous number of the *Gray's Inn Journal* of 13 October 1753, Charles Ranger expresses his surprise that Garrick had countenanced the playing of a pantomime on the Drury Lane stage after his well-canvassed dislike of the purely physical comedy. 26 December 1751 saw the first performance of *Harlequin Ranger* at Drury Lane by Henry Woodward, with Woodward in the title role. This was the second of six pantomimes by Woodward that Garrick reluctantly staged in the 1750s in order to compete with the rival Covent Garden stage and John Rich's fame as an author, performer and manager of pantomime. More than likely, Harlequin's powers of escapology and gymnastic prowess entailed some stage business with a rope ladder in the production. Murphy is then comically referencing his own impersonation of Ranger and claiming a kinship with Garrick's standout performance of a part that combined verbal and physical agility, by association with Woodward's pantomimic imitation. In so doing, he both defers to and promotes Garrick's claims to be enhancing and promoting polite and gentlemanly comedy. Garrick was often referred to as 'Roscius' by pundits and admirers. Quintus Roscius (c.126 BC–62 BC), the Roman actor, was born a slave but rose to pre-eminence for his skill in mimicry; he was especially admired for elevating Roman acting from coarse comic clowning to moderate art.

In 1801, twenty-two years after Garrick's death, Arthur Murphy published his two-volume *Life of David Garrick*. By the time he composed this work, Murphy had enjoyed the benefit of working closely with Garrick. A

---

[33]   *The Suspicious Husband*, Act 4, scene 1, p. 47.

friendship with Samuel Johnson, commenced in 1754, led to Murphy taking to the Covent Garden stage as an actor to try and address a £300 debt. Garrick was the manager who staged a number of his plays at Drury Lane in the late 1750s.[34] Murphy continued to write for the periodical press with a special interest in theatrical criticism. However, his biography of Garrick came late to a crowded field and one that had consistently elided Garrick's life with his most famous roles and that of Garrick's *éminence grise*, William Shakespeare.[35]

Edward Kimber, traveller, travel-writer and editor of the *London Magazine* from 1755, published in 1756 a two-volume fictionalised biography of Garrick with the title *The Juvenile Adventures of David Ranger, Esq.* This was the third of those works Simon Dickie terms 'ramble novels' (episodic, comic novels)[36] in which Kimber was to build such reputation as he did as a novelist: *The Life and Adventures of Joe Thompson* had already enjoyed great success in 1750 and went into six editions. *The Life and Adventures of James Ramble, Esq.* (1755) was set in the time of the 1715 Jacobite uprising and sent its hero on an expedition to Cuba.[37] The title of this third work in the same vein – a young man gets into comic scrapes in his travels – was surely meant to attract readers who may have thought they were offered a peek into the life of David Garrick or the backstory of one of his famous roles, Ranger, or some version of both. In the event, they got neither, although the early and later parts of the narrative do suggest some relation to the known facts of Garrick's life despite giving him an Irish origin and extended kinship that Garrick did not in fact share. The title page claims the work to be that of an original manuscript found in the collection of an old Lord and sets a quotation by Shakespeare ('All the World's a Stage!') above another from Garrick's prologue to his adaptation of the former's *Winter's Tale*:

---

[34] *The Apprentice*, a farce, was performed on 2 January 1756 at Drury Lane. Other plays staged there were the farce *The Spouter*, the tragedy *The Orphan of Tragedy* (21 April 1759), *The Desert Island* and *The Way to Keep Him* (both 1760).

[35] Thomas Davies, *Memoirs of the Life of David Garrick* (London: for the Author, 1780), was the first of many. See Cheryl Wanko, 'David Garrick and the Authority of the Celebrity', in her *Roles of Authority*; on the numerous portraits and Garrickiana, see Shearer West, *The Image of the Actor: Verbal and Visual Representation in the Age of Garrick and Kemble* (New York: St Martin's Press, 1991).

[36] Simon Dickie, 'Tobias Smollett and the Ramble Novel', in *The Oxford History of the Novel in English: Volume Two: English and British Fiction 1750–1820*, ed. Peter Garside and Karen O'Brien (Oxford: Oxford University Press, 2015), pp. 92–108.

[37] J.A. Downie, 'Novels of the 1750s', in *The Oxford Handbook of the Eighteenth-Century Novel* (Oxford: Oxford University Press, 2016), pp. 252–63, p. 258.

Hence, for the choicest Spirits flow Champaign,
Whose sparkling Atoms shoot thro' ev'ry Vein;
Hence, flow, for martial minds, Potation strong,
And sweet Love Potions, for the Fair and Young.
For you, my Hearts of Oak, for your Regale,
Here's good Old English Stingo mild and stale.

Hoadly's Ranger is first introduced to his audience after a long night's drinking and he aspires to be considered a womaniser. As we have seen, Garrick turned politeness into an art form that raised common and popular traditions into new gentility. Here, English 'stingo', a dark brown ale, is offered to a British audience (the 'Hearts of Oak'). Shakespeare is both a familiar form of entertainment (good old English ale) and a new one, or one made new by Garrick (expelling French fashionable stimulants such as champagne and potions administered to soldiers and young lovers). Here too, the effect is one of assimilation and appropriation.

Likewise, Kimber's hero David Ranger is celebrated in the same terms as Garrick had been: as a naturaliser of performance and as a reformer of the morals not only of the members of his acting company but also his audience. By the tenth chapter of the second volume, David Ranger has been elevated to manager of the London Theatre Royal:

> the publick began to see performances introduced, whose natural abilities and talents were adapted to the parts they exhibited; who were, by nature, form'd to inculcate moral instruction; and who, in private life, were inoffensive and amiable, who, in short, followed the example of their master. Those dramatick productions, which do honour to our nation and language were revived, and the immortal *Shakespear* shone with that lustre and fire that none but a *Ranger* could have given him. But the taste of the town was so perverted to the unmeaning buffoonery of pantomime and entertainment, that, even, against his will and judgment, something of that kind was to be reserved – the vulgar of the twelvepenny gallery must still have somewhat to propagate the roar: However, even these exotic productions were new modelled, and made more subservient to good sense and contrivance.[38]

High and low (Shakespeare and pantomime) are remodelled by David Ranger/Garrick, Kimber argues, in ways that promote national virtue. In

[38] Edward Kimber, *The Juvenile adventures of David Ranger, Esq.*, 2nd ed., 2 vols (London: J. Stevens, 1757), vol. 2, pp. 217–18.

this respect, Kimber follows suit, shaping a new kind of fiction ('ramble fiction') not only from the familiar genres of picaresque and romance, but also the theatrical fragments of Garrick's reputation as an actor and manager. Central to this process is the recollection of one of Garrick's most celebrated roles: the young warm-hearted rake Ranger. Ranger's rambling spirit is especially well-suited to the picaresque tradition that Kimber revives here for a modern audience deeply literate in the Georgian stage.

The Critical Review warned its readers:

> The Title of this Piece, together with the Motto annexed, is a mean artifice apparently made use of to mislead the reader into an opinion, that these are the secret memoirs of our modern *Roscius*.... The character hath not the least resemblance to the person so artfully squinted at in the first page of it, being nothing but a heap of ridiculous adventures, and some bad poetry by the author; with scraps of plays, ballads, &c. quoted to eke out a trifling and miserable performance.[39]

Kimber's Ranger, like other libidinous young heroes with essentially good hearts in the picaresque tradition, is largely engaged in romantic scrapes. Those scrapes point both to David Garrick and to the role of Ranger. Richard Ranger, a Cork merchant, lives in Playhouse Street with his wife Penelope who raises David, the youngest of five children, with a passion for tragedy:

> One effect of his mamma's bent of mind, it was not possible to guard him against; she had not only read plays before him, but had initiated her son into the tragick stile and manner. Already he pronounced the word *farewell* in the accent and with the emphasis of the stage, could soliloquy with *Hamlet,* and stab himself with *Cato,* and what the good gentlewoman seem'd only to suffer him to be diverted with, soon became the passion of his soul. In dying agonies he had already measured every carpet in the house and, young as he was, was become a finish'd lover, which his innocent sister had often experienced in a tender embrace, and every glass had witness'd *attitudes* that were surprizingly perfect for his years.[40]

David Ranger, like Garrick, perfects the art of stage dying. Like Garrick he is short and energetic with mobile features that charm: 'tho' his stature was

---

[39]   *The Critical Review: or, Annals of Literature. By a Society of Gentlemen* (London: R. Baldwin, 1756), vol. 2, Article 19, p. 379.

[40]   Ibid., vol. 1, chapter 2, pp. 14–15.

not of the most elevated, yet the symmetry and proportion of his limbs and features, and the easy *je ne sçay quoy* politeness of his behaviour, suffer'd that disadvantage to slip the observation of all those who saw him.'[41] Like Garrick he engages in affairs with fellow actors: Maria McCarthy, Irish heiress who runs away to join Ranger in pursuing a career on the stage, appears to be a version of Garrick's mistress, Peg Woffington. Miss Amiable, the young actress he trains but ultimately refuses as a wife because of her promiscuity, may point to George Anne Bellamy who played Juliet at the age of nineteen to his thirty-three-year-old Romeo at Drury Lane in 1750.

Like Hoadly's Ranger, Kimber's David Ranger is a loyal friend and enabler of other men. More particularly, like Garrick, he forms a close friendship with a fellow actor. Captain MacKenzie, the strolling player David meets in a tavern and whose acting company he joins for his first professional stage appearances, is a version of the Irish actor, Charles Macklin. In the second volume of the *Juvenile Adventures*, Davy saves MacKenzie from attempted suicide and restores him to mental equilibrium. Macklin appeared with Garrick on many occasions at Drury Lane, but he did also appear with him when Garrick played Ranger; Macklin took the part of Strictland for the first performance at the rival house, Drury Lane, of *The Suspicious Husband* of 5 December 1747. Before that, however, he had composed and seen into production for one night only a short play, *The New Play Criticiz'd*, which was performed on 24 March 1747 at Drury Lane, only a month after *The Suspicious Husband* had debuted at Covent Garden.[42] Here, the envious critic Canker waits at his house hoping that the audience at Covent Garden will be disappointed by the performance underway of *The Suspicious Husband*. Mrs Chatter visits and raves about the charms of Ranger, considering his talk of ropes and the leaving of his hat as the funniest part of the performance:

> I think M[r]. Ranger the Templer is a charming Fellow! O Lud! I protest I shou'd not care to trust myself with him in his Chambers – well he made me laugh a thousand times tonight, with his going up the Ladder of Ropes, and then into the Ladies Chamber, and his dropping his Hat, and his going to Ravish Jacyntha, and a thousand comical things – but he brings all off at last.[43]

---

[41]   Ibid., p. 15.
[42]   MSS *The New Play Criticiz'd; or, The Plague of Envy (The Suspicious Husband Criticized; or, The Plague of Envy)*, LA64, The Huntington Library, San Marino, California, p. 3.
[43]   Ibid.

Harriet, Lady Critick's independent-spirited niece, is equally charmed and declares that she only needs a rope ladder and breeches to emulate Jacintha and escape the match her aunt plans for her with Canker. She offers Canker an ultimatum: to attend the new comedy and applaud it to show his good temper, or abandon his aspiration to her hand. His inability to comply leaves her free to pursue her romance with the attractive Heartly.

Macklin's script invokes a particular charm of the character of Ranger: the physical and verbal agility that positioned him between pantomime harlequin and rake-hero at the forefront of the new stage comedy. These characteristics also made him an attractive figure to adapt to the mid-century novel. Like Tom Jones, David Ranger is a likeable innocent abroad in a recognisable contemporary landscape. He can serve as the vehicle for a new kind of polite heteronormative masculinity, assimilating the rake's energies while still promoting virtuous domestic union and re-imagining the stage repertory company as honest family rather than vagrant robbers.

In 1760, Ranger featured in another miscellaneous work, although not one of prose fiction: *Ranger's Progress: Consisting of a Variety of Poetical Essays, Moral, Serious, Comic, and Satyrical. By Honest Ranger, of Bedford-Row*. The collection of poems mixes elements from Hoadly's play (including two poems addressed to the ever-popular Jack Meggot) and elements utterly unrelated (a poem to William Pitt, another to one Mr Doggrel). The anonymous author defends his own preface by distinguishing between his own propriety and the failures of his namesake. Unlike Hoadly's Ranger this Ranger announces himself with a measure of rectitude:

> To let a new Book bounce into the World without a Preface, is like a Person's running into a strange House without first knocking at the Door; therefore I think it just in me to say something by way of introducing my Performance. And first, I beg of all such Readers as I am a Stranger to, to peruse with *Patience*, to judge with *Tenderness*, and condemn with *Mercy*.[44]

Here the rhetorical trope of *occupatio* (an assertion made in the act of disavowal) serves to mark the persistent presence of the Ranger character in mid-century fiction; and also the passage of a stage performance in the embodied form of a celebrity actor (Garrick) into a recurrent persona for the new mediations of print narrative. Murphy, Kimber, the anonymous

---

[44] 'Preface', in *Ranger's Progress: Consisting of a Variety of Poetical Essays, Moral, Serious, Comic, and Satyrical. By Honest Ranger, of Bedford-Row* (London: Printed for the Author, 1760), p. iii.

compiler of Honest Ranger's 'poetical essays' reform Ranger himself. The latter confesses that he has not taste for gambling, drinking, or traducing the fair sex. His sole compulsion is an 'itch for scribbling'.[45] Writing rather than performance has become the signature mark of Ranger's character.

We have seen, then, Ranger's expansion from a debut part for David Garrick to a fictional presence in a variety of other plays and into prose fictions. As with *Pamela* the passage from corporeal to textual performance is attended by strengthened claims for the character's capacity to reform: and by extension for the 'new' forms he occupies to reform the stage. In this case, however, an actor's self-conscious projection of a form of authorial presence interacts with the character of the role he played, a character clearly written with that actor in mind. Leslie Mitchell speaks of Garrick's '[s]elf-manufactured anticipatory critique' in establishing his control over his contemporary mediascape.[46] Garrick owned newspapers and magazines and actively deployed a variety of media to promote his career and the institutions he managed. As we have seen in the case of the stage Licensing Act of 1737, control of media is not always or only effected through censorship. *Occupatio*, disavowal as a form of assertion, generates presence-effects that endow a character with agency. Indeed, the passage from unconcealment to withdrawal is everywhere evident in Garrick's self-characterisation: as, for example, in his description of the period of Ranger's composition in which both actor and part oscillate between wakefulness and sleep. Bringing Ranger to life, into being, shapes the presence-effect of the performer and the part. Periods of life-lessness, of rest, of pausing, are part of that process: a process we shall see Laurence Sterne turn into an integral part of his narrator, Tristram Shandy's, self-invention through the imitation of and encounter with David Garrick.

[45] Ibid.
[46] Leslie Mitchell, *David Garrick and the Mediation of Celebrity* (Cambridge: Cambridge University Press, 2019), p. 8.

Chapter 11
The Play of Character: Tristram

Laurence Sterne owned a copy of Kimber's *The Juvenile Adventures of David Ranger*.[1] It may have spoken to his own keen sense of the pleasures found in playful slippage between performance and person. *The Life and Opinions of Tristram Shandy, Gentleman* (1759–67) is an example of a version of character we have yet to encounter: where the author is 'so adeptly grafted' to the main protagonist or character of his work that the two can hardly be distinguished.[2] Here, character becomes a kind of play-acting, a game of presence and absence performed on the page and in person in ways that promote a sense of a 'real' body manifesting a fictional identity through a variety of signature moves – which were nonetheless understood to bring a new form of naturalism and authenticity to the world of fiction.

Character as play is manifest in the comical transference of a set of qualities from one generation to another in Sterne's fiction, presented as a form of family resemblance learned through proximity rather than the effect of genetic inheritance (after all Tristram's biological, as well as his authorial, legitimacy is repeatedly questioned). The play of these characteristics across a variety of characters intra- and extra-diegetic has the curious effect of making eccentricity a shared and levelling mark: a family resemblance in fact. And yet, as we shall see, this is nonetheless serious play, a kind of humorous exchange that promotes ethical exchange between kin and kind despite different temperamental casts of mind. For Sterne, co-presence – an awareness of being with others at the same time and place – is the necessary basis of ethical connection, feeling with and recognising (if not necessarily understanding) the value(s) of others.

Tristram's is a 'novelty act' – both a one-off and an original and also an exception that proves a rule: every character in *Tristram Shandy* and every character it touches becomes (pre)occupied by their own hobby-horsical

---

[1] See Laurence Sterne, *A Facsimile Reproduction of a Unique Catalogue of Laurence Sterne's Library* (London: J. Tregaskis, 1930).

[2] Frank Donoghue, *The Fame Machine: Book-Reviewing and Eighteenth-Century Literary Careers* (Redwood City, CA: Stanford University Press, 1996), p. 69.

interpretation of the work. The emergent genre of the novel is profoundly changed after the publication of the first volume of *Tristram Shandy* in December 1759 as was the stage after Garrick's first appearances in November 1741. And in not unrelated ways. Both men deliver a highly individuated and mannered performance (the play of absence and presence, speech and silence, behavioural tics and cognitive generality) which becomes the ground of what appears as a transformative naturalism. Central to that performance is the pause: its presence in *Tristram Shandy*'s typographic (ellipses), narratological (digressions) or simply descriptive (something that characters do when they speak or act) is a mark that invites the reader to play, and play along with, Tristram, to be with him without insisting on arriving anywhere in particular.

Sterne's innovation as novelist was, then, closely related to that of Garrick as actor. Laurence Sterne came to London in the spring of 1760 after the first two volumes of his work had been published in York in December 1759. He successfully sought the patronage of David Garrick to introduce him to society, and he confided to Garrick, in a letter from Paris in 1762, that he 'Shandy[ed] it away fifty times more than I was ever wont'[3] playing the jester parts of Tristram and Parson Yorick in company and on paper.

Perhaps unsurprisingly, given the richly allusive texture of Sterne's masterpiece, the character of Tristram Shandy, so inextricably wound into that of his creator Sterne, incorporates aspects of all three examples of character that we have discussed so far: outdoing (Townly), sway (Pamela), expansion (Ranger). All three of these characters play a part in the making of *Tristram Shandy*. At Christmas 1762 Laurence Sterne organised and performed a Christmas amateur adaptation of Colley Cibber's *The Provok'd Husband* when he was overwintering in Toulouse. Walter Shandy's attempts to keep his metropolitan-obsessed wife at home for her pregnancy and lying-in echo the frustrations of Lord Townly.

Colley Cibber's autobiography was an explicit reference point for Sterne in composing Tristram's account of his conception, birth and being of Tristram. As Julia Fawcett identifies, when Laurence Sterne informs a friend after the publication of his novel's first two volumes 'I wrote not [to] be *fed*, but to be *famous*', he inverts Cibber's defence of the *Apology for the Life of Colley Cibber* (published in a pamphlet of 1742): 'I wrote more to be Fed, than to be Famous'.[4] As a hands-on author-protagonist, Sterne may

---

[3]   Laurence Sterne to David Garrick 19 May 1762, in *Letters of Laurence Sterne*, ed. Lewis Perry Curtis (Oxford: Oxford University Press, 1935), letter 86, pp. 156–8.

[4]   See Julia H. Fawcett, *Spectacular Disappearances: Celebrity and Privacy, 1696–1801* (Ann Arbor, MI: University of Michigan Press, 2016), pp. 98–9. The letters concerned are: Laurence Sterne, 'Letter to Unknown Gentleman', Wednesday 30 January 1760,

have seen affinities between his own ambitions and the career of an actor-manager-playwright such as Cibber. However, as the parody of Cibber suggests, by the late 1750s there were more modernising (and openly critical of Cibber) models to emulate, in particular that of David Garrick.

David Garrick is addressed by name four times in the course of *Tristram Shandy* (references discussed in more detail later in this chapter). As we have seen, his patronage in London society was actively sought by Laurence Sterne. The attraction of Garrick as mentor may have also lain in the attraction of Garrick as model. Like Garrick, Sterne sought to gain and manage his public celebrity through association with his characters, especially those of Parson Yorick and Tristram. The part of Ranger was associated with Shandy in April 1760 when the *London Magazine: Or Monthly Intelligencer* published extracts from recent comical poems under the title *Two LYRICK EPISTLES, one to my Cousin Shandy on his coming to Town and the other to the Grown Gentlewomen, the Misses of ****, being lately published.*[5] The 'misses' inclined to the attractions of fairy imaginings are warned that enchanters will assume masculine form to seduce them; the attorney's clerk will seek possession, but:

> You are in no less danger
> From Hamlet and Ranger,
> The enchanters of the stage.[6]

Pamela too serves as a model. Like her, Tristram is both author and 'main' protagonist; unlike her, however, he writes to shape a public persona for others to consume and, unlike her, he admits a desire to be read, to acquire a posterity. The characters of author (Sterne) and protagonist (Tristram) are discursively related, whereas the roles of editor (Richardson) and protagonist (Pamela) are carefully distinguished. Although *Tristram Shandy* does not mention Pamela by name, her practice of writing to the moment is everywhere subject to hermeneutic pressure and comic exposure. Tristram is so busy writing his life, so enwrapped in his relation with his readers at the moment of writing, that he has no life other than in and of writing. The moment of that writing, and of any recounted action, is

in *Letters of Laurence Sterne*, letter 47, pp. 88–91; and Colley Cibber, *A Letter from Mr. Cibber to Mr. Pope* (Dublin: A. Reilley, 1742), p. 5.

5   The author was Sterne's friend, John Hall-Stevenson. See Mary-Céline Newbould, *Adaptations of Laurence Sterne's Fiction: Sterneana, 1760–1840* (London: Ashgate, 2013), p. 18.

6   'Poetical Essays in April, 1760', *London Magazine: Or, Gentleman's Monthly Intelligencer*, vol. 29, p. 212.

always pressed on by anterior actions and the question of their causality. In the third volume, as he describes the moment that his father learns that Tristram must have an artificial bridge built for his flattened (as a result of a forceps delivery) nose, adult Tristram comments:

> From the first moment I sat down to write my life for the amusement of the world, and my opinions for its instruction, has a cloud insensibly been gathering over my father. – A tide of little evils and distresses has been setting in against him. – Not one thing, as he observed himself, has gone right: and now is the storm thicken'd, and going to break, and pour down full upon his head.[7]

And yet, the writing of these passages provides a kind of ease, a relaxing of authorial muscle, as the author opens his heart and moves his pen gently to communicate sorrow and sympathy:

> I enter upon this part of my story in the most pensive and melancholy frame of mind, that every sympathetic breast was touched with. – My nerves relax as I tell it. – Every line I write, I feel an abatement of the quickness of my pulse, and of that careless alacrity with it, which every day of my life prompts me to say and write a thousand things I should not. – And this moment that I last dipp'd my pen into my ink, I could not help taking notice what a cautious air of sad composure and solemnity there appear'd in my manner of doing it.[8]

Writing, as in *Pamela* and for Pamela, is a source of relief, a form of healing. It is also a vehicle for performance, in which the writer watches him or herself in action. For Tristram, of course, writing *is* action rather than record. Tristram's hand and gesture is separated from his consciousness while it composes that consciousness. So too what has value in that consciousness owes its origin to *Pamela*; the power to move a reader, to prompt a sympathy that results in submission to a character otherwise without resources or authority.

The paradox of *Tristram Shandy*, or one among its many paradoxes, is this sense that the apparent contemporaneity of novelistic and theatrical performance, of writing and acting, makes character into something beyond representation. Tristram produces his own presence in the act of being read. His writing to the moment puts under impossible pressure the

[7]   Laurence Sterne, *The Life and Opinions of Tristram Shandy, Gentleman*, ed. Melvyn New and Joan New (London: Penguin Books, 1997), vol. 3, chapter 28, p. 175.
[8]   Ibid., p. 175.

act of *re*-presentation, providing the reader only a dynamic relationship with a writing presence itself constantly under pressure to communicate a self through a secondary print technology. While serial publication to some extent closes the gap between (hand)writing Tristram and print Tristram, there is still an unbridgeable gap, albeit a productive one. Indeed, presence might be produced in that causal pause.

Hans Gumbrecht notes that 'our desire for presence will be best served if we try to pause for a moment before we begin to make sense – and if we then let ourselves be caught by an oscillation where presence effects permeate the meaning effects.'[9] He describes the 'marvellous quieting effects' of Japanese Noh and Kabuki performance.[10] Pausing delays the 'leap' to meaning, to Cartesian evidence of mind, inviting us to linger with the material, the present, what is before us. And it is just this kind of playful lingering, while acknowledging our compulsion to move forward into interpretation to infer meaning, which is the performance style of Tristram Shandy as character-who-narrates.

Pausing was a thespian technique particularly marked in the performances of David Garrick, and it is the description of such pausing which summons Garrick's presence on the page of *Tristram Shandy*. Garrick appears early in the third volume, as part of Sterne's concerted campaign to court the great actor to aid his plans for promotional appearances in London soon after the production of the novel's second instalment. Tristram embarks on a digression concerning the tormenting practice of critics. The digression itself leaves the reader paused in the pursuit of the main action of the story of Tristram's birth: Dr Slop, with the gentle support of Uncle Toby, is cursing the servant Obadiah when the door 'hastily opening in the next chapter but one – put an end to the affair.'[11] Before we can learn who is entering the room (in fact Susannah with news of the [lack of] progress in baby Tristram's delivery at the hands of the midwife), Tristram impersonates the tendentious and ungenerous words of critics in relation to works of art: a new fashionable book, an epic poem, a picture, Garrick's delivery of soliloquy and an epilogue. Sterne is answering back to the bewildered lack of empathy that he felt critics had shown to his own eccentric first two volumes of *Tristram*. Garrick here stands in for Tristram and for Sterne: an artist whose characteristic artistry lies in a mannered performance that nonetheless brings a new naturalism to the medium in which he works.

---

[9] Gumbrecht, *The Production of Presence*, p. 126.
[10] Ibid., p. 149.
[11] Sterne, *Tristram Shandy*, vol. 3, chapter 11, p. 147.

This performance is distinguished by acts of hesitancy that enhance the aesthetic experience of the work, but which critics brand as failure:

> – And how did *Garrick* speak the soliloquy last night? – Oh, against all rule, my Lord, – most ungrammatically! Betwixt the substantive and the adjective, which should agree together in *number, case* and *gender*, he made a breach thus, – stopping, as if the point wanted settling; – and betwixt the nominative case, which your lordships knows should govern the verb, he suspended his voice in the epilogue a dozen times, three seconds and three fifths by a stop-watch, my Lord, each time. – Admirable grammarian! – But in suspending his voice – was the sense suspended likewise? Did no expression of attitude or countenance fill up the chasm – Was the eye silent? Did you narrowly look? – I look'd only at the stop-watch, my Lord. – Excellent observer![12]

Garrick was famous for his lengthy pauses in which he varied his expression and 'pointed', to draw attention to the lines that were to follow. The critic is criticised because his attention is turned away from the physical presence of the performer, which he gauges against two inappropriate measures of stage presence: the laws of grammar and the laws of time (the script and the stopwatch). The reader is aware that these forms of tyranny have impeded or altered the course of Tristram's conception and birth. His mother distracted his father from sexual coitus by asking whether he had wound the clock. His father's obsession with writing lengthy documents that promote traditional hierarchies and make the case for the government of subordinate terms by dominant ones distracts him from the familial and paternal duties that would allow his household to flourish. Art is to be measured and valued, Tristram argues, by abandoning oneself to the moment of performance. Thus, he concludes his digressive diatribe against rebarbative criticism:

> I would go fifty miles on foot, for I have not a horse worth riding on, to kiss the hand of that man whose generous heart will give up the reins of his imagination into his author's hands, – be pleased he knows not why, and cares not wherefore.[13]

Tristram's opening example of unjust criticism at odds with the temperament of the art form on which it comments – the critic of Garrick's

---

[12] Sterne, *Tristram Shandy*, vol. 3, chapter 12, p. 148.
[13] Ibid., p. 149.

performance – also serves to illustrate the topsy-turviness of Tristram's sense of aesthetic value which rests in the person of the performer. Garrick is the artist in this instance and not the playwright. Indeed, neither playwright nor play are named, nor need they be since the 'soliloquy' must of course be the only soliloquy which does not require author or name to be mentioned, Hamlet's 'To be or not to be'. The text Garrick delivers is at the service of his character as performer rather than vice versa. So too, the digressive, eccentric Tristram is the elusive presence we should seek to travel with, despite his apparent lack of a governing principle (a hobby-horse) to drive his text forward. The impossibility of such a task is rapidly becoming clear to the reader, but there is a pleasure in the play of absence and presence.

And a similar pleasure is found in the transposing of expectations regarding the ephemerality of character between theatre and novel. Emily Hodgson Anderson investigates the intermediary roles of Hamlet and Yorick in the telling of *Tristram Shandy* to support the arguments about the latter's aspiration to integrate theatrical styles – and especially those of Garrick – into prose fiction. In particular, re-enactments, such as Toby's of his fateful experience in battle, are attempts in *Tristram Shandy* – as they are in *Hamlet* – to serve as 'both monumental record and live performance': hence, Anderson concludes:

> *Tristram Shandy* challenges our understanding of memorialization as dependent on a sense of static fixity, and challenges the association of the novel with the material fixity of print. In the eighteenth century, the ubiquitous influence of theatre urges us to read novels, and to see eighteenth-century readers reading novels, as often akin to live events.[14]

(Dramatic) pausing may be related to a potent kind of absenting of character that Sterne evidently used as a playful ploy to call attention to himself. Volumes three and four, Sterne informed Garrick in a letter of 27 January 1760, would be 'still more dramatick' than the first two. And he imagines a 'Cervantic Comedy' made out of the materials, promising that 'half a word of Encouragement would be enough to make me conceive, & bring forth something for the Stage (how good, or how bad, is another Story)'.[15] That half a word does not seem to have been forthcoming, but Garrick certainly

---

[14] Emily Hodgson Anderson, '*Hamlet*, David Garrick, and Laurence Sterne', in *Shakespeare and the Legacy of Loss*, pp. 73–2.
[15] Laurence Sterne, *Letters*, letter 46, pp. 86–7.

did befriend and promote Sterne himself, giving him a 'character' to launch him in the circles the actor moved in. Sterne had secured a reference for his character from his actress-amour, Catherine Fourmantel, who sent Garrick a letter at the beginning of the month composed by Sterne as though from her. Sterne has Fourmantel stand as surety for the character of his book and its author. Her giving of that character rests on the gratitude Sterne has her voice for his own patronage when she came as a stranger to York:

> There are two Volumes just published here which have made a great noise, & have had a prodigious Run; for in 2 Days after they came out, the Bookseller sold two hundred – & continues selling them very fast. It is, The Life & Opinions of Tristram Shandy, which the Author told me last night at our Concert, he had sent up to London, so perhaps you have seen it; If you have not seen it, pray get it & read it, because it has a great Character as a witty smart Book, and if You think it is so, your good word in Town will do the Author; I am sure great Service; You must understand, He is a kind & generous friend of mine whom Providence has attached to me in this part of the world where I came a stranger – & I could not think how I could make a better return than by endeavouring to make you a friend to him & his Performance. – this is all my Excuse for this Liberty, which I hope you will excuse. His name is Sterne, a gentleman of great Preferment & a Prebendary of the Church of York, & has a great Character in these Parts as a man of Learning & wit. the Graver People however say, tis not fit for young Ladies to read his Book. so perhaps you'l think it not fit for a young Lady to recommend it; however the Nobility, & great Folks stand up mightily for it. & say tis a good Book tho' a little tawdry in some places, –[16]

Character is here something that is passed from hand to hand in letters of 'reference'. The author is being given a 'character' by his referee to someone who might further his career in town (like a rustic servant seeking employment), and he brings with him a 'great' character from his own locality for which the referee stands surety. The work she references for is described as a 'Performance' and the first two volumes of *Tristram*, like a successful stage play have had 'a good run'; hence its author would be appropriately promoted by the most well-known actor-manager of the time.

Yet, this kind of character struggles to manifest as stage performance and is somehow cheaper and easier to handle in manuscript circulation – one conceit in the novel is that Tristram is composing a handwritten

[16] Laurence Sterne, *Letters*, letter 45, pp. 85–6.

manuscript being read simultaneously by his reader, and Fourmantel's letter of reference is constructed as a letter from one grateful character to another potential patron. Sterne may be adopting a position of false modesty in his apprehension of inadequacy as a writer of stage comedy in the letter to Garrick. That pose of inadequacy and impotence is of course consistent with the character of Sterne's alter-ego Tristram himself. But it seems Sterne was indeed nervous of his success as a playwright, and that his uneven temperament impeded his success in a field which might have offered him some financial advantage. Joseph Cradock (1742–1826), man of letters and friend to Garrick, records:

> Sterne never possessed any equal spirits. He was always either in the cellar or the garret, and once meeting him at Drury-lane Theatre, I said to him, "As you are so intimate with Garrick, I wonder that you have never undertaken to write a Comedy". He seemed quite struck, and after a pause, with tears in his eyes, replied, "I fear I do not possess the proper talent for it, and I am utterly unacquainted with the business of the stage." – "The latter," I said, "would readily be supplied." I found, however, that he was at that time under embarrassment, and that a successful Comedy would have been particularly serviceable to him.[17]

Here, Sterne becomes the sentimental subject of the anecdote. His tears are a sign of his sensibility but also an indicator of his need. The characteristic 'pause' described in Cradock's anecdote may be an imitation of the many signs of the gap so central to the representation of a sentimental hero: between the ideal and the embodied reality of sensibility, between a fantasy of pure sympathy (unsullied imaginative identification with the suffering of others) and the sensualist drives of embodiment (the pleasure of experiencing a physical response to the feelings of others play out on our own flesh). So too the sentimental actor on stage must display feeling – must feel with his character – but he does so in order to embody feeling for a paying audience and to maintain his livelihood. The pause is not only one of performance on the stage in front of the author's audience (here Cradock) but also a temporal one (it is not until later that Cradock realises Sterne's financial 'embarrassment' that would have made a successful stage comedy a real relief to his circumstances).

---

[17]   Joseph Cradock, *Literary and Miscellaneous Memoirs* (London: for the Author, 1826), vol. 1, pp. 207–8.

Pausing is of course also central to the serial production of *Tristram Shandy*. It was in the pauses between one set of volumes appearing and the next that other writers and performers seized the opportunity to imitate and parody Sterne's cult work.[18] Gaps and pauses are spaces in which to insert foreign matter. In *Tristram Shandy* the author tells us that he has purposefully provided such gaps for the reader to have an opportunity to collaborate in the production of meaning. The aposiopesis is the most obvious typographical sign, but the invitation to the reader to 'fill out' the figure of the Widow Wadman in the absence of a specific description is a more obvious characterological illustration of the same intention.

It is certainly striking that despite the author's and the work's many affinities with the theatrical world, Sterne's central character, Tristram, does not have a flourishing stage afterlife. He was thoroughly eclipsed by the appeal of Uncle Toby, the traumatised, gentle-spirited, tender-hearted retired military officer whose innocent lunacy captured the hearts of Sterne's audience. The only stage adaptation of the novel does not give Tristram place among its *dramatis personae*; Leonard MacNally's two-act farce, *Tristram Shandy*, which enjoyed relative success as an afterpiece (seven performances in the spring season of 1783 at Covent Garden, including its debut performance on 26 April), did not include either Tristram or Parson Yorick as characters.

This afterpiece concerned a double courtship plot: Toby and the Widow Wadman serve as the older couple, with Corporal Trim and Susannah (who ousts Bridget from this position in the source) as the young servant pairing. Walter Shandy conspires to lead his brother to a declaration of love while he receives reports of the disastrous series of offstage events that lead to his son's birth with a crushed nose and a misreported Christian name (Tristram instead of Trismegistus). The play's subtitle points to the playful treatment of its source material: *a Sentimental, Shandean bagatelle, in two acts*. A bagatelle is a game in which small balls roll down a sloping board to numbered holes to achieve a score if they evade the obstructions of pins. Figuratively it refers to a thing of unimportance, not worth consideration. Newbould observes that the play – perhaps in line with the game from which the subtitle derives 'plots a more definitive route for Sterne's meandering lines to follow so as to achieve a specific destination.'[19] If that destination is the two unions with new wives of master (Toby) and man (Trim), not achieved in the source novel, it was nonetheless arrived at through different directions and orderings – if the various states of the play text that

[18]   See Newbould, *Adaptations of Laurence Sterne's Fiction*.
[19]   Newbould, *Adaptations*, 'the bagatelle... plots a more definitive route for Sterne's meandering lines to follow so as to achieve a specific destination', p. 130.

survive are anything to go on. The manuscript submitted to the Licenser (Larpent) with the title *Tristram Shandy, a Farce in Two Acts* in advance of the first performance varies hugely from the published text, which went into a second edition 21 October 1783.[20]

In the manuscript of the play submitted to the Licenser, Dr Slop appears as a predatory villain making advances to Susannah, whereas in the printed version he is closer to the comic bumbler of the source novel. Trim and Susannah's comic discovery in amorous play under Toby's bridge at his fortifications takes place at the end of the first act in the Larpent and the end of the second in the printed play. The Larpent manuscript contains songs delivered by the Widow and Toby not found in the printed play text; it also indicates that Mrs Kennedy played the part of the Widow Wadman for the benefit, but Mrs Morton is listed in the printed play (all other parts remain the same). Margaret Kennedy also delivered an epilogue which was published separately from the play in the *Morning Herald and Daily Advertiser* of 7 May 1783. This praised the ways in which 'the Language of looks can speak life to the soul!', while Kennedy turned her own fine eyes to the boxes to crave their indulgence.[21] Finally, the Larpent manuscript for performance offers a much more jingoistic celebration than the printed play of British military might as the American revolutionary wars drew to a disappointing close for loyalists to the English crown.[22]

MacNally's dramatic adaptation draws on the language and scenes of *Tristram Shandy* but in so doing it reattributes and reorders in ways that often change their character. Tristram's characteristic speech acts are given to the characters who do appear on stage. Chapter thirteen of the eighth volume of *Tristram Shandy* finds Tristram meditating on the discombobulating effects of love. The Widow Wadman, he has observed in chapter eleven, can neither give up on her passion for Toby nor advance it (since Toby does not love her back). Tristram says he too is caught between such conflicting feelings and finds in chapter twelve his imagination heated by the very metaphors he enlists to describe their oscillation. In chapter thirteen he asserts that those who think about love concur that:

[20] See Leonard MacNally, [[Tristram]] [[Shandy]], LA621, The Huntington Library, San Marino, California.

[21] See also 'A favorite song sung by Mrs. Kennedy in Tristram Shandy' (London: Longman and Broderip, 1783). The Widow Wadman sings a song from a sonnet written by her first husband.

[22] Warren Oakley, 'The Redeployment of Uncle Toby', chapter 3 of *A Culture of Mimicry: Laurence Sterne, his Readers and the Art of Bodysnatching* (London: Maney, 2010), pp. 53–76.

LOVE is certainly, at least alphabetically speaking, one of the most

A gitating

B witching

C onfounded

D evilish affairs of life – the most

E xtravagant

F utilitous

G alligaskinish

H andy-dandyish

I racundulous (there is no K to it) and

L yrical of all human passions: at the same time, the most

M isgiving

N innyhammering

O bstipating

P ragmatical

S tridulous

R idiculous – though by the bye the R should have gone first – But in short 'tis of such a nature, as my father once told my uncle Toby upon the close of a long dissertation upon the subject – "You can scarce," said he, "combine two ideas together upon it, brother Toby, without an hypallage".[23]

Tristram's alphabet imitates the list in *Don Quixote* of the requirements of a good lover, but also mocks the absurdity of that romance rhetoric in the choice of obscure and newly coined comical adjectives. The list is itself incomplete and resistant to the alphabetical ordering it ostensibly embraces. There is no J, an absence Tristram does not allude to although he acknowledges that there is no K to include and he thinks the R should have come first since the adjective 'ridiculous' is the paramount and defining one. Walter's conclusion to his own (and different) dissertation on love is harnessed to the end of Tristram's list in a moment of awkward coupling that mimics the very impossibility of firmly attaching an adjective before so elusive a noun, and the larger impossibility of the coupling of the Widow and Toby, man and woman. 'Hypallage' is the literary device whereby two elements in a sentence are subjected to unexpected change, most often in the form of a transferred epithet (Walter goes on to describe it as putting the cart before the horse). The Widow's love has improperly come before Toby's; the adjectival list attempts to gloss love but in fact comes to define it,

---

[23] Sterne, *Tristram Shandy*, vol. 8, chapter 12, pp. 460–1.

or rather indicate the difficulty of settling love in a stable relation between two elements.

MacNally reorders the elements of this alphabetical scene in ways that make us aware of the different terms of mediation in the spoken and mimetic drama by comparison with the written and diegetic novel. Tristram's meditations are turned into a conventional courtship exchange between an amorous couple. The printed edition of the play appears to have sought to provide the descriptive account of the posture of the actors (John Edwin the elder played Trim and Sarah Maria Wilson played Susannah[24]), either to recall the ways in which the two actors performed their roles on stage or Sterne's minute description of the gestures and postures of his characters in the printed fiction; there are no such stage directions in the Larpent manuscript.

In this scene early in the first act, Susannah comments on the distress of Mrs Wadman and asks Trim if he knows the marks of love:

> *Trim.* Know them, I have felt them, Susannah, *(pressing her hand.)* But say, what dost thou think of love thyself, my girl?
> *Sus.* I can tell you what it is through the whole alphabet; parson Yorick taught me. You must give me the letter, Mr. Trim, just as you give the word of command – begin with A.
> *Trim.* Very well; – now mind the word – take care. *(as he gives the word he exercises with his stick, and as she answers, she reckons with the forefinger of her right hand upon her left hand.)*
>
> *Trim.* A!
> *Sus.* Agitation.
> *Trim.* B!
> *Sus.* Bewitching.
> *Trim.* C!
> *Sus.* Charming.
> *Trim.* D!
> *Sus.* Delightful, or dev'lish, which you please; in short, Love is the most E – extravagant F – funny, G – gigglish, H – humorous, I – interesting, K – O there is no key to it!

---

[24] John Edwin the Elder (b. 1749) was a lead actor under contract with Harris at Covent Garden from 1779 until his death in 1790 (Highfill, *Biographical Dictionary*, vol. 5, pp. 20–5). Mrs Richard Wilson (Sarah Maria, née Adcock, 1752–86) was known as Mrs Wilson (Highfill, *Biographical Dictionary*, vol. 16, pp. 173–8), but was not married to the Mr Richard Wilson who played Captain Toby Shandy in the same production.

> *Trim.* What no key to love, Susannah? O there is a key! – Well, go on. –
> *Sus.* Love is the most L – longing, M – misguiding, N – natural, O –
> the O expresses its own meaning, its the same with the heigh ho!
> *(sighs)* P – pleasant, Q – quarrelsome, R – rapturous – but here comes
> Obadiah, so the next time we
> meet, I'll give you the S, T, U, W, X, Y, and Z, of love.
> *Trim.* With the *et cætera*, I hope, Susan – for the *et cætera* is worth the
> whole alphabet.[25]

Like Tristram, Susannah omits the 'K' (explaining the pun that Sterne likely intended 'there is no K or key to love'). Like him, she omits the 'J' without comment. She also omits the 'V' from her promised list of the rest of the alphabet of love. Otherwise her alphabetical list is more pragmatic, more girlish, and the adjectives she repeats more positive than the strange coinings and tortures of Tristram's choice. Susannah recites a learned exercise, playing the part of a dutiful student (of the amorous and absent Parson Yorick). This recital might be rendered as a sign of her innocence (she does not know or understand what she repeats) or a knowing performance of that innocence designed to kindle the spirits of her suitor.

While Susannah's recital is quite unlike and incompatible with Tristram's display of learning, which spirals into its own ridiculous coinings, she and Trim nonetheless recall the familiar figures of Sterne's novel. Trim engages in his characteristic stick play, while Susannah carefully reckons with her fingers (Tristram minutely observes the hand gestures of his characters as they speak). The exchange concludes with a pun not found in Sterne. The 'et cetera' Trim anticipates points to the frequent use of the term to signify female genitalia. Susannah has already invoked this idea in the other frequent term for the vagina, the 'O' which 'expresses its own meaning'.[26]

MacNally here turns the written scene in which Tristram engages in conversation with his absent reader into one for performance and exchange between two acting bodies who engage in a dialogue of courtship, while their physical bodies (Susannah's hand reckons, Trim's stick wavers) mark their mutual attraction and understanding. The act of hypallage referred to in the written 'source' shadows the exchange in that it is not clear which term or character leads, Susannah or Trim, in the play of language and the game of innuendo. In this bagatelle, Tristram's words are taken over by

[25] MacNally, *Tristram Shandy*, pp. 4–5.
[26] See Amelia Dale, 'Dramatic Extraction and Polly Honeycombe's &c.', Beauchamp Prize for Literature, University of Sydney, http://hdl.handle.net/2123/8726 [accessed 20 February 2020].

secondary characters, his presence displaced by theirs. But nonetheless, the self-conscious play with language that is the mark of *Tristram Shandy* is maintained. MacNally selects a scene that has to do with alphabetical character. The written marks of feeling in the novel are translated into a set of spoken ones accompanied by bodily gestures that nonetheless recall the aspiration of the novel that print mimics the form of embodied expression.

There were no other direct adaptations of Sterne's *Tristram Shandy* into plays of the eighteenth century, but the novel indisputably informed the character of dramatic productions that followed. Not least in its energetic mixing of sentiment and comedy, which contributes to the new life given to the sentimental comedy in the early 1770s, a few years after Sterne's death. One explicit allusion to *Tristram Shandy* in a sentimental comedy demonstrates that the novel exerted its influence not through bringing its narrator to dramatic life but by referring to the compelling power of its secondary characters and by the 'extracting' of particularly potent sentimental scenes. Here, as in the novel itself, the sentimental character (or the character of sentiment) plays across and into the performances of other minor characters. Sentiment has an infectious capacity to slip from one person to another as well as from text to person.

Richard Cumberland's sentimental comedy, *The West Indian* (opened by David Garrick at Drury Lane Theatre, 19 January 1771), deploys reference to an offstage character from *Tristram Shandy* to demonstrate the sentimental virtues of its onstage cast. The elderly soldier, Captain Dudley, has come to London with his daughter Louisa and son Ensign Charles Dudley. The family are poor (it transpires that Captain Dudley's aunt, Lady Rusport, has kept the information of a will and inheritance from him to her own advantage). And they take lodgings at the house of an ostensible bookseller named Mr Fulmer; Fulmer and his wife are in fact fences for stolen goods. Dudley's beautiful daughter, Louisa, catches the eye of a young and wealthy Creole immigrant from the West Indies, Belcour, while her brother, Charles, honourably suppresses his passion for his cousin, Charlotte Rusport, because he cannot offer her a financially stable union. The two marriages are secured through the intervention of a wild but generous-hearted Irish Major, Dennis O'Flaherty, who reveals the true content of the will. The hero, Belcour, is in the course of the play reunited with his long-lost father, the merchant Stockwell. The hero of the play, Belcour, proves himself to have a feeling heart despite his rakishness, and his resemblance to the popular character of Ranger was noted by contemporaries.[27]

---

[27] Stanley Thomas Williams, 'Richard Cumberland's *West Indian*', *Modern Language Notes*, 35, no. 7 (November 1920), 414.

We meet Captain Dudley in person in the first scene of the second act, where he mentions his admiration for *Tristram Shandy* to his villainous landlord, Fulmer. He tells Fulmer that he has borrowed the sixth 'volume of my deceased friend Tristram'. Sterne died in 1767 leaving his work apparently incomplete; Dudley equates the author Sterne with his narrator Tristram and counts the latter as a 'friend' because of his long acquaintance with him through the book. Dudley has selected the sixth volume of a favourite work rather than chancing upon it:

> DUDLEY. Mr. Fulmer, I have borrow'd a book from your shop; 'tis the sixth volume of my deceased friend Tristram: he is a flattering writer to us poor soldiers; and the divine story of Le Fevre, which makes part of this book, in my opinion of it, does honour not to its author only, but to human nature.[28]

The story of the tragic death of Lieutenant Le Fever is told in the sixth volume of *Tristram Shandy* in chapters six to ten. There, Corporal Trim acts as envoy and reporter to Uncle Toby when the sickness and poverty of Le Fever, attended only by his young son Billy, is brought to their attention by the landlord of the inn in which Le Fever lies dying. Uncle Toby acts as Le Fever's executor, raises the young boy and procures him a commission, but after four years in service against the Turks, Billy's health is broken, and Toby proposes him as a tutor for the young Tristram. The scene of Le Fever's death was especially celebrated for its sentimental affect. Nonetheless, it is also shadowed by the sense of the narrator Tristram's impatience that the story of one father and son has displaced his own; he pens chapter eleven promising 'I am so impatient to return to my own story, that what remains of young *Le Fever's*... shall be told in a very few words, in the next chapter.'[29] The substitution of secondary characters for primary ones is both a form of digression that pauses the progress of the main plot but also a means of deepening the sentimental force of the work as a whole. Le Fever and his son substitute for Walter and his son. The former has brought his child up with him in the army while Walter has been so preoccupied with writing his account of how to bring up his son that he has failed to fulfil the role he describes. So too in Cumberland's play one father and son plot (that of Dudley and his son) appears to be a digression or a pause in the delivery of a main plot concerning another father and son (the West Indian Belcour and

---

[28] Richard Cumberland, *The West Indian* (London: W. Griffin, 1771), Act 2, Scene 2, pp. 17–18.

[29] Sterne, *Tristram Shandy*, vol. 6, chapter 11, p. 354.

his father the merchant Stockwell). Dudley's son, like Le Fever's, follows in his father's footsteps and his health is also broken. Dudley's innocence is contrasted with the calculated worldliness of his landlord, but the book's presence in Fulmer's shop and the fact that he stocks it is also an indication of its character: *Tristram Shandy* is not only a success in the affective force of its sentiment but also in commerce and trade. The novel's currency is feeling, and a capacity for feeling is demonstrated in its pages by the generosity that leads someone who learns of another's distress to relieve it.

Cumberland's play contrasts this generosity of spirit (Belcour, O'Flaherty) with self-interested thieving (Lady Rusport, Fulmer). Dudley's sensibility contrasts with Fulmer's pragmatism:

> FULMER. He is an author I keep in the way of trade, but one I never relish'd; he is much too loose and profligate for my taste.
> DUDLEY. That's being too severe: I hold him to be a moralist in the noblest sense; he plays indeed with the fancy, and sometimes perhaps too wantonly; but while he thus designedly masks his main attack, he comes at once upon the heart; refines, amends it, softens it; beats down each selfish barrier from about it, and opens every sluice of pity and benevolence.
> FULMER. We of the catholic persuasion are not much bound to him. – Well, Sir, I shall not oppose your opinion; a favourite author is like a favourite mistress; and there you know, Captain, no man likes to have his taste arraigned.
> DUDLEY. Upon my word, Sir, I don't know what a man likes in that case;'tis an experiment I never made.[30]

The exchange tells us the nature of Dudley's investment in the work, which in turn indicates the kind of cultural capital *Tristram Shandy* had accrued by the early 1770s. Dudley sees himself and his kind reflected in the representation of Le Fever; Tristram/Sterne is also a 'friend' in the sense of a writer who promotes the interest of soldiers who have given much in war but find themselves dependent on the charity of others on return from service.

As other critics have noted, *Tristram Shandy* is a work composed and published through a time of war (1759–67), the Seven Years' War. Uncle Toby, Le Fever and Billy Le Fever all have their health broken by action in wars of earlier decades, but they serve as affective character types for an audience encouraged to appreciate the sacrifice and nobility of their

---

[30] Act 2, scene 2, p. 18.

army. The figure of the weeping soldier had especial symbolic resonance: it suggests that war is an act taken to protect the weak rather than one of belligerence and self-aggrandisement.[31]

And the exchange with Fulmer also illuminates the ethical position promoted by the play, in which Sterne's novel features as meaningful prop. Fulmer pretends to virtue and complains that Sterne is too loose for his tastes. He asserts that Tristram is no friend to those of his religious persuasion: Dr Slop's Roman Catholicism is the target of much of the book's satire. The audience of *The West Indian* have already met Fulmer and his wife in an earlier scene and they know that the pair are opportunist villains and not legally married. Dudley defends freedoms in wit, while he is innocent of the extramarital freedoms at which Fulmer not-so-slyly winks.

Dudley is, like Uncle Toby, a sexual innocent with a sensibility that responds to wit and to feeling. The audience of the play, like the audience of the novel, are invited to admire this innocence and gentleness, while retaining a knowing scepticism that allows them to see through a character like Fulmer where Dudley (and Toby) would fail. The allusion to *Tristram Shandy* does not simply serve to illuminate local relationships, but also to foster a certain kind of interpretive practice in an audience, drawing on what they know of the novel to understand the contrast of character(s). Where theatre audiences might previously have expected to rely on dramatic convention and generic norms to anticipate likely outcomes in the course of a plot, they are now assumed to have in their own interpretive repertoire an understanding of the ethics of the successful prose fictions of their time. The 'line' that is traced through the play can be one derived from a non-dramatic work, and especially from a successful prose fiction text.

Of course, this interpretive confidence might not be expected to be available to those who were very familiar with *Tristram Shandy*. The novel has long been celebrated and maligned for its oddity: an eccentric, self-generating artefact beyond classification by genre or media. We oversimplify when we characterise it as a work resistant to theatrical adaptation, or as a novel that draws on theatrical techniques. Its own governing binary seems to be between oral and written performance, between embodied being and textual being. In this respect it is unsurprising that 'character' is the common denominator in the many types of performance on which

---

[31] See Carol Watts, *The Cultural Work of Empire: The Seven Years War and the Imagining of the Shandean State* (Edinburgh: Edinburgh University Press, 2007). See also Simon Parkes, 'Wooden Legs and Tales of Sorrow Done: The Literary Broken Soldier of the Late Eighteenth Century', *Journal for Eighteenth-Century Studies*, 36 (2013), 191–207.

the book draws: prose fiction narrative, philosophical fiction, the sermon, comedy, tragedy.

Tristram Shandy is 'new' in the sense that Garrick's acting was 'new': a kind of naturalistic performance that visibly and self-consciously breaks with conventions and reflects overtly on that departure from the conventional. The two performances were hybrid products, located between the sentimental and the ironic, the comic and the tragic, and able to play both – simultaneously or at least sequentially. This hybrid figure draws its shape from both theatrical and prose fictional sources; he is the 'motley' jester who is at the same time the Harlequin of pantomime (escape artist, agent of chaos), the 'fool' of Shakespearean drama, and the Quixotic hero of prose fiction who determinedly pursues his own fantasy of the fictional real against the hard facts and bodies of the everyday.

The 'presence' of Sterne's text, however, lies not in its theatrical references (and there are many – to curtains being drawn, parts being played, scenes of discovery), but rather in its performance of the kind of serious play that vindicated the apparently immoral climate of a commercial theatre in the period: the ethical claim to provide audiences with an experience of co-presence. Plays acted out forms of connection between characters who otherwise perpetually 'miss' each others' meaning, and between role and audience who find themselves in the same space for a short period of time with different 'intentions' but nonetheless profoundly bound to each other. In *Tristram Shandy* the forceful connection of feeling for others frequently overcomes the separations of imaginative worlds. Although Walter and Toby cannot communicate and repeatedly misunderstand each other, their fellow-feeling averts conflict. Natural and authentic performance in the novel is formed in *relationship* between characters and between character/narrator and his audience/reader.

This kind of co-presence, the mutual making of relationship, is a special kind of kinship that is figured in *Tristram Shandy* through the feeling for kin between the male protagonists. Chapter twelve of the second volume sees Walter snap at Toby when the latter insists that 'curtins' are to do with fortifications (the scene of his trauma) as opposed to 'bedspreads' (the scene of his brother's, at which Dr Slop's laughter at the term 'curtins and horn-work' hints). Toby gives Walter a patient look of suffering, which produces a responsive twinge of guilt in Walter. Toby:

> turned his head, without the least emotion, from Dr. *Slop*, to whom he was addressing his discourse, and look'd up into my father's face, with a countenance spread over with so much good nature; – so placid; – so fraternal; – so inexpressibly tender towards him; – it penetrated

my father to his heart: He rose up hastily from his chair, and seizing hold of both my uncle *Toby*'s hands as he spoke: – Brother *Toby*, said he, – I beg thy pardon; forgive, I pray thee, this rash humour which my mother gave me.[32]

This is also a world that excludes women – curtains are drawn, doors closed, on the female characters; indeed, Walter promulgates a theory of geniture that women are unrelated to the children they bear and deliver. Such a world seems to mirror the masculine world of exchange and competition between men in the actor-manager dominated sphere of eighteenth-century theatre. However, the representation of the creative world as one of exchanges between men was, as *Tristram Shandy* shows in the absurd awkwardness of Walter Shandy's theory of geniture, achieved only by great efforts to conceal the contribution and presence of women as performers (whether as authors, actors or audience).

The co-presence of characters who form a connection draws the audience into the affective space of the theatre. And it is this co-presence that repeatedly redeems and succeeds in underpinning the world of *Tristram Shandy*, otherwise always under threat of spinning out into a series of unconnected threads. The world of *Tristram Shandy* is a world of wayward lines. Tristram is an unfortunate child, his conception only narrowly achieved, his nose broken in delivery, his foreskin removed in an accident with a falling sash-cord window. He may be premature, he may be illegitimate. He does not appear to be married or likely to reproduce. The patrilineal line of inheritance his father so jealously guards is in jeopardy. So too the conventional lines of print of prose fiction – which neutrally communicate story without apparently being subject to formal devices such as the line breaks and metre of verse – are interrupted by uses of print technology that call attention to the struggle to make meaning in and through language: the black page that marks Parson Yorick's death (black lines of print overscored to obscure textual markings of black against white); the marbled page of liquid pigments suspended in oils to make swirling colourful lines that signify the 'motley' of Tristram's performance; and other typographical devices (asterisks, changes of print forms, manicules).

Tristram Shandy fails to follow the usual line of plot in the bildungsroman, from birth to happy marital union. It departs into other kinds of writing: philosophical speculation, anecdote, sermon. *Tristram Shandy* is a novel that resists falling into line as a novel. It is full of erudite references to the earlier literary works from which it derives its own lineage: the tradition

---

[32]   *Tristram Shandy*, vol. 2, chapter 12, pp. 92–3.

of learned wit associated with Erasmus (*In Praise of Folly*), Rabelais (*Gargantua*) and Cervantes (*Don Quixote*) – and particularly Jonathan Swift, also Irish-born and an Anglican clergyman (*The Tale of a Tub* and *Gulliver's Travels*). But if Sterne's novel is satire in this tradition, it is not quite clear *what* it satirises. And, unlike these predecessors, the work was admired as much for its 'sentimental' attitudes as for its bawdy comedy. So although *Tristram Shandy* seems to take some of its energy from the literary tradition of satire, it also appears to be a departure from this: moving more into the terrain of the sentimental novel, in stimulating its readers to cry and to laugh in sympathy with suffering, rather than to see that suffering as the deserved result of vice or folly.

But finally – and perhaps less obviously to modern critics, who tend to see theatre and novel as entirely different forms of fiction-making or life-writing – the traditional 'lines of business' are both stubbornly held to by novel characters, and subject to departures and digressions despite their best efforts. An actor's 'lines of business' are the established category of type or role he or she consistently plays. They make it easier to recognise the character's function in the plot, and for the actor to play in a dizzying and demanding daily revolution of performances: leading business, leading lady, juvenile lady, first and second low comedy, chambermaid, etc.[33]

Actors continued to take these parts, indeed owned a kind of property in them, regardless of how their physical appearance and experience might change. In MacNally's 1783 bagatelle of *Tristram Shandy*, Richard Wilson, celebrated for his comic parts, apparently stepped 'out of line' when he took on the sentimental role of Uncle Toby in that play. Arguably, however, it was the hybrid blend of the comic and the sentimental characteristic of Sterne's novel that Wilson's reputation and performance would have brought to life on stage.[34]

Nonetheless, lines of business were hierarchical and successful actors could expect to move up through the hierarchy. We can see that Sterne's *Tristram Shandy* both marks individual characters by their individual traumas and the hobby horses that drive them as a result (giving them lines of business) *and* confuses its audience by leaving it unclear which of these characters 'leads' the narrative. Tristram, ostensibly the main character of his drama, struggles to arrive at the point of narrating his own birth. Toby might appear to play the part of second-fiddle to the brother in whose

---

[33]   See James C. Burge, *Lines of Business: Casting Practice and Policy in the American Theatre, 1752–1899* (New York: Peter Lang, 1986).

[34]   Mary-Céline Newbould, *Adaptations*, p. 131. Newbould observes that Wilson had delivered in May 1783 (a few weeks before he took the part of Uncle Toby) 'JOE HAYNE'S EPILOGUE, To be spoken by Mr WILSON, riding on an Ass', p. 134.

household he lives and whose domestic drama is apparently the mainspring of the action. But audiences quickly became attached to the gentle, open lunacy of the second part and more interested in his line of plot in pursuing and evading the attractive Widow Wadman. All the male characters in *Tristram Shandy* attempt to hold to their lines of business: Toby to his military history; Walter to his paternal authority; Tristram to his life as a writer and in writing; Trim to his service. And yet all uncannily mirror each other, substitute for each other and cross the lines of their distinctions through their passionate attachment to each other. Character has become a transferable commodity, a vehicle for affect that is passed from hand to hand, from role to role, from actor to actor – and from medium to medium (novel and play). And the dramatic pause has become a playful currency for performers in both media to afford their readers with opportunities to linger with those newly natural characters who had become serial presences in their lives.

Chapter 12
From Character to Consumer

Paradoxically, the 'persons' who emerge with most presence in the history of theatre and novel traced in this book are wholly fictional. Those who make works of art and those who consume them are real embodied persons in time. Yet they prove tantalisingly elusive, inclined to disappear as 'beings' when we attempt to retrieve them from behind (or anticipate them beyond) the texts or performances that appear to 'represent' them. In contrast, invented characters – 'persons' who are most distant from real embodied people in the making of a work of fiction – are those with most apparent 'presence' to us. In this sense too, characters 'occupy space': they are more tangible, extend further into our apprehension, than authors or readers. In particular, the *dramatis personae* discussed in the preceding section of this book extend beyond the 'role': they become 'themselves' rather than stand for, or in the place of, a position in an aesthetic system. Nonetheless, character – like the other forms of person in art (artist and consumer) – also achieves an effect of presence through the process of unconcealment and withdrawal.

The characters discussed here occupy both stage and page to the extent that they become more absorbing to us than the stories in which they feature. They impede rather than advance both 'plot' and 'meaning-effects' through their pausing, digressing, departing or preventing the actions of others. Of course, such impediments also generate plot. And characters also thicken the environment so as to make plot more plausible, or to turn our attention away from the implausibility of plot by creating a sense that they, as characters, are real. Blakey Vermeule notes the 'portability' of literary characters, they are:

> more flexible than other pieces of literary code, such as plot and allusion. They can jump between media – from print to stage to film – and between genres – from fiction to drama to poetry – quite easily. Characters have lives that extend infinitely in serial form.[1]

---

[1]   Blakey Vermeule, *Why Do We Care about Literary Characters?*, p. 49.

Character portability enables readers to reason offline, to address the problem of other minds in environments where they can 'reason about the social contract under conditions of imperfect access to relevant informa- tion.'[2] My analysis points, however, away from character as an affordance for reasoning. Or, at least, that consumers learn to reason through charac- ter by acknowledging the impact of the effect of presence – the sense of the material, the embodied – in making judgement. Pamela is perhaps the most powerful character in this regard: a character whose withdrawal from the theatrical stage in her determined anti-theatricality only increases her sway, a presence-effect that has the power to bring about ethical transformation.

We have looked at four ways of occupying space performed by four characters: outdoing (Lady Townly), sway (Pamela), expansion (Ranger), play (Tristram). We can see in each case that they have a presence-effect that occupies spaces beyond a single text or genre. And in these cases, there is a particular and productive tension in the process of unconcealment and withdrawal between theatre and novel. These characters not only extend their own lives, but they extend the capacity of the genres they occupy to invoke presence, to move beyond type and meaning to communicate embodied experience and ethical complexity. Lady Townly's compelling fascination in public performance contrasts with Pamela's sway as an anti-theatrical presence, able to make the domestic space one rich with dramatic possibility. Ranger's energetic invasion of stage space is paralleled with Tristram's attempts to manage the space of the printed page. Yet both characters are marked by an alternation between vigorous activity – so vigorous indeed in meddling with generic habitat (whether stage props and scenery or novel print and type) that they threaten to undermine it completely – and moments of pause and rest (which threaten in a reverse motion entirely to arrest the progress of plot).

Characters only become characters when they exceed role or type, whereas artists and consumers, authors and readers, are most themselves *in* role and function. Consumers are elusive in a different way than authors and characters in that single instances of reception reported at a particular time or by an individual person cannot serve as evidence of reception as a whole. One report of the experience of attending a theatre or of reading a novel does not indicate the reception of the work for all who encountered it at any one moment. Value and judgement shift through time and, indeed, may vary among an audience or group of readers gathered together to con- sume a single work at a single moment in time. Large digital resources of

[2]   Ibid., p. 55.

record such as the *Reading Experience Database 1450–1945*[3] can only offer a collection of possibilities. This is not to claim that all reading is subjective and every interpretation different: as cognitive studies have shown, the processes of mental reasoning are shared by humans and it is likely that our responses to art are relatively predictable. But rather that, in the case of the consumer of art, the association of a person with an aesthetic process (of unconcealment and withdrawal) distracts from rather than explains 'Being'.

We think of readers and audiences as a group or commonality. In the eighteenth century especially so, given that solitary reading remained an unusual experience and performance contexts such as the theatre and the sermon were the most common means of accessing narrative. An individual testimony is, then, not sufficient to capture the 'character' of the response to a work. In what follows. I turn to look at the ways consumers were imagined as fictional presences at moments of the consumption of art work. I also examine the methods by which a commonality of being (for readers and audiences) was shaped, often through warning against negative or dangerous forms of consumption and often through the complaint that a rival genre was more likely to foster such forms. Hence 'novel readers' and 'theatre audiences' become fictional presences inclined to misdirect the ethical forms of consumption fostered in each other's territory.

---

[3]   *Reading Experience Database 1450–1945*, www.open.ac.uk/Arts/reading/UK/ [accessed 20 February 2020].

PART 3

Consumers: What is Seen

Chapter 13
Introducing Consumers

I think it is appropriate to associate the vertical dimension in the
movement of Being with its simple being there (or, more precisely
with its emergence into being there and with occupying a space),
whereas the horizontal dimension points to Being as being perceived,
which also means to Being offering itself to somebody's view (as an
appearance and as an "ob-ject," as something that moves "toward" or
"against" an observer).[1]

What is seen matters; the scene on the page and on the stage offers itself
to view. The eye traces prose along the lines of the page, watches
the bodies of performers moving in space on the stage. We grasp Being
through an idea produced by a presence that we see. Equally, art anticipates
its future consumption by a viewer, and it reflects retrospectively on what
happened in the moment of consumption, or what it knows of that happening. In this section, we look at fictions of the presence of consumers and
the rival claims to presence at and with the act of consumption offered by
novels and plays in their competition for the market of fiction.

It is the presence of an *audience* that most distinguishes the fiction of
the stage from that of the page in the long history of anti-theatrical sentiment and consequent censorship. As late as 1909 the UK Parliament's Joint
Select Committee on Stage Plays (Censorship) stresses that the presence
of an audience – and especially the shared experience of affect between
them – exacerbates the influence of ideas.

The existence of an audience, moved by the same emotions, its members conscious of one another's presence, intensifies the influence of
what is done and spoken on stage... The performance, day after day,
in the presence of numbers of people, of plays containing [indecency,

---

[1]   Gumbrecht, *Production of Presence*, p. 69.

libel and blasphemy] would have cumulative effects to which the con-
veyance of similar ideas by print offers no analogy.[2]

Wc can see in this early twentieth-century judgement the privileging of a
model of art as an act of communication between 'author' and 'audience'.
The Select Committee understands 'what is done and spoken on stage' as
a conduit for a set of ideas. In this model of communication, actors and
genre, as much as print text, mediate 'ideas' that exist before their manifestation. Georgian theorists rather saw things the other way around: that the
'author' of a play or a novel, and the actors in a drama, respond to and try
to serve the 'ideas' of the audience. Lisa Freeman puts it well:

> This was... a theater of interaction in which the audience was as much
> a part of the performance as the players. No single controlling gaze
> regulated the space of performance in the eighteenth century; the
> power of performance was routinely shared and exchanged between
> audience and performers.[3]

Audience presence should be distinguished from the 'liveness' that is an
evident quality of theatre by comparison with other forms of mimesis (such
as film and television). 'Liveness' has more to do with the embodied co-ex-
istence of *actors* and audience, since in all forms of representation a living
audience or reader is a necessary presence to complete the work of art.
In other words, a necessary precondition of consumption is that a living
person be in the presence of a work of art whether or not the assemblage
of the artwork is constituted wholly or partly by the bodies of performers.
The distinction between liveness and non-liveness only became possible
once performances could be recorded and circulated through other forms
of media than the theatre-space.[4] However, the experience of being present
at a theatrical performance and the sense of being present when reading a
work of fiction is surely ontologically different. Indeed, it was precisely this
difference that those who promoted the competing modes of theatre and
novel sought to exploit in the minds of a culture-hungry audience.

---

[2]   *Report from the Joint Select Committee of the House of Lords and the House of Commons on the Stage Plays (Censorship)...Ordered by the* House of Commons *to be
Printed 2 November 1909* (London: His Majesty's Stationery Office by Wyman and
Sons, 1909), p. 188.
[3]   Lisa Freeman, *Character's Theater*, p. 5.
[4]   Philip Auslander, *Liveness: Performance in a Mediatized Culture* (London: Routledge, 1999).

In performance, the actor sees the audience and responds to their reaction. At the end of the production, an actor delivers his or her epilogue enlisting the audience's applause so that the play can be repeated the next night. Novelists of the period consistently express anxiety about their inability to be present at their audience's reaction. This is not to say that the material addressing audience behaviour in the theatres – including printed epilogues and prologues, periodical accounts, memoir and diary entries, letter entries – can be seen as unproblematic witnesses. As Betsy Bolton comments, 'Georgian audiences were made, not born: they were co-produced, in part through descriptions offered up in theatrical prologues, epilogues, scenes, and prefaces.'[5] Equally, while novelists tend to imagine a solitary reader immersed in an intimate experience of identification and excitation in the consumption of a novel, evidence leads us to conclude that fiction read in domestic settings was probably shared by being read out loud – or at the very least consumed in a room where other family members were present and other activities underway.[6] Practical considerations such as the limited amount of light available in eighteenth-century rooms, and the high cost of books, increased this likelihood.

Reading fiction could be a thoroughly sociable affair. A work of fiction selected by the family on the basis of shared taste – a capacity to please all its members and then shared around a single candle – might have offered more opportunity to enjoy the co-presence of fellow-consumers than a night at the theatre with a huge audience made up of members of very different social classes and conventions. In *Evelina*, Burney captures the misery of being obliged to attend a performance with unlike relations and in crowded unfamiliar circumstances. Evelina has dressed for the pit to visit the Haymarket opera house with her genteel friend, Miss Mirvan, but is forced by her grandmother into accompanying her vulgar cousins, the Miss Branghtons. Their mean father will only pay for gallery seats where Evelina is uncomfortably crowded, and embarrassed by her cousins' lack of feeling in response to fine opera singing in Italian. Indeed, they mock her for her own response when the soprano – castrato Giuseppe Millico (1737–1802) – sings so finely:

5   Betsy Bolton, 'Theorizing Audience and Spectatorial Agency', in Julia Swindells and David Francis Taylor, ed., *The Oxford Handbook of the Georgian Theatre 1737–1832* (Oxford: Oxford University Press, 2014), p. 32.
6   See Abigail Williams, chapter 2 'Reading and Sociability', in her *The Social Life of Books: Reading Together in the Eighteenth-Century Home*, The Lewis Walpole Series in Eighteenth-Century Culture and History (New Haven, CT: Yale University Press, 2017), pp. 37–64.

This song, which was slow and pathetic, caught all my attention, and I leaned my head forward to avoid hearing their observations, that I might listen without interruption: but, upon turning round, when the song was over, I found that I was the object of general diversion to the whole party; for the Miss Branghtons were tittering, and the two gentlemen making signs and faces at me, implying their contempt of my affectation.

This discovery determined me to appear as inattentive as themselves; but I was very much provoked at being thus prevented enjoying the only pleasure, which, in such a party, was within my power.[7]

Evelina herself becomes the show that the spectators at the theatre watch in fascination. Her solitary and enraptured immersion in the pleasure of the music differentiates her from the others in the audience around her, reminding us of Evelina's lonely struggle in a predatory world but also of the norms of *novel* reading. *Evelina* counters the common-sense claim that the collective experience of attending the theatre can check and regulate the dangerous seductions of an aesthetic sense-experience, by illustrating that being part of an audience can also mean exposure to the lowest and most vulgar tastes (because these are least concerned about their public display). The novel can allow a private dynamic union and communion of the artist's and the reader's mind(s).

Informing Georgian accounts of the reception of the performing arts, however, was a kinetic model of the passions that derived from classical and scholastic accounts. This model had been widely disseminated in the new theories of acting that came into print in the first decades of the eighteenth century. As Daniel Larlham summarises, 'the felt truth of theatrical performance depended not upon the interpretative comparison between onstage and offstage worlds, but upon the *mimetic experience of passion*, modelled by the actor and undergone vicariously by the spectator.'[8] According to the post-Cartesian epistemology of affect, the interior motions of the mind agitate the actor's physical body (the actor animates emotions), and these in turn move through space to excite a corresponding bodily sensation in the audience. The passions, excited by the inner motions of the soul, become contagious when registered on the body in ways that spectators cannot help but mirror.

---

[7]   Burney, *Evelina*, ed. Susan Kubica Howard, letter 23, p. 196.
[8]   Daniel Larlham, 'The Felt Truth of Mimetic Experience: Motions of the Soul and the Kinetics of Passion in the Eighteenth-Century Theatre', *The Eighteenth Century*, 53, no. 4 (2012), 435.

However, as Joseph Addison explains in his description of the pleasures of the imagination, the consumer of sense experience cultivates his mind to move from gross sense through the imagination to arrive at the higher order of understanding. Addison's hierarchy indicates that increased *distance* from the stimulating object itself (the beautiful, the sublime, or the novel) enables a more cultivated imagination to achieve knowledge. The presence of the being that stimulates imaginative pleasure can thus impede rather than advance reason and understanding. Addison's account (published in numbers 411 to 421 of *The Spectator* in June and July of 1712) was to provide fertile ground for advocates of the novel seeking to promote its superior aesthetics: especially in claiming the novel's capacity, precisely by virtue of distance from embodied performance, to turn sensation into aesthetic experience.

Nonetheless, the contagious nature of the passions can also arrest the consumer in that primary relation: trapped in a compulsion to repeat without understanding in order to achieve the same sensory high of first experience. Distance, then, was an important element in the achievement of genuine 'presence'. Without some distance from the contagious feeling body, consumers risk simply mirroring physical affect. Or resisting that affect by separating themselves entirely from the spectacle. David Garrick's decision to remove the opportunity for his audience to sit on the stage at Drury Lane in the early 1760s, a decision swiftly also adopted by Covent Garden and the unlicensed stages, may be an indication of this sense of distance being a necessary element of the fiction of presence.[9]

We cannot know the minds of eighteenth-century consumers of the novel and theatre. It is impossible to recapture the presence of an eighteenth-century reader of a novel or a member of the audience at an evening's performance. However, we can explore the 'fictions of presence' generated in and by the evidence that remains: accounts of theatregoing and novel-reading in the works themselves, in reviews, in diaries, memoirs, letters. And it tells us much about the kind of presence both media sought to fashion: one receptive to their influence, one flattered, cajoled, instructed and reformed into acts of judgement that conform to the 'spirit' of the work (rather than abide by the 'letter' of genre or decorum).

---

[9]   Garrick took spectators off the front of the stage in 1762, three years after Voltaire had successfully lobbied for architectural changes at the *Comédie Française* that had the same effect. See Bruce McConachie, 'Theatres for Knowledge through Feeling, 1700–1900', in Philip B. Zarrilli, Bruce McConachie, Gary Jay Williams and Carol Fisher Sorgenfrei, *Theatre Histories: An Introduction*, 2nd ed. (New York and London: Routledge, 2010), p. 243.

This was especially true for 'novel' works – whether those produced on a stage or a page – which by definition lacked a model against which to be measured. Novel fictions cannot be assessed in terms of expectations of genre (comedy, tragedy) or character type. Their novelty constitutes their status as curiosities but also their precarity. Since both theatre and novel relied on an audience's desire for more material *and* variety within it, 'new' works always risked disappearing without trace after first appearance or encounter. To be 'new' is a kind of unconcealing, an announcement of a presence not hitherto recognised or made fresh in the moment, always attended by withdrawal. Newness passes swiftly into convention; it is by definition an unsustainable presence.

Imaginative shaping of an hospitable audience is, then, integral to bringing the work into being and it is often performed by a process of negative definition. The ideal, often termed 'candid', reader or spectator is shaped by comparison with what he or she is *not*. And the two types with which the ideal consumer is contrasted fall along increasingly gendered lines of difference in the course of the eighteenth century: the critic (foolish, egotistic, unfeeling, usually male) and the mimic (foolish, vain, unthinking, usually female). Novels and plays frequently conjure the presence of these two types, especially in prologues and epilogues, in order to call on their consumers to give the artworks fair hearing. You, reader, or you, spectator, have come to this work to participate: to find an equilibrium between judgement (the critic) and affect (the mimic), an equilibrium that will enable the fiction you are experiencing to live on its own and in its fullest terms.

The critic and the mimic share a characteristic, as consumers of the work of art. They are instinctive conformists, driven by rules that make it impossible for them to understand the art work as a composite, living whole. They judge by a set of rigid conventions inappropriately applied in all circumstances. Aesthetic experience, Gumbrecht explains, involves 'moments of intensity' and there is nothing 'edifying in such moments, no message, nothing we could really learn from them'.[10] We have seen in our discussion so far how often such 'moments of intensity' are described in novels through scenes where the main protagonist attends the theatre and is observed in a state of heightened feeling, immersed in the art work.

It is the tension between presence-effects and meaning-effects that produces an aesthetic experience: sense (of the presence of others as embodied or potentially embodied beings) is in continuing tension with sense (of the meaning of the narrative in which persons – author, character and consumer – are co-present). We can see this process modelled with great care in

[10] Gumbrecht, *Production of Presence*, p. 98.

Maria Edgeworth's 1817 novel, *Harrington*, a work she composed expressly to answer criticism of anti-Semitism by a young reader of her work. Rachel Mordecai (1788–1831) wrote to Edgeworth from a village in North Carolina in the summer of 1816 complaining that Edgeworth's children's stories represented Jews as 'by nature mean, avaricious and unprincipled'.[11]

Harrington's experience in the theatre is one of intense response to the presence of an actor on stage and the presence of a young Jewish woman offstage in the box next door to his own. His oscillation of response between meaning-effects and presence-effects is described with minute particularity in his first-person narration. The audience is expecting a comedy but the illness of the principal actor has meant that *The Merchant of Venice* is substituted at the last minute and the kerfuffle in the neighbouring box makes Harrington aware that Miss Berry whom he had thought at first to be an 'East Indian' is in fact a Jewess, a 'Jessica' (Shylock's daughter) as Harrington's companion puts it. Harrington confides 'I... stationed myself so that I had a better view of my object, and could observe her without being seen by any one', but as soon as Shylock, played by Charles Macklin, appears:

> I forgot every thing but him – such a countenance – such an expression of latent malice and revenge, of every thing detestable in human nature! Whether speaking or silent, the Jew fixed and kept possession of my attention.... In my enthusiasm, I stood up, I pressed forward, I leaned far over towards the stage that I might not lose a word, a look, a gesture.[12]

When the act finishes, Harrington turns to look again at Miss Berry, who is endeavouring to hide behind a pillar to avoid the curious gaze of the

---

[11]   Letter from Rachel Mordecai Lazarus to Maria Edgeworth, 7 August 1815, in *The Education of the Heart: The Correspondence of Rachel Mordecai Lazarus and Maria Edgeworth*, ed. Edgar E. MacDonald (Chapel Hill, NC: University of North Carolina Press, 1977), p. 341. See also Catherine Craft-Fairchild, '"The "Jewish Question" on Both Sides of the Atlantic: Harrington and the Correspondence between Maria Edgeworth and Rachel Mordecai Lazarus', *Eighteenth-Century Life*, 38, no. 3 (2014), 30–63. Edgeworth wrote an adult novel in response in which the hero Harrington is brought up to fear Jews in the bedtime stories told him by a malign nursery-maid. He begins the process of adjusting his ideas when he comes to London as an adult around 1780 and sees Charles Macklin perform as Shylock in Shakespeare's *The Merchant of Venice*.

[12]   Maria Edgeworth, *Harrington*, in *Leonora. Harrington*, ed. Marilyn Butler and Susan Manly, *The Novels and Selected Works of Maria Edgeworth*, general ed. Marilyn Butler and Mitzi Myers, vol. 3 (London: Pickering and Chatto, 1999), chapter 5, p. 214.

audience, and he apologises for blocking her view, but she begs him not to quit his place:

> But now my pleasure in the play was over. I could no longer enjoy Macklin's incomparable acting; I was so apprehensive of the pain which it must give the young Jewess. At every stroke, characteristic of the skilful actor, or of the master poet, I felt a strange mixture of admiration and regret. I almost wished that Shakespear had not written, or Macklin had not acted, the part so powerfully: my imagination formed such a strong conception of the pain the Jewess was feeling, and my inverted sympathy, if I may so call it, so overpowered my direct and natural feelings, that at every fresh development of the Jew's villainy I shrunk, as though I had been myself a Jew.[13]

Here, the response of one audience member prompts a transformation in the response of another: an intellectual conversion begins to be facilitated by an act of identification with feeling. The intimate flow of sympathy prompted by the presence-effect of Miss Berry breaks the focus of attention on a powerful stage performance. This kind of interruption is a requirement, Jacques Rancière argues, for the production of 'dissensus', the conversion of an aesthetic experience of performance into a potential for radical political change:

> Breaking away from the phantasms of the Word made flesh and the spectator turned active, knowing that words are only words and spectacles only spectacles, may help us understand how words, stories, and performances can help us change something in the world we live in.[14]

Edgeworth uses the medium of the novel to reproduce the presence-effect of theatre not only by describing this scene but also by inviting her readers to undergo the same conversion she herself experienced in her encounter with Rebecca Mordecai. The distance of geographical space between North Carolina and Ireland, between temporalities (Edgeworth's past children's writing and her present novels, Harrington's world of 1780 and the present of author and reader in 1817) is bridged by the immediacy of this scene of affect. But the scene is also given in a printed narrative

---

[13]   Ibid., p. 215.
[14]   Jacques Rancière, 'The Emancipated Spectator', *Artforum International*, 45, no. 7 (2007), 280.

which enables a turn away, or enough of a turn away, from the corporeal 'seen' to the textual 'seen' to produce a reflective repudiation of political prejudice. To produce, in Gumbrecht's terms, 'an intellectually and aesthetically productive tension between meaning effects and presence effects'.[15]

Moreover, Edgeworth provides us with a scene in which traditional gender dynamics are remediated. Most commonly in novels, first-time visitors to the theatre who become immersed in its presence-effects are women: indeed, this is Miss Berry's first visit to the theatre, Harrington is informed. Here, however, it is the male theatregoer who focalises the narrative and whose immersive experience we readers are also immersed in. The traditional gender dynamics of anti-Semitic prejudice nonetheless inform the scene: the Jew Shylock is the stock picture of malice and avarice, his daughter Jessica – brought to life offstage in the person of Miss Berry – mitigates that villainy and provides a bridge to the gentile world: indeed, prompts a passionate love in a gentile admirer.

Maria Edgeworth and Rebecca Mordecai provide an alternative model of encounter: an older and younger woman meet on the terrain of the letter which Edgeworth converts into a public performance of remediation: of political injustice. Edgeworth invites us to 'see' consumers of fictions of stage and page and the fiction of what consuming such fictions can mean from a new, and more complex, perspective. What is seen is not immaterial in this process. There is a dynamic relationship between the story seen whether on the page or on the stage and the ethical perspective of the one who sees (reader or audience-member).

In the next two chapters, I look at two fictional presentations of consumers that feature in both plays and novels: the mimic and the critic. Both are characterised as 'errant' forms of consumer, their behaviours a kind of present admonition to audiences and readers that helps to shape an absent 'ideal'. Here too, a person is unconcealed and then withdrawn, brought into being and then negated as being, because he/she fails to find in art a way of living. Rather, both mimic and critic bring perspectives not appropriate to the work of art – derived from elsewhere – to form a relationship with the work that is out of touch with its own principles of being. In each case – that of the female mimic and that of the male critic – I chart the sense of a rivalry between the modes of theatre and novel. The theatre casts the mimic as a (female) novel reader who walks on to the stage and applies a set of unreal norms to the 'real' world she inhabits. The novel casts the mimic as a (female) theatre-addict too vulnerable to affect and unable to achieve the critical distance required to assure moral behaviour in the 'real'

---

[15]   Gumbrecht, *Production of Presence*, p. 19.

world that prose fiction claims to represent. The theatre casts the critic as a (male) reader of dramatic theory preoccupied with letter over spirit. And the novel casts the critic as a (male) consumer of theatre preoccupied with his own performance.

The 'types' of critic and mimic are negative constructions serving to re-instantiate the borders of genre, to contain and manage the 'new' opportunities for imagining presence afforded by both theatre and novel in response to each other and to the new determinants of the Licensing Act of 1737 and the growth in the market for and forms of print. Hence in this section I look at how the persons of the 'mimic' and 'critic' are used to differentiate media of theatre and novel. I also look at the ways in which these terms tend to be gendered. The mimic is female and the critic male and when men or women adopt either role transgressing these gender expectations they are also seen as 'crossing' genders themselves: the female critic is masculinised, the male mimic feminised. The borders of genre and of gender are policed and identities are shaped simultaneously. Moments of transitivity or transgression further the business of cultural 'border-patrol'. The male critic runs the risk of being no more than an empty mimic of the theories of theatre he has absorbed and the female mimic only reveals her own intellectual shortcomings when she attempts to perform the role of a critic.

Chapter 14
The Mimic

What shall I sing – at this contagious time,
When ev'ry son of ribaldry and rhime
Struts forth, with self applause to act this part?
Up, muse, and chaunt the Mimic's various art.
That human ape, who, mirror-like, reflects
Our shapes, our faces, beauties, and defects:
We meet him heedless, but with wonder find,
That when we part – we leave ourselves behind.[1]

To imitate is an attempt to 'be there', to enter into someone else's role. Equally, we might understand it as an act that distances us from that present and presence. As we have seen with Samuel Richardson's Pamela (see Chapter 9), the author's claim was for his heroine's inimitability. Others look and behave like her but the measure of their failure to match up is shown in that they do not command the same sway: in fact, they do not invite imitation as she does. However, imitation also puts the original under threat, the threat of erasure, the accusation that the authority it claims is empty if it can be exactly copied by others. Homi Bhabha describes mimicry as an effective destabilising practice in colonial discourse:

> Mimicry emerges as the representation of a difference that is itself a process of disavowal. Mimicry is, thus, the sign of a double articulation; a complex strategy of reform, regulation, and discipline, which "appropriates" the Other as it visualizes power.[2]

Mimicry was a staple technique of the eighteenth-century theatre for a number of reasons. It was an effective procedure for a partisan stage and a competitive market. Overt partisan, sexual or libellous reference in a play text risked censorship, whereas an impersonation of the gestures and style

---

[1] Samuel Foote, *The Mimic, A Poem. By the Author* (London: J. Scott, 1761), pp. 9–10.
[2] Homi Bhabha, 'Of Mimicry and Man: The Ambivalence of Colonial Discourse', *October*, 28 (1984), 126.

of a well-known public figure would not be recognised in an otherwise unmarked playscript. After the Licensing Act, unlicensed or temporarily licensed stages attracted audiences by mocking the two theatre managements (Covent Garden and Drury Lane) that held licences. Actors' power to mimic could be a source of revenue and fame – as well as infamy.

Mimicry was central to Samuel Foote's career as a playwright, actor and manager. The poem *The Mimic* which serves as the epigraph to this chapter, was composed by an admirer of Foote and was published accompanied by a preface addressed to Foote. Foote's most controversial satire, *The Minor* (first performed in Crow Street, Dublin, in January 1760 and transferred to the Little Theatre, Haymarket, on 28 June 1760), took Methodism and its power to generate imitation as its target. George Whitefield's persuasive oratory made preaching a greater theatrical draw than the theatre industry under licensing restriction could offer. Whitefield is presented in Foote's play as Dr Squintum, the Methodist preacher whose spiritual excitations are easily compatible with the sexual ones trafficked by his follower, the brothel-madam, Mrs Cole.

In the main plot of the play, a young man about town, Sir George Wealthy, is brought back to morality through the combined play-acting powers of his father, uncle, and a hired mimic, Shift; George undergoes a moral conversion and leaves off bad company as well as saving from forced prostitution his virtuous cousin, Lucy, whom he takes as his wife. Foote took three parts in the play: the mimic Shift; an actor-turned-preacher named Smirk; and Mrs Cole. In the latter part, Foote dressed in drag and impersonated the well-known Scottish bawd Jenny Douglas (c. 1700–61) to whom he was said to bear some resemblance.[3]

The play serves as a virtuoso demonstration of Foote's talents. His powers of mimicry assert his presence in the theatrical scene, his command and control of performance to hit several satiric targets at once. Simultaneously he mocks those who lack this kind of command, for whom imitation is a sign of their absence of self-control: Mrs Cole espouses Methodism to allow her to continue her trade as brothel-madam with absolution. Gout-ridden, obese, greedy Mrs Cole mouths the language of grace 'in my last illness, I was wish'd to Mr. Squintum, who stepp'd in with his saving grace, got me with the new birth, and I became, as you see, regenerate, and another creature'.[4] Foote, then, claimed to use his powers of mimicry to bring a town run mad by Methodism to its senses, to see in theatrical performance imitating enthusiastic embodiment the falsity of the claims

---

[3]   Ian Kelly, *Mr Foote's Other Leg* (London: Picador, 2012), p. 375.

[4]   Samuel Foote, *The Minor* (London: J. Coote et al., 1760), Act 1, p. 46.

to presence that the townspeople failed to recognise when they attended religious assemblies.[5]

Mimicry was not just a matter of persons; it could also relate to genres and in particular complaints that individual works simply mimicked others or reproduced a type. In a two-act comedy entitled *The Author* which opened at Drury Lane on 5 February 1757, Foote turned to the familiar matter of satirising the business of print and publication as an industry built on plagiarism. As Mrs Cole does, it wraps up old wares in new packaging to hoodwink its customers. Foote had a specific target, John Apreece, who had offered Foote money in exchange for good publicity; he appears as Cadwallader, a foolish vain and over-fond husband whose sister Arabella is the object of the penniless author, young Cape's, affections. Here, though, we also see the actor's art of mimicry associated with the reproduction and repetition of literary works. In both cases there is a distinction between empty imitation as a result of stupidity or cupidity and a well-wrought act of reforming mimicry. The bookseller Vamp is commissioning work from his authors and asks young Cape for two octavos ready for the spring. Cape's friend, Sprightly, asks:

> *Spri.* Upon what Subject?
> *Vamp.* I leave that to him; Master *Cape* knows what will do, tho' Novels are a pretty light Summer reading, and do very well at *Tunbridge, Bristol*, and the other watering Places: No bad Commodity for the *West-Indies* Trade neither; let 'em be Novels, Master *Cape.*
> *Cape.* You shall be certainly supply'd.[6]

Novels have a special place in the economy of eighteenth-century comedy. The generic title 'novel' suggests something entirely new but the claim to newness, like the claim to fashion, is revealed to be in fact an act of empty imitation. All novels are in fact the same, are easily substitutable for each other. And they, like those who imitate the behaviour within their covers, are easily seen through: they excuse selfish pleasure and teach mimicry rather than independent and ethical thought.

The best-known example of this critique of the novel in the theatre is Richard Brinsley Sheridan's *The Rivals* (first performed at Covent Garden on 17 January 1775). Jack Absolute is courting silly novel-reader Lydia

---

5   Misty Anderson, 'Actors and Ghosts: Methodism and the Theatre of the Real', chapter 4 of *Imagining Methodism: Enthusiasm, Belief, and the Borders of the Self* (Baltimore, MD: Johns Hopkins University Press, 2012).
6   Samuel Foote, *The Author* (London, R. Francklin, 1757), Act 1, n.p.

Languish. He confides to his friend that he is not only a rival for her affections with the country bumpkin Bob Acres and the Irish soldier Sir Lucius O'Trigger:

> *Abs:* [Acres] is likewise a rival of mine – that is of my *other self's*, for he does not think his friend Capt. Absolute ever saw the lady in question; – and it is ridiculous enough to hear him complain to me of *one Beverley* a concealed skulking rival, who –
> *Falk:* Hush! he's here.[7]

Absolute reveals that the hidden and true rival to Jack Absolute in his courtship of the novel-besotted Lydia Languish is himself. In a play that pits Absolute against two rivals for Lydia's affections (Bob Acres, Sir Lucius O'Trigger), it becomes apparent that the only serious contender is his own entirely fictional creation, Ensign Beverley – a dashing impoverished soldier who promises adventure and elopement by comparison with Jack Absolute, worthy young heir and approved suitor. In the manuscript submitted to the Lord Chamberlain prior to performance, a passage that was excised in the first printed edition underlines the fictional nature of this rivalry through the words of Sir Lucius O'Trigger in the final scene (Act 5, scene 3).[8] When Lucius realises that his amatory correspondent is in fact Lydia's ageing aunt, he concedes:

> Captain Absolute, I ask your pardon for the trouble I have given you. Mrs Malaprop has very agreeably convinc'd me of my error! We were only Rivals by Mistake, and Mr Acres, too, (my other Rival that was) I must beg your pardon for – unless you make pretensions to this Lady [i.e. Mrs Malaprop] also.[9]

Absolute uses techniques from the drama to counteract the dangerous influence of the novel that drives his wayward beloved to risk their union, maintaining his part as Beverley to Lydia and his other role as Absolute to his father and her aunt.

---

[7] Richard Brinsley Sheridan, *The Rivals*, ed. Richard Little Purdy (Oxford: Clarendon Press, 1930), Act 1, sc.1, p. 25.

[8] Sheridan revised the play after one performance (17 January 1775). He tempered some of the extravagance of language, double entendre, references to duelling and considerably altered the roles of Sir Lucius (played by John Lee, who did not know his lines) and Sir Antony Absolute to which reviewers objected. The revised play opened with Lawrence Clinch playing Lucius on 28 January to acclaim.

[9] Sheridan, *The Rivals*, ed. Purdy, p. 117.

The story of an obsession with novels on the part of foolish girls and adult women was a familiar one to comic drama. Polly Honeycombe – the eponymous heroine of George Colman the Elder's well-established one-act farce (first performed at Drury Lane on 5 December 1760) – refuses to give up on her 'novel' admirer, Scribble, even after he is revealed not to be the honourable suitor he claims but a simple attorney's clerk. The farce is left unresolved with Mr Honeycombe's preferred suitor, the pompous Mr Ledger, retiring from his courtship, Polly's co-conspiratorial nurse exposed as the aunt of Scribble seeking to promote his interest, and Scribble threatening to sue Honeycombe claiming that his union with Polly complies with the strictures of the 1753 Marriage Act.[10] The only possible resolution is in the unlikely hands of Polly's so-far-ineffectual and alcohol-dependent mother, who advises her husband: 'You are too violent – Go, my dear, go and compose yourself, and I'll set all matters to rights.'[11]

While Polly and Scribble are evident antecedents of Lydia and Beverley/Absolute, Polly is an unusual heroine, with no trace of her successor's sentimentality. It is the adventure of the novel, indeed its down-to-earthness, that attracts this young woman. The prologue delivered by Mr King, the actor who played Scribble, makes visible the transition from the familiar satire of the smitten romance reader to that of the livelier novel addict. Novel, we are told, is 'The younger Sister of ROMANCE':

> Less solemn is her air, her drift the same,
> And NOVEL her enchanting, charming, Name.
> ROMANCE might strike our grave Forefathers' pomp,
> But NOVEL for our Buck and lively Romp![12]

Instead of the bulky folios of romance we have 'Two Neat Pocket Volumes', sentimental in style and full of incident in each chapter. This Polly is a 'pocket' version of the romance reader, just as the one-act afterpiece is a miniaturised or pocket version of the mainpiece three- or five-act comedy that usually precedes its performance. The preface to *Polly Honeycombe* provides an account of the reservations of the author's mother about the play, as well as an amusing anecdote about events that persuade her his satire on the novel is well-deserved and necessary. Colman's mother's reservations

---

[10] Under Lord Hardwicke's Marriage Actthose under the age of twenty-one had to have parental consent if they married by licence; marriages by banns, by contrast, were valid as long as the parent of the minor did not actually forbid the banns.

[11] *The Rivals: Richard Brinsley Sheridan; and Polly Honeycombe: George Colman the Elder*, ed. David A. Brewer (Peterborough, ON: Broadview Press, 2012), pp. 108–9.

[12] Ibid., p. 68.

are, interestingly, that the play itself fails to conform to the rules of comic *drama*: indeed, that this satire upon the novel is too novelistic:

> She is astonished at my attempting to violate the received laws of the
> Drama – that the *Catastrophe* (that was really her word) is directly
> contrary to all known rules – that the several Characters, instead of
> being dismissed, one by one, should have been industriously kept
> together, to make a bow to the audience at the dropping of the curtain.[13]

Novel and theatre are not, it seems, simply rivals for the same audience but also rivals for the laurels of 'realism' and 'probability'. While the play itself argues that novel-reading leads women to delusive visions of the reality of courtship and marriage, the preface here suggests that dramatic conventions lead to improbable unions and unlikely closure, which an allusion to the less predictable outcomes found in a 'new' form of narrative make visible.

Half an Hour after Supper: A New Novel (1789), an anonymous one-act interlude, was likely composed and produced in self-conscious debt to *Polly Honeycombe*. It was first performed as an afterpiece in May of 1789 at the Haymarket, and it was – according to the preface of the published work – written by a woman who enjoyed the patronage of the theatre manager; it is not clear whether the patron the playwright refers to is George Colman the Elder or Younger, who were both active in the theatre in the spring before the father's mental collapse, but it seems more likely that it is the Elder since the 'Authoress' (as she terms herself) speaks of the manager's being 'revered by all' and having already given 'delicate and kind encouragements' to the 'gentle and the fearful'.[14]

Contrasting sisters, the vivacious Sukey and the sentimental Eliza, keen to imitate the heroines they admire in modern fiction, and aided by a resourceful nurse, plan to elope with their suitors, Captain Berry and George Bentley (the son of a baronet), in the half-hour after supper. Their novel-obsessed aunt, Tabitha, discovers the suitors hidden beneath the table when she returns to the parlour to retrieve a volume of her favourite novel and is fooled into believing that Bentley has been admitted to the house in order to court her. Swiftly persuaded to concede to his violent passion, she leaves to enter the waiting carriage, but, before the girls can escape also, their father, upright merchant Mr Sturdy, interrupts them.

---

[13] Brewer, ed., *Polly Honeycombe*, p. 60.
[14] *Half an Hour after Supper: An Interlude, in One Act, as Performed at the Theatre Royal, Haymarket* [London: J. Debrett, 1789], n.p.).

When Sturdy expresses a willingness to consider the matches, Berry leaves not prepared to engage in anything but an elopement, but Bentley confesses himself the ordinary son of a businessman and the play concludes with the likely promise of his employment with Sturdy and eventual union with his beloved Eliza, as well as the discovery that Tabitha has willingly departed in the postilion with Berry. A note prefixed to the printed version of the play finds the authoress express a hope that her own script will come to rival the novels in the closets of her female readers:

> The favourable reception with which this little sketch has been honoured by a generous publick, demands the most grateful acknowledgements of its authoress; who now commits it to the press, in the hope it may not offend, or lose its value, in the closets of her fair countrywomen – whose literary pursuits, though she ever regrets to see them terminate in FEMALE PEDANTRY would, in her opinion, be still more to their honour, were they not too frequently engaged in the dangerous detail of amorous adventures, or, at best, tending to idle and frivolous amusement.[15]

The Monthly Review echoed the reference to the closet in its response to the published play, interestingly suggesting that it likely worked better as a stage play than a substitute for novel reading in a closet: 'We hope, for the sake of the moral, that, on the stage, it possessed some little interest; of which, we are sorry to say, it is totally deficient in the closet.'[16] Indeed, the novel-reading portrayed in this afterpiece is largely performative and sociable; Tabitha reads to the family interrupted by her impatient brother who is no martinet and refuses to lead his family by force and prohibition; the servant Frank, who reads snatches of the novels discarded in the family parlour, complains that they are covered in grease and ink from the hands of previous borrowers from the circulating library. Novels are not handsome and pristine volumes enjoyed in solitary communion, but grubby, much passed around, shared sources of collective pleasure for women and servants. The 'moral' of the drama suggests that the novel's power is dissipated in this diffusion. It is Tab, the spinster aunt, we note, who returns alone to retrieve her volume of the novel and it is Tab who is conveniently taken off the family's hands at the close of the play. Novels appear to have resolved rather than broken a family crisis by precipitating action.

---

[15] *Half an Hour after Supper*, n.p.
[16] Ralph Griffith, 'Art. 59 Half an Hour after Supper: An Interlude, in One Act', *Monthly Review*, 81 (1789), 284.

The sentimental heroine in *Half an Hour after Supper* is rewarded for her virtue and loyalty with a happy marriage. The sprightly impulsive heroine in the same play (Sukey) is disappointed in her choice of man, while a similar character type, her forebear, Polly, is won by default. But perhaps most importantly, these performances anticipate their own reception by relying on an audience recognising allusion to another 'rival' system of representation, especially that of the novel.

Rivals for mimesis: theatrical treatments of the novel

Half an Hour and *Polly Honeycombe* provide new variants on a familiar theme: the danger of imitative reading, especially for women. Recent cognitive theory has been especially attracted by the neuro-scientific evidence concerning 'mirror' neurons: that imitation or performance of emotion, or watching an imitation or performance of an emotion, stimulates the same response in the brain as the primary experience of that emotion.[17] Eighteenth-century cultural commentators were engaged in a similar (if more value-laden) debate about the tendency to 'mirror' representation among a (newly) literate and theatregoing public, especially in the metropolis of London, where the two media flourished side by side. In this respect, the proliferation of theories of acting and of criticism of theatre relates productively to the lively and ongoing conversation about the 'novel' as a prompt for incendiary or affective or sociable response. Here, however, I explore a different 'mirror' effect: that plays about the power of prose fiction to prompt imitative behaviour in female readers mirror novels about the power of dramatic performance to prompt imitative behaviour in a female audience, and (of course) vice versa.

In eighteenth-century England, the most familiar theatrical representation of a female mind swayed by fiction (early recognised as the female equivalent of Cervantes' Don Quixote) was Richard Steele's successful play, *The Tender Husband* (1705). Steele's play (a performance of which Pamela attends and criticises as we saw in chapter 9) drew a comic portrait of Biddy Tipkin, a merchant's daughter obsessed with romances who is tricked into a marriage with an impoverished aristocrat passing himself off as a hero from the fictions she so admires.

---

[17]   See Giacomo Rizzolatti, Corrado Sinigaglia and Frances Anderson, *Mirrors in the Brain: How Our Minds Share Actions, Emotions, and Experience* (Oxford: Oxford University Press, 2008).

Two plays of the mid-eighteenth century continue with the plot of the misguided romance heroine fooled into marriage. However, there is a significant new relationship announced in a familiar narrative at this point: with the published novel and *its* claims to act as an antidote to the romance. A two-act comedy entitled *Angelica; or Quixote in petticoats* was printed for its anonymous author in 1758 with a dedicatory preface to David Garrick, which explains that the Drury Lane actor-manager had turned the play down for performance because of its similarity to Steele's *Tender Husband.* The phenomenon of the published play text that has seen *no* performance suggests another form of 'mirroring': that the play might be consumed under similar circumstances to the novel, indeed serve as a surrogate for the novel.

The advertisement asserts that the character of Angelica and 'the heroic part of Careless, is not only borrow'd, but entirely taken, from the female Quixote, of the ingenious Mrs. Lennox'.[18] In Charlotte Lennox's 1752 novel, *The Female Quixote: or, the Adventures of Arabella,*[19] the heroine is persuaded to abandon her delusion that romance narratives are a true representation of life by transferring her attachment to novels. The novel is presented to her as a more rational and credible mimetic performance than the works from her dead mother's library that she came to admire and model her own life upon.

A 1777 play by the actor Robert Hitchcock entitled *The Coquette; or, the Mistakes of the Heart,* performed at the theatres of Hull, the Haymarket and York also took its source or at least acknowledged its debt not to another play (or play tradition) but from a novel: Eliza Haywood's *History of Miss Betsy Thoughtless* (1751).[20] Haywood's work was a near contemporary to the *Female Quixote* and equally concerned to bring down a peg or two a heroine over-persuaded by the theory rather than practice of romance courtship.

Neither *Angelica* nor *The Coquette,* however, bears a close relation to its acknowledged source; indeed, both plays pursue plot lines familiar from the drama rather than the novel. Unlike Lennox's Arabella, Angelica has a sister, Melinda, pursued by her suitor's friend, Modeley. Where Arabella has a simple and trusting maid, Angelica's maid, Maria, is a familiar figure

---

[18] Anon., *Angelica; or Quixote in Petticoats. A Comedy, in Two Acts* (London: Printed for the Author, 1758), n.p.

[19] Charlotte Lennox, *The Female Quixote: or, the Adventures of Arabella,* ed. Margaret Dalziel (Oxford: Oxford University Press, 2008).

[20] Robert Hitchcock, *The Coquette; or, the Mistakes of the Heart* (Bath: R. Cruttwell, 1777); Eliza Haywood, *The History of Miss Betsy Thoughtless,* ed. Christine Blouch, Broadview Literary Texts (Peterborough, ON: Broadview, 1998).

from the comedy of intrigue. Feisty and scheming, if equally ignorant of romance conventions, Maria makes a good profit by accepting bribes from her mistress's suitors and eventually wins herself a husband in the wily servant of one of the suitors, George. Unlike Lennox's Angelica, the play's heroine does not convince all who meet her of her sense and understanding. She is – like Biddy Tipkin – inclined only to an antique style of speech, a tendency to call all her suitors 'presumptuous', and an inconvenient commitment to the romance tradition's expectation of many years of chaste courtship prior to marriage.

The Coquette is only distantly related to its source, borrowing some plot motifs and a few characters. The popular comical character in the novel of an elderly sea captain named Hysom, who courts Betsy only in sailing metaphors, becomes the figure of Captain Helm in the play, suitor to Flora Younglove (who shares her first name and the burden of a lustful widowed mother with the character of Flora Mellasin, Betsy's cousin and rival in Haywood's novel). Frederick Fineer is reprised in the role of the dressmaker Mrs Fashion's son, who passes himself off as the enamoured aristocrat Lord Flamwell in an effort to trick the play-heroine (renamed Miss Bloomer) into marriage. However, Betsy's unhappy marriage to Mr Munden and her reconciliation with her first suitor, Mr Trueworth (only after he has himself loved and lost a first wife), finds no place in this conventional if rather rambling comedy.

Neither Betsy nor her theatrical counterpart, Miss Bloomer, is a novel reader. Both are young women of fashion over-persuaded of their sway in the world by the deference that their suitors pay them before marriage. It is noteworthy that the long history of representing the female Quixote figure in the drama often draws parallels, indeed suggests some uncanny mirroring, of the woman of fashion and the romance reader – despite the former's addiction to the novel and the latter's addiction to the antique. Here, as elsewhere, we see how often the romance – its old-fashionedness, its capacity to prompt unthinking imitation – serves as a surrogate generic rival, whether for advocates for the 'new' form of storytelling (the novel) or advocates for another established medium for storytelling (the drama). The romance is easily cast as an old and outworn form overtaken by new and more present, more embodied, experiences of consuming fiction.

The transition from the figure of the female romance to the female novel-reader (or in the case of Miss Bloomer in *The Coquette* to the 'modern miss') is not a smooth one. Its rough passage rather illustrates the active rivalry between two modern forms: the revived Georgian theatre and the mid-century domestic novel. The novel heroine is impatient and busy, sexually and socially aware by comparison with her idealising, often platonic, forebear. She will not wait or expect a ten-year courtship from her lover. She runs the risk of seeming fast or debauched but can also represent a modernising force who educates an indulgent father-figure (Sturdy and Absolute if not Honeycombe) in the new sociable forms of authority emerging during the mid-eighteenth century. She might also be seen to have learned something from the theatrical context in which she so often appears. Theatre audiences cannot be expected to wait a long time for the 'catastrophe' of their plots. Getting smartish to a conclusion – as the proliferation of short-form dramas such as the interlude, the afterpiece, and the burletta indicates – was a necessary requirement to ensure that an evening's entertainment was busy and varied. An author such as Sheridan received a critical panning for an over-length five-act play that was to become a huge favourite once it was cut down to size.

Moreover, the female novel 'mimic' on stage is not only curtailed in terms of the time she is allowed to occupy, but also contained by the very business of being represented on stage and in the presence of a discerning audience. Georgian audiences, we should perhaps remind ourselves, were always conscious of the theatrical space in which they saw these narratives acted out and they were especially aware of the irony that actresses known for sexual dalliance and for their financial shrewdness were playing the parts of innocent heroines at risk. The theatres themselves were understood to be places of risk and exposure for women.

By contrast, the danger of the novel was most often articulated in terms of the risk attending *not* being on public view; intimate relations with the written text could take part in a private boudoir without the surveillance of other family members. The assumed tendency among women to mimic popular narrative representations, whether encountered on the public stage or in the private boudoir, is a vehicle for early formulations of audience response. Novelists who paid attention to the experience of women at the theatre experiment with representations of the capacity of the theatre to prompt imitation, experiments that also restage a ubiquitous rivalry between novelistic and theatrical narrative.

Rivals for mimesis: novelistic treatments of the theatre

Richard Steele's long-estranged friend, Delarivier Manley – who began her public career as a writer with two stage plays in 1696 (*The Lost Lover* at Drury Lane and *The Royal Mischief* at Lincoln's Inn Fields) – highlighted the risk that the affective power of theatre might prompt imitation in its female audience in her influential scandal novel, *Secret Memoirs and*

Manners...From the New Atalantis (1709). At the end of the first volume, readers encounter the story of Louisa, who is, like her author, persuaded into a bigamous marriage. Louisa is a young orphan of whom Hernando Volpone's wife is very fond and whom she has raised on the principles of strictest virtue in their family home. Hernando, now jaded with his wife and seeking to triumph over her, determines to set about seducing Louisa. When Louisa is courted by a young man named Wilmot who invites her to the opera, Volpone insists on accompanying them. In her depiction of Louisa's response to an opera fortuitously concerned with a woman's guiltless bigamy, Manley focalises through the lascivious Volpone:

> Louisa, who did not see such Representations, became extremely mov'd at this: Her young Breasts heav'd with Sorrow; the Tears fill'd her Eyes, and she betray'd her Sense of their Misfortune with a Tenderness that Hernando did not think had been in her; he was infinitely pleas'd, and employ'd a world of pains to applaud, instead of ridiculing, as his Lady did, that sensibility of Soul; when they came away, he took care that her Hand should fall to his share: As they were going home, he sat over against her, in the same manner as before. At Supper, the Play was their Subject: His Wife was reasoning about the Accident of the double Marriage, and said it was necessary the Poet should dispatch her out of the way, for loaded with such a Misfortune, 'twas impossible she should live without being infamous, and consequently detesting her self. Hernando was not of the same Opinion, and upon that Head, in his eloquent manner, introduc'd a learned Discourse of the lawfullness of double Marriages.[21]

The 'opera' Louisa attends is most likely reference to the best-known play concerning bigamy of the period – Thomas Southerne's *The Fatal Marriage* (1694), based on Aphra Behn's novella, *The History of the Nun; or, the Fair Vow-Breaker* (1689). If so, for the reader in the know, Hernando's eventual success in persuading Louisa to espouse bigamy as a conscious and (for her) moral choice, is especially remarkable: both play and novel concern a woman who is an unwitting bigamist, persuaded into marrying a second

[21]   Delarivier Manley, *Secret Memoirs and Manners of several Persons of both Sexes. From the New Atalantis*, in *The Selected Works of Delarivier Manley*, ed. Rachel Carnell and Ruth Herman, 5 vols (London: Pickering and Chatto, 2005), vol. 2, p. 132. The separately published key indicates that the scandal to which Manley is referring concerned William Cowper, first Earl Cowper, Whig MP for Hertford Castle and rumours that he seduced Miss Elizabeth Culling or Cullen of Hertingfordbury Park, Hertfordshire, while married to Judith Cowper, née Booth.

suitor after she has been convinced of the death of her first husband on the battlefield.

The incommensurability between the dramatic content and the actual circumstances of Louisa's seduction is not an oversight on Manley's part. Rather, the 'anti-theatricality' of the story lies in the argument that the affective power of the performance and play prompts an imitative response in a female audience member that makes her vulnerable to seduction. Hernando's arguments are many and carefully outlined, but only serve to remind the reflective reader (as opposed to the merely 'reflecting' or 'mirroring' female theatregoer) that the case for more than one spouse is designed to advantage a predatory male, rather than to provide the heroine with an opportunity for tragic authority and sway:

> he own'd that in all Ages, Women had been appropriated, that for the benefit and distinction of Children, with other necessary Occurrences, Polygamy had been justly deny'd the Sex, since the coldness of their Constitution, the length of time they carry'd their Children, and other Incidents seem'd to declare against them; but for a Man who possess'd an uninterrupted Capacity of propagating the Specie, and must necessarily find all the Inconveniencies above-mention'd, in any one Wife; the Law of Nature, as well as the Custom of many Nations, and most Religions, seem'd to declare for him.[22]

If Manley warns that the experience of the theatre may stimulate a desire to emulate the affective force of the tragic actress in women, other writers warn there are behaviours and pleasures that women may imitate in the theatre not portrayed on stage. More common, perhaps, in the novel is the representation of the loose and sexualised environs of the pit as a dangerous lure to women. In Eliza Haywood's the *History of Miss Betsy Thoughtless* (1751), it is Betsy's thoughtless behaviour at the theatre that further estranges her suitor, Mr Trueworth.[23] He arrives at her house to find Betsy dressed to go to the theatre with her disreputable friend, Miss Forward. She intends to attend the first night of a tragedy at Lincoln's Inn Fields, despite Trueworth's warning that she should not be seen 'with a woman of her fame, in a place as public as the playhouse'.[24] Betsy receives a letter from Miss Forward confirming a box is procured and sets off with

[22] Ibid., pp. 132–3.
[23] Eliza Haywood, *The History of Miss Betsy Thoughtless*, ed. Christine Blouch, Broadview Literary Texts (Peterborough, ON: Broadview Press, 1998), vol. 2, chapters 9 and 10.
[24] Ibid., vol. 2, chapter 9, p. 231.

the internal conviction of being prudent given the reservations of a man she trusts. However, their late arrival means the box is lost and they must content themselves with the third row in the pit. All too soon Betsy forgets her serious intentions:

> the brilliant audience, – the musick, – the moving scenes exhibited on the stage, and above all the gallantries, with which herself and Miss Forward were treated, by several gay young gentlemen, who, between the acts, presented them with fruits and sweet-meats, soon dissipated all those reflections, which it was so much her interest to have cherished, and she once more relapsed into her former self.[25]

Two rakes invite the ladies to dine at a tavern to which Miss Forward agrees; however, when one of the rakes makes advances and realises Betsy's innocence he takes pity on her and conducts her honourably home. This story is retold from Trueworth's rather than Betsy's perspective two chapters later (chapter eleven) and we learn that he also attended the theatre in a black periwig and muffled in a cloak, placing himself in 'a part of the middle gallery, which had the full command of more than half the boxes'.[26] Trueworth has to move to another post in the theatre in order to spot the two ladies and watches the sly nods and winks among the regular pit members at the behaviour of Betsy. At the end of the play he stands at the door and sees her leave with two men he knows are utter strangers to her in a hackney coach.

This incident leads Trueworth to reason he must give Betsy up despite his continuing love. Accordingly, he embarks on an affair with Flora Mellasin, the besotted and lustful stepdaughter of Betsy's guardian. This affair loosens the bonds of his affection for Betsy and makes possible a new and honourable attachment to Harriot Loveit, the sister of his friend, Sir Bazil. Harriot is an aristocratic countrywoman who dislikes London, finds court dull and masquerades too inclusive. Nonetheless, she admires plays and opera and considers they can be improving. When absent from London, she finds means to 'enjoy in theory all the satisfaction the representation could afford' through private performance:

> "This is somewhat extraordinary, indeed madam," cried Mr. Trueworth; "be so good as to let us know by what method." "It is this, sir," answered she; – "as for the plays, I have a very good collection of old ones by me, and have all the new ones sent down to me when they

25   Ibid., vol. 2., chapter 9, p. 236.
26   Ibid., vol. 2, chapter 11, p. 245.

come out; – when I was last in London, I was several times at the theatre, – I observed how the actors and actresses varied their voices and gestures, according to the different characters they appeared in on the stage; – and thus, whilst I am reading my play, am enabled to judge pretty near how it shews in representation. – I have, indeed, somewhat more difficulty in bringing the opera home to me, yet I am so happy as to be able to procure a shadow of it at least; – we have two or three gentlemen in the neighbourhood, who play to great perfection on the violin, and several ladies, who have very pretty voices, and some skill in music; – my sister touches the bass viol finely, and I play a little on the harpsichord; – we have all our parts in score before us, which we execute to the best of our power: – it serves, however, to divert ourselves, and those friends who think it worth their while to come and hear us."

Mr. Trueworth cried out, in a kind of rapture, as soon as she had done speaking. – "Who would not think himself happy to be one of the audience at such a performance?"[27]

Haywood effectively translates the space of the theatre with the risks that have been so evident in Betsy's experience to that of the domestic home. Harriot is secure in the company of a virtuous married sister when she attends the theatre in London but is also able to engage in a reflective imitative relation to metropolitan theatrical performance in the security of her own home with gentlemen and ladies she knows. It comes as no surprise that Trueworth makes her his bride, although Haywood finally engineers a conclusion that allows a chastened Betsy (after a failed marriage) and grieving Trueworth (on the death of his virtuous bride) to be united. The novel, then, does not refute or refuse the theatre's capacity to stimulate affective response, but it contains or reframes this within the form of the book. Haywood also presents the home and its known quantities of family and locality as the most appropriate space for women to imitate and experience again those responses.

One reader of *Betsy Thoughtless*, at least, saw a connection between this novel and the debate over poetic justice and women's ethical capacity to resist the lure of imitation – which began in theatre criticism but had by the mid-eighteenth century, largely through the vehicle of Samuel Richardson's *Clarissa* (1747–48), migrated also to the genre of the novel. Anne Donnellan wrote to Samuel Richardson on 11 February 1752: 'Who the author of Betsy Thoughtless is, I don't know, but his [*sic*] poetic justice I think very

---

[27]   Ibid., vol. 2, chapter 22, pp. 317–18.

bad: he kills a good woman to make way for one of the worst, in my opinion, I ever read of.'[28]

The debate over poetic justice in the early eighteenth century concerned the stage genre of tragedy. The gauntlet in the debate was thrown down by Joseph Addison in 1711 in *Spectator* no. 40 (Monday 16 April).[29] Addison denounces poetic justice as implausible and false because in life virtue is not always rewarded or vindicated. Art should imitate life, he asserts. John Dennis in a 'Letter to the Spectator' (1711) argued by contrast that tragedy must emphasise the rewards of virtue and ensure that evildoers are punished during the performance. Richardson explicitly evoked this debate in his postscript to *Clarissa* (1748–49).[30] He was responding to those readers who had written requesting a happy ending to the novel as it appeared in serial volume publication and he deployed Addison to defend his decision not to comply.

It is, no doubt, this postscript that another of Richardson's admirers, the actress turned novelist Frances Sheridan, expected would come to mind for readers of the opening pages of her novel, *The Memoirs of Miss Sidney Bidulph* (1761); 'The Editor's Introduction' stages a framing debate about the plausible and moral limits of the endings of drama and prose fiction. The fictional editor introduces us to a company in a domestic house in Buckinghamshire, who make their evening's entertainment the private reading of John Home's *Douglas* (1757). *Douglas* was a tragic play written by a minister of the Church of Scotland who was forced to resign due to Presbyterian outrage that a clergyman should be a playwright. Home asked the earl of Bute, Scottish mentor of the future George III, to support him in placing the play when he sent the manuscript in 1755 to Garrick for Drury Lane, but it was rejected. The work was nonetheless successfully staged two years later in Edinburgh (December 1757) and then by John Rich at Covent Garden three months after that.[31]

The play concerns a noble young hero, Norval, heir to one Lord Douglas. The child of a secret marriage abruptly ended by the death of his father in battle, Norval is brought up by simple folk but reunited as an adult with his long-lost aristocratic mother, now Lady Randolph. She had thought her child lost in a flood along with his nursemaid, but Norval was in fact

[28] *Correspondence of Samuel Richardson*, ed. Anna Laetitia Barbauld (London: Printed for Phillips by Lewis and Rodem, 1804), vol. 4, p. 56,
[29] Joseph Addison and Richard Steele, *The Spectator*, ed. Donald F. Bond (Oxford: Oxford University Press, 1965), vol. 4, p. 503.
[30] Samuel Richardson, 'Postscript', in *Clarissa; or, the History of a Young Lady*, ed. Angus Ross (London: Penguin, 1985), p. 1495.
[31] John Home, *Douglas* (London: A. Millar, 1757).

raised by a kindly peasant whose name he now bears. Lady Randolph's heir, Glenalvon, raises the suspicion of Lord Randolph that his wife has taken a young lover. Norval is killed and his mother commits suicide by throwing herself from rocks. The play was made successful in London by the powerful performance of Sarah Siddons as the distressed mother.

Garrick's letter to Bute defending his rejection of the play indicates that the actor-manager recognised the essential anti-theatricality of this overblown piece and his comments suggest it was more likely to be at home in the pages of a novel than on the public stage:

> when the Story is rather told than represented; when the Characters do not talk or behave suitably to ye Passions imputed to them, & the Situation in Which they are plac'd; when the Events are such as cannot naturally be suppos'd to rise; & the Language too often below the most familiar Dialogue; these are the insurmountable Objections, which in my Opinion, will Ever make Douglas unfit for ye Stage, In short there is no one Character or Passion which is strongly interesting & supported through ye five Acts.... I have consider'd ye Performance by Myself, I have read it to a Friend or Two with all the Energy & Spirit I was Master of but without the wish'd for Effect – the Scenes are long without Action, the Characters want strength & Pathos, and the Catastrophe is brought about without ye necessary & interesting preparations for so great an Event.[32]

The gathered company described in 'The Editor's Introduction' to *Sidney Bidulph* are also preoccupied with the catastrophe of the tragedy. A worthy lady visitor complains that the hero should have been rewarded, but her elderly hostess retorts that we should only expect reward for our virtue in heaven (taking Addison's and Richardson's line). As proof, the hostess offers the story of the unrewarded patience and virtue of a particular female friend of hers, available in manuscript largely from the female protagonist's own account:

> We are indeed so much used to what they call poetical justice, that we are disappointed in the catastrophe of a fable, if everybody concerned in it be not disposed of according to the sentence of that judge which we have set up in our own breasts.

[32] David Garrick to Earl of Bute, *The Letters of David Garrick*, ed. David M. Little and George M. Kahrl (London: Oxford University Press, 1968), vol. 1, letter 166, pp. 244–7, p. 246.

The contrary we know happens in real life; let us not then condemn what is drawn from real life. – We may wish to see nature copied from her more pleasing works; but a martyr expiring in tortures is as just, though not as agreeable, a representation of her, as a hero rewarded with the brightest honours.

We agreed with the venerable lady in her observations; and her son taking occasion from her mentioning that unfortunate person, who was her friend, told her, he would take it as a particular favour, if she would oblige me with the sight of that lady's story.

She answered, that as we had fixed upon the next day for our departure, there would not be time for me to peruse it, but that she would entrust me with it to town, that I might read it at my leisure. It is drawn up, said she, for the most part, by the lady herself.[33]

Sidney's letters tell her friend Cecilia of her courtship by the apparently virtuous Mr Faulkland brought to an unhappy close by the discovery that he has already fathered a child with an (undeserving) mistress. Sidney persuades him to honour his obligations and she herself marries another but neither enjoy happiness in their unions.

Sidney Bidulph appears to have been one of the sources for the play that was to bring the author's son his greatest stage success, *The Rivals*. In that play the sentimental nicety of Faulkland, namesake of Frances' hero, is the cause of great unhappiness to his fiancé, Julia, almost resulting in their separation. *The Rivals* may have been responding in other ways to the novel tradition in which his mother was writing: providing a lively comedy responsive to the demands of the stage (Sheridan swiftly rewrote the play after its first night was not well received) by comparison with a sentimental novel preferring moral realism to the provision of a satisfactory conclusion.

However, in doing so, Richard Sheridan rolls back the case made in his mother's novel that women might be agents of change at the forefront of the 'new' ethical revolution, whereby they resist and refuse to imitate conventional plots. In Frances Sheridan's novel, Sidney (the source of her own story) and the elderly friend – who places the manuscript in the hands of readers over-stimulated by the tragic excesses of a play read out loud in company – advocate acting according to principles not modelled on the stories already rehearsed on the stage or page. Here, women are not mimics but advocates of autonomous behaviour judged according to a Christian

---

[33] Frances Sheridan, *Memoirs of Miss Sidney Bidulph*, ed. Heidi Hutner and Nicole Garret, Broadview Literary Texts (Peterborough, ON: Broadview, 2011), p. 45.

ethics. Ironically enough, it is the model of another novel heroine, Richardson's Clarissa, whom (female) readers are invited to imitate.

As we have seen, both the novel and the theatre in the mid-eighteenth century featured female characters whose experience as readers or theatre-goers translated into imitative behaviours that put their reputations at risk. Both sought to claim that familiarity with and confidence in navigating plots, gained through a close acquaintance with their own generic conventions, could produce ethical (female) agents. In particular, the reflective powers of living with novel fiction in the home, demonstrated in Frances Sheridan's 'Editor's Introduction' to *Sidney Bidulph*, was imagined to form an instructional ethics for women readers. Where mimicry was praised as a technique with satiric as opposed to ethical sway it was usually when it was performed by men, as we saw in the case of Samuel Foote. The male mimic commands his material, satirises the thing he mimics; his presence-effect lies in the critical distance he achieves from his object. The female mimic is often contrasted with the male one, because she lacks this distance and is forced only to re-present, repeat without the capacity to reform others or herself. Male mimicry is then a form of criticism. As we shall see, the critic was another familiar type who travelled between theatre and novel. The male mimic may, however, be seen as a positive version of the critic. If women were often seen as vulnerable to affect, inclined to lose their moral compass in the dizzy excitement of feeling with extreme emotion depicted on stage or on the page, men were often cast at the opposite end of the spectrum of representation: stony-hearted critics who fail to feel *with* characters or who fall in love with their own performances so that they are blind to the aesthetic achievements of others.

Chapter 15
The Critic

Thomas Parnell characterises the critic as a 'Book-Worm' (1714), a cankerous creature who lives off and in the paper texts of the works the poet loves; he must be hunted out and destroyed if art is to thrive:

> On ev'ry corner fix thine eye,
> Or ten to one he slips thee by.
> See where his teeth a passage eat:
> We'll rouse him from the deep retreat.[1]

The critic has no creative genius himself (he may never have produced a creative work or may have been disappointed in his attempts to succeed doing so) and can only apply the words of others to works that he has not – in the main – even read. His presence is, unlike that of the female mimic, not flamboyant but insidious. It is marked by traces that slowly eat into the texts he lives off. Indeed, it is arguable that the critic's presence is only found, is only there, in the signs of destruction left with the works he has handled (or attended). In this way the critic's 'presence-effects' are both more elusive than those of the author and more impactful. In any case they are always out of time with the artwork he feeds off: either belated (the signs of their effect show up after the event) or anticipated (earlier principles of literature are applied to a present work inappropriately).

The female novel reader and the male theatre critic were both 'new' species of the eighteenth century, albeit forged from earlier 'types': the romance reader or the ancient satirist. The 'type' of the modern critic was Zoilus, envious antagonist of Homer, whose literal-minded commentary on the *Iliad* and the *Odyssey* survived only in fragments.[2] Despite that

---

[1] Thomas Parnell, *Collected Poems of Thomas Parnell*, ed. Claude Rawson and F.P. Lock (London and Toronto: Associated University Presses, 1989), pp. 162–4, p. 162. The poem was published in Parnell's *Poems on Several Occasions* (1722) but probably composed in 1714.

[2] See Thomas Parnell's octavo pamphlet of 16 May 1717 printed in *Homer's Battle of the Frogs and Mice, with the Remarks of Zoilus. To which is prefix'd, The Life of the*

ancient lineage, eighteenth-century writers tended to see critics as symptomatic irritants of the modern culture industry, deformed beings made by media phenomena that played to the lowest tastes and understanding. If the female novel reader happily imitated the heroines she met on the page, the male theatre critic refused to recognise himself in the follies that were mocked on stage. Both figures cannot match the creativity they respond to. If the female novel reader blindly imitates the work she admires, the male critic as myopically disparages it.

Criticism, unlike mimicry, always originates elsewhere, is always foreign to its object. While mimicry is an art intrinsic to the industry of theatre, critics take their cue from (other critical) texts. Critics adopt a set of rules that they apply rigidly to works of art, killing all creative genius in their path. Above all, critics consistently fail to travel with the spirit of works and only assess them by the strict letter of the rules and systems they have adopted from classical and foreign sources. Critics in eighteenth-century culture are everywhere both absent and present. They hide their identities behind ignorant and pseudonymous printed publications, and yet when satirised they are often depicted in drawing rooms and parlours, in boxes and the pit at theatres, pontificating on the failures of the works they have recently attended or read. In particular, they drain the pleasure and humour that ordinary people of taste take in literary works by their rule-bound and bad-tempered judgements. Periodical writing, paratextual theatrical material, novels and rehearsal or performance plays, abound with encounters with critics who are first allowed to voice their clichéd judgements and then hounded from the scene. Even when the work they criticise is weak, critics are rarely portrayed as justified or as figures to be admired. Their criticism is vainglorious rather than a heroic voicing of aesthetic standards.

The critic's malice is contrasted with the 'candour' that is invited from consumers of works who open themselves up to the true 'spirit' of the work. David Garrick's short satirical 'A Recipe for a Modern Critic' (1756) illustrates the contrast when criticism is described as made up 'Of candour a grain, and of scandal a ton'.[3] The internal half-rhyme of 'candour' and 'scandal' indicates both proximity and distance between these two kinds of reading, the latter outweighing the former in the scales of judgement. Garrick's poem concludes with advice to the author to 'Take this dose' so that he 'quickly will do/For *Critical, Monthly*, or any *Review*.'[4]

---

said *Zoilus* (London: Bernard Lintot, 1717). Zoilus is described as tall, lean, slovenly dressed and his voluminous work filled with 'cold Jests and trifling Quarrels' (p. 101).

[3]   David Garrick, 'A Recipe for a Modern Critic', in *The Universal Visiter* 3 (March 1756), 191.

[4]   Ibid., p. 192.

The growing significance of the novel as a literary player in the market-place coincides with the emergence of review journals. The *Monthly Review* was launched by Ralph Griffiths, Nonconformist publisher, in 1749 and its more conservative rival, the *Critical Review* by one-time contributor and novelist, Tobias Smollett, in 1756. Numerous published authors (as playwrights, writers of fiction and other works) including Oliver Goldsmith, John Cleland and Theophilus Cibber contributed to both journals. Here too the proximity between the versions of the writer as parasitic, carrion critic and as thriving, spirited independent creative genius is marked.

The 'new' form of the periodical not only offered a new form of mediating criticism, in the shape of the review of literary works, it was also the place where the 'new' critic was satirically represented as a character and where new forms of collective literary authority were both imagined and mocked. Samuel Johnson invents Dick Minim in his *Idler* in 1759 in order to illustrate two points: any fool can be a critic and, while it is deeply malicious, in the end criticism cannot harm true genius. When the young brewer's apprentice (apprentices are commonly represented as easily bedazzled by the theatre) inherits a fortune in stocks from his uncle, he determines to become known as a man of wit and humour, but he educates himself through second-hand knowledge:

> That he might be properly initiated in his new character, he frequented the coffee-houses near the theatres, where he listened very diligently day, after day, to those who talked of language and sentiments, and unities and catastrophes, till by slow degrees he began to think that he understood something of the Stage, and hoped in time to talk himself.
>
> But he did not trust so much to natural sagacity, as wholly to neglect the help of books. When the Theatres were shut, he retired to *Richmond* with a few select writers, whose opinions he impressed upon his memory by unwearied diligence; and when he returned with other wits to the town, was able to tell in very proper phrases, that the chief business of art is to copy nature; that a perfect writer is not to be expected, because genius decays as judgment increases, that the great art is the art of blotting; and that according to the rule of Horace, every piece should be kept nine years.[5]

He swiftly acquires an audience for his hackneyed judgements, is admitted to rehearsals and begins to influence the choices made in productions.

---

[5]   Samuel Johnson, *The Idler*, 60 (Saturday 9 June 1759), in *The Idler*, 2 vols (London: J. Newbery, 1761), vol. 2, p. 41.

Minim's presence at the theatre begins to eclipse the performance. He has 'advanced himself to the zenith of critical reputation; when he was in the Pit, every eye in the Boxes was turned upon him'. Puffed up with his self-importance:

> He has formed a plan for an Academy of Criticism, where every work of Imagination may be read before it is printed, and which shall authoritatively direct the Theatres what pieces to receive or reject, to exclude or to revive.[6]

Minim's academy does not come into being. He satisfies himself by pigeon-holing young men, and regaling them with instruction to follow the example of his favourite (and it seems largely unread) poet, John Milton.

Critics stalk the stages and pages of plays and novels. The generic rivals of novel and theatre were not slow to cast their competitors as dull critics to contrast with their own genius. Novels abound with set-piece conversations between caricatures who set themselves up as theatre critics. The action of many comic plays is impeded by the presence of tiresome inattentive critics or failed-playwrights-turned-critics who only know theatrical life-forms through paper manifestations and their subscription to the dead letter of rules.

Theatrical treatments of the critic

Imagining the critic as a hidden canker prompts an obsession with flushing out his presence at the theatre. The speakers of prologues and epilogues rail against the critics who lurk among well-disposed theatregoers; audiences are beseeched to give the play a candid hearing, to round off the evening with enthusiastic clapping so as to drown out the noise of malicious judgement from the critics and ensure a further night's performance of the play. And if they cannot be spotted offstage, fictional versions of the critic are a frequent presence on it. Metatheatrical comedies feature critics who watch plays in rehearsal or in production. These are often malicious, self-interested or vain figures, sometimes rival writers but sometimes also speakers of truth to a foolish manager or playwright. Their presence refers to a set of rules or expectations that exist offstage by which the performance is measured.

---

[6]   Samuel Johnson, *The Idler*, 61 (Saturday 16 June), vol. 2, p. 47, pp. 47–8.

The conceit of the rehearsal play is that the audience is absent from the performance. It is being prepared for consumption. The actual audience is given a supposed glimpse of the play in production. More often than not the rehearsal play serves a satirical purpose, often partisan. Rival playhouses, playwrights and managers are targeted but they also represent politicians, our peep behind the performance giving us insight into the corruption and self-interest behind the political authority or integrity on public display. This was the rationale behind the series of rehearsal and performance plays that Henry Fielding mounted at the Little Theatre in the Haymarket in the mid-1730s, which prompted Robert Walpole's introduction of the Licensing Act in 1737: *Pasquin: A Dramatic Satire on the Times* (1736), *The Historical Register for the Year 1736* (1737) and *Eurydice Hiss'd; or, A Word to the Wise* (1737).[7]

In each of these plays, a critic attends rehearsals that expose the incompetence, vanity and idiocy of the management. In all of them, there is no virtuous position for the spectator or producer of theatre. The names of the critics – Sneerwell in *Pasquin*, Sowrwit in *The Historical Register* and *Eurydice Hiss'd* – indicate their propensity to malice, but their function in the plays is to ask questions that reveal the playwright's stupidity. These critics are ironic versions of the satirical playwright who mocks his rivals as well as his political 'masters' and exposes the playwright who composes 'by the book' and without genius. Sneerwell is introduced to *Pasquin* only in the fourth act and observes the rehearsal of Fustian's tragedy (he sees nothing of Trapwit's comedy); he comments with concern that Fustian's ham-fisted allegorical tragedy about the attempts to murder the goddess Common-Sense by her courtiers is too 'emblematical' for the audience to follow.[8]

Samuel Foote set himself in opposition to Fielding by using his powers as a mimic and actor to dispel rather than collude with the voice of critics on or off stage. In *Tragedy-a-la-Mode*, first performed on 7 April 1761, Foote promoted his reputation as a mimic who appropriated and dispelled the power of his critics and stage rivals whether authors or actors. Here, the tragedian Fustian (named after Fielding's original) confides in the critic Mr Manly that he plans to cast his plays with one actor only and the remainder of the parts will be played by puppets. Fustian declares that Manly and his friend the man of fashion, Mr Townly, are 'the men I wish to please, the *Primores Populi*; a fig for the *Populuum Tributum* – Your voices outweigh a

---

7   Henry Fielding, all in *Plays, Volume III, 1734–1742*, ed. Thomas Lockwood (Oxford: Oxford University Press, 2011).

8   Ibid., *Pasquin*, Act 4, scene 1, p. 296.

theatre.'⁹ Since audiences only attend to catch a glimpse of the main actor, all other parts will be occupied by silent pasteboard. Fustian's plan was in fact executed by Foote. He performed with life-size pasteboard puppets at his Little Theatre in his *Diversions of the Morning* which opened on Wednesday 22 April 1747; Foote played both a man and a puppet on stage.[10] Further, Foote was asserting in *Tragedy-a-la-Mode*, his command over the field of satire through puppetry; his rival, Henry Fielding, had launched a satirical Punch and Judy puppet show on Panton Street, which took the moral high ground in claiming that his satire provided a general critique of hypocrisy rather than what he saw as Foote's derivative imitation of particular celebrity characters. Foote here insists on his superior power to bring to life dead figures, his power as a single actor to attract audiences to a small unlicensed theatre. Where Fielding set his crowd at odds and aligned with the critic, Foote played to the crowd, flaunting a reputation for mercilessly mimicking friends and enemies alike.[11]

Critics talk up their achievements when they walk on stage but when they encounter the stage space within the play they are quickly silenced and cut down to size, whether by the folly or the wit of the playwright-managers they encounter. As in Samuel Johnson's caricature of Minim, the critic is largely ineffectual; while satire distorts competitive spirit (in a crowded market of authors aspiring to see their plays staged) by enlarging it into the vices of outright envy and malice, it also aims to puncture and diminish that threat in the course of the play: whether by restoring order and hierarchy through the expulsion of such vices from the stage at play's end, or by suggesting that they are so petty as not to deserve attempts to reform or correct them. The theatre, then, promises its audience to chastise vice but to ensure that there is still entertainment.

Richard Sheridan's enormously successful burlesque rehearsal farce, *The Critic*, rehearsed just these alternatives when it was staged at Drury Lane from 30 October 1779.[12] At play's opening we meet Mrs Dangle who

---

⁹   Samuel Foote, *Tragedy a-la-mode*, in *The Wandering Patentee…. By Tate Wilkinson….To which are added, never published, The Diversions of the Morning, and Foote's Trial for a Libel on Peter Paragraph. Written by the late Samuel Foote*, 4 vols (London: Printed for the Author, 1795), vol. 4, Act 2, scene 1, p. 289.

[10] See Julie Park, 'Puppet Life: Voice, Animation and Charlotte Charke's *Narrative*', chapter 5 of *Self and It. Novel Objects in Eighteenth-Century England* (Stanford, CA: Stanford University Press, 2010).

[11] On the rivalry between Foote and Fielding over puppets and performance, see Ian Kelly, *Mr Foote's Other Leg* (London: Picador, 2012), pp. 117–18, pp. 125–30.

[12] Richard Brinsley Sheridan, *The Critic*, ed. David Crane, New Mermaids (London: W.W. Norton, 1989). See David Francis Taylor, '"Gross Deceptions": Newspapers,

complains at her breakfast table that her house is full of theatre hangers-on seeking promotion from her starstruck husband, Mr Dangle. As she reads newspaper reports that warn of imminent invasion by the Spanish–French alliance on English soil (Sheridan attacks here the fake news hysteria stirred up by the Foxite opposition), her husband reads theatre reviews. Mr Sneer, the critic, enters and disputes with Mrs Dangle about the purpose of the stage, the latter stating that she attends for entertainment and Sneer insisting that it has a responsibility to impart morality.

Dangle and Sneer head off in the company of neurotic playwright, Sir Fretful Plagiary, to watch the rehearsal of a new play by Puff, theatre-manager and critic, about the English rebuttal of the Spanish Armada in 1558. Puff's expertise lies in public and print oratory talking up parliamentary members, patrons and public events. His play is a mere vehicle for these activities: he shows no concern about the integrity of the unities, consistency of plot, of character, of setting and action. Puff is the antithesis of Sneer, all panegyric to the latter's contempt. Neither mode, Sheridan suggests, is in sympathy with the true demands of theatre and the nature of its pleasures. Puff and Sneer, while apparently antithetical types, like all critics, incline to turn plays into fragments of meaning. They are always and insistently distant from the real presence of theatre because they approach it from the imperatives of textual mediation (whether oratorical puffing or print reviewing).

Novelistic treatments of the critic

Paul Ricoeur distinguishes between the time of narration (utterance) and the time of what is narrated (statement):

> epics, dramas, and novels project, in the mode of fiction, ways of inhabiting the world that lie waiting to be taken up by reading, which in turn is capable of providing a space for a confrontation between the world of the text and the world of the reader.[13]

The image or ideal of the 'candid' reader suggests the possibility of bridging those times, since the candid reader reads according to the 'spirit' of

---

Theatres and the Propaganda War', chapter 2 of *Theatres of Opposition: Empire, Revolution, and Richard Brinsley Sheridan* (Oxford: Oxford University Press, 2012).

[13] Paul Ricoeur, *Time and Narrative: Volume 2*, trans. Kathleen McLaughlin and David Pellauer (Chicago, IL: University of Chicago Press, 1984), p. 5.

the text's creator, putting aside his or her own prejudices by comparison with the malicious 'critic' who ignores the larger spirit to attack the faults of constituent parts. By these lights, the candid reader is fully present or co-present with the author when they read a text. However, the presence of the 'candid' reader is also often summoned only to be expelled or disillusioned for his or her failure to accommodate the everyday and the real, which presses on ideals, idealisations and absolutes promoted by the wider 'spirit' of what he or she reads. Mid-century novels frequently turn to the idea of a 'candid' reader capable of countering the decrying habits of public criticism.

What then is 'candid' reading? In 1755 Samuel Johnson provides a definition in his *Dictionary*.[14] He tells us (correctly) that the definition is 'white' from the Latin 'candidus', but he says this is now 'very rare'. Johnson's second definition is 'Without malice; without deceit; fair; open; ingenuous'. Johnson quotes John Locke in chapter eleven of *An Essay concerning Human Understanding* (1690) ('candid and intelligent readers' will be 'led to understand the meaning of a discourse' if there is sufficient guide to explain the context in which a word is being used, despite the multiple meanings it might convey) and Alexander Pope in 'An Essay on Criticism' (1711): Johnson in fact alters the couplet giving 'A candid judge will read each piece of wit,/With the same spirit that its author writ' – Johnson changes Pope's 'perfect' to 'candid'.

Candid readers put themselves in the place of the 'spirit' of the text, its governing genius. An important reference point for the candid reader in fiction from the 1760s onwards was Voltaire's (anti-)hero, Candide, of 1759.[15] In Voltaire's *Candide*, the gullible hero puts himself not in the place of each taleteller he encounters, but judges always in relation to the principle of his tutor, Pangloss, that 'everything is for the best' despite the persistent evidence of slaughter and suffering which suggests the contrary. Candide's view of the world is sugar-coated ('candied') and he persistently refuses to swallow the bitter pill of 'real life' insisting on being guided by his tutor's patently misdiagnostic premise.[16]

In novels, the critic is often a stupid or malign figure who threatens to undermine the innocence and idealism of a central protagonist, usually a male one such as Candide: Tom Jones, Tristram, David Simple. That

---

[14] Samuel Johnson, 'Candid', in *A Dictionary of the English Language*, 2 vols (London: W. Strahan et al., 1755), vol. 1.

[15] Voltaire (François-Marie d'Arouet), *Candide and other Stories*, ed. Roger Pearson (Oxford: Oxford University Press, 2008).

[16] Mary Claire Randolph, 'Candour in XVIIIth-Century Satire', *The Review of English Studies*, 20, no. 77 (January 1944), p. 53.

protagonist is often a surrogate for the reader him or herself, learning to navigate the new form of the novel where outcomes are not certain because not predictable by familiar generic conventions. The novel prides itself as a form on its *lack* of the kind of generic norms governing our expectations that tragedy will end in death and comedy in reconciliation. And the critic's apprenticeship in his art is nearly always learned (as it is for Johnson's Minim) through attending theatre and associating with theatre people. Here, the critic develops his own vanity; the 'mirror' of the stage is, he fantasises, reflecting his own superior powers of judgement. As we have seen, those powers are in fact simply second-hand imitations, repetitions, of worn-out clichés.

Novels provide us with young male innocents who encounter metropolitan culture and either resist the lure of a critical culture or succumb to it. Encounters with critics often provide vivid set pieces that showcase the hero's virtue while they satirise urban vice. Sarah Fielding's *The Adventures of David Simple* (1744) includes several chapters in its second book that introduce the idealistic young hero, David, to metropolitan culture through the medium of criticism. David's new friend, Spatter, introduces David to a tavern Critic – here too, the satire of the critic is communicated by absenting him from the site where he might see the art form he discusses in practice. His location is the tavern outside the theatres from which space he pontificates on work at which he has never been present, that he has experienced only in textual form, and then only through the clichés of others writing about plays. The tavern critic embarks on a stream of analogy, comparison and metaphor. Jonson and Shakespeare cannot be compared since the one is a regular garden and the other a wilderness; Corneille, the French Shakespeare, is a fiery courser and Racine plods forward majestically. Waller's verse is a gentle cooling stream, while Dryden's genius is 'like a rapid River, ready to overleap its Bounds; which we view with Admiration and find, while we are reading him, our Fancy heighten'd to rove thro' all the various *Labyrinths of the human Mind*'.[17]

Just under a decade later, Sarah Fielding was to return to the metaphor of art as a form of investigation of the mind's labyrinth and to claim it as the special quality of her co-authored (with Jane Collier) novel, *The Cry*. We must assume, then, that she thought it a good quality. It is the Critic's repetition without purpose and accumulation of cliché that marks his

---

[17] Sarah Fielding, *The Adventures of David Simple and Volume the Last*, ed. Peter Sabor, Eighteenth-Century Novels by Women (Lexington, KY: Kentucky University Press, 2015), book 2, chapter 3, p. 71.

folly, rather than the sentiments he expresses. He stops mid-flow when his breath begins to fail:

> For he had utter'd all as fast as he could speak, as if he was afraid he should *lose his Thread,* and *forget* all that *was to come.* When he had ceased, his *Eyes rolled with more than usual Quickness,* to view the *Applause* he *expected,* and thought he so well *deserved,* and he look'd bewilder'd in his own Eloquence.[18]

Sarah Fielding draws her reader's attention to the issue of performance. We are reminded that poor acting, a performance not in command of meaning and unable to communicate the presence of the action, undermines the best and most original script. The framing power of a judicious narration, it is suggested, brings familiar truths to life in a fresh way.

In the next chapter, Fielding takes care to introduce David, who has become weary of Spatter's cynicism, to a Mr Varnish, who is the complete contrast, always inclined to paint character in the best light. David struggles to arrive at judgement finding all that he has encountered either 'touched by the Pencil' or 'daubed with Mud'.[19] He determines to break off his friendship with Spatter after a particularly painful conversation in which the latter insists on the pleasures of revenge. The tables turn again, however, when Mr Varnish reveals to David that in fact Spatter only *speaks* bile and malice. His verbal vindictiveness hides a truly generous soul who does his best secretly to aid those he maligns (chapter five). Here too, Sarah Fielding defuses the apparent threat of criticism not by demonstrating that it is ultimately ineffectual, but rather by suggesting that it is a form of self-protection for those who are in fact genuinely sensitive to the sufferings of others.

In *The Adventures of Peregrine Pickle* (1751), Tobias Smollett describes a 'College of Authors' that his young hero joins. The authors puff each others' works and publicly savage works by those not admitted to their circle. They are led by an old man whose theatrical productions have been damned beyond redemption and who has resorted to translation of the classics to support himself. Twenty members meet at an alehouse and dress the temples of speakers with wreaths of laurel; arguments result in violent physical conflict in the dark (a satirist almost bites off the ear of a lyric bard). The metaphor of savage mangling of art through satire is here turned into a 'literal' element of plot. The critics do not confine themselves to discussion of

[18]   Ibid., p. 71.
[19]   Ibid., chapter 4, p. 74.

texts. Much of their talk concerns stage-playing and performance style and the second chapter has two critics deliver their verdicts on performances of established plays: *The Fair Penitent* by Nicholas Rowe and *The Revenge* by Edward Young. Their censorship is of poor performances: the villain Lothario has the gestures of a puppet master and an actor mangles the sense of a line by inserting a period in its middle. This set piece of satire includes the world of puffing, reviewing and criticism as one of a series of town vices to which the scoundrel hero is introduced and which he embraces before he undergoes reform at the conclusion of the novel. Criticism is here a symptom rather than a cause of ethical atavism.[20]

In 1767 an anonymous work entitled *The Adventures of an Author*, a homage to the metafictional comedy of Sterne's *Tristram Shandy*, introduced Jack Atall's career as an aspiring writer and his ill-treatment at the hands of criticism. Atall is a target for exploitation by theatre-folk and critics alike when he determines to abandon his work as a legal clerk to become an actor. He joins a spouting club (a meeting for aspiring amateur actors from the labouring classes to rehearse parts) and makes an appointment with 'a genius and critic' named Mr Hyper who introduces him to Mr G--- (Garrick). Garrick, true to his reputation for fobbing off approaches from aspiring actors and playwrights, advises Atall that he must learn to dance and fence and undergo an operation to loosen his tongue so as to conquer a speech impediment. Hyper undertakes to instruct Atall in the former and the aspiring actor undergoes the necessary surgery. Unsurprisingly, an acting career is not forthcoming. It transpires that Hyper has no real influence with Garrick and is cultivating Atall only to secure someone who will pay for his meals at a tavern. Atall decides to be Virgil rather than Roscius and becomes a 'magazine poet and hebdomadal rhymer'.[21] Neither he nor Hyper flourish and Atall is obliged to live off the meagre earnings of his mistress, a milliner, until she leaves him for a more lucrative partner. After a series of adventures in Spain and Germany, and continued efforts to make a living by writing, Atall inherits a subsistence from his uncle and retires from his efforts. The critic is less fortunate: 'Mr Hyper, having been the dupe to men of fortune, in every sense of the word, had been stript of all his cash, and from being almost as rich as a little nabob, he was condemned in the Fleet for a small sum at his taylor's suit and here he supported himself with his pen.'[22]

---

[20] Tobias Smollett, *The Adventures of Peregrine Pickle*, 4 vols (London: Printed for the Author, and sold by D. Wilson, 1751), vol. 4, chapters 101–2.

[21] *The Adventures of an Author written by Himself and a Friend*, 2 vols (London: Robinson and Roberts, 1767), vol. 1, chapter 9, p. 75.

[22] Ibid., vol. 2, p. 198.

Relations of dependence and patronage are radically unstable in the mediascape of eighteenth-century London. Hyper presents himself as patron while he is in fact on the make. Later he becomes himself the victim of exploitation by others when he does have money to spare. In Frances Brooke's *The Excursion* (1771), the critic features as an honourable figure in a corrupt world, the chivalrous saviour of an aspiring female author cruelly fobbed off by the great theatre-manager of the day (Garrick).[23] Maria Villiers, as did the author Frances Brooke, wants to see her tragedy into production, but her confidence in her work begins to waver and she recruits her landlady to engage an intermediary to assess its worth:

> One of the sublimest poets, and most judicious critics, this enlightened age has produced, had, it seems, lived a year in her house before she came to Berner's-street.
>
> The candor and beneficence of his mind, his advanced time of life, his birth (for he was of a noble family), and the extreme respectability of his character, to which Maria was no stranger, rendered him the properest person on earth to consult.
>
> He was the more so, as he had himself declined writing for the theatre, and had consequently no interest to warp his judgement.[24]

As we can see, Mr Hammond the critic has all the qualities that equip him to be a true judge: he is not vain of his own reputation and writings, he is well-born and hence does not need to earn a living from his literary endeavours. The precious term 'candor' is the first characteristic of his mind. Maria is tortured with apprehension as she awaits his judgement on the work she has sent to him and gratified when he affirms that she has 'literally a *Muse of fire*' and that he likes especially the 'little strokes of tenderness and passion which seize so instantaneously on the heart'.[25]

Hammond promises to use his interest to get her play read, since it is improper that she should wait on the manager in person to do so. However, the manager does not even read it.[26] Hammond steps in where everyone else fails Maria. He sends her one hundred pounds under anonymous

---

[23]   See Katherine G. Charles, 'Staging Sociability in *The Excursion*: Frances Brooke, David Garrick, and the King's Theatre Coterie', *Eighteenth-Century Fiction*, 27, no. 2 (Winter 2014–15), 257–84.

[24]   Frances Brooke, *The Excursion*, book 4, chapter 6, p. 59.

[25]   Ibid., p. 60.

[26]   In the second edition after some furore, Brooke revised her treatment of Garrick in response to criticism of what was seen as her sour grapes. Maria is asked to send the work again in 20 months for consideration, a time which is nonetheless an age to the

cover to alleviate her financial difficulties, prevents a private letter from public circulation and prevents publication of a libel – both of which might undermine her reputation in London. He takes Maria home, for a tour of the country, and provides her with a husband in his relative Captain Herbert. Hammond also proposes that he should live with Maria in her country estate where Col. Dormer, her uncle and guardian, 'shall build us a theatre; and Miss Villiers and I will, in defiance of managers, write tragedies, and play them ourselves.'[27]

Hammond and Hyper are two sides of the same coin, it appears. They promise to enable authors whose literary merits and interests are close to their own. Neither in the end does have such power to wield. As we have seen in this exploration of the representation of the male (theatre) critic, satire tends to exaggerate his power and then diminish it. Neither Maria nor Atall, however different they are as authors, obtain success in a metropolitan London milieu and the critic can neither defend nor ruin them. The individual male critic is weak by comparison with the sites of real power: the audience or reading public and/or the managers and publishers. If the latter are represented as driven by profit motives rather than aesthetic ideals, the former can often be seen as an undifferentiated and easily swayed mass. How, then, might an artist with ethical and aesthetic ambition imagine shaping an audience hospitable to a new ethics of virtuous presence, and could such an artist exploit the energies of the liveness of theatrical performance and the reflective communion of mind with novelistic text?

The hack critic, Grubstreet, in Charles Macklin's *The New Play Criticiz'd* (1747) urges his fellow critics, Plagiary and Canker, to return to the company at an evening soiree to persuade them to turn against Benjamin Hoadly's *Suspicious Husband*: 'they will', he says, 'serve to fill up the Cry, which you know is the present Test of Right and Wrong.'[28] Grubstreet's reference may have provided the idea for Sarah Fielding and Jane Collier's representation of the prejudiced and partisan court of judgement in the work they subtitled 'a new dramatic fable' of 1754. In this work we can see the figures of male critic, female mimic and candid consumer act out in dramatic allegory the stakes of reception between theatre and novel. That Fielding and Collier's *The Cry: A New Dramatic Fable* of 1754 has disappeared so thoroughly from the history of the rise of the novel until recently may be a measure of its avant-garde position, or of a road in the end not travelled: one in

---

ambitious and impecunious Maria. See appendix to *The Excursion*, ed. Backscheider and Cotton, pp. 171–8.

[27] Ibid., p. 152.
[28] MSS Charles Macklin, *The New Play Criticiz'd*, LA 64, p. 11.

which the ways that the two media of theatre and novel were received, were transparently tested and contested on the same ground.

The Cry plays with the mutual dependence of the mimetic and diegetic, performance and narration.[29] Its virtuous heroine, Portia, is called before the Cry, a large audience wedded to error; Portia's sole ally is the one virtuous auditor, an allegorical figure named Una (who stands for simplicity or truth). Over the course of three volumes, Portia counters the Cry's attempt – aided by Una's nemesis, Duessa – to ridicule and denigrate her. Along the way she delivers the story of her love for Ferdinand, his twin sister, Cordelia, and sufferings at the hands of their evil elder brother, Oliver, their foolish father, Nicanor, his conflicted mistress Cylinda, and her jealous friend, Melantha.

Fielding and Collier reanimate here in their modern hybrid novel the characters of not only Shakespeare's romance dramas – Portia from *The Merchant of Venice* and twins named Ferdinand (*The Tempest*) and Cordelia (*King Lear*) – but also Edmund Spenser's Elizabethan romance epic, *The Faerie Quene*. Una is the virtuous lady and allegorical embodiment of the Christian church whom the Knight of the Redcrosse protects, while Duessa is the witch who adopts Una's form to seduce and distract the Knight from his purpose. Portia's truth-telling is contrasted with the error into which her opposite, Cylinda, is led as a result of her intellectual vainglory.

The Cry turns not just stage plots, but also theatrical conventions and the cognitive ecology of the stage, into prose fictional form. In the world of *The Cry*, a single, virtuous member of the audience (Una) can resist the majority verdict more effectively than in the playhouse. Plays, after all, were only guaranteed a continuing life if the audience clapped sufficiently to secure a further performance the following night. So too a single, apparently errant interpretation can, through diegetic narration, have authority conferred upon it. This experiment in fiction assesses, addresses, and attempts to bridge the gap between the stage play's cognitive advantage (real bodies represent personages) over that of the prose fiction (print is the medium that conjures the impression of character). Portia, true to her namesake, the legal cross-dresser of Shakespeare's *Merchant of Venice*, speaks truth to power but has more success in converting her extradiegetic than her intradiegetic audience. *The Cry*'s Portia is also the voice of a resistance to the imitative reproduction of familiar meanings. She coins new words – 'turba' for disturbance of mind and 'sinistra' for deviance of mind by comparison

---

[29]　Sarah Fielding and Jane Collier, *The Cry. A New Dramatic Fable*, ed. Carolyn Woodward, Eighteenth-Century Novels by Women series (Lexington, KY: University Press of Kentucky, 2018).

with 'dextra' – the pursuit of the good but also a 'dextrous' management of speech. And she resists lazy use of quotation or instrumental treatments of allegory.

Words in *The Cry* have the capacity to be experienced through the body. See, for example, the fourth scene of the third part, where Portia warns the Cry not to indulge in angry feelings and to try to be 'agreeable'. Do not, she warns:

> invite into your breasts such evil passions as are, according to *Shake-spear* in his *Winter's Tale*,
> – *Goads, thorns, nettles, tails of wasps* – [30]

The quotation refers to the pangs of jealousy that torment Leontes when he suspects Hermione of infidelity in Shakespeare's play. We are told that:

> The *Cry*, conscious of the force of Portia's quotation by the pains they felt within, yet resolutely bent on not confessing their folly in being thus their own tormentors, with lowering brows, with raised voices, and every technical mark of anger, declared that Portia was to them the highest object of contempt, and that they despised her from their very souls.[31]

Later, in scene six of the same part, Portia tells the Cry about a proposal she received from a sly and self-interested suitor, Oliver. Oliver is brother to the man she really loves, Ferdinand (their names recall the violent brother of Orlando in *As You Like It* and Miranda's devoted suitor in *The Tempest*). Oliver depends on the 'force of his wise maxims' to pursue his amours:

> He had invented and remember'd political maxims enough to have filled a large volume on the methods of gaining women's hearts. The difference of their positions he never consulted; for he had read,
>   *That women have no characters at all:*
> and no sooner had he read this assertion than the truth of it gained in his mind an unlimited credit. For that the author of the above verse confessed an exception to his own general rule, by addressing the poem to a lady, was an observation that could never enter into the head of such characters as *Oliver*.[32]

---

[30] Fielding and Collier, *The Cry*, part 3, scene 4, p. 153.
[31] Ibid.
[32] Ibid., part 3, scene 6, pp. 157–8.

Portia both resists Oliver's application of a quotation to her case and proves its appropriateness in ways he and the Cry fail to understand. She demonstrates to Una and her extradiegetic audience her superior understanding of the quotation's place in the work from which it comes, Alexander Pope's *Epistle to a Lady* (1735), a poem addressed to Martha Blount in which Pope is in fact praising his female friend because she is the exception to this 'rule'. Further irony missed by Oliver is that the statement is in fact the lady's and only quoted by Pope who then proceeds to delineate the different 'characters' of those women from whom she differs. Portia puts herself in sociable alliance with an audience absent – with the honourable exception of Una – from the stage on which she is performing.

The Cry stages a series of such disputes about the inappropriate 'relocation' of elements from one work to another (quotation used out of context), within a work that operates by just such a process (taking names, words, elements from dramatic works and repurposing them for a printed prose fiction). The distinction is, however, presented as one between a mechanical application of terms to fulfil a collective intention, and what the 'Cry' often represents as a 'candid' openness to pursue meaning for its own sake and in sympathetic alliance with the terms of the advocate (Portia).

In the Prologue to the third of the five parts of *The Cry*, Fielding and Collier differentiate between our willingness to correct our sense-perception and unwillingness to seek forms of assistance such as their own fable, to ensure we arrive at intellectual truth:

> Invention then is truth pretty much the same with having eyes and opening them in order to discern the objects which are placed before us. But the eye here made use of must be the mind's eye (as *Shakespear*, with his peculiar aptness of expression, calls it) and so strictly used is this metaphor, that nothing is apparently more frequent than a perverse shutting of this mental eye when we have not an inclination to perceive the things offered to our internal view. I know not likewise, why a short-sighted mind's eye should not be as good an expression as a short-sighted body's eye. But in this we are much kinder to our sense than to our intellect; for in order to assist the former we use glasses and spectacles of all kinds adapted to our deficiency of sight, whereas in the latter we are so far from accepting the assistance of mental glasses or spectacles, that we often strain our mind's eye, even to blindness, and at the same time affirm that our sight is nothing less than perfect.[33]

---

[33] Ibid., p. 133.

The book is here represented as a tool, in analogy with a pair of spectacles; it serves as a substitute for the deficiencies of the cognitive activity in the 'mind's eye'. Perhaps it should not surprise us that the metaphor is attributed to Shakespeare and that it originates in *Hamlet* and specifically to the dead father's supernatural manifestation in that play. Hamlet records that he sees his father in his 'mind's eye' and this is the prompt for the entrance of the ghost of Old Hamlet. Here, Fielding and Collier suggest an analogy between theatrical embodiment (the actor makes Old Hamlet flesh) and textual presence (the book): both concretise and externalise our longing to make 'solid' those truths that we often prefer not to see.

And allegory, the process of turning aspects of mind into characters, is the formal mechanism for this process. *The Cry* proclaims itself a new form of allegory. It provides a fiction of an animated mind at work, in place of the theatrical or (old) romance actor whose psychological conflicts are depicted through action and allegorical embodiment. In their preface, Fielding and Collier reject the obvious allegory of the 'romance' for the new allegorical psychology of their work in which the authors themselves feature as the heroic protagonists who defend the mind from error in collaboration with their reader:

> If the heroine of a romance was to travel through countries, where the castles of giants rise to her view; through gloomy forests, amongst the dens of savage beasts, where at one time she is in danger of being torn and devoured, at another, retarded in her flight by puzzling mazes, and falls at last into the hands of a cruel giant; the reader's fears will be alarmed for her safety; his pleasure will arise on seeing her escape from the teeth of a lion, or the paws of a fierce tiger:.. But the puzzling mazes into which we shall throw our heroine, are the perverse interpretations made upon her words; the lions, tigers, and giants, from which we endeavour to rescue her, are the spiteful and malicious tongues of her enemies...
>
> Thoroughly to unfold the labyrinths of the human mind is an arduous task; and notwithstanding the many skilful and penetrating strokes which are to be found in the best authors, there seem yet to remain some intricate and unopen'd recesses in the heart of man. In order to dive into those recesses, and lay them open to the reader in a striking and intelligible manner, 'tis necessary to assume a certain freedom in writing, not strictly perhaps within the limits prescribed by rules. Yet we desire only to be free, and not licentious. We wish to give our imagination leave to play; but within such bounds as not to

grow mad. And if we step into allegory, it shall not be out of sight of
our reader.[34]

Fielding and Collier here open the vein of analogy which runs throughout
the work between the image schema of the eye that traces the written word
across the page and the 'mind's eye' that is strengthened to recognise truths
through the experience of reading (their own fable). The prose work and
the experience of its reading lay bare its mechanisms to the reader. The
authors do nothing 'out of sight' of their reader. While the theatrical performance appears to give us a more powerful visual experience, it is also an
act of concealment because it absents the narrating consciousness. Again,
Hamlet seems to be evoked in the shadows here: a man driven mad by the
visual proof of his father's murder through a ghostly visitation. Reason can
be maintained if we can participate in framing the critical consciousness of
the fable in which we are immersed.

In their claim to make visible to the reader the workings of narration,
the authors of *The Cry* seek to fuse the experience of reading on the page
with the performative immediacy of the drama to construct a new but
also radically unstable 'blend'. That blend is also one which redirects and
reforms the energies of 'errant' forms of consumption. The 'malice' of the
critic will be turned toward acts of candid judgement. The female mimic
will recognise the dangers that await her in public life and know to tread
carefully by imitating the ethical behaviour of the heroine of this work.
And the 'new' form of the novel is also one that captures the collective
and collaborative energies of the theatre audience while guiding them
toward reformed ends. The work is composed by more than one hand and
addressed to a collective audience.[35]

[34] Fielding and Collier, *The Cry*, pp. 41–2.
[35] For the external evidence of joint composition between Jane Collier and Sarah Fielding found in the commonplace book of Jane Collier's sister, see Michael Londry,
'Our Dear Miss Jenny Collier', *Times Literary Supplement*, 5 March 2004, pp. 13–14.
And for a general discussion of authorship see Carolyn Woodward, 'Who Wrote
The Cry?: A Fable for Our Times', *Eighteenth-Century Fiction*, 9, no. 1 (1996), 91–7.
Rebecca Anne Barr argues that the utopian image of clarity of language promoted
in the work is satirically undermined by a sense of the barriers to clear exchange
between the sexes represented in *The Cry*. See Rebecca Anne Barr, '"Barren Desarts
of Arbitrary Words": Language and Communication in Collier and Fielding's *The
Cry*', *Women's Writing*, 23, no. 1 (2016), 87–105. Barr speaks of the 'hobbled happiness' of the concluding union between Portia and her lover, Ferdinand, who tests her
through his dissimulating letters (p. 102), a conclusion unsatisfying to readers such
as Lady Mary Wortley Montagu and Samuel Richardson.

We have come increasingly to recognise the innovative and proto-feminist aspects of *The Cry*. Rebecca Anne Barr identifies another source in James Harris's critique of the moral redundancy of empirical (Lockean) approaches to agreeing meaning in language in his *Hermes: or, a Philosophical Inquiry Concerning Language and Universal Grammar* (1751). However, collective communal fantasy represented on a moralised stage was, of course, also the stock in trade of Georgian theatre. As Betsy Bolton summarises, Georgian theatregoers conceived of the stage as a mirror that taught 'the audience to desire itself in a mode of representative, often chastised, communal identity'.[36] Fielding and Collier attempt to reproduce the sense of co-presence of audience, actors and authors (plural collaborators in the making of a theatrical event) on the page of *The Cry*. The commercial but also the ethical success of the novel in the mid-eighteenth century rested on imagining ways in which it could match this collaborative and collective presence known from the theatre, rather than contest it by alternative modes.

[36] Bolton, 'Theorizing Audience and Spectatorial Agency', p. 33.

Conclusion

We attempt to make the past 'present' by presenting it in space, as though it were happening again and before us, before our eyes. We long for the past to be present to us, tangible. Museum exhibitions, re-enactment, historical fictions on stage and screen, the material turn in humanities scholarship, all – as Gumbrecht terms it – expand the range of the present. 'Presentification' consists of 'techniques that produce the impression (or, rather, the illusion) that worlds of the past can become tangible again'.[1] The turn to the corporeal, the material, and away from the spirit, the abstract, is a symptom of the fear of an imperilled future over which our imaginings and anticipations appear to have little purchase:

> In our present, the epistemological disposition to fashion a figure of self-reference that is more strongly rooted in the body and in space meets up with a yearning that emerged in reaction to a world determined by excessive emphasis on consciousness.[2]

Presentification extends the possibility of being with the dead and touching the objects of the world. And we have seen it present itself most often and recurrently in those moments in prose and drama where a ghost appears and when persons appear to become puppets. Between life and death, between being persons and ideas (the ghost), or between being persons and machines (puppets), the not-quite-not-personhood of these figures presents to their audience the productive tension of unconcealment and withdrawal that is 'Being'. The importance of the imagining of an audience, a collectivity to be with even in difference – and hence the difficulty of dislodging the theatre as the primary space of presence – is evident in the urge to seek out companionship that inevitably accompanies the encounter with ghosts. Conversely, the encounter with puppets tends to produce a

---

[1] Gumbrecht, *Production of Presence*, p. 94.
[2] Hans Gumbrecht, *Our Broad Present. Time and Contemporary Culture* (New York: Columbia University Press, 2011), p. xiv.

desire to assert individuality and eccentricity, an ability to reflect on one's quirkiness not shared by mechanical forms of being.

Let us look more closely at two such moments, one describing an encounter with a fictional ghost and another an encounter with fictional puppets, to understand better the ways that, in the eighteenth century, non-corporeal beings in and of the theatre prompt a compulsion to be with others. These examples invite us to see more clearly how the novel might have been perceived as a successor to theatrical presence, as a way of providing those presence-effects without the hindrance of body.

First, one of the most familiar encounters with that most familiar of stage ghosts, Old Hamlet. In her *Anecdotes of the Late Samuel Johnson* (1786), Hester Piozzi (previously Thrale) relates a story Johnson told her of his childhood:

> I have heard him relate another odd thing of himself too, but it is one which everybody has heard as well as me: how, when he was about nine years old, having got the play of Hamlet in his hand, and reading it quietly in his father's kitchen, he kept on steadily enough till, coming to the Ghost scene, he suddenly hurried upstairs to the street door that he might see people about him.[3]

As he reaches the point in his reading when Hamlet first encounters his father's ghost, Samuel leaps to the door on to the street in desperate need to find company, to be with people. Samuel wants to see people and be seen by them. Hester Piozzi goes on:

> Such an incident, as he was not unwilling to relate it, is probably in every one's possession now; he told it as a testimony to the merits of Shakespeare. But one day, when my son was going to school, and dear Dr. Johnson followed as far as the garden gate, praying for his salvation in a voice which those who listened attentively could hear plain enough, he said to me suddenly, "Make your boy tell you his dreams: the first corruption that entered into my heart was communicated in a dream." "What was it, sir?" said I. "*Do* not ask me," replied he, with much violence, and walked away in apparent agitation. I never durst make any further inquiries.[4]

---

[3]   Hester Lynch Piozzi, *Anecdotes of the Late Samuel Johnson, LL.D. during the Last Twenty Years of his Life* (London: T. Cadell, 1786), p. 20.

[4]   Ibid.

Hester Piozzi concludes that Johnson did not share the story only with her: it is 'in the possession' of many others. She cannot help but echo here, given the context of the story, a fear of being possessed by a story rather than possessing it, which the young Johnson acts out for us.

This anecdote though, prompts another in which Johnson refuses to pass on a story he possesses: in place of the story about a dream that prompted his first experience of corruption, Samuel provides an instruction to Hester to insist that another child deliver *his* story to her: that her son should tell her his dreams. Piozzi uses the *Hamlet* anecdote to demonstrate 'a warmth of imagination little consistent with sound and perfect health' which is confirmed in the story that follows it. Johnson's search for companionship as a way of healing mental disorder now becomes a form of coercive surrogation in which another child in the present substitutes for the child he was in the past. Telling or sharing the fictions we imagine dispels their power to corrupt, but the opportunity of that moment is passed for Johnson and only available to new audiences: through the *Anecdotes.*

Five years after Piozzi published her *Anecdotes,* James Boswell added in his *Life of Dr Johnson* an allusion to *Hamlet* in order to flesh out a description of his first meeting with Samuel Johnson. In this account, meeting Johnson is for Boswell like Hamlet meeting the ghost of his father. Boswell had long sought an introduction and it was enabled finally when he visited the bookshop run by the bookseller and part-time actor Thomas Davies, who had told Boswell that Johnson was a frequent visitor of the shop:

> At last on Monday 16th May when I was sitting in Mr Davies' back parlour having drunk tea with him and Mrs Davies, Johnson unexpectedly came into the shop; and Mr Davies, having perceived him through the glass door in the room in which we were sitting, advancing towards us, announced his aweful approach to me, somewhat in the manner of an actor in the part of Horatio when he addresses Hamlet on the appearance of his father's ghost: 'Look, my Lord, it comes.'[5]

This account was not given in Boswell's journal, so we know he added it retrospectively, perhaps to invoke and make present to himself the experience of finding his calling (as a biographer) through a form of re-enactment of the well-known scene. It may be that Davies' calling, that of an actor, also summons up the reference as an appropriate one, a dramatic entry into an encounter otherwise framed by books and print. The theatrical scene

---

5   James Boswell, *The Life of Samuel Johnson, LL.D,* 2 vols (London: Henry Baldwin for Charles Dilly, 1791), vol. 1, p. 211.

nestles in the printed pages of the biography. And, of course, it also introduces two men who were to be close companions for the rest of Johnson's life.

Hamlet, and in particular this scene of the paternal ghost, seems to have had a spectral quality to enter and animate the pages of print representations of personhood and the formation of being. And the entry of the ghost prompts a search for company; it instigates literary relationship; it introduces being with others as a form of defence against 'awefulness' and solitary, potential, madness. As we have seen, Johnson sought company as a means of alleviating his own pressing mental fears. Those who gathered and reanimated his presence for readers after his death, pressed him into the same service for others.[6]

Spectrality was often contrasted on the London stage with the materiality of puppets, and yet these figures served a similar function of estrangement and the search for human company and presence as compensation. Ghosts were performed on stage by corporeal bodies. Henry Fielding makes fun of this contradiction in his *Pasquin* (1736), in which the rehearsal of a tragedy is delayed because the actor playing the first ghost has a cough.[7] Spectral bodies would not be subject to such corporeal limitations, of course. The actress who plays the goddess Common Sense forgets to take her own life on stage before she rises from the grave, her face covered in flour to indicate her change in state. The author, Fustian, rebukes her and she answers, 'I ask Pardon, Sir, in the Hurry of the Battle I forgot to come and kill my self.'[8]

Puppets are often contrasted with ghosts in theatrical productions because they are not subject to such corporeal failings (as a cough) or nonsensical forgettings (giving a ghost scene before a death scene) as actors. The perfection of the puppet fiction promises a presence-effect that real bodies cannot attain. And in this respect puppets gesture toward the capacity of the novel – precisely because it does not have to deal with corporeality – to make Being. Julie Park reminds us that the word 'fiction' derives from the Latin 'fingere': to make with one's hands. Fiction is a fabrication of the mind and hands, and character with the increasing cultural authority of the novel, is turned into something made by hand in the process of handpress printing.[9] Puppets are of course both worked by hands in their making

[6]   See Helen Deutsch, '"Look, my Lord, it comes": Uncritical Reading and Johnsonian Communion', in *Loving Dr Johnson* (Chicago, IL: University of Chicago Press, 2005), pp. 105–54.

[7]   Henry Fielding, *Pasquin*, in *The Plays, Vol. 3: 1734–1742*, ed. Lockwood, Act 1, scene 1, p. 254.

[8]   Henry Fielding, *Pasquin*, Act 5, scene 1, p. 308.

[9]   Julie Park, *The Self and It*, p. xviii.

and in their performances. Joseph Drury reminds us that men begin to be thought of as machines in the post-Cartesian world of the seventeenth century; he quotes physician George Castle who concludes that man does not differ much 'from those pieces of Clock-work, which are to be seen at every Puppet-play'.[10] By the eighteenth-century, Drury concludes, the novel was thought of as a philosophical machine that demonstrated the workings of (human) nature.

Puppets and ghosts are often played by real beings on the London stage. Equally, the mistaking of puppets for real beings was a familiar incident in accounts of the London stage and in prose fiction. *Don Quixote* provided an early example of a scene in which puppets are mistaken for real beings. In the second part, chapter twenty-six, Master Peter puts on a puppet show at an inn for Don Quixote and the knight is so convinced that the show is real that he destroys the set in his attempt to assist the puppet-knight in his rescue of his puppet-wife. Samuel Foote may have recalled Cervantes' satire on romance errantry to support his attack on the sentimental comedy through puppetry in 1773. The double target here was David Garrick's naturalism and the popularity of sentimental comedy at Garrick's theatre in Drury Lane. Foote offered *The Primitive Puppet Show* at the Haymarket, in the form of his send-up of dramatic adaptations of *Pamela* under the title *The Handsome Housemaid, or Piety in Pattens*.

Foote provided an 'Exordium' to *The Primitive Puppet Show* which he delivered to the huge assembled crowd on the opening night of Monday 15 February 1773. Here, he recalls that conventional set piece we have seen so often elsewhere; the first-time visitor to the theatre is deeply absorbed by the experience of theatre's presence-effects. He tells the story of 'a raw country girl' who:

> Being brought by her friends for the first time to a puppet-shew, she was so struck with the spirit and truth of the imitation, that it was scarce possible to convince her, but all the puppets were players: being carried the succeeding night to one of the theatres, it became equally difficult to satisfy her, but that all the players were puppets.[11]

---

[10]   George Castle, *The Chymical Galenist* (London: Henry and Timothy Twyford, 1667), p. 6. See Joseph Drury, *Novel Machines*, p. 50.

[11]   Samuel Foote, 'Exordium to the Primitive Puppet Shew', in *The Town and Country Magazine, or, Universal Repository of Knowledge, Instruction and Entertainment*, Issue 5 (June 1773), p. 320.

Foote tells his story so that his audience will be able to distinguish his performance from others that might rival it, to allow them to see the distinction where the raw country girl cannot:

> I could wish there was no other Puppet Shew in this town but my own, and that no nobler hands were employed moving wires and strings than what are conceded by that curtain. There are puppets, though formed of flesh and blood, full as passive, full as obedient as mine; but that mine may not have the disgrace of being confounded with those of that composition, permit me to desire, that you will profit by the error of a raw country girl.[12]

Foote's imitation of Garrick alongside an imitation of *Pamela* mocks both as country figures who lay claim to an inimitability, to a natural authority which exercises sway over others to the extent that those others become puppets in their hands. His own puppets will show the strings and wires, by contrast.

Garrick, according to report, sneaked into the performance with the general crush and laughed heartily at the impersonations. This 'new species of entertainment', according to *The Gentleman's Magazine*, virtually caused a riot:

> The Novelty of it brought such a crowd to see it, that the Haymarket was impassable for over an hour; the doors of the theatre were broke open, and great numbers entered without paying any thing for the admission. Several hats, swords, canes, cloaks, &c. were lost among the mob; three ladies fainted away and a girl had her arm broke in endeavouring to get into the pit.[13]

Foote's wooden leg and his wooden puppets are alike impervious to the kind of harm experienced by another girl in the audience.

The actors at this performance have no access to the kind of feeling that traditionally communicates presence; acting theory of the early eighteenth century understood acting as the transmission of a passion experienced by the actor identifying with role to the audience. Foote's celebration of their perfection as actors is a satirical dig at the admiration of Garrick's acting talent and its naturalism. Denis Diderot, having observed Garrick's acting,

---

[12]   Ibid., pp. 320–1.
[13]   *Gentleman's Magazine* (February 1773), vol. 43, p. 101. See Ian Kelly, *Samuel Foote's Other Leg*, pp. 274–6.

composed his *Paradoxe sur le Comédien* (written c. 1773 but not published until 1830) in a refutation of Aaron Hill's then hegemonic theory of the mechanistically impassioned contagious acting body. For Diderot, the actor, like the novelist, inhabits a 'puppet' body which he manipulates to move his audience. Diderot argues that the actor's body is his or her puppet and its mechanically performing rehearsed gestures act as a conduit for the *appearance* of authentic presence.[14]

However, the corporeality of audience members and performers is also their route to an experience of presence not shared by puppets and unfeeling surrogate body parts. Presence is a theatrical quality found in company. To be there is to be with others. In the case of *The Primitive Puppet Show*, this puts the corporeal company (as opposed to the actor's mechanical and wooden one) at risk. The experience of reading fiction on the page was often, as we have seen, promoted as a surrogate experience of companionship – that of being with other minds who have the same experience of reading the same text – without the danger of shared corporeal presence described in the account of Foote's frenzied first night here.

I turn in conclusion away from the past of eighteenth-century fiction to think about what it tells us about our present. And in particular the present state of criticism. The dominance of historicism in our criticism is, I suggest, inclined to fetishise the primary state of a text's 'being': first composition, first publication, first performance. The implication is that the meaning of a work is best excavated through reconstituting its first conditions of production and reception.

The primacy of the primary has been long recognised as a problem: is the first or the last authorial 'state' the best used for copy-text? The first might suggest the author's 'first' idea, but the last a more 'perfected' or 'corrected' instantiation. So too we tell the story of genres and characters as though they formed a linear sequence. Yet we know that our experience of building our acquaintance with a genre or a character or an author is never a calculated progress from earliest to latest work. Late eighteenth-century audiences were likely to have read *Evelina* before they saw a production of or read a version of Hoadly's *The Suspicious Husband*, for instance. Our progress – if progress it is – through culture is often reactive and in-the-moment; even the most organised plan of reading/consumption will be subject to whim and opportunity. This is especially the case where theatre is involved, since attending a theatrical performance depends on programming, season and our own availability.

---

[14] Aaron Hill, *The Actor: a Treatise on the Art of Playing* (London: R. Griffiths, 1750); Denis Diderot, Paradoxe sur le Comédien (Paris: A. Sautelet, 1830).

I am not saying that we should be more systemic and synchronic in our reading and entertainment habits: far from it. Rather we should aim to shape a criticism that is more able to acknowledge and assess the 'presence-effects' of works, on and with their consumers – on every occasion of contact. Put simply, works only exist or come to existence at the moment when they connect with and inhabit the same moment of consciousness as do their producers (actors, authors and other agents) and their readers or audiences. Our characterisation of criticism as interpretation and our tendency to view art as acts of communication too often avert attention from the dynamic mutual presence of producer, character and consumer as beings-in-time-and-space, which is the effect of aesthetic experience.

When I read, I read in the present. When I attend the theatre, the play is acting in real time and I am present with it. Ghosts and puppets when they enter the scene only remind me of my own presentness: in the theatre with others, in the book with its characters. Company has its own presence-effect. I travel with those novels and those plays in my everyday life and they surface to my attention when what happens in the world seems to coincide with my experience of those works. A criticism that provides its readers with ever-more-distant and distancing contexts of information to 'explain' the works they consume will find itself ever more solitary: such criticism cannot travel with and live with others. And the desire to 'be there', if it means anything, means only this: the desire to be with others.

Bibliography

Primary sources

Manuscript

Burney, Frances, Undated Camilla manuscript, Egerton 3696 fols 27–73, British Library, London.

Colman, George, LA179, The Huntington Library, San Marino, California.

Covent Garden Theatre Ledger, Egerton MS 2274, British Library, London.

Goldsmith, Oliver, *The Novel; or, Mistakes of a Night*, LA349, The Huntington Library, San Marino, California.

Hoadly, Benjamin, *The [[Rake]]*, LA63, The Huntington Library, San Marino, California.

Macklin, Charles, *The New Play Criticiz'd; or, The Plague of Envy (The Suspicious Husband Criticized; or, The Plague of Envy)*, LA64, The Huntington Library, San Marino, California.

MacNally, Leonard, [[Tristram]] [[Shandy]], LA621, The Huntington Library, San Marino, California.

Stage Licensing Act 10 Geo II c 28.

Print

Addison, Joseph and Richard Steele, *The Spectator*, ed. Donald F. Bond, 5 vols (Oxford: Oxford University Press, 1965).

Anon., *The Adventures of an Author written by Himself and a Friend*, 2 vols (London: Robinson and Roberts, 1767).

Anon., *Angelica; or Quixote in Petticoats. A Comedy, in Two Acts* (London: Printed for the Author, and sold by the booksellers of London and Westminster, 1758).

Anon., 'A favorite song sung by Mrs. Kennedy in Tristram Shandy' (London: Longman and Broderip, 1783).

Anon., *The Critical Review: or, Annals of Literature. By a Society of Gentlemen*, 2 vols (London: R. Baldwin, 1756).

Anon., *The Daily Advertiser*, 28 April and 2 May 1741.

Anon., *The Disguise, a Dramatic Novel*, 2 vols (London: J. Dodsley, 1771).

Anon., *Half an Hour after Supper: An Interlude, in One Act, as Performed at the Theatre Royal, Haymarket* (London: J. Debrett, 1789).

Anon., *London Magazine: Or Monthly Intelligencer*, vol. 29 (April 1760).

Anon., *The Monthly Review* 38 (February 1768), Art. 43–44, 159–60.

Anon., *Morning Chronicle*, 1 October 1778.

Anon., *Public Advertiser*, 27 January 1787.

Anon., *Ranger's Progress: Consisting of a Variety of Poetical Essays, Moral, Serious, Comic, and Satyrical. By Honest Ranger, of Bedford-Row* (London: Printed for the Author, 1760).

Anon., *Reasons why David Garrick, Esq. should not appear on the Stage, In a Letter to John Rich, Esq.* (London: J. Cooke, 1759).

Anon., *Report from the Joint Select Committee of the House of Lords and the House of Commons on the Stage Plays (Censorship)...Ordered by the House of Commons to be Printed 2 November* 1909 (London: His Majesty's Stationery Office by Wyman and Sons, 1909).

Anon., 'Theatrical Intelligence', *St James' Chronicle*, 18–21 February 1769.

Baker, David Erskine, *Biographia Dramatica, Or, A Companion to the Playhouse*, 4 vols (London: Longman et al., 1811).

Banks, John, *Vertue Betray'd: or, Anna Bullen* (London: R. Bentley and M. Magnes, 1682).

Barbauld, Anna Letitia, *The British Novelists*, 50 vols (London: F.C. and J. Rivington, 1810).

Bickerstaff, Isaac, *The Maid of the Mill* (London: Newbery and others, 1765).

Boaden, James, *Memoirs of Mrs. Inchbald*, 2 vols (London: R. Bentley, 1833).

Boswell, James, *The Life of Samuel Johnson*, 2 vols (London: Henry Baldwin for Charles Dilly, 1791).

––, *Life of Johnson*, ed. G.B. Hill and L.F. Powell, 6 vols (Oxford: Oxford University Press, 1934–50).

Brewer, Anthony (Thomas), *The Countrie Girl* (London: A.R., 1646).

Brooke, Frances, *The Excursion*, ed. Paula R. Backscheider and Hope D. Cotton, Eighteenth-Century Novels by Women (Lexington, KY: University Press of Kentucky, 1997).

Brumoy, Pierre, *The Greek Theatre of Father Brumoy*, trans. and ed. Charlotte Lennox, 3 vols (London: Millar et al., 1759).

Burney, Frances, *Camilla, Picture of Youth*, ed. Edward A. Bloom and Lillian Bloom (Oxford: Oxford University Press, 2009).

––, *The Court Journals and Letters of Frances Burney. Vol. 1*, ed. Stewart J. Cook and Peter Sabor (Oxford: Oxford University Press, 2011).

––, *Early Journals and Letters: Vol. V 1782–1783*, ed. Lars E. Troide and Stewart J. Cooke (Oxford: Oxford University Press, 1988).

––, *Evelina, or a Young Lady's Entrance into the World* (1778), ed. Susan Kubica Howard, Broadview Literary Texts (Peterborough, ON: Broadview Press, 2000).

––, *The Wanderer, or Female Difficulties*, ed. Margaret Doody (Oxford: Oxford University Press, 2001).

Byron, Medora Gordon, *Celia in Search of a Husband* (London: Minerva Press, 1809).

Caines, Michael et al., *Lives of Shakespearian Actors*, Series editor Gail Marshall, 2 parts, 5 vols (London: Pickering and Chatto, 2012–15).

Castle, George, *The Chymical Galenist* (London: Henry and Timothy Twyford, 1667).

Charke, Charlotte, *A Narrative of the Life of Mrs. Charlotte Charke* [1755], ed. Robert Rehder (London and New York: Routledge, 2016).

Cibber, Colley, *An Apology for the Life of Colley Cibber: With an Historical View of the Stage During his Own Time*, ed. B.R.S. Fone (Ann Arbor, MI: University of Michigan Press, 1968).

––, *A Letter from Mr. Cibber to Mr. Pope* (Dublin: A. Reilley, 1742).

––, and John Vanbrugh, *The Provok'd Husband; or a Journey to London* (London: J. Watts, 1728).

––, and John Vanbrugh, *The Provok'd Husband*, Regents Restoration Drama Series, ed. Peter Dixon (London: Edward Arnold, 1974).

Clarke, Norma, *Dr Johnson's Women* (London: Random House, 2011).

Collier, Jane, *An Essay on the Art of Ingeniously Tormenting*, ed. Audrey Bilger, Broadview Literary Texts (Peterborough, ON: Broadview, 2003).

Colman, George, *Polly Honeycombe. A Dramatic Novel* (London: T. Becket; and T. Davies, 1760).

––, *The Rivals: Richard Brinsley Sheridan; and Polly Honeycombe: George Colman the Elder*, ed. David A. Brewer (Peterborough, ON: Broadview Press, 2012).

Congreve, William, *The Works of William Congreve*, ed. D. F. McKenzie and Christine Ferdinand, 3 vols (Oxford: Oxford University Press, 2011).

Cradock, Joseph, *Literary and Miscellaneous Memoirs*, 2 vols (London: for the Author, 1826).

Cumberland, Richard, *The West Indian* (London: W. Griffin, 1771).

Curll, Edmund, *A Compleat Key to the Dunciad* (London: A. Dodd, 1728).

Davies, Thomas, *Memoirs of the Life of David Garrick* (London: for the Author, 1780).

Delany, Mary, *The Autobiography and Correspondence of Mary Granville, Mrs. Delany: With Interesting Reminiscences of King George the Third and Queen Charlotte*, ed. Augusta Hall Llanover, second series, 3 vols (London: R. Bentley, 1862).

Diderot, Denis, Paradoxe sur le Comédien (Paris: A. Sautelet, 1830).

Drennan, William, and Samuel McTier, *The Drennan-McTier Letters 1776–1819*, ed. Jean Agnew, 2 vols (Dublin: The Women's History Project, 1999).

Edgeworth, Maria, *Belinda*, ed. Kathryn J. Kirkpatrick (Oxford: Oxford University Press, 1994).

——, *Belinda*, ed. Siobhán Kilfeather, *The Novels and Selected Works of Maria Edgeworth*, general ed. Marilyn Butler and Mitzi Myers, 12 vols, vol. 2 (London: Pickering and Chatto, 2003).

——, *The Education of the Heart: The Correspondence of Rachel Mordecai Lazarus and Maria Edgeworth*, ed. Edgar E. MacDonald (Chapel Hill, NC: University of North Carolina Press, 1977).

——, *Harrington*, in *Leonora. Harrington*, ed. Marilyn Butler and Susan Manly, *The Novels and Selected Works of Maria Edgeworth*, general ed. Marilyn Butler and Mitzi Myers, 12 vols, vol. 3 (London: Pickering and Chatto, 1999).

——, *Memoirs of Richard Lovell Edgeworth, esq. begun by himself and concluded by his daughter, Maria Edgeworth*, 2 vols (London: R. Hunter, 1820).

Fielding, Henry, *An Apology for the Life of Mrs. Shamela Andrews* (1741), in Catherine Ingrassia, ed., *Shamela and Anti-Pamela* (Peterborough, ON: Broadview Press, 2004).

——, *The History of Tom Jones: A Foundling*, ed. Fredson Bowers and Martin C. Battestin. The Wesleyan Edition of the Works of Henry Fielding, 2 vols (Oxford: Oxford University Press, 1974).

——, *Joseph Andrews*, ed. Martin Battestin, The Wesleyan Edition of the Works of Henry Fielding (Oxford: Oxford University Press, 1966).

——, *Miscellanies by Henry Fielding, Esq. Vol. 1*, ed. Henry Knight Miller, The Wesleyan Edition of the Works of Henry Fielding (Oxford: Oxford University Press, 1972).

——, *Miscellanies by Henry Fielding, Esq. Vol. 2*, ed. Bertrand A. Goldgar and Hugh Amory, The Wesleyan Edition of the Works of Henry Fielding (Oxford: Oxford University Press, 1993).

——, *Plays*, ed. Thomas Lockwood, The Wesleyan Edition of the Works of Henry Fielding, 3 vols (Oxford: Clarendon Press, 2011).

Fielding, Sarah, *The Adventures of David Simple and Volume the Last*, ed. Peter Sabor, Eighteenth-Century Novels by Women series (Lexington, KY: Kentucky University Press, 2015).

——, and Jane Collier, *The Cry. A New Dramatic Fable*, ed. Carolyn Woodward, Eighteenth-Century Novels by Women series (Lexington, KY: University Press of Kentucky, 2018).

Foote, Samuel, *The Author* (London, R. Francklin, 1757).

––, *The Dramatic Works of Samuel Foote, Esq; to Which Is Prefixed a Life of the Author*, 4 vols (London: J.F. and C. Rivington et al., 1788 [1789?]).

––, 'Exordium to the Primitive Puppet Shew', in *The Town and Country Magazine, or, Universal Repository of Knowledge, Instruction and Entertainment*, Issue 5 (June 1773), 219–321.

––, *The Handsome Housemaid, or Piety in Pattens* (1773), *Samuel Foote's Primitive Puppet-shew, Featuring Piety in Pattens; a Critical Edition*, ed. Samuel N. Bogorad (Pittsburgh, PA: University of Pittsburgh Press, 1973).

––, *The Mimic, A Poem. By the Author* (London: J. Scott, 1761).

––, *The Minor* (London: J. Coote et al., 1760).

––, *Tragedy a-la-mode*, and *The Diversions of the Morning*, in *The Wandering Patentee.... By Tate Wilkinson...... To which are added, never published, The Diversions of the Morning, and Foote's Trial for a Libel on Peter Paragraph. Written by the late Samuel Foote*, vol. 4 (London: Printed for the Author, 1795).

Fordyce, James, *An Essay on the Action Proper for the Pulpit* (London: R. and J. Dodsley, 1753).

Garrick, David, *Miss in Her Teens; or the Medley of Lovers* (Dublin: S. Powell, 1747).

––, *The Letters of David Garrick*, ed. David M. Little and George M. Kahrl, 3 vols (London: Oxford University Press, 1963).

––, 'A Recipe for a Modern Critic', *The Universal Visiter* 3 (March 1756), 191–2.

Gay, John, John Arbuthnot and Alexander Pope, *Three Hours After Marriage*, ed. John Fuller, in *John Gay, Dramatic Works*, 2 vols, vol. 1 (Oxford: Clarendon Press, 1983).

Genest, John, *Some Account of the English Stage: From the Restoration in 1660 to 1830* (Bath: H.E. Carrington, 1832).

Giffard, Henry, *Pamela. A Comedy* (London: J. Robinson, 1742).

Goldsmith, Oliver, *Collected Works of Oliver Goldsmith*, ed. Arthur Friedman, 5 vols (Oxford: Clarendon Press, 1966).

––, *The Collected Letters of Oliver Goldsmith*, ed. K.C. Balderston (Cambridge: Cambridge University Press, 1928).

––, *The Letters of Oliver Goldsmith*, ed. Michael J. Griffin and David O'Shaughnessy (Cambridge: Cambridge University Press, 2018).

Griffiths, Ralph, 'Art. 59 Half an Hour after Supper: An Interlude, in One Act', *Monthly Review* 81 (1789), 284.

Hatchett, William, *The Rival Father: or, the Death of Achilles* (London: William Mears and Thomas Corbett, 1730).

Haywood, Eliza, *Anti-Pamela* (1741), in Catherine Ingrassia, ed., *Shamela and Anti-Pamela* (Peterborough, ON: Broadview Press, 2004).

——, *Dalinda: or, The Double Marriage* (London: C. Corbett and G. Woodfall, 1749).

——, *The Dramatic Historiographer*, in *The Dramatic Historiographer and The Parrot*, ed. Christine Blouch, Alexander Pettit and Rebecca Sayers Hanson, in *Selected Works of Eliza Haywood*, Set II, vol. 1, gen. ed. Alexander Pettit, 6 vols (London: Pickering and Chatto, 2001).

——, *The History of Miss Betsy Thoughtless*, ed. Christine Blouch, Broadview Literary Texts (Peterborough, ON: Broadview, 1998).

——, *Love in Excess*, ed. David Oakleaf, 2nd ed. (Peterborough, ON: Broadview, 2000).

——, *The Masqueraders, or Fatal Curiosity, and the Surprize, or Constancy Rewarded*, ed. Tiffany Potter (Toronto: University of Toronto Press, 2015).

——, *A Wife to be Lett, A Comedy* (London: Dan. Browne and Sam. Chapman, 1724).

——, *Secret Histories, Novels and Poems*, 4 vols (London: Charles Hitch, Daniel Browne, Samuel Birt and R. Ware, 1725).

——, *The Works of Mrs Eliza Haywood*, 4 vols (London: D. Browne and S. Chapman, 1724).

Hill, Aaron, *The Actor: a Treatise on the Art of Playing* (London: R. Griffiths, 1750).

——, *An Essay on the Art of Acting* (London: Printed for J. Osborn, 1746).

——, *The Prompter* 66 (27 June 1735).

Hitchcock, Richard, *The Coquette; or, the Mistakes of the Heart* (Bath: R. Cruttwell, 1777).

Hoadly, Benjamin, *The Suspicious Husband* (London: J. and R. Tonson and S. Draper, 1747).

Home, John, *Douglas* (London: A. Millar, 1757).

Inchbald, Elizabeth, 'To the Artist', in *The Artist: A Collection of Essays Relative to Painting, Poetry, Sculpture, Architecture, the Drama, Discoveries of Science, and Various Other Subjects*, 1, no. 14 (1807), 9–19.

Johnson, Charles, *The Country Lasses, or, The Custom of the Manor* (Dublin: S. Powell, 1727).

Johnson, Samuel, *A Dictionary of the English Language*, 2 vols (London: W. Strahan et al., 1755).

——, *The Idler*, 2 vols (London: J. Newbery, 1761).

Kelly, Hugh, *False Delicacy* (London: Baldwin, Johnston and Kearsly, 1768).

Keymer, Thomas and Peter Sabor, ed., *The Pamela Controversy: Criticisms and Adaptations of Samuel Richardson's* Pamela *1740–1750*, 6 vols (London: Pickering and Chatto, 2001).

Kimber, Edward, *The Juvenile adventures of David Ranger, Esq.*, 2nd ed., 2 vols (London: J. Stevens 1757).

Kirkman, J.T., *Memoirs of the Life of Charles Macklin*, 2 vols (London: Lackington & Co., 1799).

Lamb, Charles, 'On the Tragedies of Shakespeare Considered with Reference to Their Fitness for Stage Representation', *The Reflector: A Quarterly Magazine, on Subjects of Philosophy, Politics, and the Liberal Arts*, 2, no. 4 (1811), 298–313.

Leanerd, John, *The Country Innocence: or, The Chamber-Maid Turn'd Quaker* (London: Charles Harper, 1677).

Lennox, Charlotte, *Charlotte Lennox: Correspondence and Miscellaneous Documents*, ed. Norbert Schürer (Lewisburg, PA: Bucknell University Press, 2012).

––, *The Female Quixote: or, the Adventures of Arabella*, ed. Margaret Dalziel (Oxford: Oxford University Press, 2008).

––, *Henrietta*, ed. Ruth Perry and Susan Carlisle, Eighteenth-Century Novels by Women series (Lexington, KY: University Press of Kentucky, 2008).

––, *The Sister* (London: J. Dodsley and T. Davies, 1769).

Lillo, George, *The London Merchant: or, the History of George Barnwell* (London: Printed for J. Gray, 1731).

––, *Silvia; or, The Country Burial* (Dublin: S. Powell, 1730).

MacNally, Leonard, *Tristram Shandy, a Sentimental, Shandean bagatelle, in two acts* (London: S. Bladon, 1783).

Manley, Delarivier, *Secret Memoirs and Manners of several Persons of both Sexes. From the New Atalantis*, in *The Selected Works of Delarivier Manley*, ed. Rachel Carnell and Ruth Herman, 5 vols, vol. 2 (London: Pickering and Chatto, 2005).

Montagu, Lady Mary Wortley, *Essays and Poems and Simplicity, a Comedy*, ed. Isobel Grundy and Robert Halsband (Oxford: Clarendon, 1977).

Murphy, Arthur, *The Gray's Inn Journal, by Charles Ranger, Esq.* (London: W. Faden and J. Bouquet, 1753).

––, 'The Life of the Author', in *The Works of Henry Fielding, Esq: With the Life of the Author*, 12 vols, vol. 1 (London: W. Strahan, J. Rivington and Sons, 1783).

––, *The Life of David Garrick*, 2 vols (London: J. Wright, 1801).

Oakley, Warren, *A Culture of Mimicry: Laurence Sterne, his Readers and the Art of Bodysnatching* (London: Maney Publishing, 2010).

Parnell, Thomas, *Collected Poems of Thomas Parnell*, ed. Claude Rawson and F.P. Lock (London and Toronto: Associated University Presses, 1989).

−−, *Homer's Battle of the Frogs and Mice, with the Remarks of Zoilus. To which is prefix'd, The Life of the said Zoilus* (London: Bernard Lintot, 1717).

−−, *Poems on Several Occasions...Written by Dr. Thomas Parnell* (London: Bernard Lintot, 1722).

Piozzi, Hester Lynch, *Anecdotes of the Late Samuel Johnson, LL.D. during the Last Twenty Years of his Life* (London, T. Cadell, 1786).

Pope, Alexander, *The Dunciad: In Four Books*, ed Valerie Rumbold, 2nd ed. Longman Annotated Texts (Abingdon: Routledge, 2014).

−−, *The Poems of Alexander Pope. Volume III, the Dunciad (1728) & the Dunciad Variorum (1729)*, ed. Valerie Rumbold, Longman Annotated English Poets (Harlow: Pearson/Longman, 2007).

−−, 'A Project for the Advancement of the Stage', in *Peri Bathous: Or the Art of Sinking in Poetry*, in *Miscellanies in Prose and Verse. In Two Volumes. By Jonathan Swift, D.D. And Alexander Pope, Esq.* (London: Sam Fairbrother, 1732).

Richardson, Samuel, *Clarissa; or, the History of a Young Lady*, ed. Angus Ross (London: Penguin, 1985).

−−, *Correspondence of Samuel Richardson*, ed. Anna Letitia Barbauld, 6 vols (London: R. Phillips by Lewis and Rodem, 1804).

−−, *Pamela, or, Virtue Rewarded, Virtue Rewarded*, ed. Albert Rivero, The Cambridge Edition of the Works and Correspondence of Samuel Richardson, vol. 2 (Cambridge: Cambridge University Press, 2011).

−−, *Pamela in Her Exalted Condition*, ed. Albert Rivero, The Cambridge Edition of the Works and Correspondence of Samuel Richardson, vol. 3 (Cambridge: Cambridge University Press, 2012).

−−, *A Seasonable Examination of the Pleas and Pretensions of the Proprietors of, and Subscribers to, Play-Houses* (1735), in *Early Works*, ed. Alexander Pettit (Cambridge: Cambridge University Press, 2012), vol. 1 of The Cambridge Edition of the Works and Correspondence of Samuel Richardson.

Savage, Richard, *An Author to Be Lett. Being a Proposal Humbly Address'd to the Consideration of the Knights, Esquires, Gentlemen, and other Worshipful and Weighty Members of the Solid and Ancient Society of the Bathos. By their Associate and Well-Wisher Iscariot Hackney* (London: Alexander Vint, 1729).

−−, *The Authors of the Town: A Satire, Inscribed to the Author of the Universal Passion* (London: J. Roberts, 1725).

−−, *The Bastard: A Poem, Inscribed with all Due Reverence to Mrs. Bret, once Countess of Macclesfield* (London: T. Worrall, 1728).

Sheridan, Frances, *Memoirs of Miss Sidney Bidulph*, ed. Heidi Hutner and Nicole Garret, Broadview Literary Texts (Peterborough, ON: Broadview, 2011).

Sheridan, Richard Brinsley, *The Critic*, ed. David Crane, New Mermaids (London: W.W. Norton, 1989).

––, *The Rivals, a Comedy: As It Was First Acted at the Theatre-Royal in Covent-Garden*, ed. Richard Little Purdy (Oxford: Clarendon Press, 1930).

––, *The Rivals: Richard Brinsley Sheridan; and Polly Honeycombe: George Colman the Elder*, ed. David A. Brewer (Peterborough, ON: Broadview Press, 2012).

Smith, Adam, *The Theory of Moral Sentiments*, ed. D.D. Raphael and A.L. Macfie, *Glasgow Edition of the Works and Correspondence of Adam Smith*, vol .1 (Indianapolis, IN: Liberty Fund, 1982).

Smollett, Tobias, *The Adventures of Peregrine Pickle*, 4 vols (London: Printed for the Author, and sold by D. Wilson, 1751).

Steele, Richard, *The Tender Husband; or, the Accomplished Fools* (London: Jacob Tonson, 1705).

Sterne, Laurence, *A Facsimile Reproduction of a Unique Catalogue of Laurence Sterne's Library* (London: J. Tregaskis, 1930).

––, *Letters of Laurence Sterne*, ed. Lewis Perry Curtis (Oxford: Oxford University Press, 1935).

––, *The Life and Opinions of Tristram Shandy, Gentleman*, ed. Melvyn New and Joan New (London: Penguin Books, 1997).

––, *A Sentimental Journey through France and Italy and continuation of the Bramine's journal: The text and notes*, ed. M. New and W.G. Day, The Florida Edition of the Works of Laurence Sterne, 6 vols (Gainesville, FL: University Press of Florida, 2002).

Voltaire (François-Marie d'Arouet), *Candide and other Stories*, ed. Roger Pearson (Oxford: Oxford University Press, 2008).

Walpole, Horace, *The Yale Edition of Horace Walpole's Correspondence*, ed. W.S. Lewis, 48 vols, vol. 9 (New Haven, CT: Yale University Press, 1937–83).

Williams, David, *A Letter to David Garrick, Esq. On his conduct as Principal Manager and Actor at Drury-Lane* (London: S. Bladon, 1772).

Women's Theatrical Memoirs. Part 1, ed. Sharon Setzer, 5 vols (London: Pickering and Chatto, 2007).

Women's Theatrical Memoirs Part 2, ed. Sue McPherson, and Julia Swindells, 10 vols (London: Pickering and Chatto, 2008).

Zunshine, Lisa, ed., *Acting Theory and the English Stage, 1700–1830*, 5 vols (London: Pickering and Chatto, 2009).

Secondary sources

Anderson, Emily Hodgson, *Eighteenth-Century Authorship and the Play of Fiction: Novels and the Theatre from Haywood to Austen* (London: Routledge, 2009).

––, *Shakespeare and the Legacy of Loss* (Ann Arbor: The University of Michigan Press, 2018).

––, 'Theatrical *Tristram*: Sterne and *Hamlet* Reconsidered', in *Georgian Theatre in an Information Age: Media, Performance, Sociability*, ed. Daniel O'Quinn and Gillian Russell, *Eighteenth-Century Fiction*, Special Issue 27, nos. 3–4 (2015), 661–80.

Anderson, Misty, *Imagining Methodism: Enthusiasm, Belief, and the Borders of the Self* (Baltimore, MD: Johns Hopkins University Press, 2012).

Auslander, Philip, *Liveness: Performance in a Mediatized Culture*, 2nd ed. (London: Routledge, 2008).

Backscheider, Paula, 'Shadowing Theatrical Change', in *Players, Playwrights, Playhouses: Investigating Performance, 1660–1800* (Basingstoke: Palgrave Macmillan, 2007), 78–101.

Balderston, K.C., 'A Manuscript Version of *She Stoops to Conquer*', *Modern Language Notes*, 45 (1930), 84–5.

Ballaster, Ros, 'Passing Judgement: The Place of the Aesthetic in Feminist Literary History', in *Women's Writing, 1660–1830. Feminisms and Futures*, ed. Jennie Batchelor and Gillian Dow (London: Palgrave Macmillan, 2016), 11–32.

––, 'Rivals for the Repertory: Theatre and Novel in Georgian London', *Restoration and Eighteenth-Century Theatre Research*, 27, no. 1 (Summer 2012), 5–24.

Barr, Rebecca Ann, '"Barren Desarts of Arbitrary Words": Language and Communication in Collier and Fielding's *The Cry*', *Women's Writing*, 23, no. 1 (2016), 87–105.

Batchelor, Jennie, 'The "Latent Seeds of Coquetry": Amatory Fiction and the 1750s Novel', in *Masters of the Marketplace: British Women Novelists of the 1750s*, ed. Susan Carlile (Bethlehem, PA: Lehigh University Press, 2011), 145–64.

––, *Women's Work: Labour, Gender and Authorship, 1750–1830* (Manchester: Manchester University Press, 2014).

Battestin, Martin C. and Ruthe R. Battestin, *Henry Fielding: A Life* (London: Routledge, 1989).

Bhabha, Homi, 'Of Mimicry and Man: The Ambivalence of Colonial Discourse', *October*, 28 (1984), 125–33.

Bolton, Betsy, 'Theorizing Audience and Spectatorial Agency', in *The Oxford Handbook of the Georgian Theatre 1737–1832*, ed. Julia Swindells and David Francis Taylor (Oxford: Oxford University Press, 2014), 31–52.

Brewer, David A., *The Afterlife of Character, 1726–1825* (Philadelphia, PA: University of Pennsylvania Press, 2005).

Brock, Claire, *News, Biography, and Eighteenth-Century Celebrity* (Oxford: Oxford University Press, 2016).

Brown, Gillian, 'The Quixotic Fallacy', *NOVEL: A Forum on Fiction*, 32 (1999), 250–73.

Burge, James C., *Lines of Business: Casting Practice and Policy in the American Theatre, 1752–1899* (New York: Peter Lang, 1986).

Carlile, Susan, *Charlotte Lennox: An Independent Mind* (Toronto and London: University of Toronto Press, 2018).

––, 'Henrietta on Page and Stage', in *Masters of the Marketplace: British Women Novelists of the 1750s*, ed. Susan Carlile (Bethlehem, PA: Lehigh University Press, 2011), 128–41

Carlson, Marvin, *The Haunted Stage: The Theatre as Memory Machine* (Ann Arbor, MI: University of Michigan Press, 2003).

Carson, James P., '"The Little Republic" of the Family: Goldsmith's Politics of Nostalgia', *Eighteenth-Century Fiction*, 16, no. 2 (January 2004), 173–96.

Charles, Katherine G., 'Staging Sociability in *The Excursion*: Frances Brooke, David Garrick, and the King's Theatre Coterie', *Eighteenth-Century Fiction*, 27, no. 2 (Winter 2014–15), 257–84.

Clarke, Norma, *Brothers of the Quill: Oliver Goldsmith in Grub Street* (Cambridge, MA: Harvard University Press, 2016).

––, *Dr Johnson's Women* (London: Random House, 2011).

Cordner, Michael and Peter Holland, ed., *Players, Playwrights, Playhouses: Investigating Performance, 1660–1800: Redefining British Theatre History* (Basingstoke: Palgrave Macmillan, 2007).

Craft-Fairchild, Catherine, '"The "Jewish Question" on Both Sides of the Atlantic: *Harrington* and the Correspondence between Maria Edgeworth and Rachel Mordecai Lazarus', *Eighteenth-Century Life*, 38, no. 3 (2014), 30–63.

Davidson, Jenny, 'Restoration Theatre and the Novel', in *The Oxford History of the Novel in English. Volume 1: Prose Fiction in English from the Origins of Print to 1750*, ed. Thomas Keymer (Oxford: Oxford University Press, 2017), 435–49.

DeLanda, Manuel, *A New Philosophy of Society: Assemblage Theory and Social Complexity* (London and New York: Continuum, 2006).

Deleuze, Gilles and Félix Guattari, *A Thousand Plateaus: Capitalism and Schizophrenia*, trans. Brian Massumi (Minneapolis, MN: University of Minnesota Press, 1987).

DeRitter, Jones, *The Embodiment of Characters: The Representation of Physical Experience on Stage and in Print, 1728–1749*, New Cultural Studies (Philadelphia, PA: University of Pennsylvania Press, 1994).

Dickie, Simon, 'Tobias Smollett and the Ramble Novel', in *The Oxford History of the Novel in English: Volume Two: English and British Fiction 1750–1820*, ed. Peter Garside and Karen O'Brien (Oxford: Oxford University Press, 2015), 92–108.

Donkin, Ellen, *Getting into the Act: Women Playwrights in London, 1776–1829* (London: Routledge, 1995).

Donoghue, Frank, *The Fame Machine: Book-Reviewing and Eighteenth-century Literary Careers* (Redwood City, CA: Stanford University Press, 1996).

Downie, J.A., 'Novels of the 1750s', in *The Oxford Handbook of the Eighteenth-Century Novel* (Oxford: Oxford University Press, 2016), 252–63.

Drury, Joseph, *Novel Machines: Technology and Narrative Form in Enlightenment Britain* (Oxford: Oxford University Press, 2017).

Evans, James E., '*Evelina*, the Rustic Girls of Congreve and Abington, and Surrogation in the 1770s', *The Eighteenth Century*, 52, no. 2 (Spring 2011), 157–71.

Fawcett, Julia H., *Spectacular Disappearances: Celebrity and Privacy, 1696–1801* (Ann Arbor, MI: University of Michigan Press, 2016).

Forster, E.M., *Aspects of the Novel* (San Diego, CA: London: Harcourt Brace, 1927).

Frank, Marcie, 'Melodrama and the Politics of Literary Form in Elizabeth Inchbald's Works', in *Eighteenth-Century Fiction: Georgian Theatre in an Information Age: Media, Performance, Sociability*, ed. Daniel O'Quinn and Gillian Russell, special issue *Eighteenth-Century Fiction*, 27, nos. 3–4 (2015), 707–30.

––, *The Novel Stage: Narrative Form from the Restoration to Jane Austen* (New Brunswick, NJ: Rutgers University Press, 2019).

Freeman, Elizabeth, *Time Binds. Queer Temporalities, Queer Histories* (Durham, NC and London: Duke University Press, 2010).

Freeman, Lisa A., *Anti-Theatricality and the Body Public* (Philadelphia, PA: University of Pennsylvania Press, 2016).

––, *Character's Theater: Genre and Identity on the Eighteenth-Century English Stage* (Philadelphia, PA: University of Pennsylvania Press, 2002).

Frow, John, *Character and Person* (Oxford: Oxford University Press, 2014).

The Georgian Playhouse: Actors, Artists, Audiences and Architecture 1730–1830, Catalogue of Exhibition devised by Iain Mackintosh assisted by Geoffrey Aston (London: Hayward Gallery, 1975).

Gerrard, Christine, *Aaron Hill: The Muses' Projector, 1685–1750* (Oxford: Oxford University Press, 2003).

Gollapudi, Aparna, *Moral Reform in Comedy and Culture, 1696–1747* (Farnham: Ashgate, 2011).

Goodall, Jane, *Stage Presence* (London and New York: Routledge, 2008).

Gooding, Richard, 'Pamela, Shamela, and the Politics of the *Pamela* Vogue', *Eighteenth-Century Fiction*, 7, no. 2 (1995), 109–30.

Greenblatt, Stephen, 'The Improvisation of Power', in *Renaissance Self-Fashioning: From More to Shakespeare* (Chicago, IL: Chicago University Press, 1980), 222–54.

Guillory, John, 'Enlightening Mediation', in *This Is Enlightenment*, ed. Clifford Siskin and William B. Warner (Chicago, IL: University of Chicago Press, 2010), 37–63.

Gumbrecht, Hans Ulrich, *Our Broad Present. Time and Contemporary Culture* (New York: Columbia University Press, 2014), 1–10.

––, *Production of Presence: What Meaning Cannot Convey* (Stanford, CA: Stanford University Press, 2004).

Hanlon, Aaron, 'Maids, Mistresses, and "Monstrous Doubles": Gender-Class Kyriarchy in *The Female Quixote* and *Female Quixotism*', *The Eighteenth Century*, 55, no. 1 (2014), 77–96.

––, *A World of Disorderly Notions: Quixote and the Logic of Exceptionalism* (Charlottesville, VA and London: University of Virginia Press, 2019).

Harkin, Maureen, 'Goldsmith on Authorship in *The Vicar of Wakefield*', *Eighteenth-Century Fiction*, 14, nos. 3–4 (April–July 2002), 325–44.

Harris, Jocelyn, 'Introduction', in *Richardson's Published Commentary on Clarissa 1747–1765. Volume 1 Prefaces, Postscripts and Related Writings*, ed. Thomas Keymer (London: Pickering and Chatto, 1998), vii–xcv.

Havens, Hilary, 'Omitting Lady Grace: The Provok'd Husband in Frances Burney's Camilla and the Wanderer', *Journal for Eighteenth-Century Studies*, 38 (2015), 413–24.

Heidegger, Martin, *Being and Time*, trans. Joan Stambaugh, rev. Dennis J. Schmidt (Albany, NY: State University of New York Press, 2010).

Highfill, Philip H., Kalman A. Burnim and Edward A. Langhans, *A Biographical Dictionary of Actors, Actresses, Musicians, Dancers, Managers and Other Stage Personnel in London, 1660–1800*, 16 vols (Carbondale, IL: Southern Illinois University Press, 1973–93).

Hume, Robert D., 'The Economics of Culture in London, 1660–1740', *Huntington Library Quarterly*, 69 (2006), 487–533.

——, 'Goldsmith and Sheridan and the Supposed Revolution of 'Laughing' against Sentimental Comedy' (1972), rpt in *The Rakish Stage: Studies in English Drama, 1660–1800* (Carbondale, IL: Southern Illinois University Press, 1983), 312–55.

Hutson, Lorna, 'Liking Men: Ben Jonson's Closet Opened', *English Literary History (ELH)*, 71, no. 4 (2004), 1065–96.

Jensen, Kristin, 'Reforming Character: William Law and the English Theophrastan Tradition', *Eighteenth-Century Fiction*, 22 (2010), 443–76.

Jones, Emrys and Victoria Joule, ed., *Intimacy and Celebrity in Eighteenth-Century Literary Culture: Public Interiors* (Basingstoke: Palgrave Macmillan, 2018).

Kavanagh, Declan William, *Effeminate Years: Literature, Politics, and Aesthetics in Mid-Eighteenth-Century Britain* (Lewisburg, PA: Bucknell University Press, 2017).

——, '"Of Neuter Gender, Tho' of Irish Growth": Charles Churchill's Fribble', *Irish University Review*, 43 (2013), 119–30.

Kelly, Gary, *The English Jacobin Novel 1780–1805* (Oxford and New York: Clarendon Press, 1976).

Kelly, Ian, *Mr Foote's Other Leg* (London: Picador, 2012).

Kenny, Shirley Strum, 'Two Scenes by Addison in Steele's "Tender Husband"', *Studies in Bibliography*, 19 (1996), 217–26.

Keymer, Thomas, 'Henry Fielding's Theatrical Career', *The Cambridge Companion to Henry Fielding*, ed. Claude Rawson (Cambridge: Cambridge University Press, 2007), 17–38.

——, 'Pamela's Fables: Aesopian Writing and Political Implication in Samuel Richardson and Sir Roger l'Estrange', *Bulletin de la Société d'Etudes Anglo-Américaines des XVIIe et XVIIIe Siècles*, 41, no. 1 (1995), 81–101.

Keymer, Thomas and Peter Sabor, ed., *Pamela in the Marketplace: Literary Controversy and Print Culture in Eighteenth-Century Britain and Ireland* (Cambridge: Cambridge University Press, 2005).

King, Kathryn R., 'Eliza Haywood, Savage Love, and Biographical Uncertainty', *The Review of English Studies*, New Series, 59.242 (2008), 722–39.

——, 'New Contexts for Early Novels by Women: The Case of Eliza Haywood, Aaron Hill, and the Hillarians, 1719–1725', *A Companion to the Eighteenth-Century Novel and Culture*, ed. Paula R. Backscheider and Catherine Ingrassia (Oxford: Blackwell, 2005), 261–75.

——, *A Political Biography of Eliza Haywood, Eighteenth-Century Political Biographies* (London: Pickering and Chatto, 2012).

Kinkead-Weakes, Mark, *Samuel Richardson: Dramatic Novelist* (London: Methuen and Co., Ltd., 1973).

Kinservik, Matthew J., *Disciplining Satire: The Censorship of Satiric Comedy on the Eighteenth-Century London Stage* (London: Bucknell University Press, 2002).

——, 'Reconsidering Theatrical Regulation in the Long Eighteenth Century', in *Players, Playwrights, Playhouses: Investigating Performance, 1660–1800*, ed. Michael Cordner and Peter Holland (Basingstoke: Palgrave Macmillan, 2007), 152–74.

Konigsberg, Ira, 'The Dramatic Background of Richardson's Plots and Characters', *Periodical of the Modern Languages of America (PMLA)*, 83, no. 1 (1968), 42–53.

——, *Samuel Richardson and the Dramatic Novel* (Lexington, KY: University of Kentucky Press, 1968).

Kramnick, Jonathan Brody, *Actions and Objects from Hobbes to Richardson* (Stanford, CA: Stanford University Press, 2010).

Kukkonen, Karin, *4E Cognition and Eighteenth-Century Fiction. How the Novel Found Its Feet* (Oxford: Oxford University Press, 2019).

——, 'The Literary Designer Environments of Eighteenth-Century Jesuit Poetics', in *The History of Distributed Cognition: Enlightenment and Romanticism*, ed. Miranda Anderson, George Rousseau and Michael Wheeler, Edinburgh History of Distributed Cognition (Edinburgh: Edinburgh University Press, 2019), 187–203.

——, *A Prehistory of Cognitive Poetics: Neoclassicism and the Novel* (Oxford: Oxford University Press, 2017).

Kurnick, David, *Empty Houses: Theatrical Failure and the Novel* (Princeton, NJ: Princeton University Press, 2012).

Larlham, Daniel, 'The Felt Truth of Mimetic Experience: Motions of the Soul and the Kinetics of Passion in the Eighteenth-Century Theatre', *The Eighteenth Century*, 53, no. 4 (2012), 432–54.

Latour, Bruno, *Reassembling the Social: An Introduction to Actor-Network-Theory* (Oxford: Oxford University Press, 2007).

Levine, Caroline, *Forms: Whole, Rhythm, Hierarchy, Network* (Princeton, NJ: Princeton University Press, 2015).

Liesenfeld, Vincent J., *The Licensing Act of 1737* (Madison, WI: University of Wisconsin Press, 1984).

Lipking, Lawrence I., *Abandoned Women and Poetic Tradition*, *Women in Culture and Society* (Chicago, IL: University of Chicago Press, 1988).

Londry, Michael, 'Our Dear Miss Jenny Collier', *Times Literary Supplement* (5 March 2004), 13–14.

Luckhurst, Mary and Jane Moody ed., *Theatre and Celebrity in Britain, 1660–2000* (Basingstoke: Palgrave Macmillan, 2005).

Lynch, Deirdre Shauna, *The Economy of Character: Novels, Market Culture, and the Business of Inner Meaning* (Chicago, IL: University of Chicago Press, 1998).

Mannheimer, Katherine, 'The Scriblerian Stage and Page: *Three Hours After Marriage*, Pope's "Minor" Poems, and the Problem of Genre-History', *Comparative Drama*, 43, no. 1 (2009), 63–88.

Marcus, Sharon, *The Drama of Celebrity* (Princeton, NJ and Oxford: Princeton University Press, 2019).

McConachie, Bruce, 'Theatres for Knowledge through Feeling, 1700–1900', in *Theatre Histories: An Introduction*, ed. Bruce McConachie, Carol Fisher Sorgenfrei, Philip B. Zarrili and Gary Jay Williams (London: Routledge, 2010), 235–67.

McGirr, Elaine, *Eighteenth-Century Characters: A Guide to the Literature of the Age* (Basingstoke: Palgrave Macmillan, 2007).

––, *Partial Histories: A Reappraisal of Colley Cibber* (London: Palgrave Macmillan, 2016).

Mitchell, Leslie, *David Garrick and the Mediation of Celebrity* (Cambridge: Cambridge University Press, 2019).

Milhous, Judith and Robert Hume, *The Publication of Plays in London 1660–1800: Playwrights, Publishers and the Market, The Panizzi Lectures* (London: The British Library, 2015).

Motooka, Wendy, *The Age of Reasons: Quixotism, Sentimentalism, and Political Economy in Eighteenth-Century Britain, Routledge Studies in Social and Political Thought* (London and New York: Routledge, 1998).

Nancy, Jean-Luc, *The Birth to Presence* (Stanford, CA: Stanford University Press, 1994).

Nellhaus, Tobin, 'Performance Strategies, Image Schemas, and Communication Frameworks', in *Performance and Cognition: Theatre Studies and the Cognitive Turn*, ed. Bruce McConachie and F. Elizabeth Hart, (London: Taylor and Francis, 2006), 77–94.

Newbould, Mary-Céline, *Adaptations of Laurence Sterne's Fiction: Sterneana, 1760–1840* (London: Ashgate, 2013).

Nussbaum, Felicity, *Rival Queens: Actresses, Performance, and the Eighteenth-Century British Theater* (Philadelphia, PA: University of Pennsylvania Press, 2010).

––, 'Owning Identity: The Eighteenth-Century Actress and Theatrical Property', in *Mediating Identities in Eighteenth-Century England: Public Negotiations, Literary Discourses, Topography*, ed. Isabel Karremann and Anja Müller (London: Routledge, 2016), 71–110.

Orr, Leah, 'The Basis for Attribution in the Canon of Eliza Haywood', *The Library*, 12, no. 4 (2011), 335–75.

Park, Julie, *Self and It. Novel Objects in Eighteenth-Century England* (Stanford, CA: Stanford University Press, 2010).

Parkes, Simon, 'Wooden Legs and Tales of Sorrow Done: The Literary Broken Soldier of the Late Eighteenth Century', *Journal for Eighteenth-Century Studies*, 36 (2013), 191–207.

Parsons, Coleman O., 'Textual Variations in a Manuscript of "She Stoops to Conquer"', *Modern Philology*, 40, no. 1 (1942), 57–69.

Paulson, Ronald, *Don Quixote in England: The Aesthetics of Laughter* (Baltimore, MD: Johns Hopkins University Press, 1998).

Phelan, Peggy, *Unmarked: The Politics of Performance* (London: Routledge, 1993).

Powell, Manushag, *Performing Authorship in Eighteenth-Century Periodicals* (Lexington, KY: Bucknell University Press, 2012).

Power, Cormac, *Presence in Play: A Critique of Theories of Presence in the Theatre* (Amsterdam and New York: Rodopi, 2008).

Randolph, Marie-Claire, 'Candour in XVIIIth-Century Satire', *The Review of English Studies*, 20, no. 77 (January 1944), 45–62.

Rancière, Jacques, 'The Emancipated Spectator', *Artforum International*, 45, no. 7 (2007), 271–80.

Ricoeur, Paul, *Time and Narrative: Volume 2*, trans. Kathleen McLaughlin and David Pellauer (Chicago, IL: University of Chicago Press, 1984).

Rizzolatti, Giacomo, Corrado Sinigaglia and Frances Anderson, *Mirrors in the Brain: How Our Minds Share Actions, Emotions, and Experience* (Oxford: Oxford University Press, 2008).

Roach, Joseph, 'Afterword: What Now?', in *Eighteenth-Century Fiction: Georgian Theatre in an Information Age: Media, Performance, Sociability*, ed. Daniel O'Quinn and Gillian Russell, special issue *Eighteenth-Century Fiction*, 27 (2015), 707–30.

––, *Cities of the Dead: Circum-Atlantic Performance* (New York: Columbia University Press, 1996).

––, *It* (Ann Arbor, MI: University of Michigan Press, 2007).

––, 'Performance: The Blunders of Orpheus', *Periodical of the Modern Languages of America (PMLA)*, 125, no. 4, Special Topic: Literary Criticism for the Twenty-First Century (October 2010), 1078–86.

––, *The Player's Passion: Studies in the Science of Acting* (Ann Arbor, MI: University of Michigan Press, 1993).

Robinson, Terry F., '"Life is a Tragicomedy!": Maria Edgeworth's *Belinda* and the Staging of the Realist Novel', *Nineteenth-Century Literature*, 67, no. 2 (September 2012), 139–76.

Rumbold, Valerie, 'Cut the Caterwauling: Women Writers (Not) in Pope's Dunciads', *The Review of English Studies*, 52, no. 208 (2001), 524–39.

Russell, Gillian, 'The Novel and the Stage', in *The Oxford History of the Novel in English. Volume 2: English and British Fiction 1750–1820*, ed. Karen O'Brien and Peter Garside (Oxford: Oxford University Press, 2015), 513–28.

Saggini, Francesca, *Backstage in the Novel: Frances Burney and the Theater Arts* (Charlottesville, VA: University of Virginia Press, 2012).

Sells, A. Lytton, *Oliver Goldsmith: His Life and Works* (London: George Allen & Unwin, 1974).

Sherman, Stuart, 'Garrick among Media: The "Now Performer" Navigates the News', *Periodical of the Modern Languages of America (PMLA)*, 126, no. 4, Special Topic: Celebrity, Fame, Notoriety (October 2011), 966–82.

Siskin, Clifford, *System. The Shaping of Modern Knowledge* (London and Cambridge, MA: MIT Press, 2017).

Skinner, Gillian, '"An Unsullied Reputation in the Midst of Danger": Barsanti, Propriety and Performance in Burney's Early Journals and Letters', *Women's Writing*, 19, no. 4 (2012), 525–43.

Smitten, Jeffrey R., 'Gesture and Expression in Eighteenth-Century Fiction: *A Sentimental Journey*', *Modern Language Studies*, 9, no. 3 (1979), 85–97.

Solomon, Diana, *Prologues and Epilogues of Restoration Theater: Gender and Comedy, Performance and Print* (Newark, DE: University of Delaware Press, 2013).

——, 'Tragic Play, Bawdy Epilogue', in *Prologues, Epilogues, Curtain-Raisers, and Afterpieces: The Rest of the Eighteenth-Century London Stage*, ed. Daniel J. Ennis and Judith Bailey Slagle (Newark, DE: University of Delaware Press, 2007), 155–78.

Spedding, Patrick, *A Bibliography of Eliza Haywood* (London: Pickering and Chatto, 2004).

——, 'Imagining Eliza Haywood', *Eighteenth-Century Fiction*, 29, no. 3 (2017), 345–72.

Stevenson, John Allen, *The Real History of Tom Jones* (Basingstoke: Palgrave Macmillan, 2006).

Staves, Susan, 'Don Quixote in Eighteenth-Century England', *Comparative Literature*, 24 (1972), 193–215.

Suarez, Michael F., 'Toward a Bibliometric Analysis of the Surviving Record, 1700–1801', in *The Cambridge History of the Book in Britain: Volume 5: 1695–1830*, ed. S.J. Michael, F. Suarez and Michael L. Turner (Cambridge: Cambridge University Press, 2009), 39–65.

Swindells, Julia and David Francis Taylor, ed., *The Oxford Handbook of the Georgian Theatre 1737–1832* (Oxford: Oxford University Press, 2014).

Taylor, David Francis, *Theatres of Opposition: Empire, Revolution, and Richard Brinsley Sheridan* (Oxford: Oxford University Press, 2012).

Thomas, David, David Carlton and Anne Etienne, *Theatre Censorship: From Walpole to Wilson* (Oxford: Oxford University Press, 2007).

Tierney-Hynes, Rebecca, *Novel Minds: Philosophers and Romance Readers, 1680–1740*, Palgrave Studies in the Enlightenment, Romanticism and the Cultures of Print (Basingstoke: Palgrave Macmillan, 2012).

Turner, James Grantham, 'Novel Panic: Picture and Performance in the Reception of Richardson's *Pamela*', *Representations*, 48 (1994), 70–96.

Turner, Victor, *From Ritual to Theatre: The Human Seriousness of Play* (New York: PAJ, 1982).

Vermeule, Blakey, *Why Do We Care About Literary Characters?* (Baltimore, MD: Johns Hopkins University Press, 2010).

Wanko, Cheryl, *Roles of Authority: Thespian Biography and Celebrity in Eighteenth-Century Britain* (Lubbock, TX: Texas Tech University Press, 2003).

Watson, Carly, *Miscellanies, Poetry, and Authorship, 1680–1800*, Palgrave Studies in Enlightenment, Romanticism, and the Cultures of Print (London: Palgrave Macmillan, 2020).

Watts, Carol, *The Cultural Work of Empire: The Seven Years War and the Imagining of the Shandean State* (Edinburgh: Edinburgh University Press, 2007).

Warner, William B., *Licensing Entertainment: The Elevation of Novel Reading in Britain, 1684–1750* (Berkeley and Los Angeles, CA: University of California Press, 1998).

Widmayer, Anne F., *Theatre and the Novel from Behn to Fielding*, Oxford University Studies in the Enlightenment (Oxford: Liverpool University Press, 2015).

West, Shearer, *The Image of the Actor: Verbal and Visual Representation in the Age of Garrick and Kemble* (New York: St Martin's Press, 1991).

Wiles, David, *The Masks of Menander: Sign and Meaning in Greek and Roman Performance* (Cambridge: Cambridge University Press, 1991).

Williams, Abigail, *The Social Life of Books: Reading Together in the Eighteenth-Century Home*, The Lewis Walpole Series in Eighteenth-Century Culture and History (New Haven, CT: Yale University Press, 2017).

Williams, Stanley Thomas, 'Richard Cumberland's *West Indian*', *Modern Language Notes*, 35, no. 7 (November 1920), 413–17.

Wilputte, Earla, 'Haywood's Tabloid Journalism: *Dalinda: or, The Double Marriage* and the Cresswell Bigamy Case', *Journal for Early Modern Cultural Studies*, 14, no. 4 (2014), 122–42.

––, 'Wife Pandering in Three Eighteenth-Century Plays', *Studies in English Literature 1500–1900*, 38, no. 3 (1998), 447–64.

Winchester, George, ed., *The London Stage 1660–1800: Part Four 1746–1777*, 3 vols (Carbondale, IL: Southern Illinois University Press, 1962).

Wong, Bethany, 'Pamela, Part ii: Richardson's Trial by Theatre', *Eighteenth-Century Fiction*, 29 (2016), 179–99.

Woodfield, Ian, *Opera and Drama in Eighteenth-Century London: The King's Theatre, Garrick, and the Business of Performance* (Cambridge: Cambridge University Press, 2001).

Worrall, David, *Celebrity, Performance, Reception: British Georgian Theatre as Social Assemblage* (Cambridge: Cambridge University Press, 2013).

Woodward, Carolyn, 'Who Wrote *The Cry?*: A Fable for Our Times', *Eighteenth-Century Fiction*, 9, no. 1 (1996), 91–7.

Web-based sources

Amory, Hugh, 'Lennox, (Barbara) Charlotte (1730/31?–1804)', *Oxford Dictionary of National Biography* (Oxford: Oxford University Press, 2004); online edn, May 2009, http://ezproxy-prd.bodleian.ox.ac.uk:2167/view/article/16454 [accessed 20 February 2020].

Ballaster, Ros, 'Enter the Novel: Prose Fiction in the Georgian Theatre'. *Eighteenth Century Drama: Censorship, Society and the Stage* (Marlborough: Adam Matthew, 2016), www.eighteenthcenturydrama.amdigital.co.uk/Explore/Essays/Ballaster [accessed 20 February 2020].

Boyes-Maconaghie, Harriet, 'A Critical Edition of Benjamin Hoadley's "the Suspicious Husband" (1747)', (ProQuest Dissertations Publishing, 1984). Paper 1348. Scholarship@Western, http://ir.lib.uwo.ca/digitizedtheses [accessed 20 February 2020].

Brown, Susan, Patricia Clements and Isobel Grundy, ed., 'Medora Gordon Byron', in *Orlando: Women's Writing in the British Isles from the Beginnings to the Present* (Cambridge: Cambridge University Press Online, 2006), http://orlando.cambridge.org/ [accessed 20 February 2020].

––, 'Eliza Haywood', in *Orlando: Women's Writing in the British Isles from the Beginnings to the Present* (Cambridge: Cambridge University Press Online, 2006), http://orlando.cambridge.org/ [accessed 20 February 2020].

Dale, Amelia, 'Dramatic Extraction and Polly Honeycombe's &c', Beauchamp Prize for Literature, University of Sydney, http://hdl.handle.net/2123/8726 [accessed 20 February 2020].

Dickinson, H.T, 'Yonge, Sir William, Fourth Baronet (c. 1693–1755), Politician', *Oxford Dictionary of National Biography* (23 September 2004), https://ezproxy-prd.bodleian.ox.ac.uk:3030/view/10.1093/ref:odnb/

9780198614128.001.0001/odnb-9780198614128-e-30232 [accessed 20 February 2020].

Eighteenth Century Drama: Censorship, Society and the Stage, Adam Matthew Digital, www.eighteenthcenturydrama.amdigital.co.uk/ [accessed 20 February 2020].

Journal of the House of Lords: Volume 22, 1722–1726 (London, 1767–1830), 343-61, British History Online, www.british-history.ac.uk/lords-jrnl/vol22/pp343-361 [accessed 20 February 2020].

Milling, Jane, 'Oldfield, Anne (1683–1730), Actress', *Oxford Dictionary of National Biography* (23 September 2004); https://ezproxy-prd.bodleian.ox.ac.uk:3030/view/10.1093/ref:odnb/9780198614128.001.0001/odnb-9780198614128-e-20677 [accessed 29 February 2020].

Reading Experience Database 1450–1945, www.open.ac.uk/Arts/reading/UK/ [accessed 20 February 2020].

Shakespeare, William, *Hamlet*, Act 1, scene 1, line 111, *Modern Critical Edition*, ed. G. Taylor, J. Jowett, T. Bourus and G. Egan (The New Oxford Shakespeare) (Oxford: Oxford University Press, 2016). Oxford Scholarly Editions Online doi:10.1093/actrade/9780199591152.book.1 [accessed 20 February 2020].

––, *The Tempest*, Act 4, scene I, lines 148–50, *Modern Critical Edition*, ed. G. Taylor, J. Jowett, T. Bourus and G. Egan (The New Oxford Shakespeare) (Oxford: Oxford University Press, 2016). Oxford Scholarly Editions Online. doi:10.1093/actrade/9780199591152.book.1 [accessed 20 February 2020].

Thomson, Peter, 'Garrick, David (1717–1779), Actor and Playwright', *Oxford Dictionary of National Biography* (23 September 2004), https://ezproxy-prd.bodleian.ox.ac.uk:3030/view/10.1093/ref:odnb/9780198614128.001.0001/odnb-9780198614128-e-10408 [accessed 29 February 2020].

Index

Printed and bound by CPI Group (UK) Ltd, Croydon, CR0 4YY

09/06/2025